# BAHRAIN'S UPRISING

## ABOUT THE EDITORS

ALAʾA SHEHABI is a Bahraini writer and researcher. She is a co-founder of Bahrain Watch, an NGO that advocates for accountability and social justice in Bahrain. She has a PhD in economics from Imperial College London and studied at University College London and Warwick University. She previously worked as a policy analyst at RAND Corporation and as a lecturer at the Bahraini Institute for Banking and Finance during the 2011 uprising. Her husband was imprisoned during that period and she visited the prisons and military court in the country. She appears in the media and has written for *The Guardian,* Al Jazeera, *Jadaliyya,* openDemocracy, and *Foreign Policy.* Various parts of the book were written during a visiting position at Lund University and a fellowship at the Arab Council for Social Sciences.

MARC OWEN JONES is a writer and PhD candidate researching political repression in Bahrain at Durham University. In addition to teaching Middle East politics, Marc is a member of the advocacy NGO Bahrain Watch and writes a blog on Bahrain. He spent most of his formative life in Bahrain and has worked and studied in both Sudan and Syria. Since completing his MSc in Arabic and Arab World Studies, Marc has written extensively about Bahrain for outlets such as CNN, openDemocracy, Index on Censorship, *Muftah, Your Middle East,* and *Middle East Eye.* He is also a regular contributor to the Economist Intelligence Unit and has written academic articles on various topics related to Bahrain, including social media, satire, and diplomacy. In 2011, he helped to expose fake journalist Liliane Khalil and appeared on Al Jazeera and France 24 to discuss how PR companies are using such figures to spread government propaganda.

# BAHRAIN'S UPRISING

## Resistance and repression in the Gulf

EDITED BY ALA'A SHEHABI AND MARC OWEN JONES

Zed Books

LONDON

*Bahrain's Uprising: Resistance and Repression in the Gulf* was first published in 2015 by Zed Books Ltd, Unit 2.8 The Foundry, 17 Oval Way, London SE11 5RR, UK

www.zedbooks.co.uk

Editorial copyright © Ala'a Shehabi and Marc Owen Jones 2015

Copyright in this collection © Zed Books 2015

Chapter 2 is from *Allah ba'da al-'ashira*. Copyright © 'Ali Al Jallawi 2011. By arrangement with the author. Translation copyright © Ayesha Saldanha 2011. Published August 2011 by Words Without Borders (www. wordswithoutborders.org) and reprinted with permission. All rights reserved.

The rights of Ala'a Shehabi and Marc Owen Jones to be identified as the editors of this work have been asserted by them in accordance with the Copyright, Designs and Patents Act, 1988

Typeset by Swales & Willis Ltd, Exeter, Devon, UK
Index by John Barker
Cover designed by Kazimir Iskander

A catalogue record for this book is available from the British Library

ISBN 978-1-78360-434-0 hb
ISBN 978-1-78360-433-3 pb
ISBN 978-1-78360-435-7 pdf
ISBN 978-1-78360-436-4 epub
ISBN 978-1-78360-437-1 mobi

# Contents

# Acknowledgements

The editors wish to acknowledge the commitment and scholarship of all the contributors to the book and to show gratitude to the many people interviewed for the various chapters.

We especially wish to thank to Christine Rothman and Leif Steinberg for their generosity in providing working space at the Centre for Middle East Studies at the University of Lund. Kim Walker, our editor at Zed Books, has been keen to publish this collection from the day it was first proposed to her. We are grateful for her encouragement, support, and advice.

We would also like to thank the Issam Fares Institute and the Asfari Institute at the American University of Beirut, and in particular Fateh Azzam, Mark Levine, Lisa Hajjar, Rayyan Alamine, and Omar Dewaichi for their academic and financial support through the Research, Advocacy and Public Policy collaboration project between AUB and Lund University, through commission of the research on human rights. In particular, the feedback that was received in the May 2014 workshop of the RAPP research team in Lund was most useful.

Particular thanks go to Dr Abdulhadi Khalaf for input and feedback on parts of the book and to Ayesha Saldanha for her help with the translation of Ibrahim Sharif's speech. Finally, thanks to Anne Alexander for her continuous feedback and supportive advice.

This work is a product of the digital collective that is Bahrain Watch, established in 2012, and its members – John Horne, Luke Bhatia, Bill Marczak, Reda Al-Fardan, Ahmed Ali, Ali Abdulemam, Fahad Desmukh, and the co-editors – whose collegial spirit has created a self-perpetuating energy that has kept us all going for the past three years and has driven the success of some seemingly impossible campaigns, such as the ban on tear gas exports from South Korea, and serious technical investigations into the use of surveillance technology that have been discussed in the book. We have discovered amongst ourselves the unbounded possibilities of voluntary collective work. Ala'a would in particular like to thank Ghazi and Sarah for their patience and support. Marc would also like to thank his family and friends for being so wonderfully supportive throughout.

# About the contributors

ʿ**Ali Al Jallawi** is a renowned Bahraini poet, researcher, and writer. His early work was characterised by revolutionary and political ideas, and he was imprisoned for three months at the age of seventeen after writing a poem in which he criticised the Bahraini regime. He was arrested again in 1995, during the uprising in Bahrain, and imprisoned until 1998, which was the period covered in his memoir, *God after Ten O'Clock*. He has also written books on the Baha'i and Jewish communities in Bahrain, and ran a research centre in Manama dedicated to raising awareness of Bahrain's minority communities. He has also presented his poetry at dozens of literary festivals, both in the Arab world and elsewhere. During the 2011 Bahraini uprising, he fled to Europe to avoid further imprisonment. In May 2012, he was living in Germany as a fellow of the Akademie der Künste in Berlin. His collections of poetry include *Al Madina Al Akhira*, *Dilmuniyat I*, *Dilmuniyat II*, and *Tashta'il karazat nahd*. He is now working on a novel called *Yadallah's Shoes*.

**Luke Gokal Gandhi Bhatia** is a PhD researcher at the University of Manchester and a member of the research and advocacy group

Bahrain Watch. His research is concerned with social movements in authoritarian regimes with a particular focus on the Middle East. Luke is a rights specialist, having formerly worked for the Equality and Human Rights Commission and Commission for Racial Equality in the UK. He is a former long-term resident and frequent visitor to the Gulf.

**Zoe Holman** is a writer, journalist, and researcher specialising in international politics and democratic change in the Middle East. She has lived in and reported on a variety of regional countries, including Lebanon, Syria, Jordan, Iraq, Egypt, and Bahrain, and her journalism and writing have appeared in, amongst others, *The Economist*, VICE News, *The Guardian*, openDemocracy, Al Jazeera, the *Sydney Morning Herald*, and the Institute of War and Peace Reporting. Her PhD thesis examines British foreign policy in the Arab Middle East since the 2003 Iraq War.

**John Horne** is a PhD student at the University of Birmingham, researching representations of torture in the Middle East and North Africa as encountered in the West. He is a member of the research and advocacy organisation Bahrain Watch and has written on Bahrain for openDemocracy, *Muftah*, and *Jadaliyya*. John is also the co-coordinator of the Connecting Tear Gas Research initiative with Dr Anna Feigenbaum and co-founder of Screening Rights with Dr Michele Aaron.

**Abdulhadi Khalaf** is professor emeritus at Lund University's Department of Sociology and one of Bahrain's most renowned intellectuals. Born in Manama, Bahrain, he obtained his doctorate in Sociology in 1972 from Lund University. Following a year-long stint as a lecturer in Lund University, he returned to Bahrain to participate in the country's first parliamentary election and was elected in December 1973. However, he was imprisoned in Bahrain without trial for eight months in 1974–75 and for three

months in 1976. Between 1976 and 1990, he has consulted for
several institutions including Team-International and United
Nations Commission for West Asia (now UN-ESCWA). In
1990, he returned to Lund University, where he resumed an academic career at the Department of Sociology. Until retirement
in 2012, he also worked as a senior researcher at the Centre for
Middle East Studies, Lund University. His academic research
and political interest in social and political change in the Middle
East are reflected in several books, journals, and publications.
His frequent political commentaries are published regularly in
Arab periodicals.

**Amal Khalaf** is a Bahraini artist and the assistant curator of the
Serpentine Gallery's Edgware Road Project, an international resi-
dency and site-specific research programme based in the Edgware
Road neighbourhood of London, linking artists with local people and issues. Khalaf holds an MA in Visual Cultures from
Goldsmiths, University of London. Her curatorial and research
activities address themes of urbanism, community media activism, and art through participatory projects and media initiatives.
In her work as a researcher and curator, she has been involved
in collaborative programming with artists and community groups
in the Gulf, London, and Cairo, in addition to running activities ranging from screenings, performances, seminar series, and
conferences.

**Tony Mitchell** is an Australian English instructor who has taught
in Thailand, Oman, and most recently Bahrain. He lived on the
doorstep of the Pearl Roundabout and was present during the
violent security crackdown on protesters that occurred on 17
January 2011. His videos of that event and the days that followed
were broadcast on the BBC and CNN and his recollections were
published on *The Atlantic* in the United States.

**Ibrahim Sharif** is an imprisoned opposition political activist and is the General Secretary of the National Democratic Action Society (Waʿad). Hailing from the island of Muharraq, Sharif was a student activist and a member of the underground leftist Popular Front for the Liberation of the Occupied Arabian Gulf (PFLOAG) in the 1970s. He studied at the American University of Beirut and in the United States, and later became a banker in Bahrain. He ran for election twice, in 2006 and 2010, and lost, believing that the elections were gerrymandered. He was outspoken on issues of corruption and political reform. In 2011, he was among the protesters who occupied the Pearl Roundabout. Sharif was sentenced to five years in prison on 22 June 2011. In September 2012, an appeal court upheld his sentence, despite determining that the evidence against him had been obtained by means of torture. He endured sleep deprivation and other acts of degrading treatment. He is due for release in 2016.

# Foreword

## On the prelude to the 14 February Uprising

## Abdulhadi Khalaf

Bahraini activists are probably justified when they complain that their side of the Arab Spring has not received its due in terms of media and academic attention. There have, however, been some interesting attempts to examine the Bahrain Uprising and the conditions that provoked *and* constrained collective action in this small, shaykhly rentier state.[1] In the following introductory notes, however, I have a narrower ambition, as I focus mainly on the prelude to that uprising.

## Prelude

A previously unknown network of young Bahrainis, the 14 February Movement, started calling for a 'Day of Rage' to coincide with the date of the plebiscite (a national referendum) held a decade earlier. Preparations for the day were openly discussed in electronic forums, where participants reflected, rather romantically, on events in Egypt and Tunisia, which they hoped to emulate.[2] While most outsiders reckoned that the call would fail, or at best be short-lived, it was enthusiastically backed by a number of highly respected, but marginalised, opposition figures. Most prominent among those were Abdulwahab Hussain and Hassan Mushaima.[3]

The regime did not seem particularly worried. In the weeks leading up to 14 February, local media echoed the official line: 'Bahrain is not Tunisia or Egypt', declaring the royal family's conviction that it could handle the impending challenge. The regime's confidence may have been bolstered by the official opposition's decision in 2005 to moderate their criticism of the King's unilateral proclamation of a new constitution in 2002,[4] as well as their decision to end their boycott of parliamentary elections.[5] While controversial, both decisions were celebrated as necessary steps to revive the process of political reform.[6]

## A shift in tactics of protest and repression

Veterans of past uprisings, including Hussain and Mushaima, provided the 14 February Movement with credibility, prestige, and political pedigree. The Movement, in turn, brought with it anonymity, numbers, and social media savvy. Each side was able to reach far beyond its ordinary spectrum of activists and supporters.

This collaboration between marginalised veterans and youth networks, I contend, is an interesting case study of an alliance between two understudied actors in collective action: the radical flanks[7] and the contingent accelerators.[8] The two sides were interested in (a) exposing both the brutality and ineffectuality of the security forces; (b) ending the modus operandi between the official opposition and the royal family; (c) lowering the personal cost endured by ordinary individuals likely to participate only occasionally in the collective protests; and (d) minimising the hold of Al Wefaq (a registered Islamic opposition society) and its clerical backers on opposition public discourse and activities. These objectives were illustrated in the open and intense debates on the political and security virtues of decentralised leadership, grassroots protest initiatives, and overcoming the barrier of fear.

For the regime's part, it relied on the same repertoire of repression that it had used since 1954. That repertoire includes the mobilisation of three key elements: (1) the security services' use of brutal force to disperse protesters, followed by sweeping police raids to arrest known activists and leaders of protest; (2) use of the media and traditional notables to discredit protest leaders and their lack of 'patriotism'; (3) dispensing promises of political reforms in combination with offering lavish *makramāt* (royal gifts bestowed by the King) to protest leaders perceived as 'moderate'.

## Changes in protest repertoires

Under these banners of decentralised leadership, grassroots initiative, and overcoming the barrier of fear, the participants in the uprising renewed the usual stale repertoires of protest in Bahrain. In light of this, they did not start by petitioning the royal family for reforms, by seeking mediation by traditional notables, or by instigating riots. Furthermore, and unlike previous uprisings since 1954, organisers of the 2011 uprising have largely been successful in guarding their anonymity. On the first day, 14 February, marches were spread all over the country in both urban neighbourhoods and villages. These small, geographically scattered marches succeeded in reducing the ability of the security forces to contain the protests. By midday, it became quite obvious that the regime had not taken seriously the change in the protest leadership and its repertoire.

While groups of marchers chanted *'silmiyya, silmiyya'* (peaceful, peaceful) and held banners declaring their adherence to non-violence, the security forces fired tear gas and live bullets. However, their attempts to prevent the spread of the protests simply added fuel to the flames. The fall of the first fatality, twenty-one-year-old ʿAli ʿAbdulhadi Mushaymaʿ, generated popular anger and drove more people to the streets. By then, protesters had started congregating at the Pearl

Roundabout, Bahrain's iconic landmark. Two days later, the public security forces, backed by the Bahrain Defence Force and other security agencies, forced protesters to evacuate the Roundabout. Four people were killed and around two hundred others injured,[9] and 17 February 2011 has now become known as 'Black Thursday'. The killings caused more anger and generated nationwide sympathy for the protesters. Al Wefaq's newly elected MPs resigned in protest, as did several Shi'a officials, including ministers, judges, and members of the Shura Council.

Exposed and uncharacteristically on the defensive, leading members of the royal family made a number of contradictory statements. The Crown Prince appealed to both security forces and protesters 'to show restraint'.[10] King Hamad appeared on local TV to eulogise the victims, before visiting the HQ of Bahrain's Defence Forces to thank them for their work. During that period of political turmoil, the protesters succeeded in making the Pearl Roundabout the focal point of their protests. They started organising rallies to various sites considered symbolic of the might of the state, including the Ministry of Interior, the Royal Palace at Safriya, and the Financial Harbour. Those rallies, it was argued, would also help recruit more participants to the protests and would foil attempts by the security forces to contain protests within the perimeters of the Roundabout. The sit-ins were an audacious departure from the protest-and-run tactics of the past and these new tactics limited the risk of making the protest contingent on the safety of a militant core. Furthermore, the Roundabout created an open space for protest where anyone could participate for a duration and intensity that they felt comfortable with. Indeed, people were able to attend for a short visit or, alternatively, join the campers within the perimeters of the Roundabout. For the next four weeks, the country was in a political gridlock, with an escalation of protests, a flurry of secret talks, and the plotting of a counter-revolution by the military.

## A final note

Four years after the Saudi and Emirati military interventions, and the imposition of martial law in Bahrain, the Al Khalifa regime remains unstable and in daily confrontation with protesters. I contend that the 14 February Uprising was a public announcement of the demise of rentier politics in Bahrain. The regime that thrived for decades on using the relatively enormous resources of the state to manage the vertical segmentation of society has had to surrender its autonomy and seek direct Saudi–Emirati military intervention to crush the uprising. I further contend that the current crisis in Bahrain is another indication of the inherent weaknesses of rentier politics itself. The Bahraini regime has lost its ability to mobilise its own infrastructural and repressive capacities to deal with domestic challenges.[11]

The trajectory of the 14 February Uprising, its strengths, failures, and political choices, have been shaped by the combined effects of the *contingent accelerators,* represented by youth networks, and the *radical flank,* represented by Hussain, Mushaima, and other veterans. The combined effects may also explain the continuing revolutionary relevance of the Pearl Roundabout, even after the site itself was erased following Saudi and Emirati military interventions on 15 March 2011. Crucially, without the collaboration of the two marginalised groups, 14 February 2011 would have been just another short-lived episode in the contentious politics that has marked the history of Bahrain over the past century.

Our path, as you know,
Is thorny, rugged and difficult,
Death on either side
But we will march onward
Onward, onward we will march
To a free nation and a contented people.
                – a poem written by Ahmed al-Shamlan in 1965 and composed
                                    into a song by Majeed Marhoon in prison in 1985

# Bahrain's uprising

## The struggle for democracy in the Gulf

Ala'a Shehabi and Marc Owen Jones

> Bahrain experienced near-revolution. Its opposition trend was massive in size, cross-sectarian (at least at the outset), and existentially threatening to the regime. At the height of the unrest in February 2011, well over a hundred-thousand Bahrainis marched in protest, an astonishing number, given the tiny island country's citizen population of less than 570,000. If Charles Kurzman's estimate that modern revolutions seldom involve more than 1 percent of the population is true, then what transpired was proportionally one of the greatest shows of 'people power' in modern history.[1]

Before Egyptians had managed to affirm their occupation of Tahrir Square in Cairo after protests erupted on 25 January 2011, a user called 'Sahib al-Ahbar' (owner of the ink) on the popular online political forum Bahrain Online wrote, 'let us choose a day to start the popular revolution in Bahrain, for there is no dignity without blood, and blood is victorious over the sword. Our people must sacrifice so that the next generation can inherit a future that is better than the present we are living in'.[2] A date had to be chosen quickly and the immediate response from another user was the suggestion of 14 February 2011, 'the day that promises were broken and the constitution was overturned'. Someone else added, 'February 14 will be our day of rage in Bahrain . . . Do not be afraid of your small number . . . it will

**Running Man:** A running man carries a flag bearing the word 'freedom' as he overcomes hurdles representing the years that have elapsed since the first hurdle, which was 2011. The Pearl Monument can be seen in the background.

inevitably grow the more you sacrifice and give up . . . for what does it mean to live in oppression and deprivation'. 14 February 2011 was chosen because it was the tenth anniversary of the National Action Charter referendum and the ninth anniversary of the promulgation of a new constitution that was rewritten by Hamad bin 'Isa Al Khalifa, who also used the Yes vote to upgrade his title from Emir, to King.

The administrators of the website, who had taken over from the imprisoned owner, Ali Abdulemam, were urged to adopt the calls for a revolt. The forum had hundreds of thousands of users, offered the space and security for anonymous discussions, and allowed people a digital locale to charter the political travails of the previous decade. Crucially, at that point in time, Bahrain Online still carried functional salience that other social media platforms like Twitter (which still had a relatively low uptake) and Facebook (which used public identities) had not yet achieved; it provided a space for discussion and organisation under the protection of anonymity.

The anonymous administrators of the Bahrain Online site decided to adopt and encourage the calls for a 'Day of Rage', urging people to protest on 14 February to demand a 'new constitution written by the people'. The statement went on to explain the reasons:

> We have been suffering the ills of unmitigated corruption and brutal oppression for far too long, established under an irresponsible and unaccountable regime. The grievances may diverge but the cause is one. The regime has grown accustomed to creating crisis after crisis under the constructed banner of sectarianism, escaping accountability and suppressing the legitimate rights of the people. The plunder of the nation's wealth has reached unprecedented proportions, including the expropriation of public land and sea. They have used foreign security forces to humiliate and attack citizens, and endemic corruption has seeped throughout the state's institutions. Our thoughts and voices have been controlled through censorship and press control, while political naturalisation to change the population of the country has reached unprecedented levels. Anger and frustration is boiling amongst us all.[3]

It was at this point that the discussion went from the fanciful imaginations of excitable users to serious conviction that the time had come. A page set up by a group calling itself the 'February 14 Youth Coalition' quickly gained tens of thousands of followers. The government, fearful of these revolutionary rumblings, announced a 1,000 dinar payout to every family. However, people responded by saying, 'not 1,000 or 2,000, our reckoning is on Monday'. Soon after, users began discussing logistical matters for the Day of Rage: should people attempt to congregate at the targeted central location from day one or should they protest in their local neighbourhoods first?[4] On 31 January 2011, one enthusiastic user wrote about the possible locations of a central protest, proposing three sites; the Pearl Roundabout, King Faisal Corniche, or the Marina Club in Manama. Then, on 5, 6 and 7 February, another voluntary user ventured out and conducted several field studies of the three proposed sites of protest, posting photographs and citing the relative merits of each location.[5] Eventually, users agreed that the Pearl Roundabout was most ideal given its accessibility, centrality, and proximity to villages. The site itself was of no historical or symbolic importance at that point, but served as a notable landmark for tourism and postcards. Many would later joke that it was the first time that they had ventured to take a photo by the Pearl Monument, as it had previously carried little value for most Bahrainis.

14 February 2011, the Day of Rage, arrived. Protests began very early that morning across several villages with hundreds of citizens participating. They were met with tear gas and birdshot. By the evening, the protests had spread into the capital Manama and its suburbs. By nightfall, news and images of the first death emerged: ʿAli ʿAbdulhadi Mushaymaʿ, 21 years old, shot in the back with birdshot. The next day, during his funeral, another participant, Fadhel al-Matruk, was again shot in the back. The funerals turned into massive protests and mourners, having just buried Mushaymaʿ in the village of Al-Daih, turned their sights to the Pearl Roundabout that happened to be just one kilometre away. A mixture of good timing, luck (given the location of funeral), and the imaginings posted earlier on Bahrain Online came together to unite people in an unplanned march towards the Pearl Roundabout. As they marched, news spread and others spontaneously left their cars to join in. Approaching the Roundabout, or *al-dawār*, as it later became known, the crowd chanted 'silmiyya, silmiyya' (peaceful, peaceful) and 'the people and the land are furious, our demand is a contractual constitution (*dustūr ʿaqdi*)'.

With not a policeman in sight, the Pearl Roundabout welcomed its new guests. Thousands swarmed into the space euphorically, some bowing and kissing the ground. Ibrahim Sharif, one of the older veterans to arrive at the Pearl that day, was carried along by the thronging crowds like a groom on his wedding night. A former banker, Sharif would later describe in his letters how he became consumed by this experience at the Pearl and how it allowed him to fulfil those revolutionary dreams of his youth. He spent day and night at the roundabout, becoming heavily involved in behind-the-scenes negotiations. However, it was in the early hours of the night, in small tents discussing strategies for the future with protesters and youth leaders, that Ibrahim Sharif emerged as a revolutionary leader.

Three days later, just as protesters were settling down in their tents, the unexpected shooting began. Without warning, the area was drowned with tear gas and old and young were shot in a pre-dawn raid by the security forces. Four were killed in cold blood that night. Ibrahim Sharif, having barely slept the previous two nights, ferried the injured to hospital. Tony Mitchell, an Australian expatriate, gives a blunt account of what he saw that night in Chapter 3. From his block of luxury apartments, aptly named the Pearl Towers, Mitchell had a vantage point over the roundabout. Grabbing his camcorder, he simply filmed what he saw. He did not intend to be a 'citizen journalist', nor a participant in the protests, but the next day the video footage he recorded was aired by international news channels. What was to happen to Tony after that was to change both his views and his life.

As the hospitals filled up with the dead and injured, footage of stunned doctors, agonised relatives, and the bullet-ridden bodies of young and old men punctured the stereotype of Bahrain as a calm, oil-rich Gulf backwater. Collective shock and disbelief soon escalated into collective rage. Undaunted, a few brave protesters attempted to return to the *dawār*, which was now besieged by tanks. This was a totally different situation to that of a few days ago. Now protesters, much smaller in number, faced the inevitable prospect of confrontational state violence. In a video that was shared millions of times over, shots fired from a barricade of tanks were seen killing a young man in a green T-shirt. His name was ʿAbd al-Redha Buhmayd. An order was given for the army to withdraw and the protesters almost immediately returned to the Pearl Roundabout.

The encampment was rebuilt, but the innocent euphoria of reaching *al-dawār* on 15 February was now replaced by a melancholic and righteous defiance. Both times, the protesters were victorious in reclaiming their now sacralised territory, but at greater cost and sacrifice – literally transcribing the path in the blood of 'martyrs' and adorning every corner with their images. These were needless victims but, at the same time, there was an agency in their choice to participate in protests, an exercise in individual sovereignty that nourished the moral faith in a popular movement. Time, resources and care were invested in the construction of a settlement of tents, stages, and sound systems. The camp represented an array of identities and purposes, and pre-existing political leftist groups as well as human rights groups, artists, and women's groups. A media centre, and a lost and found tent, as well as plentiful food and drink were available. The palm trees circling the monument were numbered to serve as signposts and meeting points, and a media centre was installed. Village identities emerged as a focal point of congregation, whilst religious or sectarian markers were visibly absent. Press conferences were organised in the morning and seminars were held in the evenings, and a central stage was used for public expression all day. Protesters even brought air conditioners in preparation for the hot summer: 'we will protest until the regime falls' ( *'itiṣām ḥata isqāṭ al-niẓām*). Notable was the equal presence of women as both protesters and organisers, as discussed by Frances Hasso.[6] Yet they were to stay there for only another three weeks.

On 14 March 2011, the Gulf Cooperation Council Peninsula Shield Force (GCCPSF), an armed force representing the ruling class of this eponymous coalition of five neighbouring states (excluding Oman), entered via the highway linking the island to Saudi Arabia, Bahrain's pernicious protector. Qatar chose to send 10 intelligence officers whilst Kuwait, facing resistance from its citizens, sent a few small naval ships. The following day, the Government of Bahrain (GoB) declared a 'State of National Safety', a euphemism for martial law. As in Libya, Bahrain was now confronted with direct foreign intervention. While the GCCPSF attempts to confer some sense of regional consensus, who ultimately made the decision to send in troops remains debatable, as well as who has the legitimate right to order foreign troops when a 'sovereign' regime is embattled with its own people reveals a glaring gap in international law. Writing in *The Independent*, Fisk stated, 'they [the Saudis] never received an invitation . . . They simply invaded and received a post-dated invitation'.[7] Indeed, what has been a decades-long process of Saudi cultural and political encroachment suddenly became what many opposition activists called 'an invasion', with some, including Ibrahim Sharif, referring to the Saudi troops as *quwāt al-iḥ tilāl* (the forces of occupation) in the perception that the primary goal was to quell the protests by regaining the territorial control of the spaces appropriated by protestors. This was quickly confirmed with the immediate clearance of al-dawar and the destruction of the Pearl Monument. The state media, however, painted these troops as saviours, playing nationalistic and celebratory song on radio and TV.

With their Saudi enablers, the Bahraini regime began to manufacture the pretext that the brutality of the crackdown and the entrance of Saudi troops were necessary in protecting Bahrain's sovereignty from Iranian interference. The government wished to paint the movement as an Iranian-sponsored, exogenously instigated uprising and a smokescreen intent on using democracy to install a Shiʿa theocratic state in Bahrain – a tactic that has been deployed since the Iranian Revolution in 1979. For this reason, the authorities continued to whip up sectarian discord. They demolished numerous Shiʿa religious structures and severely punished the most prominent Sunnis who participated in the protests, including a former military officer, Muhammed al-Buflasa, and Ibrahim Sharif of the National Democratic Action Society, whose speech before the Court of Appeal forms Chapter 1 of this book.

On 21 March 2011, King Hamad announced that the security forces had foiled a foreign (read Iranian) plot. As government confidence increased, so did their assertiveness on the alleged Iranian link. The die was cast and the authorities were now unabashedly pushing the sectarian line that the opposition were agents of Iran, further inflaming sectarian tensions in Bahrain and the region as a whole. Even when the King's appointed commission of inquiry ruled that it found no evidence of Iranian involvement, state discourse barely changed. With the authorities positioning themselves as defenders against a foreign threat, repression continued with muted international criticism. As American comedian Jon Stewart noted, while US politicians and policymakers were busy galvanising public support for intervention in Syria and Libya, their message to the Bahraini government was simply, 'Hey, tone it down will ya'.[8] Yet the Bahraini government did anything but tone it down. Between February 2011 and May 2014, the Bahrain Center for Human Rights reported that up to ninety-eight people were killed directly by the government's excessive use of force.[9] This figure now is likely to be higher due to recent killings by the state security services.[10] In addition to physical coercion, killings, and the torture of activists, the government has resorted to multilayered tactics of repression to discourage dissent. During February and March 2011, at least 2,075 public sector employees and 2,464 private employees were dismissed from work 'for their support for or participation in strikes during the protests'.[11] However, it was revealed by an independent team of legal experts in the Bahrain Independent Commission of Inquiry (BICI) report that the strikes 'were within the permissible bounds of the law'.[12] Other punitive measures included withdrawing scholarships from students on government stipends who engaged in dissent. Hundreds of students were even dismissed from university for their alleged role in demonstrations and criticism of the regime.[13] In one case, a student was reportedly dismissed for simply liking a comment on Facebook that criticised the regime.[14] Indeed, this broad spectrum repression targeted everything, from the banal tweet to the Pearl Monument itself.

The sheer scale and resonance of the Arab uprisings of 2011 was met with boundless enthusiasm around the world. Amplified by social media and the ability to track events in real time, it was a social and political phenomenon not seen in the world for decades. But when protests reached the shores of the small Gulf state of Bahrain, the response, as projected by the media, was 'different' - reflecting various biases and agendas of the corporate media. In a documentary called *Shouting in the Dark*, one of the few films produced about the uprising, Al Jazeera described Bahrain as being 'abandoned by the Arabs, forsaken by the West and forgotten by the world'. The Bahraini Uprising was inconvenient, exceptional, and an anomaly. Framed in sectarian terms, the narrative of most reporting was around 'Shiʿa' protesters struggling against a Sunni ruling family. Beyond this ahistoricism, the myriad grievances, including unemployment, land usurpation, corruption, and the politics of exclusion, were concealed. Yet, these were critical factors that united Bahrainis at the start, until state repression temporarily crushed the momentum of the movement. It is widely believed that Western silence on foreign intervention in Bahrain was quid pro quo for GCC military support in Libya. In her memoir, Hilary Clinton says, 'Frankly, when we have a situation with our armed forces in Bahrain it's hard to participate in another operation if our armed forces' commitment in Bahrain is questioned by our main ally'.[15] The Telegraph reported that 'Saudi officials say they gave their backing to Western air strikes on Libya in exchange for the United States muting its criticism of the authorities in Bahrain.' With the benefit of hindsight, we now know that Bahrain was in fact a harbinger of the counter-revolutionary forces that would sweep the region, the shifting geopolitical alliances justifying different foreign interventions, the instrumentalisation of sectarianism, criminalisation, intensive persecution, and further marginalisation of opposition groups particularly in Egypt.

This book is driven by three main motivations. First, to harness the emancipatory power of storytelling, not just to 'give a voice' to the oppressed, but to enable others to hear these voices, voices that have been ignored and effectively erased through imprisonment or banishment. Second, to chart the configurations and reconfigurations of dissent and the changing spaces of representations, be they physical, digital, or organisational. Third, to look at changing modes of repression, the institutional processes of violence, and the transnational nature of the uprising. These three motivations are divided into three broad sections:

## Part I: Voices of the condemned

Storytelling and the narration of lived experience is an important approach towards the humanisation of condemned subjects. The first part of the book, therefore, explores the precarious position of citizen-subjects. Here, we begin with Ibrahim Sharif in Chapter 1. Once described as the 'most dangerous man in Bahrain',[16] Sharif is a secular activist who believes in the principles of non-violent protest. His 'dangerousness' does not stem from any disposition to violence, but merely from the fact that he is a Sunni politician whose appeal transcended the Sunni–Shiʿa sectarian divide that the regime was so adamant in imposing. Crucially, Sharif's danger lay in his ability to unite Bahrain's disparate political and religious groups against Al Khalifa, making him a particular threat to them, and even more of a 'traitor'.[17] Incarcerated by the regime, beaten, sexually assaulted, and sentenced to five years' imprisonment, Sharif's speech before the Supreme Court of Appeal has been included here, due not only to its eloquence, but also to its comprehensive summary of many points of contention held by the opposition at large. Being one of the most important yet least-known statements made, we publish it here both for its explanatory power and for archival purposes. As Omar Shehabi states, 'And so the island – and the region as a whole – more than ever needs individuals like Ibrahim Sharif: those gifted enough to fend off despotism, imperialism, and the sectarianism which is its handmaiden, and exemplify a struggle that can lead poor Shi'i and poor Sunni of Bahrain, Damascus, and Baghdad alike to see that what they have in common is more important than what is different between them.'[18]

As one of the most talented poets in the country, 'Ali Al Jallawi's story in Chapter 2 is an evocative description of his prison experience in the nineties. Little has changed since then. His story is a tragicomedy par excellence, an account that gives colour and humour to what is a depressing and difficult subject to tackle. To imagine that up to 20,000 men, if not more, of all classes, professions, and ages could have passed through prisons and experienced or witnessed torture directly at some point, in such a small country, is to understand how the simple statistics of arrests do not reflect the personal transformations described or the kind of prison solidarity that forms. Prison becomes a meeting place where friendships are forged and where acts of kindness, and not money, are the real currency, and where wearing somebody else's wet trousers becomes a life-long debt. By subtly unpicking certain ironies, Jallawi's writing interweaves the trivial with the tragic, evoking both laughter and tears.

Our final testimony is by Tony Mitchell. A former lecturer in English at the Bahrain Polytechnic, Mitchell could be considered by many to be a typical 'Western expatriate' who enjoyed a tax-free employment package and a luxury apartment. Unfortunately, his apartment's 'great view' just happened to overlook the Pearl Roundabout – a blessing that became a bane. His story charts the bizarre journey of an accidental witness, carrying out a common everyday act, to being dragged into the conflict. Mitchell's account is striking in its honesty and simplicity. His account is almost the contrast of Hannah Arendt's idea of 'the banality of evil'. Instead of looking the other way like many of his highly paid Western colleagues, Mitchell's seemingly naive deeds highlight too the 'banality of good' in the sense of Hannah Arendt. While the majority of Bahrain's population are low-paid migrant workers from

South Asia, including several who were shot dead by the police and Bahraini Army, Mitchell's account comes from the other end of the class spectrum. It does, however, highlight that, even though Western expatriates are the highest paid in the country, all migrants, regardless of class or race, are seen by the regime as dispensable. One step in the wrong direction (namely threatening political acts), and deportation occurs almost immediately.

Overall, these stories provide us with a new set of vocabulary, where existing narrative structures, particularly those embedded in regurgitative sectarian paradigms, have become oppressive. These stories enable narrators to convey meanings from their reality instead of reducing them to mere objects in relatively impersonal news or NGO reports. The narrators of these testimonies also have another feature in common – their accounts are open-ended. As with real life, their stories may not have a happy ending or a fairy-tale resolution. Spoiler alert: Sharif was only released in June 2015, and serious reports are emerging of a dreadful crisis in the prison where Sharif was being held. (At the time of writing, Ibrahim Sharif was arrested again almost immediately after his release, for allegedly inciting people against the regime.) While Mitchell was deported, Jallawi was eventually forced into exile. Just like these stories, this book has no real denouement, reflecting the episodic and ongoing nature of a people's quest for self-determination and sovereignty. Through these voices, the innate human desire for dignity and equality is understood in the transformative experiences that lead to radical efforts by Bahrainis to move from being oppressed subjects to free citizens.

## Part II: Configuring dissent – charting movements, space, and self-representation in Bahrain

> Since the twenties, protests and rebellions have become expected features of Bahraini polity, as if they were seasonally ongoing processes. – Fuad Khuri[19]

It is important to acknowledge that what has happened in Bahrain since 2011 is not simply as a result of a government inexperienced in dealing with repression - simply a 'police training' or a 'security' problem. Repression and contentious politics have marred almost every decade of Bahrain's history throughout the 20th and 21st centuries. It is safe to assume that the mass protests of 2011 were part of this historical trajectory, if not almost historically determined, as well as the wider Arab uprisings. The uprising has been called several things. It is self-referentially called the *thawrat al-Lu'lu'*, 'the Pearl Revolution', or, more commonly, *thawrat arb'atāshar febrāyir*, the '14 February Revolution'. By loyalists and adversaries, it is referred to as *al-ahdāth*, 'the Events', or *al-azma*, 'the Crisis'. Frances Hasso described the uprising and these revolutionary moments as the 'politics of multiple emancipatory enactments and transgressions whose results are new gendered imaginaries, subjectivities, and ways of inhabiting space'.[20] Badiou describes such a happening as an 'event' that is an extraordinary social rupture akin to a 'rip in the fabric of being, and/or of the social order. It is traumatic for the mainstream, and exhilaratingly transformative for participants'.[21] But, more importantly, 'the event is the sudden creation, not of a new reality, but of a myriad of new possibilities'.[22] The Pearl Roundabout became the realm of possibilities:

> [Participants] experienced, however briefly, rare moments of feeling free, engaged in unfettered spaces of self-realization, local self-rule, and collective effervescence. As a consequence, some of the most entrenched hierarchies were challenged. Women's extraordinary public presence threatened patriarchal sensibilities . . . Revolutionary youths charged their elders with apathy and complicity, at the same time that they gained the respect and recognition of the older generation for their own remarkable activism and sacrifice. Workers demanded accountability from their bosses, students from their mentors, and citizens from the moral and political authorities.[23]

Previous contentious episodes in Bahrain have all spawned their own monikers, with the unrest in 1956, 1965, and the 1990s all being referred to as *(intifādāt)*, or 'uprisings'. While they may have chipped away at the political order, and prompted some degree of reform, they did not radically alter the regime or create a crisis within the ranks of the ruling elite. As Bayat adds, there ought to be a distinction between 'revolution as movement' and 'revolution as change'.[24] While the latter term refers to actual political change, the former refers to movements that are borne of 'dramatic episodes of high solidarity and sacrifice, of altruism and common purpose'.[25] The Gulf ruling class certainly saw the uprising as an extremely serious threat and responded by mobilising foreign allies and loyalists, and by deploying extreme repression in order to stifle the development of any kind of popular revolutionary change. Crucially, the uprisings over the course of the past century in Bahrain can be understood as the beginnings of a revolutionary process, where the majority of those participating initially believed that reform of the old system was possible. It was persistent government repression, the backtracking on pledges of reform over the previous decade, that prompted some veteran leaders to call for a republic as one option, both as a political manoeuvre and to resurrect the radical idea of the illegitimacy of absolute hereditary monarchical rule. This was not a new demand; calls for a republican system existed in the sixties when wars in Yemen and Dhofar between Arab Nationalists and monarchical forces were raging. Reasserting such a demand at that particular moment was controversial, but reflected the desire by the veteran political leaders to be the radical flanks that would empower the registered opposition groups like Al Wefaq to negotiate hard for a genuine constitutional monarchy in their secret talks with the Crown Prince during the start of the protests. In the end, all groups were outflanked by an extreme reactionary violent assertion of power by the regime and the GCC who put an end to any political scenario of democratic transition. At the same time, unleashing malicious anti-opposition propaganda to a domestic constituency living in fear of uncertainty (using, for example, the idea of an Islamic republic as a replacement if regime change were to occur).

Ibrahim Sharif points out in his speech that most of those protesting for change in Bahrain had demands that revolved around a number of key issues: an accountable executive (elected prime minister and cabinet), a fully empowered legislature, equal representation (one person one vote), fair distribution of wealth, an end to anti-Shi'a discrimination, an end to political naturalisation, and an end to corruption. In order to do this, the majority of citizens advocated a representative form of democracy, a fact demonstrated by the 98.4 per cent of the voters who supported the pledge of democratic reform in 2001, which in itself was a testimony to a natural spirit of unity among Bahrainis. Yet, despite these 'reforms', what followed was a constitutional coup in which the King promulgated a constitution stipulating an appointed upper house and virtually powerless elected house. Bahrain's new political system had failed to accommodate the will of the people. Instead, power remained in the hands of the ruling Al Khalifa regime, a regime that Abdulhadi Khalaf defines as a 'despotic form of rule' to have 'gradually evolved in the aftermath of British-designed political and economic reforms in the first decades of this century'.[26] The painful memory of the constitutional coup on 14 February 2002 became an apt anniversary date to launch the latest iteration of revolt. The Day of Rage, therefore, was a commemoration of national betrayal.

## The emergent opposition since 2011

The initial Day of Rage, like elsewhere, was organised de-centrally and relied on a critical mass of individuals to invoke agency simultaneously for popular collective action. Shortly, after the Saudi intervention and during the state of emergency, the February 14 Youth Coalition became an organised umbrella body for today's street movement. It has proven to be a powerful and salient mobiliser of protesters. Its logo – a fist and the pearl monument – with the caption *sumūd muqawama* (steadfastness, resistance) appears on banners in protests across Bahrain's villages. It has built a strong in-group identity and a protest 'brand' adorned by teenage youths and young men in their twenties who self-identify with the group. Indeed, 'the Coalition operates more as a collective than a traditional organization' and 'relies on a broad base of supporters who first generate ideas for dissent or particular kinds of activism in various digital forums. Once they achieve consensus, members turn to grass-roots campaigning'.[27] Despite thousands of its members being arrested, the networks of affinity groups across different villages have allowed the movement to continue unabated. Shehabi and Jones add:

> February 14th has demonstrated its power to mobilize time and again. In late September [2011] it inspired activists who tried to breakout from the security cordon to re-converge on the Pearl Roundabout. Demonstrators were pushed back by heavy security, but they made clear their determination to continue to test the government's resolve. The February 14th youth maintain a weekly protest schedule (under the theme of 'self-determination') and have also taken up other kinds of civil disobedience. In September [2011] activists launched a campaign known as 'dignity belt' that disrupted car traffic across the country . . . In October thousands of activists participated in a symbolic act of dissent in which they successfully evaded security forces and passed over 15 'torches of freedom' from one embattled village to another. Villagers have also taken to burning tires, turning the country's sky black when all else has proven impossible. Mostly recently, the organization called for what turned into the most widespread day of protests in months. Deemed the 'Decisive Movement,' what started off as a coordinated day of family picnics outside their front doors, escalated to a call for everyone to take to the main road.[28]

The movement in its first year managed to sustain the energy and capacity for creative resistance,[29] to think out of the box in a difficult security environment in which the anonymity of participants is critical. Now in its fourth year, protest has become routinised. Al Wefaq, Bahrain's largest registered opposition party, holds rallies most weeks, but only if it is given authorisation by the police. As protests in the capital are banned, these occur in rural areas and tend not to cause disruption or tarnish Bahrain's tranquil facade. Since the jailing of the head Al Wefaq in December 2014, no protests have since been authorised. The Coalition now relies on a swathe of male youth protesters drawn mainly from Bahrain's villages, forming a youth subculture that relishes police confrontation. Their tactics of burning tyres, roadblocks and Molotov cocktails are used on such a scale that, after sunset, they produce spectacular performative face-offs, usually filmed from several angles. Bare chested, using T-shirts to mask faces, and wearing flip-flops, the common attire of a restive and fearless youth contrasts sharply with the idea of a 'good subject' and they are routinely referred to as 'brainwashed vandals'. The demographic youth bulge, with around 60 per cent of Bahrainis under the age of thirty, means that the political views of this important social segment are increasingly relevant. Their attitudes are defined by the legacies of struggle, prison experiences of their own or of relatives, the systematic disenfranchisement in opportunities and the provision of services, and the acute awareness of the inequality in wealth distribution through usurpation of oil revenues and land.

> The calls for the fall of the ruling al-Khalifa family have hardened, garnered greater support, and gained legitimacy. As February 14th moves in this more revolutionary direction, it will most likely pull the rest of the opposition along. Bahrain's future will be determined by a test of wills between a government unwilling to accommodate change and an increasingly politicized youth movement unwilling to surrender.[30]

In understanding how power from above and below inscribes itself an individual bodies and spaces, Hasso studies the changing gender dynamics within the protests:

The 14 February Uprising marks a historical turning point
in Bahrain's contentious politics. To a large extent, it has
transformed relations between bodies and space, loosened
gendered restrictions, and produced new sex-gendered
subjectivities, embodiments, and tensions. Among the Uprising's
notable dimensions is a rise in women-led confrontational street
politics, one that has not necessarily been authorized by Bahraini
opposition men. This has produced sublimated tensions not
captured by images of orderly gender-segregated marches. For
their part, Bahraini state officials and their supporters strategically
deploy conservative ideologies of sexual respectability,
homophobia and purity to discredit women and men activists.[31]

The traditional opposition groups remain in their pre-14 February
structures that existed prior to the uprising and that are still patriarchal and unrepresentative of both women and youth; yet, faced
with a stifling security environment – their leadership behind bars,
their activities criminalised – there is very little space for change in
their ranks.

The chapters collected in Part II all explore various aspects of dissent in 2011. Chapter 4 looks at the transforming terrain of Bahrain's
social movements and expounds on how the 2011 uprising has
resulted in new forms of activism with emerging post-Islamist and
post-sectarian discourses by populist movements that focus on
human and civil rights, and a discourse against oppression. It builds
on the work of scholars like Kristin Diwan and Jane Kinninmont,
who have extensively studied opposition movements in Bahrain.
In offering a brief topography, the chapter charts the emergence of
multiple organisations and groups with differing and overlapping
roles and the challenges that they face. These sometimes blurred
roles, along with external restrictions on freedom of mobility and
opinion, have complicated the linearity of the movement and
denied its singularity. Yet they have also seen creative tactics of civil
disobedience emerge, along with a salient discourse focused on

human rights. While these different actors have similar objectives, their relatively different stances are not unproblematic and the government has sought to capitalise too on the human rights discourse to position itself as a bulwark against partisan expansionism. Yet, for opposition and government alike, there are considerable challenges facing the reconciliation of populist human rights discourse with Bahrain's economic and cultural constructs. This is particularly true with regard to the role of women, migrant workers, and sectarian divisions. This chapter also argues that changing discourses does not necessarily interpret this uprising as a triumph of liberalism or a desire for the West, but that it is a discourse that has been bourne of Bahrain's history and charismatic leaders.

Amal Khalaf's literary essay in Chapter 5 looks at the profoundly spatialised staging of dissent and explores the symbols of the uprising, particularly that of the Pearl Roundabout monument. Khalaf examines how the little-known monument came to take on new meaning by exploring its many 'afterlives' and how, even after its vindictive destruction by the government, its spirit lives on as a symbolic form of resistance. She shows that space and territory were central to the process of challenging the structuring principles of the established order and how the protests undermined the image of 'business-friendly Bahrain' and its liberal facade of hypermodernity: 'In demolishing the roundabout, it became clear to all who watched that this speechless stone monument, which had once bore witness to the Bahraini uprising and once symbolized state-sanctioned progress, had since become an enemy of the state. Its punishment was erasure.' Indeed, in an age where Islamic State (ISIS) is destroying historical monuments, Khalaf's piece sheds light on the lesser known, yet equally insidious, attempt by an authoritarian regime to erase history.

In Chapter 6, John Horne, using critical theory, elaborates on how the strategic relationship between Bahrain and the West has converged to both marginalise and skew the popular media discourse on the uprising. Despite new technologies, the media-heavy 'visual rush' of the Arab uprisings was often filtered by this concatenation of mediating forces. This discourse has become dominant and forms part of the artificial and constructed notion of what has been labelled in the mainstream as the 'Arab Spring'. The reach of the spectacle of the 'Arab Spring' is pervasive, yet social media and the democratisation of image production has allowed activists to puncture the hegemonic narrative or, indeed, perforate the 'field of representability'. However, even puncturing this field with images of torture may not elicit more than sympathy. For this reason, Horne argues that *Tn Tn Ttn*, a video representation of torture made by anonymous activists, goes further than just eliciting sympathy. Instead, it elicits solidarity by exposing structures of power, forging new social relations and undermining the homogenising discourse of the 'Arab Spring' spectacle. Bahrain today continues to be racked by protests on a daily basis, despite reports of an 'aborted', 'quelled', or 'crushed' uprising in the media. Horne urges the observer to look beyond both the discourse of the media and sometimes the graphic images of death and torture disseminated by activists, again, so that we may understand oppressive structures underpinning the established order.

## Part III: Suppressing dissent in an acceptable manner – modes of repression, colonial legacies, and institutional violence

> Suppressing dissent is not something most countries have problems with; it is doing so in an acceptable manner that poses the challenge, and that is where the UK's efforts in Bahrain can help. – RUSI[32]

Today, if you were to say *al-rabī ʿal-ʿarabī* (Arab Spring) anywhere in the Arab world, you would probably get a sneer if not an outright tirade. Nearly all of the Arab countries with populist movements have faltered into a spectacle of varying speeds of death. With war, violence, and repression raging in Syria, Yemen, Libya, Egypt, and

Bahrain, autocracy has either been entrenched or replaced by many smaller autocrats (militias or terrorist groups), but now without the mantra of 'stability'. Egypt and Bahrain, strong central states, have used 'a survival ideology that blends national chauvinism with, on the one hand, neoliberal globalism, and on the other, a conservative religiosity and moral politics of the Salafi sort that it supposedly disdains'.[33] The Bahraini regime knew that meaningful political change entailing any change to structures of power would not protect their position of privilege – one they have enjoyed since invading Bahrain in late 1782. Given that even minor political concessions would be perceived as weakness, the vast apparatus of coercion, built on various mechanisms of everyday structural violence, were easily projected in a modus operandi of explicit and unashamed repression. As such, the counter-revolutionary response was predicated on a need to securitise and re-impose the police state in order to prevent a new political creation or a new social order forming.

Unsurprisingly, the counter-revolutionary response was harsh and within the space of just three months, 0.5 per cent of a population was arrested, almost 1 per cent sacked from work, hundreds tortured, and dozens killed. Yet the Al Khalifa did not act alone. Like Egypt, Bahrain has relied on massive foreign political, military, and economic patronage. The GCC pledged $10 billion in economic aid. In Bahrain's case, the role of the British is of particular interest. British overlordship and protection was, and remains, a galvanising aspect of contentious politics within Bahrain. Continuity in the nature of the postcolonial relations and the extent of British involvement is staggering and forms much of the discussion in the final part of the book. It is apt, therefore, that this book will go to press at a time when both the British and Bahraini governments are bracing themselves for year-long celebrations of the bicentenary of British–Bahraini relations in 2016.

We argue in this book that state violence is institutionalised and predicated on the enforcement of hierarchical subordination of different social groups. Although we focus on the security sector in the book, this argument applies to health, education, housing, land distribution, labour, and business. Yet, to understand repression, we must look at the intersection of a myriad of factors to truly comprehend what forms structural and epistemic violence takes. This section, therefore, addresses the nature of that repression and the factors that drive it. By understanding repression, we can understand what factors are stymying the emergence of social justice in Bahrain.

## *Institutional roots of violence*

First, though, it is important to understand the institutional roots of this violence and repression. To understand 'deep authoritarianism' in Bahrain, we need to begin with the power structures that maintain this status quo. The regime's reluctance to share power stems from the Al Khalifa's perception of themselves as the 'conquerors' of Bahrain, which has resulted in what Abdulhadi Khalaf describes as a 'legacy of conquest'.[34]

> This legacy refers to 1783 conquest of Bahrain by the al-Khalifa family and its tribal allies from the mainland Arabia. To this day, the ruling family in Bahrain, and of course sheikh Hamad himself, refer to that conquest as the basis for establishing the legitimacy of their dynastic rule. I am not talking here about few symbolic signifiers of this legacy such as titles or demeanours. No. The legacy of conquest is to be found in the real world of politics and business. It is to be found the daily experience that any al-Khalifa person whether senior in rank and age or not, is above the law. The legacy of conquest is found in the monthly stipend of thousands of pounds given to each and every member of the al-Khalifa. It is found in the songs and poems that Bahrain children learn to sing and recite acknowledging the conquest as an act of historic salvation. And in the monuments constructed to tell parts of the inhabitants that they are victors and tell the others that would remain the vanquished. The legacy of conquest is found in the submissive acknowledgement by an employee,

professional or otherwise, that a priority in appointment and in promotion is, naturally, reserved to one's al-Khalifa colleagues.[35]

This legacy of conquest and the subsequent 'settler-ruler'[36] approach to their rule has prevented them from integrating into the local population and this has had a corollary negative impact upon the 'life chances' of many Bahrainis. Fuad Khuri embellishes on this and notes the 'exclusiveness and nonassimilative character' of the Al Khalifa, as well as their 'claims to legitimacy of rule on the basis of historically earned rights without resort to public delegation'.[37] This exclusive, tribal, and feudal climate has resulted in a superior disposition and sense of entitlement among the ruling clan. This distance between regime and society has underlined a number of problems. Indeed, throughout history, the Al Khalifa have been responsible for all manner of gross oppression against the local population, with a number of them, such as the notorious ʿAbdullah bin ʿIsa Al Khalifa, extorting, murdering, and defrauding the Baharna throughout the early 1900s. As Marc Owen Jones notes in Chapter 8, this exclusive settler–conquerer/tribal mentality was highlighted too in the forties, when an Al Khalifa family member who became a Shiʿa was publically ridiculed by other members of the family. Due to the Al Khalifa regime's exclusivity and refusal to share key instruments and institutions of state – that is, power and wealth – with the broader population, the state and its organs have functioned largely as a cartel that ensures the continued economic and material domination by the ruling family. Indeed, the Al Khalifa dominate all important positions of government, including the Ministry of Interior, the Foreign Ministry, and the Ministry of Defence.

As Abdulhadi Khalaf suggests in the Foreword, 2011 represented an important shift in contentious politics in Bahrain and, even if it did not lead to regime change, it has exhausted the regime's usual repertoire of repression. It is no surprise then that the Al Khalifa have struggled with a legitimacy crisis and with what Shehabi[38] calls a 'sovereignty crisis', and their authoritarianism has led to the patrimonial and selective/discriminatory distribution of services. In this crisis, power has inscribed itself in economic domination that has been underlined by a number of key events, most recently the revelation by the *Financial Times* that the ruling family has an investment vehicle that has amassed large shares in a $22 billion real-estate empire.[39] Much of this has been gained through lands bestowed upon the King, by the King himself – acquiring at least 65 square kilometres of reclaimed land and destroying beautiful palm groves and natural coastlines that were a feature of the island. Indeed, in 2002, 'the king issued a law giving himself the sole authority to grant state land rights'. This appropriation of land followed decades of what H.V. Mapp described as 'shovelling oil royalties into the Khalifa's family treasure chest'.[40] Evidence indicates that, between 1926 and 1971, the Al Khalifa took a quarter of Bahrain's GDP.[41] What has emerged in Bahrain is essentially a kleptocratic ethnocracy, where one ethnic group, the Sunni Al Khalifa, has captured the instruments of state in order to protect their position of material and political privilege. As a result of this, a system of domination is reproduced through social, political, and legal institutions that reflect the 'norms, values and interests of the dominant ethnic group',[42] the Al Khalifa 'tribe'. Despite representing under 5,000 members, the ruling family has historically appropriated a third of economic wealth, a third of all key political positions,[43] and over a third of the land mass of Bahrain. In this unwritten consociational distribution, loyalists, mostly Sunni, would get another 30–40 per cent and the Shiʿa would get the remainder.

Adam Hanieh argues that Arab struggles are not simply just about 'human rights', they are integrally connected to the ways that capitalism and class in the Middle East have formed under the aegis of Western domination. Bahrain was 'was the principal location of the uprisings in the Gulf in 2011' because of a strong working-class base and strong labour/leftist movements, due to lower levels of oil wealth and the entrenched discrimination against the Shiʿa population.[44] He believes that the prime root cause of the uprisings can be traced to 'patterns of uneven and combined development that have characterized the region as a whole over the last two decades' and have unified and consolidated the Gulf states as imperial powers.[45] Indeed Bahrain's economy has essentially survived on economic aid from Saudi Arabia's donated share of the Abu Safa oil plant.[46] Oil income thus comprises over 80 per cent of government spending and a further economic boost from the $10 billion aid package pledged by the GCC. Leaked official documents from Saudi Arabia appear to show that specific conditions to this aid are included, including making sure that the financial support does 'not help to enrich the Shia'.

## The role of foreign actors and the shadow of empire

> Bahrain does not enjoy the independence needed to be revolutionary. – Roger Tomkys

Inextricable from the Al Khalifa regime are the influence of foreign actors who shape the nature of repression in Bahrain by aiding and abetting this deep authoritarianism. James McDougall argues that, as protectors, the British, operating at the apex of power in GCC sheikhdoms, had the striking feature of the 'crystallisation of existing social order rather than its dislocation'.[47] Challenging the Al Khalifa has always been hampered by the protection afforded to them by outside powers. As Emile Nakhleh states, Bahrain 'cannot be an independent actor in the international arena. Whether Bahrain wills it or not, by its very location it will be caught in the squeeze of international politics.'[48] Indeed, the Al Khalifa have always relied on external protection and, as a consequence, have been amenable to external influence over domestic politics by its chief protectors, namely Britain, the United States, and Saudi Arabia. The influence of these actors has, of course, shifted over time. Between the early 1800s and Bahrain's independence in 1971, Britain in particular played an enormous role in influencing the shape of governance in Bahrain and the role of opposition abroad.

Following 1971, growing American regional hegemony and increasing Saudi influence in Bahrain's politics altered the dynamics of the internal situation in Bahrain. Britain still retained an influence, especially through the security apparatus, but this had become less significant, even leading up to independence. However, it was during this period that the infamous Brit, Colonel Ian Henderson, advisor to the ruler, was head of the Security and Intelligence Service (SIS) in Bahrain. His proposition of the State Security Decree of 1974, a raft of draconian laws sanctioning arbitrary arrest and three years of detention without charge, itself supported by the British, was a source of contention within parliament. A coalition of support across the three blocs within parliament led to calls for the State Security Decree to be abolished and the American base to be evicted.[49,50] With a parliamentary majority opposing the State Security Decree, the short-lived parliament was dissolved in 1975, the initiative apparently coming from the Prime Minister with pressure from the Saudis.[51,52] Amy Austin Holmes investigates the role of the Americans and their response to two eviction notices of the US naval base. By ignoring the eviction notices to preserve its interests, Holmes acknowledges that the United States played a significant role in the 'de-democratization' of Bahrain.[53]

Today, Bahrain has three military bases: the US Fifth Fleet naval base, a British naval base, and a second headquarters for the GCCPSF. Thankful for Saudi Arabia's political and economic bailout in 2011, the regime sought to formalise this relationship through a GCC union – a union that was actually rejected by other states and was instead replaced with a proposal for a Saudi–Bahraini confederation. Though all of these proposals have been abandoned,

Bahrain's sovereignty as an island state, colonial legacies, as well as popular claims are testing the boundaries of authority and the locus of power. Without Western and Saudi Arabian patronage, the Al Khalifa regime would have most likely been overthrown long ago, as shown by British documents from the seventies, which Marc Owen Jones discusses in Chapter 10. Without the Al Khalifa, the West may have lost influence following the rise of nationalist politics in the 1950s, which sought to challenge what was seen as British colonial rule. With the return of the British 'East of Suez' policy, the new British base in Bahrain announced in December 2014 is perceived by Bahrainis as a reassertion of this historical colonial relationship. *The Economist* headline regarding the British base in December 2014 was, 'We are back'.

Yet, while Toby Craig Jones[54] has argued that the protection of foreign powers like the United States has enabled the Al Khalifa to carry out repression against the indigenous population without fear of intervention, the reality is far more complex. In particular, as is argued by Marc Owen Jones, the British have often tempered the excesses of the ruling family without actually getting rid of them completely. However, British protection has also resulted in the ossification of Al Khalifa rule and the establishment of an inherently autocratic and repressive political order.

Bahrain's precarious sovereignty and insecurity is also a business opportunity for its allies and repression has become transnationalised in a number of ways. First, multiple actors benefit from an arms trade that capitalises on insecurity and, while the United States, Britain, and Saudi Arabia play an important role, countries such as South Korea, Cyprus, France, and Brazil have all been selling weapons to the Bahraini government. Countries such as Pakistan and Jordan have contributed at least 10,000 men to the security services. What has emerged in Bahrain is not just the concept of the 'policing of transnational protest',[55] but the *international policing of local protest*. So, while the Al Khalifa regime achieved some form of legitimacy following the British reforms of the 1920s, in its modern form its represents the symbiosis of multiple players, both regional and international, all of whom have perpetuated a regime type that is inimical to the integration of state and society. It is not 'monarchical exceptionalism', the idea that, because GCC regimes are monarchies, they have been resilient to popular challenge. Instead, it is what Steven Heydemann calls the 'upgrading of authoritarianism': various circumstances and strategies that have resulted in ever-expanding forms of control (colonialism, clientalism, sectarianism, and rentierism) which must exist to preserve Al Khalifa hegemony in light of increasing challenges from below for popular participation and social justice. In this respect, the tempered, top-down 'reforms' only reflect the diverging sensibilities between American foreign policy and Saudi conservatism. In essence, the regime has survived not through a carrot and stick, but, more appropriately, a rotten cabbage and a board with a rusty nail in it.

### Cementing sectarian rule

To a large extent, international patronage allows the Al Khalifa to pursue repressive policies with limited moderation or, as the Royal United Services Institute (RUSI) advises, in an 'acceptable manner'. In the repertoire of control, the instrumentalisation of sectarianism has been an adopted divide-and-rule strategy for decades. Given that unity of opposition against it could be Al Khalifa's swan song, the regime has worked to prevent different groups forming a united front to challenge them. Consequently, those espousing unity, such as Ibrahim Sharif and Mohammed Buflasa, have been targeted, and even the well-intentioned leader of an online campaign (using the Twitter hashtag #UniteBH: 'Unite Bahrain') was arrested and interrogated by the authorities for his role in trying to cross the political divide. Attempts to overcome political differences and sectarianism, which were epitomised by the formation of an

8 km human chain of unity (a counter-mobilisation of regime loyalists called the National Unity Gathering, facilitated by the regime)
between Al Fateh Mosque and the Pearl Roundabout early on in the
protests ultimately failed, and efforts by the regime to provoke divisions increased. Attempts to spark communal conflict, especially in
mixed sect areas like Hamad Town, by unleashing *baltajiyya* thugs
were risky endeavours that would later backfire, as the sectarian ideology resonated with the extremist thoughts of ISIS that by 2013
had recruited tens of Bahrainis to Syria. Citizens complained of
sectarian harassment by the security services. One person reported
that she was ridiculed at a checkpoint by security officers for having
a 'No Sunni, No Shi'a, Just Bahraini' badge about her person.[56]
Videos even emerged of police jeeps broadcasting derogatory, anti-
Shi'a slogans.[57] Indeed, such divisive tactics have been deployed
during moments of crisis when dissent becomes visible. Since the
1950s, 'the response of the British authorities and the local rulers
would define the manner in which the regime would deal with any
organized popular political movements for the next half-century.
The strategy was simple but very effective: delay, sow division,
co-opt, and if all else fails, annihilate by force.'[58]

However, it is misleading to give the impression that all Bahrainis
are against the Al Khalifa regime. This is not the case and the Al
Khalifas, it is argued, have traditionally relied on a 'ruling core'
for support, a form of political and economic 'clientalism' and
exclusionary politics. Faced with an existential popular challenge,
as Cherif Bassiouni described it, the King faced the choice 'between
maintaining the unity of the family or the regime, or the unity of
the country'.[59] The regime immediately took all measures to
mobilise its limited supporters, mostly from the minority Sunni
sect. It facilitated and encouraged the formation of the National
Unity Gathering (NUG) on the grounds of Al Fateh Grand Mosque.
This was symbolic as much as it was useful. Ahmed Al Fatih was the
founder of the Al Khalifa state and led the conquest of the island in

the eighteenth century. This conquest was always shrouded in the language of 'enlightenment' and 'renaissance', and at the expense of the history of the indigenous Baharna Shi'a population. This divisive war of symbols took place between Al Fateh, the defender of the status quo, and *al-Lu'lu'*, the 'pearl' of freedom and democracy. At the height of the protests, this counter-mobilisation, though much smaller in size than that at *al-dawār* appeared genuine, but it quickly became clear that the mobilisation took place as a result of fear-mongering against the opposition rather than blind or sectarian loyalty to the regime. Justin Gengler writes that 'a new generation of Sunni activists has begun to demand a more efficacious role in political decision making and a larger share of state-benefits'.[60] The NUG chose not to assimilate into traditional Sunni power bases in Bahrain, such as the Al-Asalah or Al-Minbar political societies that have, on occasion, challenged the government in much the same way as the more traditional opposition has done previously. The NUG set a list of socio-economic demands, including housing and health, which the government did not fulfil. Gradually, the movement fragmented and failed to gain even a single seat in the 2014 parliamentary elections, despite the boycott of the opposition. The fizzling out of this group is indicative of a broader disillusionment amongst Sunnis in Bahrain, whose basic socio-economic demands have not been met, but also of the regime's decision to abandon and dispense of the need for its loyalists, as its security measures gradually succeed in regaining its political composure.

Regardless of this seeming sectarian polarisation, with Sunni groups representing a largely loyal opposition, questioning the regime in the limited and controlled space allowed, seeing the Bahrain issue as conflict between a Sunni minority government and a Shi'a majority population is problematic, although it does not preclude the likely possibility of that becoming a reality given the bigger regional conflicts in Syria, Iraq, and Yemen. While sectarianism matters, its analytic purpose as a paradigmatic framework is limited in its explanatory power when the main political science approaches (instrumentalism, essentialism, and realism) are conflated in a reductive narrative.[61] First, the way the sectarian arguments are set out as simply a social and communal conflict tend to undermine Bahrain's complex history, which has demonstrated clearly the importance of cross-sect cooperation in resisting Al Khalifa control in Bahrain. For example, in 1956, the National Union Committee, influenced by Arab Nationalism, attempted to expose 'sectarianism as a regressive phenomenon and as a moral degeneration, as well as being a divisive tool manipulated by British colonialism and its local allies'.[62] Therefore, the 'Sunni Awakening' in 2012 was neither new nor an awakening, and perhaps gives the false impression of historical Sunni acquiescence to Al Khalifa rule, further legitimising the sectarian paradigm. Second, as addressed by Abdulhadi Khalaf, vertical segmentation of society along sectarian lines has been a mainstay enforced over the decades and highlights the instrumentalisation of sectarianism, namely, the use of it as a tool of repression to divide society, co-opt opposition, and facilitate the crackdown.[63] In recent scholarship, Toby Matthiesen, Frederic Wehrey and the work of Kristin Diwan and Laurence Louër in the edited volume of Lawrence Potter expound on the regime's use of this sectarianised authoritarianism as a ruling strategy.[64] Finally, the sectarian paradigm conceals the transactional elements of the master–subject relationship. The work of Steffen Hertog here on 'segmentary clientalism' – the idea that the patron–client relations characterise the way the distributive/allocative oil-state has created an intricate and widespread system of 'brokers', consisting of an expanding army of bureaucrats that deal with other individuals in society – is an important idea for understanding the mechanisms of control and loyalist mobilisation around the regime beyond simply being an issue of identity politics.[65] The sectarian argument, as was highlighted by Hanieh as well, overlooks the fact that the coalition keeping the Al Khalifas in power extends far beyond Sunnis and involves an intricate web involving numerous clients and elite classes, at both local, regional, and international levels. Indeed, opposition to the regime has not been based only on sect and, while it certainly has been manipulated, it is disingenuous to imply 'colonial' forces should solely bear the brunt of responsibility in regard to manipulating sectarianism. Sectarianism, a form of racialisation, is just a facet of boundary-building underpinning the hierarchical subordination of the kind of specific 'royal sovereignty' that the ruling family has constructed over the course of a century. Like other containment tactics, sectarianism can be compared with the restriction of protests within villages via checkpoints, barricades, and concrete blocks, and is one of many layers of hierarchical subordination. Others include class boundaries enforced through gated residential developments, private islands, and privatised welfare service provisions. Institutional segregation occurs starkly in the security and military sectors (where foreign Sunni mercenaries make up the majority of foot soldiers), and in ministries, such as that of foreign affairs, and the information affairs authority. But, anecdotally, sectarian discrimination is the tangible effect of exclusionary politics that exists at many levels, from obtaining building permits, to citizenship rights and the distribution of scholarships, to school textbooks. This can even facilitate forms of collective punishment. As with Foucault's description of plague control, citizens are separated and isolated from one another socially, economically, culturally, and politically, so that they do not coalesce to confront the regime in unity.

However, repression and dissent in Bahrain have generally remained outside of research focus and dominant approaches adopted by NGOs, think-tanks, and international relations experts have tended to focus through paradigms of sectarianism, modernisation, rentierism, or even democratisation, where 'reform' and 'dialogue' have become tired idioms. Many of the perspectives that deal with autocratic governance and social control mechanisms have been limited. Indeed, Bahrain has always challenged the 'prevailing interpretation of politics in the Arab Gulf – the so-called rentier state paradigm – which holds that regimes can buy the political acquiescence of the citizenry through judicious distribution of oil revenues'.[66] Although the allocative power of the state through the distribution of oil revenues forms an important pacification function, it is overly simplistic. It is naive and patronising to assume that in the rentier theory's basic form, people aspire to little more in life than generous welfare provision and state patronage. The salience of the theory is in the use of oil wealth to build security apparatus and to feed the dependency on multinational corporations that exploit oil. Indeed, Bahrain has experienced numerous contentious episodes in its history, both before and after the discovery of oil. Where the rentier theory holds sway is in the way the regime, top-down, believes its allocative power serves to abrogate the political and human rights of its citizens, and we therefore see much of the state discourse, particularly around *makramāt* (the King's gifts) invoked in the distribution of housing, healthcare, and scholarships. All of these are seen as a reward for loyalty rather than a right.

The final section of the book (Part III) takes us on a journey through the history of repression and its development. In Chapter 7, Zoe Holman addresses Britain's special and unique relationship with Bahrain, documenting the historical and contemporary political milieus that have determined Britain's foreign policy towards Bahrain. Using archival resources and interviews with Bahraini activists, as well as press releases and news copy, Holman examines the dichotomous position of the Bahraini opposition in London, which lobbies for political change from within a country which has a relationship with Bahrain that they see as being inimical to the objectives of democratisation. Delving into this paradox, Holman exposes the intricacies of transnational repression and dissent, highlighting how the Bahraini opposition in London engages in dissent and advocates for its cause, while both Britain and Bahrain work to minimise the impact that this may have. Thus, while Britain provides space for activism and dissent, the nature of the Bahraini–British relationship enables this to be suitably contained.

Marc Owen Jones turns our attention to the growth of the security apparatus in Bahrain, from its inception as a British response to Al Khalifa 'rowdyism' to its current position as an institution fraught by accusations of abuse and wrongdoing. Tracking the complexities of Bahraini politics, Jones examines the political and international factors that explain why Bahrain's police force is predisposed towards violence. Part of the explanation stems from an increase in Saudi influence following Britain's withdrawal from Bahrain. The stakes of political change and popular representation are too high for Bahrain's perennial protectors – Britain and Saudi Arabia – and, as a result, repeated efforts for systemic reform have only seen police deviance increase. Police reform has inevitably been subordinated to political forces that demand the preservation of the status quo.

Inevitably, much repression is brutal, yet the recent violence deployed by the authorities stands in stark contrast to the Bahraini government's insistence that the country is a neoliberal safe haven: modern, sophisticated, and ripe for investment, and marketed as the centre of Islamic banking. Indeed, this juxtaposition of dozens of military vehicles and bloodied bodies next to Bahrain's glistening skyscrapers presented a horrific tableau that undermined the government's continued insistence that Bahrain is an 'oasis of peace and security'.[67] Social media was particularly important in allowing citizens, both local and global, to peak beneath Bahrain's 'flashy crony capitalism'.[68] 'Business-friendly Bahrain' was satirically replaced with 'bullet-friendly Bahrain'. Yet, the public relations spin could not hide the endless stream of videos and reports showing police beating, shooting, and attacking unarmed citizens or vandalising property, misusing tear gas, and hurling sectarian abuse. Pictures emerged showing horrific torture suffered at the hands of the state security services. Despite the prevalence of social media and other forms of documentation, so many of these 'revolutionary moments' have been erased. Social media itself, as highlighted by Marc Owen Jones in Chapter 9, has facilitated this process of intimidation and erasure through censorship and surveillance. While John Horne acknowledges the importance of social media as a place that disrupts Bahrain's PR image, Marc Owen Jones critically examines how the regime has used digital technology as a tool of repression.

## Future directions: prospects of democratisation and social justice

Staring into the mouth of the lion, the Arab world is already in the midst of yet another global war on terrorism following the rise of the Islamic State and continues to be afflicted by violent radical extremism and civil war that mirror the incredible stresses facing the region: authoritarianism, sectarianism, imperialism, unfettered capitalism, and occupation. The 'Arab Spring' chapter of history appears to be over. Social justice, the goal that thousands of people died for, seems a distant prospect, the political need of which is conveniently averted in bigger times of crisis. Few foresaw the rising power of the counter-revolution that has culminated in airstrikes on Yemen, barrel bombs in Syria, and brutal extremism in Iraq. The old order may have survived, but it now faces new times; the equilibrium point (the balance of power between the ruler and the ruled), drawing from economics, has shifted to a much lower level of stability. The reactionary forces in the region, in extolling their military prowess, have never appeared as weak or as fragile.

Whilst, on the one hand, think-tanks and international relations experts have called the situation in Bahrain a political 'impasse' or a 'stalemate', we argue in this book for the need to look more deeply at the changing embodiments of power, the praxis of statecraft, violence, and transgressive resistance. There is no risk of fetishising the revolutions here, as has happened elsewhere; the 'state' continues to be centred and de-centred, the intricacies between systems of power are explored.

At the time of writing, the heads of all registered and non-registered political groups were in jail (Ibrahim Sharif was released in June 2015, ʿAli Salman, Fadhel Abbas, Hassan Mushaima, Abdulwahab Hussain), along with human rights activist Nabeel Rajab for tweeting about the continuing torture in Jau Central Prison. The incarceration and political elimination of the opposition has left a leadership vacuum that gives further clout to violent splinter groups and decentralised organisations such as the February 14 Youth Coalition, but is also a chance for opportunists within the opposition ranks to jump in and try to shift public opinion, to pave the way for compromise.

While protester violence has been limited, there is an awareness that it plays into the hands of the regime; it also undermines attempts to garner broad-based popular support for social movements, especially in a society where loyalties remain divided. At the same time, the non-violent tactics that have been widely employed have not been enough to force change. This somewhat paradoxical situation underpins a conundrum faced by social movements around the world which are dealing with intransigent regimes. These regimes know that, by using violence to radicalise opposition that might otherwise be peaceful, they are creating more violence, which simultaneously bolsters support for the regime amongst existing loyalists or hardliners. Militarisation of the opposition is a difficult logistical option. Thankfully, there has been no contemporary history of civil war in the country and there is a lack of appetite for armed struggle; the cost of such an option, as has been demonstrated in the region, is even heavier than sticking with the status quo.

The outlook remains uncertain yet carries a sense of historical inevitability. On the surface, for any visitor to the country, the checkpoints, separation walls, barricades, and the police presence are all too visible, despite an uneasy daily working grind of 'business as usual' and the neoliberal trappings of the modern world. In the arts, Manama has been declared the 'capital of culture'; in sport, the Formula One Grand Prix resumed after a cancellation in 2011 and, in the trappings of princely hobbies, Bahrain hosts horse races and an air show. The toxicity of Gulf research funding can be seen in the portfolio of world-class universities that depend on it or have opened local franchises in the Gulf and in the support it gives to think-tanks, such as the International Institute for Strategic Studies that hosts the Manama Dialogue, a speech platform for the Crown Prince. Of course, in the world of celebrity, stars like Kim Kardashian and singers like John Legend willingly perform.

Overcoming this authoritarian statecraft will take time, a fact noted by Bayat, who draws on Raymond Williams's idea of the 'long revolution'. Here, regime change is accompanied by not simply a change in those in command, but also a 'fundamental shift from the old, authoritarian order to inaugurate meaningful democratic change, while eschewing violent coercion and injustice'.[69] For this to happen, such a revolution requires some degree of unity of principles among the opposition. However, the fragile alliance between the different opposition groups based around human rights is not enough; Hanieh believes that the 'revolutionary process must either continue to push forward to tackle capitalism itself or be silenced for another generation'.[70] All groups struggle to obliterate patterns of domination or supremacy, whether political, patriarchal, economic, religious, and so forth. While there are signs of progress, 'the journey from the oppressive "old" to the liberatory "new" will not come about without relentless struggles and incessant popular mobilization', and transnational solidarity.[71]

Although disillusionment and fatigue naturally seeps in among activists after a few years, as has happened in Egypt where the repressive course is very similar to Bahrain, it has certainly not led to disengagement on a wide scale and resistance persists. Why does resistance persist? Simply, resistance persists at the absurd spectacle of royal power and the cookie cutter version of the good subject. At police parades and at the bottom of the judge's hammer. Resistance persists on the cover of a red passport and at the oil pump. At the alliance of sectarianism with the state. Resistance persists on the gates of luxury developments and on the broken shores of reclaimed land. At the perforated holes in the skin from birdshot and at the gaze of a foreign mercenary in police uniform. At the numbers of triangles on a flag and at the perpetual myth called reform. At the meaningless diplomatic statements of concern. Resistance persists.

## This book

Bringing together Bahraini writers, residents, and interested scholars, the aim of the editors was to assemble the previously scattered works that capture, to some degree, the political spirit, thoughts and concerns of the writers during the uprising in a way that offers a useful and critical insight for anyone interested in the Gulf. By studying dissent and resistance to authoritarianism, this book is but a small glimpse into the important struggle for human freedom and one that attempts to subvert hegemonic narratives that have tried, through the course of the uprising, to stigmatise a popular movement. Indeed, 'understanding systems of oppression are legitimate targets for research'.[72] The Arab uprisings have invigorated the roles of academics, sociologists, anthropologists, economists, historians, and philosophers. Reflecting the tenets of the transformative paradigm, we ultimately hope to preserve in some way the hopes, despairs, and dreams that have existed in Bahrain over the past four years.

In many ways, this book is too little and too late. It comes to fill in a colossal hole in the Arab Spring genre of books where, to our knowledge, very little work specifically covers the Bahraini Uprising as a topic in its own right, though many of the colleagues previously mentioned have taken care to include Bahrain in wider, regionally focused, books. Because the selection of these works was based on mixed methods and literary approaches – interviews, speeches, short stories, testimonies, articles, and academic writings – the editors realise that one volume is not exhaustive of every topic and every theme. This is, therefore, by no means a comprehensive genealogy of revolution. Where we have not addressed important issues, such as gender and migration, we refer you to the relevant recent work of Frances Hasso and that of Abdulhadi Khalaf *et al.*[73] Several authors have expressed interest in contributing towards these issues and more in the future, and we look forward to seeing the fruits of the research of young scholars taking a greater interest in the region.

Despite censorship and erasure, many of the 'lost' moments from Bahrain's uprising can at least live on in some form in the following pages.

# PART ONE

# Voices of the condemned

CHAPTER 1

# A trial of thoughts and ideas

Ibrahim Sharif

TRANSLATION BY AYESHA SALDANHA

*Ibrahim Sharif al-Sayed is the General Secretary of the National Democratic Action Society (Wa'ad), a secular Bahraini political society. He was taken from his home at 2 am on 17 March 2011 by men in plain clothes, who had surrounded his house and pointed a gun in his face. For a detailed account of his brutal and humiliating experience with the state security services, please see the footnote.[1] This is his speech before the Supreme Court of Appeal.[2]*

I thank you for giving me the opportunity to speak before this esteemed court, especially after we were deprived of the right to defend ourselves in front of the two National Safety Courts. We were deprived in spite of the gravity of the charges levelled against us, and their vast divergence from the truth. The prosecution's rhetoric could not hide this truth, for their claims depended on statements extracted under torture or on testimony given by 'secret sources' fabricated by the National Security Agency (NSA). These fallacious claims were exposed following the publication of the report by the Bahrain Independent Commission of Inquiry (BICI, also known as the Bassiouni Commission), claims formulated in order to justify predetermined convictions.

## A trial against ideas

This trial, gentlemen, has been from the very beginning an attempt to try ideas and intentions. In order to prove the charges against me, the prosecution has cited a number of quotes it attributes to me, such as 'there is no legitimacy for a regime that kills its people', 'the 2002 constitution has no legitimacy', 'the regime lacks legitimacy', 'the regime has lost its legitimacy', and 'the Bahraini army is not for the nation'. In addition, I am quoted as saying that the ruling family are invaders and that they have seized the wealth of the country, and that I would prefer a republican system and have called for the fall of the representative councils. Despite the availability of a large number of visual and audio recordings of me, as well as my writings published both before and after the popular uprising began on 14 February 2011, the prosecution has failed to provide one shred of evidence that I have called for the use of violence or worked to topple the regime by force.

Ideas, gentlemen, cannot be killed or incarcerated, nor can they be defeated in this court or any other tribunal of the state. The only court that can try ideas is the court of public opinion, and the sentence issued by the court of public opinion is either one of defeat for that idea, and consequently its eradication, or one of its vindication and consequently its spread.

## The causes of the political crisis

We are here today not because of what happened on 14 February. That remarkable day in the history of Bahrain was the result of a decades-long failure of the political system that had its roots in the dissolution of the elected National Assembly in 1975. Yet in February 2001, Bahraini citizens' hopes were high. The government and the opposition had agreed to begin a new chapter in the form of the National Action Charter, whereby the King made a number of commitments, including a return to parliamentary life, the preservation of the 1973 constitution, and a move towards a higher democratic process by the creation of a constitutional monarchy 'similar to that seen in long-established democracies'. The government, however, quickly reneged on its promises. In 2002, the King unilaterally decreed a new constitution that expanded his executive powers and stipulated the creation of an appointed Shura Council. In short, these constitutional amendments all came at the expense of the people and the authority of their elected council. Since that date, the government, through legislation and other means, has been reversing the limited reforms that took place following the promulgation of the charter. This is especially true within the realm of public liberties, and the regime has rebuilt the security state through its various apparatuses that are expert at monitoring, trapping, and punishing the opposition.

Years of political tension, the absence of true popular participation, and rampant corruption amongst the ruling elite all pushed this country to the brink of a crisis. All that was needed was a spark, and this came in the form of the Arab Spring, which turned it into a popular uprising. This uprising was led by youth dreaming of freedom and dignity, who believed that sacrifice and peaceful protest would force the government to respect the will of the people. Even the Bassiouni Commission recognised that in the beginning, the movement's demand was for reforms, not for regime change. It added, however, that 'when demands for reforms were rebuffed, the demands became ones for regime change'.[3]

Bahrain was on the verge of an explosion, yet the authorities thought that they had the tools to prevent a possible 'Bahraini Spring'. However, their media propaganda machine, supported by a system that distributes benefits to the new political class formed by pro-government organisations and parliamentary and municipal representatives, was not up to the task. Neither were their tactics of dividing society along sectarian lines, expanding the state's bureaucracy, co-opting former opponents to promote state policies and, most importantly, enhancing the state's security and intelligence capabilities.

To the dismay of the authorities, the political and social build-up on the ground was far greater than the resources that they had amassed to confront the protests. Indeed, the regime had overlooked the fact that it itself was the biggest cause and instigator of this uprising. For example:

- the growing frustration amongst citizens, especially Shiʿa, with rapid demographic change brought about by the process of political naturalisation. Added to this the continued discrimination against citizens on a sectarian basis, such as restricting employment opportunities for Shiʿa citizens in the military;
- the distribution of public lands amongst the ruling elite and their transformation into private estates for senior ruling family members and their supporters;
- corruption within government bodies and the inability of the National Audit Court to curb it despite the numerous violations it records every year in its annual report, and the inability of the state to hold senior violators accountable, particularly members of the ruling family. This was evident recently with the corruption case filed in the United States against Aluminium Bahrain (Alba) which also involved the American company Alcoa, when corrupt agreements eventually caused Alba losses of about one billion dollars.

We should be proud that our young people have not ceased to dream of a more beautiful day than today, a better system than this, and a more just form of government than this. Inspired by the other Arab uprisings, our youth proved its connection to the wider Arab nation and its determination to use peaceful protest to force the regime into comprehensive reform. Instead of throwing them in jails and detention centres, the government should have engaged in dialogue with these young Bahrainis, who continued to use peaceful means despite the use of arms against them.

## An ethical stance against violence

Although the charges against me were not based on any factual evidence, nor any actions or statements that myself or my organisation Waʿad made, I was convicted in both National Safety Courts. The charges are unfounded and baseless. They are simply not aligned with my stance, nor with that of the organisation to which I belong.

Allow me to clarify my position and the position of Waʿad. It is based on the principle of rejecting the use of violence and force as an engine for political change. I believe that means and goals should be of the same nature. If a group's goal were to seize power in order to establish authoritarian or totalitarian rule, then surely the means to achieving this would have the same nature as the goal – violence, force, and bloodshed – because everything has become permissible. That group would believe that the end justifies the means. However, if the goal is democratic transformation then the way should be to turn to peaceful popular will, either through the ballot box or, if unavailable, through peaceful protests and perhaps civil disobedience. Advocates of such an approach, and I am one of them, are totally opposed to using arms, violence, or force, which all lead to severe damage to both the cause and its defenders. When Mahatma Gandhi was struggling against racist laws in India, he told his supporters, 'I am ready to die for many causes, but my friends, there is not one cause that deserves killing for'. This is how our political movement and uprising should be.

From a practical point of view, I do not need to spend much effort proving that change through force is unfeasible in Bahrain, given the large imbalance of militaristic power between an unarmed population that does not own one piece of weaponry and a government and its allies who are heavily armed and ready to intervene within just a few hours. I can say with certainty that the only beneficiary of violence is the regime, because it can use it to drag the opposition away from the battle of values and ideas, in which opposition has the upper hand, towards the battle of arms and force which the regime wins. When the two sides use force and violence to impose their will on each other, then the difference in ethics and values between the two sides almost disappears, and it becomes difficult to retain the interest of international peace and human rights organisations in the justice of our cause. In that way, we exhaust the moral advantage our people need to continue in their struggle for a just, democratic state. Violence is a culture produced by tyrants. It is a culture that will destroy a society if its people and political opposition adopt it.

## A charge of violence to suppress and exclude the opposition

Our political history has witnessed many situations in which the government used the allegation of violence to suppress the opposition and exclude it. In 1956, the leaders of the National Union Committee, ʿAbd al-Rahman al-Bakir and his companions, were tried based on charges of attempting to assassinate the ruler, attempting to blow up Gudaibiya Palace and the airport, introducing military organisations under the facade of scouting organisations in order to overthrow the government, and breaching security during demonstrations. Predetermined verdicts of imprisonment and exile to the British island of St Helena were issued by a court headed by Shaykh Daʿij bin Hamad Al Khalifa. To his right and left were two other shaykhs of the ruling family in conflict with the leaders of the Committee.

The recent history of Bahrain proves beyond doubt that the main source of violence is the state, with its security and military apparatuses, and sometimes its tribal and *fidāʾiyīn* militias.[4] By accepting the Bassiouni report, the state has partially acknowledged its responsibility for some of the violence against peaceful protesters, as well as the killing under torture of five citizens in its prisons. It is also my duty to remind the prosecution and this esteemed court that, at a time when members of the opposition face false charges and are subject to harsh verdicts in courts because of their political opinions, the families of these victims continue to wait for justice and the punishment of the torturers.

## Malicious charges

The charges against me were malicious from the very beginning, without basis or evidence to support them. The aim was to punish me for the positions I have taken and statements I have made in recent years. It is not surprising that a despotic regime uses all its bodies, from its intelligence apparatus, to its judicial system and security forces, to settle the score with its opponents. Traditionally, these apparatuses have been clever at fabricating, planting, and presenting evidence and witnesses to demonstrate the existence of 'conspiracies to overthrow the government by force'. But this time their inefficiency and their haste to issue verdicts according to the orders of their superiors have provided us the opportunity to prove the malicious nature of these allegations from their inception. Examples of this are many, including the following: according to Major 'Isa Sultan al-Sulayti of the NSA in the military prosecutor's report of 30 April 2011, myself and others 'provided material support necessary to carry out criminal plans using *khums* money'.[5] Al-Sulayti claimed that I was amongst those who participated in 'the attack on Sunni places of worship', and that my goal was to declare an Islamic republic in Bahrain. He also claimed that I had joined a group with 'a similar ideology to previous groups who had the same aim of establishing an Islamic republic beholden to Iran', and that I sought, along with others, to 'incite sectarian strife' and 'harm Sunni patients'. In addition, we had supposedly announced the establishment of an Islamic republic, and we believed in *wilāyat al-faqīh*[6] as a principle of political governance. Didn't this NSA major know that such claims about a person known for his liberal, secular ideas, and who is opposed to the very idea of a religious state, and is also a Sunni, would provoke laughter as well as pity for the low professional standards of the NSA, and its lack of scruples about concocting implausible charges? Is it possible that a person like myself, who was as dangerous as Major al-Sulayti alleged, would escape having his home, his personal computer, and his library full of political files and writings inspected? The reality is that neither my house nor anything in it was searched. As a matter of fact, the NSA men did not even come close to the door of my house, and before arresting me they even allowed me to hand over the contents of my pockets to my wife, without checking them!

The collusion of the military prosecution with the NSA regarding torture and extracting confessions was evident at every stage until 10 June 2011. The military prosecution did not allow me to meet privately with my lawyer during the investigation. I was not allowed to meet him until the commencement of the trial on 8 May 2011, 51 days after my arrest. Each investigation session with the military prosecution was preceded and followed by a session of torture, despite the fact that I informed the prosecution about it.

The prosecution officers were aware of the repeated visits we got by masked men who tortured and mistreated us. They were also aware that we were kept in solitary confinement when we were under their jurisdiction. We were beaten and insulted on the premises of the military prosecution. The military prosecution officers did not hesitate to forge our statements, attributing 'confessions' to me and other detainees that the investigation records had no evidence of.

Following the same approach, the judge of the First Instance Court of National Safety, Mansur al-Mansur, and the appeals judge, Samir al-Zayani, together sentenced us to over 362 years' imprisonment. These verdicts were reached in court sessions that lasted only a few hours. Our lawyers were able to neither deliver their arguments verbally nor present all the witnesses. In addition, none of the defendants was allowed to speak for a single minute about the torture they had undergone. In the military court building on 22 June 2011, all the defendants were beaten after the court verdicts were issued against them, simply because they had shouted at the end of the session.

## First: the charge of overthrowing the regime by force

Now allow me, gentlemen, to refute the allegations made against me by the military prosecutor and subsequently by the public prosecutor. To begin with, I am a son of the Arab Nationalist movement that overthrew the reactionary regimes associated with colonialism, and I find that my natural instinct pushes me towards hating titles and hereditary privileges. However, national political work is not based on what we like or prefer, rather on what most benefits citizens and protects their interests. This is why I have called for firmly establishing the foundations of a democratic constitutional monarchy as the best option for the country, taking into account the local and regional circumstances, the high political costs, and the uncertainty of a future with either a continued state of quasi-absolute monarchy or the end of the monarchy and a transition towards a republican system.

Although I support keeping a monarchy – as long as it meets the full requirements of a democracy – I respect the opinion that calls for a republican regime as an opinion that people are entitled to have. It also happens to be the opinion of most human beings, including those in the Arab world, where republics are prevalent. In countries that changed from a monarchy to a republican system, there are those who call for a return to the monarchy, just as there are those who call for a republican system in countries ruled by royal families. However, I have not heard of a single democratic country that criminalises such ideas. On 26 May 2012, *Al-Bilad* newspaper published the results of a poll, which showed that 22 per cent of

Britons rejected the monarchical system in the UK. If the public prosecution there acted like our prosecution here, it would have accused or convicted 14 million people on the charge of calling to overthrow the regime.

My support for the monarchy is conditional on the principle that the people are the source of all powers, which implies a full democratic transition that results in a king with no executive powers. That is, a king 'who reigns but does not rule'. During the 14 February Uprising, I called on citizens to choose slogans that demanded comprehensive reform without changing the system of hereditary monarchy. I fear, however, that the regime's continuous intransigence and rejection of democratic reform will reduce the number of supporters of the monarchy, and will instead push people to believe that this system is 'unfit and unfixable'.

I have never proposed that the regime should be overthrown; the idea of using force to resolve political (and non-political) disputes is anathema to my political beliefs, as I have already mentioned. If the prosecution is searching for someone to charge with overthrowing the government by force, then I would like to refer it to two successful attempts. The first took place in August 1975, with the issue of Amiri Decree No. 4. This suspended Article 65 of the constitution and effectively transferred full legislative powers to the amir and the prime minister for 27 years. The second was in February 2002, when the King retracted the pledges made in the National Action Charter. This included the statement regarding an elected parliament by Shaykh ʿAbdullah bin Khalid Al Khalifa, the President of the Supreme Committee of the National Action Charter, published on 9 February 2001 as headline news. With the blessing of the King, Shaykh ʿAbdullah had met with a group of opposition figures, and the front pages of the local newspapers announced, 'The elected council of representatives will be assigned the state's legislative functions, and the appointed council's sole task is to offer advice and opinion.' Based on Article 148 of Bahrain's Penal Code that states, 'Life imprisonment shall be the penalty for any person who attempts with the use of force to overthrow or change the country's constitution', the prosecution could, if it dared to perform its duties as it should, bring charges against those responsible for these two coups.

## Second: the charge of inciting hatred and contempt of the regime

Before refuting this charge, it is worth mentioning that Paragraph 1281 of the BICI report noted that Article 165 of the Penal Code, under which this charge falls, had been applied 'in a way that violates freedom of opinion and expression, by excluding from the public debate opinions that express opposition to the existing system of government in Bahrain, as well as opinions that call for any peaceful change in the structure or system of government, or for regime change'. Paragraph 1284 adds that, 'Articles 165, 168 and 169 of the Penal Code also restrict freedom of opinion and expression by criminalising incitement of hatred of the regime, or damaging the public interest, without requiring any material act that causes social or individual harm. They have been applied to repress legitimate criticism of the government.'

In Paragraph 1291, the BICI report recommends that 'all persons charged with offences involving political expression, not consisting of advocacy of violence, have their convictions reviewed and sentences commuted or, as the case may be, outstanding charges against them dropped'. According to Paragraph 1285 of the report, the Bassiouni Commission informed the Bahraini government of these views, and in Footnote 629 added that it had received confirmation that the government 'dropped the charges under these articles against the fourteen top political opposition figures convicted by the National Safety Courts'. We do not understand why the prosecution continues to hold on to these charges after the government pledged to drop them, nor why it insists on wasting both state funds and this esteemed court's time, as well as harming the credibility and reputation of the officials who issued pledges to the commission. I do not know which of my statements relate to the charges of hatred and contempt according to Penal Code Article 165, but I assume that the reference is to the audio recordings the prosecution attribute to me saying that the ruling family 'seize wealth and monopolise it', that they are 'invaders of the country', and that 'the regime has lost its legitimacy' (mentioned on page 25 of the committal order).

As you can see, all these charges relate to freedom of opinion, although they are still not difficult to refute. First, it must be said that the charges of hatred and contempt of the regime, if found, do not need an instigator from the opposition. The regime's actions are the biggest instigator. I have never in my life heard of a citizen who does not hate injustice or rampant corruption in government bodies. Our people are highly educated and cultured; they listen and they read the reports of the National Audit Court and parliamentary committees. They know about the investigations regarding reclaimed land and state property. They know about the 65 square kilometres of public land and coastlines that have been stolen, as documented by the special parliamentary commission of inquiry. They have also heard about the ruling family member accused in a billion dollar scandal, with charges filed by Alba in US courts against Alcoa and its partners for fraud and corruption. They can list the names of all the key players in the state property scandals and their projects in the Bahrain Financial Harbour, Tubli Bay, Bahrain Bay, Diyar al-Muharraq, Riffa Views, and other countless pieces of land that are worth tens of billions of dollars. And our people know full well the policies of discrimination, privilege, and political naturalisation.

As for the ruling family's invasion in the eighteenth and nineteenth centuries, one simply has to read history. Piracy, invasion, and slavery were common at that time, and they were practised by numerous Arab tribes who did not consider them dishonourable. This is an incontrovertible fact. In Article 1 of the Perpetual Truce of Peace and Friendship with Britain, signed in 1861 by the then ruler Shaykh Muhammad bin Khalifa Al Khalifa, it was specified that 'Bahraini shaykhs shall refrain from all acts of hostility, piracy and slavery at sea'. This means the Bahraini ruler admitted that piracy was committed by the Al Khalifa. As for the term 'invasion', I used it in a neutral sense like the word 'war'. It did not have a moral connotation, for an invasion could be for defence, or to spread religion, or it might just be an act of piracy, banditry or hostility. The purpose was not to slander the ruling family, rather to say that this age is not one of invasions or booty. Unfortunately some members of the ruling family still think in the old way – that Bahrain is the spoils of war 'gained by the sword', where the land, wealth, and positions of authority are to be distributed amongst the sons of the victorious tribe and its supporters. The incitement here, if it exists, is not against a family that has become an integral part of this society, but against a mentality that should have perished decades ago.

Nevertheless, I cannot see any relationship between the statement attributed to me about the 'invasion' and the 'tyranny of wealth' of the ruling family, and Article 165 of the Penal Code. That is, unless the public prosecution considers the government and the ruling family to be the same thing. This cannot be supported by the constitution or the law, even if it is the reality of the current situation. The public prosecution has not informed me of any complaints by members of the ruling family concerning the statements attributed to me. Even if such a complaint existed, that article cannot be used to charge me with 'incitement and contempt' of the regime.

As for what has been attributed to me concerning the regime 'losing its legitimacy', the public prosecution has given only half the truth and hidden the other half. Before I explain my stance on the legitimacy of the regime, I must emphasise that stating whether the regime is legitimate or not falls under freedom of speech, which should not be obstructed for any reason. As for this specific issue,

I subscribe to the principle that a democratic system derives its legitimacy from its citizens because 'the people are the source of all powers', as the first article of the constitution affirms. If a majority of citizens have lost confidence in the regime, then its legitimacy is demolished and talk of 'deficits of legitimacy' or 'lost legitimacy' is inevitable. All democratic governments in the world renew their legitimacy every four years or thereabouts, and no government exists that can maintain its legitimacy for over forty years without an election or renewal through popular consent, as has been the case in Bahrain. No legitimate government of any democratic country has continued ruling without periodic elections.

### Third: the charge of broadcasting and disseminating fabricated news and false rumours

Amongst the public prosecution's charges was one of broadcasting and disseminating false and malicious news, rumours, and propaganda about sectarian discrimination in Bahrain, and about the government's loss of control of the situation and its use of illegal practices. We can refer to the BICI report to prove that the statement regarding the government's use of illegal practices and its loss of control of the situation has been acknowledged by the government itself through its acceptance of the report and its recommendations. Yet, the public prosecution did not prove how such political opinions could have led to a 'security disturbance', a 'spread of fear amongst people', or a 'harming of the public interest'. That is surely a necessary condition for the application of the vague Article 168 of the Penal Code, which the Bassiouni Commission considered to be one of the articles used to repress legitimate criticism of the government.

As for the other part of the charge regarding sectarian discrimination in Bahrain, I can, just as numerous international reports on the matter do, provide facts to this esteemed court in order to prove the systematic discrimination against the Shi'a in government and the public sector:

1. The Cabinet of Ministers: Shi'a constitute around 24 per cent of the members of the Cabinet, whereas the ruling family makes up 40 per cent and other Sunnis make up 36 per cent.

2. The Ministry of Interior: Shi'a constitute 10 per cent of the high-ranking positions, whereas members of the ruling family make up 35 per cent and other Sunnis 55 per cent.

3. Ministry of Defence: There is not one high-ranking Shi'a (brigadier or higher). Members of the ruling family constitute half of those positions and other Sunnis make up the other half. No Shi'i sit on the Supreme Defence Council, while members of the ruling family occupy 13 of the 14 seats.

4. Government agencies, institutions and bodies: Shi'a do not constitute more than 7 per cent of their leadership, whereas members of the ruling family make up 29 per cent and other Sunnis 64 per cent.

5. State-owned and semi-governmental enterprises: once again, Shi'a do not represent more than 8 per cent of the leadership, whereas non-Bahrainis make up 19 per cent. Members of the ruling family are 27 per cent and other Sunnis 46 per cent.

6. Judicial and legal bodies: There is no representation of Shi'a in any of the upper judicial or legal institutions, whereas members of the ruling family make up 33 per cent, other Sunnis 58 per cent, and non-Bahrainis 9 per cent.

7. General managers of municipalities: Shi'a constitute 20 per cent, while members of the ruling family and other Sunnis split the remaining, with 40 per cent each.

These figures are both scandalous and shameful because this unjust sectarian division did not exist in such a way three decades ago.

They demonstrate systematic discrimination and marginalisation of the Shiʿa, who constitute at least 50 per cent of the country's citizens. This mostly benefits the ruling family, who occupy a much larger number of high-ranking posts compared with the Shiʿa, despite the fact that they do not constitute perhaps more 0.5 per cent of citizens. What all citizens call for, and what the Shiʿa youth who started the 14 February Uprising call for, is the principle of equal citizenship, which is the necessary foundation for any democratic society.

## Fourth: the charge of insulting the army

The issue of sectarianism and discrimination takes me to the accusation that I allegedly described the army as not being for the nation. Once again, the prosecution is taking my words out of context. During a panel discussion I spoke about not relying on the neutrality of the army in any internal political conflict, and said that the Bahraini army would not behave like its counterparts in Tunisia and Egypt. I explained this by saying that the current composition of the army, as shown by the statistics I've just given, includes no Shiʿa while members of the ruling family make up 50 per cent of the high-ranking posts. This makes it difficult for us to envisage a change in the army's stance or believe that it could act in the people's interest when it comes to any conflict between the people and the ruling family. Therefore, I concluded that the current composition of the army is 'un-national', in the sense that it lacks sufficient representation of the Shiʿa, who make up more than 50 per cent of Bahrain's citizens. As for the Supreme Defence Council that is in charge of defence and security-related policies, it is almost fully composed of members of the ruling family, as if it were a council for the defence of the ruling family, and not the country.

Add to this the large number of foreigners in the army and the security forces, which a few years ago the interior minister admitted make up more than 50 per cent. This violates Article 16 of the constitution, which states clearly that 'public jobs are a national service' and that 'foreigners shall not be entrusted with public posts except in those cases specified by law'. When Bahrainis are refused entry into the Bahrain Defence Force because of their sect, and foreigners are given preference instead, these Bahrainis are entitled to feel that the army does not represent them, meaning that it is not a national army for at least half of the country's citizens.

Everything that I have said in public forums and all the press statements that I have made in the period leading to my arrest were a result of my concern for the public good, a public good that is based on restoring peace and social stability by ensuring freedom, justice, and the equality of all Bahraini citizens, with the aim of constructing a civil and democratic state. Without these principles that bind humanity together, we will not be able to alleviate the injustice some of our people suffer and achieve the kind of development which would put our country in the ranks of democratic nations that respect human rights and practise democracy on a daily basis.

The way out of the political and constitutional crisis sweeping through our country requires a serious and meaningful dialogue between the government and the political opposition, a dialogue conditional on the government's delivery on the promises it has made since February 2001. These include legislative and oversight powers for the elected council that would exceed those of the appointed council, whose sole role should be to give advice and opinion, and a transition towards a system of constitutional monarchy similar to that in established democracies. The government's pledges must be implemented precisely, genuinely, and honestly to fulfil the recommendations of the BICI report. In addition, the recommendations of the UN Human Rights Council that were made in the session held on 18 May 2012 must be implemented. Transitional justice must be introduced, based on fairness, openness, and national reconciliation. There must be reparations for victims of torture, of arbitrary detention, and of unfair verdicts (which were handed down to hundreds of political and human rights activists, as well as ordinary citizens). All dismissed employees must be reinstated in the same posts they held prior to their arbitrary dismissal and must be compensated for the time away. The way out of this political crisis also requires fair constituencies that reflect the principle 'every citizen has an equal voice'. This needs to translate into a just electoral system that represents all elements of Bahraini society, whether in terms of sect, ethnic background, or political affiliation. We need an elected government representing the will of the people, an independent and impartial judiciary, and security for all, following the basic premise that national security requires the security of every citizen.

Gentlemen, we stand before you today following suffering that has lasted more than 14 months. We are certain that, as the saying goes, 'you can't give what you don't have'. A system that does not know justice is not capable of implementing it. We already know the outcome of this struggle between true justice that prevails for the oppressed, even if they are weak, and false justice that prevails for the strong, even if they are oppressors. They can arrest us, but they cannot arrest our dream, a dream of freedom and dignity for our people. Thank you for listening. May peace and God's mercy and blessings be upon you.

Ibrahim Sharif al-Sayed, Prisoner of Conscience

CHAPTER 2

# God after ten o'clock

'Ali Al Jallawi

TRANSLATION BY AYESHA SALDANHA[1]

## The State Security Building: the first arrest of the seagull

It was maybe three or four o'clock, or maybe sometime in between. Why am I trying to establish an exact time? Curses on the clock that forces me to define my movements, my sleep, my mealtimes . . . The time was _____. I think it's better that way, isn't it? I jumped up, rubbing my eyes, at the sound of violent banging on the door of the house, and looked down at the courtyard from the window of my room. My father, clearly bewildered, was opening the door. A gang of men wearing green uniforms burst in, led by others wearing traditional dress, their faces covered by white *ghutras*.[2] I thought God had sent hell's lackeys. I didn't have time to think before they entered my bedroom. Without uttering a word, which would have made them of this earth, they started to search everything. Yes, everything. I know where your minds have gone.

The next thing I knew, I was in a cold room containing two desks. Sitting on one of them was a policeman who was originally from Balochistan, which I worked out from his tortured pronunciation. It was now ten o'clock, and I wasn't sure what was happening. My blood had flowed down into the ground floor of my body, and my consciousness had taken sick leave, just like we would when skipping work, afraid of our wages being cut. (Here's a funny one: just think about this word, 'ma 'aash', income. It can be separated to match its real meaning: 'mā 'aash', he didn't live.)

*I spit on you all. I also refuse to apologize. I know that I am not a proletarian revolutionary, nor a leader with an all-embracing system. From now on I'm refusing your tiresome bullshit. I won't leave behind one kind of slavery only to be subject to the slavery of how you see things.*

*I know that you will despise me, as you have all those who have told you the truth, when they abandoned their faith and their ignorance. Maybe you will shoot me for my conviction that I am liberating myself. Maybe I am provoking you to do just that. Maybe you will crucify me, and then one of you will try to publish my teachings. I have started to dread this truth that you cannot bear. Now I know you without your party identities or your long beards, or even the insignia clinging to your shoulders. I have no desire to die for your salvation, if it means you will simply enter another kind of slavery.*

*But I stand before the strength of your stupidity, before the ready-made attributes you have for me, before your naked fear for the welfare of your concepts, beliefs, and faith. I don't threaten the security of your systems of thought, and the idols that you worship are no concern of mine. I am gladly trying to free myself from the many little men that reside in me, and to understand my sphere of existence, and I'm doing so as loudly as I can. So I will perhaps make things easier for you: I am not conspiring against anyone, and I am not asking you for power. I have just one problem, a problem that has nothing to do with you. My problem is that I am neither a believer nor stupid.*

I became aware that my great speech had not moved anyone. They were heading for their desks; Khan remained, looking at me, a confused expression on his face. Then he looked at the person occupying the desk next to me. However, this man was busy arranging rows of letters in boxes as empty as his head. He was thinking deeply. I later learned that my friend Khan didn't know Arabic. It seemed that my impressive speech had fallen on uncomprehending ears.

After they brought me back from the hospital, where they had checked whether I was physically and psychologically fit for interrogation, they kept me standing until ten at night. From time to time my mind visited the ground floor of my body, or I would shake my leg to move the blood that had taken refuge on one side. I paid the price, though, because in addition to their generous hands greeting the back of my head, their utterances could have put Al Zamakhshari's[3] eloquence to the test.

They removed my blindfold, and I found a dark-skinned man in his forties sitting in front of me. Some other men were standing next to him. He said, 'Do you know where you are?' I said that I didn't. He said, 'You are up on high.' I think he was correct, as we were on the third or fourth floor of the building, but what did it have to do with the State Security? He took a pen and on a small piece of paper wrote the word 'God'. He held it up to show me, and asked, 'What's this?' I nodded my head to show that I had understood the word. He put the paper in a drawer, and then asked, 'Where is God now?' As I was baffled and didn't have an answer he continued, 'God is in the drawer, and I am here now.' Then he asked, 'Do you know who I am?' I couldn't answer that either; I didn't know whether he was God himself, or someone else in that role. From the drawer he took out a revolver, and placed it on top of the desk. He went on, 'Outside, people are caught up in the events. I could kill you and throw your corpse in the garbage, and believe me, no one would ask about you. So confess!'

That is what I recall, or what I think happened. After that I cannot remember things clearly, except that they put on a magnificent banquet for me for six days, non-stop. The only time off from the feast was when they gave me food, or made me walk, afraid that my legs would swell. On the first day I remained silent for less than an hour; after that I succumbed to an attack of hysteria, and became unable to control my loud screams. I would swear at myself, then at them, and in turn they would try to silence me by hitting me. Then they found a better way; one of them put my socks in my mouth, and they blindfolded me. I remember that the man interrogating me was called Adel; his name, meaning 'just' or 'fair', did not fit him at all. I learned his name from a conversation between two policemen; one of them, called Abdul Nabi, was in his mid-forties, and the second, Sufyan, of Pakistani origin, was in his twenties. He was a handsome young man, with long hair that reached his shoulders. This Sufyan was terrified of Abdul Nabi. Abdul Nabi had tried on more than one occasion to establish an intimate and warm relationship with Sufyan, but Sufyan had refused, and indicated that he would inform Colonel Adel.

## The seagull's plea before the sea

On the sixth day they took me in to see a policeman in civilian clothes – of Jordanian origin. He had all the expletives in the world tripping off his tongue, and was known as 'the Curser'. He used to pronounce his r's in a dreadful way. He gave me a statement in his handwriting, saying: 'Sign here, or I will take you back to the nice party.'

I was taken after that to the 'confessions judge'; he was called that because his task was to confirm that the detainee agreed to the statement. After I had been sitting before him for a quarter of an hour while he read my statement, he asked me one question: 'Is this your signature?' He pointed to my name at the bottom of the statement.

I said, 'Yes.'

*I am no legendary hero, and I have not left the human realm. I hail from among the common people. I belong to myself; I don't have an honorific title before my name. I don't feel the pain of needing to liberate the world from its predicament, nor do I have the inclination to ascertain the magnitude of the hole in the sky, even if the angels of hell will descend from it onto our heads, as some say. As far as I am concerned, such empty talk has led to carnage, whether in the name of conquest or the elevation of one race over another, or of possessing a truth denied to all others.*

*Yes, I am proud to be a mongrel; I don't belong to a pure social class, or even a pure race, or to a tribe that can civilize me with its nobility while it imposes its authority on others by force. As far as I am concerned, I am a son of the first nucleus, which could be considered clay. From this comes my status as a human, not from the tent of a tribe, nor the school of a religious authority, and not from belonging to a noble race. If you like, I am from a species of luminous jellyfish, and perhaps it requires more than 1,400 years to become conscious of the light inside. This jellyfish belongs to the water, and there is a world of difference between the water and the desert.*

Showing no emotion, he gestured to the man standing behind me. This man took me back to the building of Lord Adel, whose angels led me from 'on high' down to a jail of four cells below the so-called national intelligence building. I was shoved into an unbearably cold cell at the end of the corridor. Dampness and the smell of decay emanated from the blankets on the pus- and bloodstained bed. Scrawled dates reposed peacefully on the grey wall with other scribblings indicating the people who had passed this way. I heard voices muttering in the neighbouring cells; one of them was asking about the new inmate who had just come in. Indeed, who was the new person brought to the cell? Was it me? And who am I, actually? I lay down on the bed, which sagged beyond my expectation; I felt my back touch the ground. The next thing I was aware of was being awoken by the sound of the guard pushing in a plate of food and a metal cup of tea. I took note of the things around me. The room had no windows, typical of those in the intelligence building. I didn't know what time of day it was, but the type of food told me. It was morning, which I realised from the beans covered with a thick layer of dust and dirt, and the barrel of tea, called a *balti*, a Hindi word meaning bucket, normally used as a vessel when bathing. It seemed that I had slept for more than twenty-four hours. I heard the same voices next door, and they were still muttering questions about the new resident. Yes, I was the new resident; I was the gentleman who had descended from 'on high' to these magnificent cells, the cells without windows, which had drawn their veils over themselves. I was the one descended from jellyfish, as Wilhelm Reich would say. What do you want from me now? Let me continue my precarious siesta, let me take a break from these questions . . . But the question was repeated insistently; it was the same question said in many different voices and ways. I answered that I was Ali Al Jallawi. A voice leaped from one of the cells: 'Jallawi! How are you?' I knew the voice; it was that of Sami Al Sharis. Sami! What was Sami doing here? I had last seen him in intermediate school.

## Cages for seagulls that might be born

In the neighbouring cells were some guys from my area. I knew only two of them; the first was Sami Al Sharis ('Sami the Vicious'), and the second was Hamza. Of the rest, Taher, Hussain, and Abdul Razzaq stood out. Abdul Razzaq asked me, 'What will they do with us now?' I didn't have an answer, but I told him, 'Nothing.' From his voice, I felt he just wanted to hear something. I was experienced in comparison with them because of my first arrest when I was seventeen, so they thought I was the only one able to answer them. I asked about the charges against them, and they had no idea what they were. (What irony and diligence in this conspiratorial game against me.) However, like me, they had signed the statements of the man with the mispronounced r. He had said to one of them, 'Wite your name, you son of a pwostitute! Or I'll make an example of you . . .'

During the night I heard a knock on the door of the neighbouring cell, and Sami Al Sharis calling the guard. I understood from the conversation that he had had a wet dream, so needed to wash himself clean of this new crime and its evidence. But he knocked again in the morning before breakfast, to ask if he could go to wash another time. It seemed that a consequence of the torture was that he ejaculated continually. I was afraid another charge would be made against him, for who knew what might happen? After breakfast he was told to prepare himself because the administration had sent for him (and by 'administration' they meant Colonel Adel). Sami asked me to lend him my trousers, because his were wet and had been hung out in the bathroom. I requested permission to go to the bathroom, and put on his trousers there. When Sami came back we were all asked to hurry and get ready; we were being transferred to some other cells. I had hung Sami's trousers in my cell because they were still wet, but there was no choice, so I put them on again and felt the dampness. Because of their size it was as if I was entering a large tent. After that they took us to the hallowed Adliya detention cells, or maybe I should call it 'Adamiyya' (non-existence), a place that destroys your ability to dream.

A long corridor, on either side tiny boxes, the numbers on them faded. The boxes were simply numbers, and the inmates within them were simply numbers. For the guards, days, months, and even years were simply numbers.

The din subsided as we entered the corridor. Heads appeared at the small openings in the centres of the cell doors, and without really concentrating you could spot the unkempt beards, and faces pale from extended lack of exposure to the sun. We were lined up next to the wall, and then asked by one of the policemen to remove our clothes. I was overwhelmed with confusion and fear – were they going to rape us?! But the policeman informed us that it was one of the security rules in 'Adamiyya', may God be pleased with it, and we would have to get used to it, as we were sure to return again and again. However, as he was undertaking the sacred duty of searching, the policeman did not miss the opportunity to assess our members and the thickness of the grass surrounding them . . . His eyes were glittering with sadistic pleasure. Then he asked us to put our hands behind our necks, and we had to stand and sit to prove that our blessed backsides were free of escape tools. I was put in a cell labelled with the number four, a cell with two bunk beds. (For every bed there is always an equal and opposite inmate.) The cells were two by two and a half metres, with a bathroom, one metre square, attached at the back. It seemed they had built it austerely, because they had forgotten to add a door. We used to enjoy the personal 'communications' from inside, and of course the details that accompanied them, part of the democratic dialogue between prisoners from various parts of the world, and different races, colours, and sects.

The walls were, as in all prisons, dark grey, covered with writing, some carved into the wall. The wall was a blackboard for the inmates of the cells, and a repository for their memories there. The strange thing was that you could find dates at the bottom of all the inscriptions. Among them, near the door, was the sentence, 'The bird does not rise far from the ground.' I didn't understand what this sentence meant; it seemed that the wise man – or the donkey – that carved it had a special view of things. Nevertheless, this sentence later opened many doors in my mind, making 'Abu Maqhur' – the name signed under it – a holy man to me.

## CHAPTER 3

# A room with a view

An eyewitness to the Pearl Uprising

Tony Mitchell

## Part one: the 'cleansing' of the Pearl Roundabout[1]

It all started for me on Valentine's Day, 2011. Monday, February 14.

Normally, on a Monday, I would have been at work at Bahrain Polytechnic, where I was employed as an English tutor. This day, however, was during the mid-semester break and I planned to spend a quiet day relaxing with my wife in our apartment on the tenth floor of the Abraj Al Lulu (Pearl Towers) apartment complex.

In the months leading up to this day there had been much political activity in Tunisia and Egypt, where outdated rulers had been overthrown. I had discovered on Facebook that a protest was set to take place at 'Lulu Roundabout' and I was looking forward to seeing what would happen. I'm rather ashamed to admit it now, but at the time I did not realise that Lulu Roundabout meant the impressive, large 'Pearl Monument' roundabout right next to us. Our apartment overlooked Dana Mall and the Lulu Hypermarket contained within. I thought that the protest was to take place at a small roundabout at the entrance to Dana Mall and so I kept looking out our window to see if anything had happened.

After a while I noticed that several police four-wheel-drive vehicles had gathered on the large vacant area opposite Dana Mall.

Not long after, I heard many loud bangs and saw a lot of white smoke. It appeared that the police had cornered a group of people in a side street near the roundabout next to Dana Mall, and I assumed that the people were the same ones who used to set fire to tyres around the Sanabis area (the area closest to Dana Mall and the Pearl Roundabout). To me, it looked like they had set off some smoke bombs and had quickly run away. Pretty harmless stuff, it seemed. By the time the smoke had cleared there was no one remaining and the police vehicles soon left the area. I later learnt that there were many other similar protests throughout Bahrain that day, including the death of one protester, which explained the rather small police presence near us.

Later that day, from my apartment window I counted at least 80 police four-wheel-drive vehicles positioned in the vacant lot opposite Dana Mall. The Pearl Roundabout had been completely blocked off and surrounded by police. I was able to see from the open car park in the bottom three floors of the Abraj Al Lulu complex that no one could get in or out of the roundabout. Police were turning back cars that had exited from the Seef highway and there was a lot of traffic held up in the surrounding streets. It was obvious that the police did not want anyone anywhere near the roundabout. The police cars on the vacant lot separated into groups of about ten and all sped off in different directions (I later learnt that these went to various Shi'a villages and fought with protesters). Apart from the traffic disruption, the rest of the day around us was quite peaceful.

The next day, Tuesday 15th, was quite strange. Still on my break from work, I was now greeted by the sight of hundreds of people streaming towards the Pearl Roundabout, parking their cars on the vacant lot and walking, carrying Bahraini flags. I ventured downstairs to the car park and looked out over the roundabout. The police had all gone and it was teeming with people. The mood was one of gaiety. People seemed happy to be there and within a short time there were tents, microphones, a stage, and even sofas! I later learnt that a popcorn machine had been installed. I was fascinated to see many women, all dressed in their black abayas, standing shoulder to shoulder with men chanting and singing songs. Soon there were so many people that cars could not use the surrounding streets. Despite this, the mood was still peaceful and calm and although I did not fully understand what was happening I felt quite safe and not threatened at all. As more public address systems were installed we were able to hear the singing, the chanting, and the speeches from our apartment and in the evening more and more people arrived, especially families. The sounds (I don't like to call it noise) continued late into the evening and I was surprised to see that many younger men had actually set up camp and were spending the night there.

The 'occupation' of Pearl Roundabout continued into the following day, Wednesday, and the number of people swelled considerably. Every square inch of the roundabout was occupied by people and a small city of tents had sprung up. A stage was erected and the day was once again taken up with speeches, singing, and chanting. Food and drink was handed out to all the people and once again the number of women involved was quite interesting. The evening brought the most visitors as many families arrived at the roundabout to join in the peaceful protests. Eventually the whole area was quiet as the people, much more than the previous day, bedded down for another evening.

3.00 am, Thursday 17th February. I was woken by my wife, who was very animated, telling me that she thought something was happening at the roundabout. Even with our windows closed we could hear many loud bangs (the same as I had heard on the 14th) and cars hurriedly leaving the vacant lots followed by many people running away. I dressed quickly and grabbed my video camcorder and rushed to the elevator. I don't have any real recollection why I took my camcorder other than I wanted to obviously film what happened because, for some strange reason, I knew that something bad was happening. While living in Australia, Thailand, and Oman, I had never been exposed to any kind of uprising or protests before and had never witnessed tear gas being used in person, so I guess I wanted to record this. But something told me that this was not going to be a simple situation of nicely asking people to pack up and move away from the roundabout. I knew it was going to be bad.

When I reached the third floor car park of our Gold Tower at Abraj Al Lulu, I was immediately hit with the strange smell of tear gas. It was not strong enough to affect me (or my wife, who had also accompanied me) and I began filming. I saw a large group of white-helmeted police moving in packs and people (all men as far as I could see) trying to stand their ground. I saw the tear gas being fired and glowing when they hit the ground, then releasing their smoke. Other loud explosions were going off, too. I later found out that these were 'sound bombs', which were much louder than those of the tear gas being shot. Tragically, I also discovered that shotguns were fired and that four men were later found dead. Despite the clouds of smoke and the general mayhem of the scene, I did not see a single protester carrying anything or fighting with the police in any way.

We moved to another part of the car park and I filmed more of the people hurrying away to their cars from the roundabout in the direction of Dana Mall. The police were chasing them and still firing tear gas. A few defiant protesters tried to stand their ground but were overcome by the fumes and eventually retreated. Soon the fumes wafted up to our position and our eyes began to sting. I thought the sensation would pass but even in the open car park the fumes lingered and we left the area to return to our apartment. My first ever contact with tear gas and I don't recommend it. Closing and rubbing your eyes has no effect, the only thing to do is seek refuge somewhere.

By the time we were inside our apartment, our eyes were pretty much back to normal and I immediately began uploading my video footage to YouTube. Why did I do this? At the time I was not aware, but now I know the reason: I was mightily pissed off. I had not expected such actions from a government that I had been led to believe were focused on progress, with a vision for the future. The tactics I saw I had only heard about in communist Europe when I was a kid. It confirmed what I briefly saw on Valentine's Day: that the security forces looked upon the protesters as something that needed to be subdued as quickly as possible.

I uploaded all I had taken. Then my wife and I watched the last of the protesters leave the vacant lot on foot, as it was impossible for them to have time to get into cars and drive away without being set upon by the police. It was obvious that the police were not content on merely clearing the area; they seemed hell bent on trying to injure as many of the protesters as possible. The last of the protesters retreated to the surrounding streets of Sanabis and yet the bangs continued, even though the primary aim of clearing the roundabout had been achieved.

It was difficult to sleep after witnessing such brutality and I was still quite upset and angry at what I had seen. I tried to monitor the events by viewing comments on Facebook and was surprised to learn that many of my friends (most of them students from Bahrain Polytechnic) had already viewed the YouTube videos. I was also surprised at all the messages of thanks I was receiving, many students passing on thanks from their parents to me. At the time, I did not understand the significance of what I had done and I also received warnings to be careful. I assured my friends that I was safe and that the violence had stopped but the warnings continued, telling me that I may be arrested if I was not careful. In my eyes, I had done nothing wrong and, if anything, I had merely recorded a successful (albeit brutal) police operation. The government should be supportive, shouldn't they? Unless, of course, they did not want others to see what had *really* happened.

During that Thursday, the roundabout was quickly cleared of anything that the protesters had taken there. The many cars that had been left by their owners were simply dragged away by a fleet of tow trucks. Most of the cars still had their handbrakes on or were engaged in gear and so there was the regular sound of car tyres screeching as they were being taken away. The cars that had been parked on streets were the first priority and this process lasted all day and into the night.

In the days that followed the 'crackdown' at the roundabout, I was contacted by CNN and the BBC by email, asking me for permission to use my videos on YouTube. I immediately allowed them to do so, the more people who saw them the better as far as I was concerned. One 'news agency' in America wanted me to give them exclusive rights to use them, which I refused. Later, my wife and I got a buzz from seeing my videos on TV as part of the excellent BBC reports. Meanwhile, the entire area around us was surrounded by police, sending a clear message that the protesters were not welcome back. I received a message from one of my students, very upset and afraid after she saw several 'tanks' being transported on the backs of trucks pass her house, headed towards Manama (the capital, right next to the Pearl Roundabout). She was adamant at what she saw and, sure enough, later the next morning there was a line of armoured personnel carriers slowly making their way towards us along the main highway.

Soon there was a large military as well as police presence in the vicinity of the roundabout. The soldiers that had arrived had set up camp (ironically, just as the protesters had done, with tents) with generators and water tanks. It appeared that they were prepared to be there for some time. Strangely, several large tanks were placed in the large vacant lot that was previously filled with protesters' cars. Also, the lot was completely fenced in with razor wire, as if the police, soldiers, and tanks were not quite enough of a deterrent. It all served as a powerful message to anyone thinking of returning to the roundabout. Despite this, my wife and I decided to walk to Dana Mall as we needed to buy some food. Several cars belonging to the protesters were still parked on the sides of the footpath, the owners abandoning them in their haste to leave. Every single one of them had had their windows smashed. We made our way to the mall and back without any problems and we continued to monitor the situation from our apartment windows and also from regular visits down to our car park.

In the afternoon on Friday the 18th I discovered from messages on Facebook that a large procession of protesters were marching from Salmaniya Hospital to the Pearl Roundabout. Salmaniya had become a refuge for the many injured protesters and their families and friends. It is here where dedicated doctors and medical staff were later accused and arrested for assisting the protesters at the expense of pro-government patients. I anticipated more violence so I ventured down to the vantage point of our car park, but my view of the protesters was obscured by trees. I zoomed in with my camcorder and could see men and a few vehicles approaching the roundabout, which by this time was manned by armoured vehicles and a ridiculous amount of police vehicles. Armed soldiers were crouched behind hedges close to the armoured vehicles. From my zoomed view, I once again saw that none of the marchers were armed in any way at all. Suddenly, there was an almost deafening volley of shots fired from the roundabout and without my camcorder I could see the protesters fleeing away back towards Salmaniya Hospital. I later learnt that several unarmed protesters had been shot by this volley and I was also 'reliably' informed by pro-government students that the injuries they suffered had actually been faked, which was nonsense. The police then embarked on their tactics of tear gas and eventually chased the protesters away from the area again. The armoured vehicles stayed where they were and the police vehicles all raced away after the protesters.

It was during this incident that I was first asked by the staff of the apartment not to use camcorders or cameras and to please go inside 'for your own safety'. The staff (mainly cleaners) told me they had been told to ask people not to film and not to be in the car park. I ignored them, naturally.

## Part two: unarmed and shot in the back – the return to the Pearl Roundabout

Unknown to me, there was a lot of activity taking place in Bahrain behind the scenes in a bid to end the unrest. The Crown Prince had become involved and was trying to broker an agreement that began by allowing the protesters back to Pearl Roundabout.

On Saturday February 19th, I was still keenly watching what was happening around our complex, moving between the car park and our apartment windows, trying to see if anything was happening, but the military seemed relaxed and staying in their positions, securing the roundabout. Messages on Facebook indicated that their presence would be withdrawn, but from my vantage point it looked to me that they would be there for some time. Nothing seemed to be happening and my wife and I managed to drive away from the area for some much-needed distraction of badminton (for my wife) and snooker (for me) at the excellent British Club, a short drive away but, once inside, a million miles from what we had witnessed.

We returned safely and without any problems to our apartment later in the afternoon and the first thing we did was to check the situation and, for me, to report to others what was happening, which was nothing. Once again, it was my wife who alerted me to something important happening downstairs after she went down later to check. She rushed into the apartment to tell me that the army had left and the police were shooting protesters again! I felt annoyed again (mainly for missing out on seeing the army leave, which I had felt was not going to happen and also for the fact that my wife got to see it before I did!) and once again raced downstairs with my camcorder to hopefully view the important events. I could not understand why the army would leave the area and yet the police would remain and be shooting the protesters.

Sure enough, when the elevator doors opened and we rushed to the edge of the car park walls we could see jubilant protesters with

Bahrain flags running around the grassed area of the roundabout, stopping to bend down and pray, hugging each other, clapping, chanting, and anything else they could think of. I saw no police and was looking quizzically at my wife whilst filming when once again the loud bangs associated with them were heard. A group of white-helmeted police had sprung out from behind the garden on one side of the roundabout and were trying to chase away the celebrators (they weren't protesting) and had managed to grab a few of them. I was puzzled at the time, but one must remember that the police fall under the jurisdiction of the Prime Minister who, it was later revealed, was not in favour of the roundabout being given back to the people. Just at that very point, one of the men had broken away from the police and was running away. One policeman simply raised his shotgun and calmly shot him in the back. The man disappeared behind a tree so we could not see what had happened to him, but he was definitely not shot with tear gas or a sound bomb. I captured it all on video and felt that the whole exercise was simply an elaborate trap. Remove the army, allow the people back and then the police move in and cut them down. I was prepared to record the whole thing and show it to the world but just then a man who I had never seen before came up to me and asked me to stop filming. He was well dressed and held a walkie-talkie. I was quite upset by seeing an unarmed man shot in the back and very angry that it was allowed to happen. More to the point, what was wrong with filming it? Surely I had a right to do so and I managed to tell this to the man, as well as quite a few words beginning with 'f'. He appeared quite shocked by my outburst (as was my wife) and he immediately spoke Arabic into his walkie-talkie and hurried away. I took that as my cue to leave and, after a quick look at the rounda-bout (the police were now leaving, being taunted by the protesters as they did so), we went to the relative safety of our apartment.

I was quite worried inside the apartment and made sure the door was securely locked. My students had warned me earlier about being arrested and told me that the police in Bahrain were nothing like the police in Australia (and that's saying something!). Some even advised me to leave our apartment. I knew that the man with the walkie-talkie had reported me to someone and sure enough there were men's voices outside our door followed by the inevitable loud knock. I must admit that they did well to locate our apartment so quickly but I refused to answer the door. I had done nothing wrong (except some swearing) and they could knock all day for all I cared. The only thing that concerned me was if they decided to break down the door, as our apartment belonged to a very nice couple who lived close by in Saudi Arabia. Eventually, the knocking stopped and the voices left our floor. My wife and I were whispering about what we should do when my phone rang and it was our landlord calling! She told me that I was in big trouble and I needed to go and see the security men immediately. She advised me not to be silly about it and also told me that Bahraini prisons were not nice places to be (how I agree with her now!).

My wife and I ventured downstairs to find the walkie-talkie man and eventually saw him in the car park talking to two other men. We walked up to them and I immediately apologised to the walkie-talkie man before the largest of the men introduced himself as the 'security manager for the apartment complex'. I had never seen any of the three men before in the 14 months that I had been living there. The security manager told me that I had put him in a very difficult position by filming the protests because he was under orders from the Bahrain Ministry of Interior (responsible for law enforcement and public safety in Bahrain) not to allow any resident from the apartments to document anything taking place around us. He said that if it was discovered that a lot of filming had taken place he had the right to go through every apartment searching for cameras and inspecting computers, etc. – and he did not want to do that. He said the best thing I could do was to delete all the film I had taken. I told him that I had already uploaded it all to

YouTube and Mr Walkie-Talkie said, 'Oh no'. The security manager then told me that I needed to assure him that I would stop videotaping. 'We know you work for the Polytechnic as an English teacher, we know your CPR (Civil Personal Record) number, we know that is your car over there, we know everything about you,' he said. I know he was trying to intimidate me and that most of this information would have been given to him by my landlady and the guy who operates the boom gate on the car park, but I had no wish to make things any worse and so I agreed to delete my videos and not to take any more.

At the time, I did not think much about it, but I am now convinced that the three men I spoke to were all connected to the Ministry of Interior. As I mentioned, I had never seen them nor heard anything from them before and I only ever saw the third member of the trio again after this day. I am sure that my footage was either noticed by the Ministry staff or was referred to it and the men were sent to the apartment towers to put a stop to it. I ask again, why was there a ban on it unless it was something the government did not want others to see?

Mr Walkie-Talkie accompanied my wife and me back to our apartment and he watched as I sat at the dining table and deleted all the video I had downloaded onto my computer. I then did the same in front of him with my camcorder. He asked if I had any other film stored anywhere else, to which I said 'no'. I then offered to give him my camcorder to prove I would stop filming. He took it and said I could collect it from him, probably in a few weeks. I must say, he was quite polite the whole time he was with us, and my wife was indeed able to get our camcorder back. I was relieved to be out of the 'hot seat' at our apartment complex but a little disappointed that I could no longer help spread the truth if any further outbreaks of brutality were to occur at the roundabout. I still monitored the situation around us closely and even visited the proceedings and festivities outside to see for myself just how peaceful it was. My 'reporting' days were over but little did I realise that my real problems were only just beginning.

## Part three: the classroom, the protests, and a foreign army

From the perspective of my wife and me, all was once again well with the world. The peaceful protesters were back at the Pearl Roundabout, there were no police, no army, no bloody tear gas, and no security personnel hanging around. Yes, it was difficult to move in and out of the complex in our car but the protesters had volunteer traffic wardens (as well as cleaners), so it was far from unbearable. I felt like I had dodged a bullet by not being arrested (I still cannot imagine what it must have been like for some families to have had their front door kicked down in the middle of the night and witnessed the head of the household being savagely beaten in from of them before being taken away to be tortured). There was also nothing controversial to videotape, so the lack of camcorder was no problem.

My wife and I visited the roundabout one evening and there was a pleasant, carnival-like atmosphere. Thousands of people united by one primary goal (something called 'democracy') were mingling happily as one group. There were free food stalls everywhere (a new popcorn machine had been installed), and a small area set aside for aspiring artists and even free haircuts were available. The pro-government trolls later claimed that these were 'sex tents' to cater for you-know-what, which was both preposterous and insulting to the large number of families, women, and children that were in attendance. Once again, at no time did we ever feel unsafe or threatened. Needless to say, we did not see any evidence of weapons on display.

I eventually returned to work at the Polytechnic, as preparations were in order to welcome our students back and there were several meetings with all staff, both academic and non-teaching. In these meetings, the CEO, Mr John Scott, stressed the fact that the

Polytechnic needed to be seen as a place where all students were able to feel safe amidst all the turmoil that had happened outside. Security was beefed up and there was a need to search students' vehicles for weapons, but John wanted everyone to know that we could not be seen to be taking sides and that we needed to remain neutral in front of our students. I fully agreed with him but, after what I had witnessed, I found it very difficult to be neutral. I really struggled with this notion because, to me, it made me feel like I didn't care. Looking back (which is always so easy to do), I know I should have spoken to more people about this but I could not bring myself to tell anyone I was neutral. In my eyes, it was like saying, 'Oh, I don't mind what happens because I'm an expat' or, 'it's your country, it's got nothing to do with me'.

The group of students that I had the privilege of teaching before February 14th were a wonderful group of young people and made my job so enjoyable. For those who may not know, Bahraini students have superb senses of humour and can speak and listen to English extremely well. I did not have the slightest idea which of my students were Sunni or Shiʻa and it did not make any difference before the unrest. Some of my students had formed their own group called 'The Catalysts', who wanted to bring about change (obviously) as well as undertaking community projects and charity work. They were all friends and we had a ball together. After February 14th, it was all gone.

My first day back at teaching saw my students sitting in different groups and the air in the classroom was cold. There were no smiles, no laughter, and I immediately knew which students were pro-government: the ones that were the most pissed off. I tried to make them welcome and wanted them to know that we had all been through a tough time but that I hoped we could still have a good semester together. I then told the class that I had been asked to be neutral about the events and that I was sorry, but I could not. I knew this would alienate many in the class but I hoped that they would understand and respect me, based on our good relationship. Wrong.

After the class I was approached by a group of pro-government male students who were very keen to tell me not to be fooled by what I had heard or been told by people from the other side. They played the Iran card, saying protesters wanted Bahrain to be a part of Iran again and that they wanted to change the country with all women covering themselves, etc., etc. I was told that the protesters were liars and had faked their injuries. I tried to state my case, that the protests were about true democracy, but I was wasting my time. I thanked the boys and made my excuse to leave.

Meanwhile, away from work I was kept busy on Facebook keeping up with the stream of information about what had been happening. To my dismay, there was a huge amount of misinformation about what had occurred. Allegations of weapons being found during the roundabout clearance on February 17th, the sex-tent rumours, the faking of injuries and photographs, etc. I was appalled that students, including some of my own, would spread such malicious gossip. I took it upon myself to try to correct some of these errors based on my own experience, living with the Pearl Roundabout on my back doorstep. I got involved in several discussions with a few students in particular, 'friends' on my Facebook account, who had severely warped and prejudiced views on the protesters and outrageous and blinkered opinions about their own government and so-called leaders. The use of the word 'terrorists' was introduced and one student classified the protesters as worse than Hitler because 'even Hitler kept the schools going'. Enough said.

As February drew to a close we were treated to the spectacle of the protest marches, the likes of which I had not seen before in 'real life'. We could see from our apartment the protesters stretched from Seef all the way to the roundabout, about two kilometres of united protest. Once again, the women were easily distinguished in their black and there was even a long Bahraini strip flag that was hundreds of metres long. As they slowly passed our building, we could hear their chants and singing and each of these marches were, once again, conducted peacefully and respectfully.

Not to appear to be outdone, the pro-government Bahrainis organised their own gatherings, ostensibly as a show of support for the ruling family but obviously a clear attempt at one-upmanship and 'anything you can do we can do better'. Unfortunately, it was discovered that many of the pro-government crowd consisted of expat labourers from the Subcontinent, who were paid in food vouchers to join in and wave small Bahraini flags. Once again, enough said.

On March 3rd things started to get ugly. There was reportedly a clash in Hamad Town between Shi'a and Sunni, and on March 10th another Sunni–Shi'a altercation occurred following an incident at a girls' school. I was informed that the Sunni involved were the naturalised ones who are imported by the government to help bolster their numbers in return for plum jobs (usually in security) and free housing. A few days after this I awoke to see a strange sight from our bedroom window: no cars at all on the normally busy Seef highway. I discovered later that it had been blocked at both ends by protesters and I knew this would eventually mean trouble. In the subsequent days, the large malls surrounding the area (Bahrain City Centre, Dana Mall, Seef Mall, Bahrain Mall) all closed as few customers could enter. Thankfully, my wife had left the country at this time but things were starting to get uncomfortable for me. The enormous numbers at the roundabout made travel in our car virtually impossible and now most of the shops in the area were shut. Two of my fellow teachers were also living in my apartment complex, and we all received an offer from the Polytechnic to move away and stay at a hotel if we wanted to, which was extremely kind of them.

On the 13th of March, the government had had enough and sent the police in to clear the protesters, but had to force their way in via the blocked highway first. I watched the events unfolding from my windows and from the car park (until tear gas intervened) and eventually the police retreated, much to the delight of the protesters. The battle had lasted for most of the morning and only ended when the police knew that they did not have the numbers.

That was to change when the King called on Saudi Arabia to help him control his own country the following day. Something told me that things would only get worse and I accepted the Polytechnic's offer and packed my bags and drove to the Gulf Hotel in order to figure out what to do. My wife at this time was understandably concerned about me and we decided a break in Thailand was called for, so I booked a flight online and flew there the next day.

## Part four: back to Bahrain and goodbye

I arrived back in Bahrain on the 2nd of April, after what should have been a pleasant stay in Bangkok with my wife. I found it difficult to relax with my thoughts focused on what would happen to the protesters at Pearl Roundabout after the King had asked for help, requesting the use of the GCCPS (Gulf Cooperation Council Peninsula Shield) troops to obviously control the situation with force. The GCCPS was set up to defend against external threats but was now being deployed against Bahrain's own unarmed civilians, and the roundabout was cleared again while I was away.

While I was in Bangkok, I learnt that the wonderful Pearl Monument had been demolished. I found this very difficult to understand but it only confirmed the Khalifa regime's determination to remove all traces of the peaceful protests that had occurred there. State television said the area needed to be 'cleansed' and the Bahraini Foreign Minister, Khalid bin Ahmad Al Khalifa, said the demolition was 'a removal of a bad memory'.

I felt a huge sense of loss when I drove my car towards Abraj Al Lulu and found there was no Lulu anymore. I had been told that, when the monument was constructed in 1982 (for the third summit of the Gulf Cooperation Council held in Bahrain), it was the tallest structure in the country at the time. It had since been dwarfed by several nearby apartment buildings but it was no less significant or impressive. Now it was gone.

The Polytechnic started up again following the break due to the 'social unrest' and there was another full meeting of staff. We learnt that the Polytechnic, formerly under the guidance of the Economic Development Board, was now to be a part of the Ministry of Education. A 'deputy CEO' had been appointed from the Ministry, Dr Mohammed Ebrahim al-Asiri (who was not present at the meeting), whose role was to liaise with the Minister in Arabic, so that the Minister could answer questions about the Polytechnic in parliament. In stark contrast to his statement of neutrality in February, John Scott then announced that the Polytechnic was now part of the government and that we should be seen to support the government. 'Like hell I will,' I said to myself. One of my colleagues summed up the situation perfectly when he said, 'He's been nobbled'. [Verb: Try to influence or thwart (someone or something) by underhand or unfair methods: 'an attempt to nobble the jury'.] Finally, John informed us that all staff and students would be 'investigated' for participation in any of the recent demonstrations just as soon as the investigations had been completed at the University of Bahrain.

I resumed my teaching at the Polytechnic, devoting my time to squeezing my English course into the time that remained in the semester. My students had been given the option of morning or afternoon classes and had used this opportunity to form themselves mainly into a morning pro-government group and an afternoon pro-democracy group. Now the tables had been turned and my morning class was upbeat and smiling, whereas my afternoon class was quiet but determined. I still tried (as always) to teach without any favouritism or discrimination, but the overwhelming arrogance of my morning class made it quite difficult for me. The students did not seem interested, some arriving very late, some not even bringing paper or pen, some simply operating their mobile phones for the duration of the lesson. I never mentioned what had happened outside the Polytechnic to them, but I feel that many of the students were aware of my feelings and had simply dismissed me. I now feel that some of them were struggling as much as I was with their own inner conflict of appearing to support the government but secretly questioning what had taken place.

In May, the investigations started as promised and the mood of the Polytechnic was difficult to explain. We learnt that Bahraini staff had been identified from photographs as having attended protests and were singled out for investigation. One of the non-teaching staff was arrested and severely beaten, but was able to resume work. I have since learnt that Facebook pages were expressly set up displaying photographs taken at demonstrations, asking for pro-government supporters to identify the circled faces so that they could be identified, traced, and arrested. One of my former students told me his terrifying story: he was called to the administration building at the Polytechnic and he, with five other students, was taken to the nearby military building where they were all put in a room. They stayed in there all night and were interrogated the next morning. My student was very fortunate, as he had been confused with another young man with a similar name, and was allowed to leave. Three of the youths (students from the University of Bahrain) were handcuffed, hoods were placed over their heads, and they were taken away on a bus, never to be seen again.

I was finding it more and more difficult coping at this time, but I tried not to think too much about what might happen to me, which was not easy. I tried to be positive and reassured myself that I had not taken part in any protests and therefore was safe. My videos from February had been dealt with by the 'security staff' at my apartment and so I felt safe about them. I know I had made comments to my 'friends' on Facebook, but they were not critical of the ruling family or the government, simply trying to correct wrong and misleading information. I did not know what the future held at the Polytechnic for me and I did not know if I could continue working for a government that resorted to unlawful arrests, torture, and now identification from social networking.

Students had now started to be expelled, including one from my afternoon class. Again, my morning class was as happy as usual, totally unaffected by what was now happening at the Polytechnic and in Bahrain. Understandably, my afternoon class was very upset and worried and I tried to give them as much leeway as I could to cope with everything. Some of my afternoon students came from villages that were now being raided by police, who were arresting suspects and damaging property. They bravely came to class, passing through checkpoints, and still continued to work hard. I found their courage very inspiring.

With every passing day that I was at the Polytechnic I was expecting to be asked to appear at an interview with the investigating committee that had been set up by the deputy CEO. And with every passing day that I wasn't asked I felt that maybe I had flown under their radar and escaped detection. It was a stressful time and I can remember being on edge and not being able to sleep well at home. Sure enough, I received a text message on my mobile phone while I was in class asking me to visit the Director of Human Resources in the CEO's office.

The meeting was direct and to the point. The Ministry of Education knew all about me, knew all about my videos and my comments on Facebook. It turns out that my 'friends' had kept copies of my comments and these were presented to me, although none of them could seriously be used to show that I had been critical of the government in any way. I knew that my number was up and there was nothing I could do. To his credit, John Scott had insisted that I not front the other investigative committee, as I was the only expat under investigation. I told him that I did not hold him responsible for what was taking place in any way, for which he thanked me. It was also obvious that the Ministry wanted me out immediately (as had happened to the students), but John said he would try to see if he could arrange for me to finish up later. I appreciated this, as I needed to assess my students before their classes finished in four weeks. We later agreed that I could finish on 30th June, which would also give me time to sell my car and arrange to pack and send all our belongings to Thailand. I was asked to please stop making any comments at all on Facebook, to which I agreed. I did not want the Polytechnic or anyone from management to get into trouble for anything I did, because they had all treated me so well in the past.

I remember walking back to my office with very mixed thoughts. I had been sacked from my job, not because of my teaching ability or for any normal disciplinary reason, but because I had taken videos and made comments on Facebook. I now had to think of my future after June 30th, look for a new job somewhere and tell my wife that we had to leave our beautiful apartment and the life we enjoyed together in Bahrain. On the other hand, I felt a huge sense of relief that I had been freed from having to work for the Bahraini government and that I would no longer have any association with them whatsoever.

I would like to take this opportunity to mention the expat staff who remain at the Polytechnic and my feelings towards them. I do not want anyone to assume that I look at them differently simply because they continue to work there. Their reasons for being there are private and to be respected and if there is anything I have learnt from my experiences this year in Bahrain, it is that personal feelings and decisions should be respected. I am still good friends with many of them.

In the weeks following my dismissal I still monitored Facebook, mainly to try to keep track of the students that had been expelled, as I was appalled to learn that many outstanding young Bahrainis and student leaders of the Polytechnic had been ordered to leave. It was during this time that several comments appeared criticising John Scott for being personally responsible for the expulsions and for going back on his word of the Polytechnic being neutral. I felt I could not allow this to happen, as I knew John's authority had been diminished by the intervention of the Ministry and that he truly had the students' best interests at heart at all times. So I posted what I thought was an innocent comment: 'I will tell you more about this after June 30th.' Bad move, Tony.

The next morning, June 14th, I was called to the HR Director's office (John Scott was on leave) and told that my Facebook post had been brought to the Minister of Education's attention (no doubt by one of my Facebook 'friends') and that he was 'up in arms about it'. I know that he would have been more upset with the Polytechnic for not controlling me but nevertheless he demanded that I leave immediately. This meant I could not assess my students but, thankfully, that was done later by two very capable tutors. So I packed up my belongings, copied all my files from my Polytechnic laptop to my external hard drive, and gave the laptop back. The Polytechnic had already booked flights to Thailand for my wife and me for July 1st and I was asked if I wanted them to change the tickets.

I didn't want to cause a fuss and I felt the extra two weeks would give us more time to pack, sell the car, say our goodbyes, and leave. The HR staff I was with at the time all looked at each other nervously and I was advised to think seriously about leaving the country as soon as possible. I didn't like the sound of that. Was I that much of a threat to the government? It was unnerving but it showed me just how paranoid those in the government had become and how determined they were to eradicate all opposition to their practices.

My wife and I flew out from Bahrain on June 23rd. We frantically managed to send all our possessions safely to Thailand and I managed to sell my car (with the wonderful assistance of my former student, the one who was arrested), but at least we had possessions and my car had not been smashed up, as was happening in many villages at the time. On the Etihad flight I had time to reflect on my three years in Bahrain, what I had experienced and what I had achieved. I also wondered what would happen to the amazing country and the brave people I was leaving behind.

# PART TWO

# Configuring dissent

Charting movements, space, and
self-representation in Bahrain

## CHAPTER 4

# Shifting contours of activism and possibilities for justice in Bahrain

## Luke G.G. Bhatia and Ala'a Shehabi

> We want neither to live in a palace nor to rule.
> We are a people killing humiliation and assassinating misery.
> We are a people destroying the foundation of oppression.
> We are a people who don't want to be held back anymore.
> – Poem read by Ayat al-Qurmezi at the Pearl Roundabout

First they came for the political leaders who led the protests, then the doctors who treated the protesters, then the athletes who represented their country internationally, then the academics who protected the students; they eventually reached the poet who recited the poem above. Twenty-year-old Ayat al-Qurmezi was arrested and disappeared on 29 March 2011, two weeks after the purge began. Even one third of the employees of the Formula One circuit were not spared. Angry at the cancellation of the race that year, the police raided the slick modern offices of the Bahrain International Circuit, rounding up Shi'a employees one by one, including females and executive directors, lining them up and beating them in the corridors. It is difficult amongst this vast list to select one symbolic story from inside Bahrain's thronging prisons, as Tahiyya Lulu[1] states:

> If the walls of these prisons could talk, they would tell tales of
> Bahrain's secular nationalist political history and speak of the
> coalition of legal minds fighting for constitutional rights and rule
> of law . . . They might also tell us the high price of providing
> medical care to protesters, or being a student participating in a
> national youth movement, a teacher practising the values they
> teach, or a unionist in a country that doesn't value the land and
> sea it rests upon, let alone the salt of its earth.[2]

Despite this unceasing repression, the response of many protesters
and political groups, reduced to 'bare life' in the Agambian sense,
was to try and rise above the political fray - the accusations of treason,
of being foreign agents, the sectarian backlash, and the minimal
regional and international support for regime-change by appealing
to a 'universal' human rights discourse and to international legal
frameworks. After four years of struggle, the movement has, for
the most part, continued to focus on non-violence and the desire
for social justice, continuing a steadfast routine of daily protests
against an increasingly sophisticated state suppression of dissent.
Prisons are severely overcrowded, protests in the entire country
are permanently prohibited, and all the main opposition leaders at
the time of writing are imprisoned, on trial, or in exile. This is, by
and large, the longest standing peaceful uprising in the Arab world,
notwithstanding a handful of violent dubious acts by unknown
parties that have killed a handful of police mercenaries.

As noted by Abdulhadi Khalaf in the foreword to this book,
different actors of various ages, persuasions, and histories have
coalesced in the face of a clear and distinct adversary that is the state.
Veteran political leaders stood side by side with youth protesters to
confront a formidable ruling family that has been in power for nearly
200 years. A distinguishing feature of this popular movement is the
way its main actors as well as its grassroot supporters have adopted
a specific human rights-based agenda and discourse. Although this
rights-based movement is not new, the 'NGOisation', however,

is much more recent and the framing of demands on a popular level according to international legal conventions illustrates a new articulation and platform for legitimacy. Rather than using human rights in its modern prosaic and NGO sense, some of which is necessary and unavoidable, human rights activists have emerged as leaders of the uprising, playing a central and pivotal role. As this chapter argues, rather than seeing this as a triumph of liberalism and a desire for the West, the human rights discourse was turned into a radical tool for change.

On a global scale, the popularity and political efficacy of this discourse is part of what Wendy Brown calls the 'moral-political project'[3] for its capacity to imagine and assert universal rights possessed by every human rather than the specific political rights of citizens or members of a particular political community. In the Bahraini context, this brand of universality is particularly appealing given the authoritarian nature of the state and the systematic exclusion of religious and migrant groups, amongst others. Such universalism was employed necessarily and opportunistically in order to undermine and contest the regime's accusations of the sectarian (Shi'i) motivations of the protesters.

Given the rupture in social relations with the state on 14 February 2011, this chapter examines how both old and new social movements on the island responded and reconfigured to the barriers and threats imposed by the state. In particular, three points are discussed. First, we look at the role of human rights discourse as an advocacy tool for local activists and situate it in the Islamist and authoritarian discourses that dominated pre-2011. Second, we look at the ways in which the regime itself attempted to co-opt the human rights discourse as a survival strategy, which echo similar attempts made a decade earlier, by the monarchy adopting a discourse of 'democracy' and 'reform'. A dichotomy arises, one in which both victims and rights abusers appeal to the same discourse, yet one that arguably reinforces the authority and position of the latter. Finally, we will discuss whether this pragmatic human rights approach can be effective as a tool for social change and whether, given the limits of these mechanisms and the geopolitical alliances between the West and the regime, human rights mechanisms force groups into procedural approaches that ultimately feed into the politics of fatigue, without ending structures of inequality or the everyday trauma and suffering. In addition, we discuss whether it is effective in filling an ideological dearth needed to make revolutions successful, one in which liberation and emancipation alter the human condition. As a reflective evaluation, Bahrain serves as an interesting case study in the ongoing debate of whether human rights are 'weapons for the critique of power' versus becoming 'part of the arsenal of power'.[4]

## Bahrain's 'advocacy revolution'

> The paradox involved in the loss of human rights is that such a loss coincides with the instant when a person becomes a human being in general – without a profession, without a citizenship, without an opinion, without a deed by which to identify and specify himself – *and* different in general, representing nothing but his own absolutely unique individuality which, deprived of expression within and action upon a common world, loses all significance. – Hannah Arendt[5]

A popular paradigm in the literature of contemporary social movements has been the political opportunities approach. Proponents of this approach stress that the timing and fate of movements and popular mobilisations for collective action are largely dependent on the opportunities afforded by shifting institutional structures and the ideological dispositions of those in power.[6] Although the Arab uprisings in 2011 did appear to seriously challenge the authoritarian forms of governance that have been in place for decades, many of the authoritarian regimes that we see across the world today can be characterised as relatively 'stable' in that these structures of power and state machinations remain intact.[7] Regimes have survived through forceful repression, strengthened regional alliances, and the instigation of societal (mostly sectarian) polarisation. The reclaiming of the political, or repoliticisation, by populations in the Arab world has been done despite the lack of political opportunities, not because of them. What is perceived as a political opportunity for a movement is interpretive and dependent on a whole host of historical, political, and cultural factors, and this manifests itself in innovative ways. All of these factors came together in a moment of collective realisation in 2011, or an 'event' in the sense of Alain Badiou.

Bahrainis took to the streets on 14 February 2011. For nearly a month, protesters occupied a central district on the outskirts of the capital. The 'Pearl Revolution', as it was named by the protesters, illustrates 'a politics of multiple emancipatory enactments and transgressions whose results are new gendered imaginaries, subjectivities, and ways of inhabiting space'.[8] The short-lived experience of occupying this once placid and insignificant transitory space was captured in the 2011 Al Jazeera documentary *Shouting in the Dark*. In it a protester in *Midan al-Lu'lu'* (Pearl Roundabout) talks of 'touching the spirit of freedom'. Indeed for those with an accumulated and shared sense of persecution, it is only in the sense of the loss of human rights that they became human beings in the way described by Arendt. Here was a place where previously unimagined possibilities of justice were conceived and where hopes of carving a new future were articulated in a new-found realm of consciousness, one that could not be eradicated by the British-made tanks carrying the Saudi and UAE troops that rolled over the causeway on 14 March.[9]

The diversity and complexity of what can be perceived as political opportunity was carved out of a space so tightly controlled and militarily fortified that the King's son could openly declare on state television that 'there is no escape for those who called for the overthrow of the regime'. This statement signalled the start of a 'cleansing operation' that led to thousands of arrests, dismissals, and nearly one hundred deaths.[10] The inability of Bahrainis to resort to local laws and mechanisms of justice prompted the opposition to reach for something higher, and the framework of human rights was seized upon as being something beyond that which was written as law in the country. It also offered transnational space and platforms on which to mobilise and act after space for dissent inside the country was effectively crushed. Thus, the shifting tactics and discourse framed around Western liberal conceptions of human rights have become a salient feature.

Risse and Sikkink use the notion of 'transnational advocacy networks'[11] and point to specific contexts in which blockages exist with regard to grievances at the local level. Local activists can then present these grievances to a transnational advocacy network and in turn awareness can be raised with international institutions, other governments, NGOs, and movements in order to bring pressure from above onto the local level.[12] With this in mind, the uprising in Bahrain could be described as an 'advocacy revolution', a term we wish to develop.

The human rights idiom has been a central advocacy tool pushing political graps and individuals to work within a particular 'professional' model of political organisation, professionalise organisations and to formulate campaigns for social and political change using social media. It has also been important for opening up new transnational spaces. This form of advocacy has given agency to individual protesters to expose daily abuses and structural injustices, and has informed their strategies for promoting social and political change. While human rights groups, such as the Bahrain Center for Human Rights (BCHR) and the Bahrain Human Rights Society (BHRS) existed prior to 2011, after the March 2011 Saudi-led crackdown, Nabeel Rajab, President of BCHR, and other activists became the loudest voices in the cacophony of oppression during the martial law period. These abuses were documented in detail in the Bahrain Independent Commission of Inquiry (BICI) report.

In an interview, Rajab notes that years of working towards the empowerment of people through human rights awareness has been successful. 'In 2004 if they had put me in jail, and Abdulhadi al-Khawaja at the same time, there would be no human rights movement. With the work that we have done, with both of us in jail, the work did not stop in 2011 and 2012, and maybe it has been even more effective.'[13]

The use of human rights discourse, in some cases, has been key to breaking through the red lines that formal political associations have not dared to break, including targeting the authority of the ruling family at the apex of the pyramid of power and condemning the impunity of elites which are responsible for human rights abuses. The best example of this would be the Wanted for Justice campaign launched by BCHR in 2013, which named and shamed senior figures within the ruling family, including the King and Prime Minister, who were held responsible for systematic human rights violations. In other cases, human rights became a tool to stop arms equipment that would be used for direct repression. The Stop the Shipment campaign by anti-corruption group Bahrain Watch forced the South Korean government to stop a shipment of tear gas to Bahrain in January 2014, citing grave human rights abuses caused by the indiscriminate and excessive use of tear gas. Legal proceedings also began in 2014 in London, which lifted the diplomatic immunity of the King's son, who was accused of torture, and possibly paving the way for prosecution under universal jurisdiction.

Bahrain, by demonstrating that human rights can become part of a broad-based grassroots movement that is committed to a longer term vision of equality and justice, therefore serves as an interesting case study in the debate currently raging that is critical of human rights. At the same time, common criticisms around funding and professionalisation have been averted, simply because Bahraini groups have not been awash with the foreign funding that pursues groups closer to the donor's foreign policy interests.

However, American funders, such as the National Endowment for Democracy (NED), US–Middle East Partnership Initiative (MEPI), and the National Democratic Institute (NDI), have been active in backing certain NGOs and political groups in the field of 'political development'. These include the Bahrain Press Association (BPA) in London and the Gulf Centre for Human Rights (GCHR).

In 2006, the Bahraini regime expelled the director of NDI, citing funding concerns. However, a WikiLeaks cable later revealed more racist concerns: 'Shaikh Abdul Aziz said that Bahrain would have no problem working with an NDI director "with blonde hair and blue eyes", remarking that such a person would not be accepted in the same way by the opposition or have as much influence as Guleid' (who, as the cable goes on to say is an American of Somali origin and would have 'an innate antipathy toward the regimes of the Gulf, defining the situation in terms of the haves and have-nots').[14] After that incident, NDI was forced to work more closely with GONGOs (government-organised NGOs), such as the Bahrain Institute for Political Development (BIPD).

In the name of 'democracy promotion', the recipients of such grants have covered a wide political spectrum in a policy perceived to be one of hedging risk regarding the possible outcome of democratic reform if it were to happen, rather than seriously attempting to effect any real change itself. Much research has gone into critical assessments of how Western funding influences the agenda and efficacy of NGOs and opposition groups; however, little is said about how both British and US funding of government initiatives has actually influenced the regime's belief in democracy from above. Foreign funding, however, is criminalised and so local groups are forced to establish offices abroad in order to be recipients. Unlike in other countries, such as Palestine, Egypt, or Jordan, the size of this funding is relatively small in comparison, reaching only tens of thousands rather than millions, based on the assumption by donors that GCC states are not of immediate concern given oil wealth and national income. Bahrain is, therefore, by no means awash with grants and it is possibly too early to talk of the political economy of NGOs. Given the accusation of Iranian support is all too frequently used in the state media, it would make sense for NGOs to become more transparent in order to allay such fears, but Western funding is also extremely problematic and feeds into the state's assertion of an American-Iranian conspiracy, whilst at the same time, any local philanthropy has to be done as secret donations for security purposes.

## Beyond borders: internationalising the human rights struggle

Organising politically on the ground has become extremely difficult as a result of physical and digital surveillance and a lack of spaces in which to meet, organise, and work. This even includes the officially recognised graps like Wa'ad and Wefaq – who have faced increasing encroachment of the state in their operations. State authorisation is implicitly required for all public events and the state routinely intervenes in trivial matters, such as when it does not approve of an announced event. An example of this was in December 2014, when Wa'ad planned to host 'Ali Salman, the leader of Al Wefaq, at a seminar on the boycotting of elections. Wa'ad was forced by the Ministry of Interior to change the title of the event and cancel Salman's participation. A few days later, Salman was arrested. The long arm of the state, therefore, reaches even mundane aspects of these organisations in a process to 'interfere, restrict, control' civil society.[15]

These restrictions on local actors have pushed groups, both underground and out of the country, utilising a growing cadre of Bahraini activists in exile, to work from the various capitals where they have sought refuge, and to open up offices. Good examples of this would be Americans for Democracy and Human Rights in Bahrain (ADHRB) based in Washington, DC, and the Bahrain Institute for

Rights and Democracy (BIRD) in London as well as the Bahrain Forum for Human Rights (BFHR) in Beirut. These transnational spaces opened up by human rights activists are important in amplifying the work of local groups, complementing, rather than replacing actual grassroots activism in the country itself.

The proliferation of the local–global NGO networks represents an important addition to the organisational capital among civil society actors, not just in Bahrain, but in the Gulf as a whole. Human Rights Watch, Amnesty International, Human Rights First, and Physicians for Human Rights are the international NGOs most active in monitoring the situation in Bahrain, albeit from afar, as their access is routinely denied unless, as Amnesty has done, they accept the stringent terms of access imposed by the government. At both local and transnational levels, the Bahraini diaspora and what Ragazzi has called the 'exiled enemy'[16] have been powerful resources in terms of leadership and mobilisation. London, a traditional opposition hub, and now Berlin and Washington, DC, have become important centres of activism for asylees as Zoe Holman discusses in Chapter 7.

The regime's repression was designed first to punish and then to reassert control over civil society, yet this has inadvertently led to the creation of stronger, better organised local NGOs which are transnationally connected and legally, financially, and politically independent from the state. This 'organisational capital' and 'learning' has had to be formed outside the boundaries and controls set by a domineering state. At the same time, the organisations that have remained 'registered' have had to be pushed into a difficult corner, with suffocating restrictions on their work, or they have become too weak to resist state co-optation. For example, BHRS, a registered NGO, has seen its former president, 'Abdullah al-Durazi, co-opted into government, as has 'Abd al-'Aziz Abul, now an appointed Shura Council member. In addition, the regime has managed to buy the silence of many, who conveniently remove themselves from the scene.

Activists that have joined the growing ranks of NGOs have represented the movement at international conferences and travelled the world to carry their message at a level and scale that is unprecedented. The transnational spaces offered by the UN Human Rights Council (UNHRC), the European parliament, or indeed the British parliament, are new frontiers in the struggle for democracy. Indeed, it is no longer a battle with just the Bahraini regime but with its UK and US allies as well. In September 2012, when the UNHRC hosted a follow-up review on Bahrain, at least seventy opposition activists travelled to Geneva, significantly outnumbering those delegates sent by the regime, who were about thirty. Ultimately, though, the ability of these arenas to change the course of events is limited to statements and procedural supervision that lack any kind of enforced sanctions, especially in the absence of Security Council support. The UN setting serves as an important symbolic political spectacle in the minds of activists, despite frustrations felt within the country over its limited effectiveness in enforcement.

## A history of a rights-based social movement

> The year ended with the government and the Ruler uneasy and disinclined to give way on any matter of substance and the Higher Executive Committee determined to continue to press its demands, a number of which were in fact reasonable. – B.A.B. Burrows, Political Resident, Bahrain, 1955[17]

Today's human rights movement has evolved from historically well-established political and labour based movements. The demands of the political opposition have changed little since the first broad-based uprisings that first emerged in the 1920s: namely, self-determination and participation in the political process, the removal of foreign interference and military forces (then the British, now Saudi Arabia), an end to corruption, and an end to labour and sectarian discrimination, to name just a few. Beginning with the rights struggles of the 1920s, decennial episodes of political contestation in Bahrain have been characterised by attempts at building united fronts in the face of what has become a banal divide-and-rule strategy based on sectarianism as a counter-revolutionary strategy instinctively employed by the regime.

Nelida Fuccaro traces the beginnings of the rights-based struggle to 'the confrontation between the "Persian" police and the "Arab" rioters in Manama "in the early twenties", which inspired a new vocabulary of "national" rights . . . popularised by intellectuals and activists in the following years. This vocabulary denounced the municipal government as "illegitimate" and celebrated the common good of the nation (*al-maslahah al-wataniyyah*)'.[18] In 1926, pearl divers, enraged at cuts to their advanced pay, protested outside the offices of the British advisor and government palaces, successfully achieving some of their demands and reinstating some of their rights. In the thirties, underground groups such as Shabab al-Aḥrar (Free Youth) and Shabab al-Umma (Islamic Youth) introduced ideas of national rights inspired by the establishment of a legislative council in Kuwait (*majlis al-ummat al-tashri'iyya*) in that year, and promoted 'a new type of political literacy which targeted the grassroots directly'.[19] It was here that graffiti, leafleting, petitions, strikes, and boycotts entered the modern repertoires of protest and became a way of life. In the thirties and forties, community leaders, youth organisations, and progressive individuals 'initiated intersectarian cooperation and introduced a new official language of popular representation and of rights for the "national" labour force. In a petition sent to Sheikh Hamad in November 1938 Sunni, Shiʻi and Hawala merchants from Manama and Muharraq demanded the formation of a labour committee and the appointment of Bahraini subjects instead of "foreigners" to the *majlis al-baladiyyah* (municipal council), while requesting the formation of an elected body of merchants to represent the urban residents.'[20]

In a display of prefigurative politics and the nationalist sentiment of the era, the National Union Committee (NUC)[21] was formed in the fifties, comprising equally Sunni and Shi'i notables. The British political agent during this period, Charles Belgrave, wrote, 'they [the NUC] declared there were no longer any differences between Sunnis and Shi'a, and that all people in Bahrain were merged in the popular movement'.[22] The NUC called upon the government to introduce an elected parliament, to allow labour to organise into unions, a codified system of law, and the removal of Belgrave and British influence from the island.[23] The NUC also established the island's first labour union, which attracted 14,000 members in the first three months of its establishment.[24] (During a meeting in Bahrain on 29 December 2014, Radi al-Musawi, Wa'ad's political leader, described his society's demands as a direct extension of the basic demands of the National Liberation Front [NLF] and the NUC. These were an elected government that represents the will of the people, a fair electoral system that represents 'one person, one vote', a legislative body with full authority, an independent judiciary, security for all, and a security sector that is inclusive and respectful of human rights.)

With the decline of traditional industries, such as pearl diving, and the discovery of oil in Bahrain in 1932, the labour force within the country had undergone a drastic transformation as a result of the transition to an oil-dependent economy. The emergence of the Bahrain Petroleum Company (BAPCO) as a major employer on the island found workers from all communities, both local and expatriate, working side by side, and it became a 'learning ground(s) for communally blind labour militancy'.[25] This came to a head in 1965 following the sacking of hundreds of workers from BAPCO, with a protest which has come to be known as *intifādāt mars* (the March Intifada). Led by the underground political movements of the NLF and Arab National Movement (ANM), demands resonated with previous uprisings with protesters calling for a democratically elected parliament, the removal of the British, the ability to form workers' unions, the release of political prisoners, and equality in Bahraini society.[26] The uprising reached its peak in 1968 with labour strike actions affecting a large number of employers on the island. Khalaf writes that, 'the duration and its violent character underlined the gap between all major sections of the population on the one hand and the British and the ruling family on the other'.[27] The prospect of secular discontent proved a significant enough challenge to Al Khalifa rule and, again, the Bahraini police and the British navy quashed the uprising. Many of the youth longed for the 'the paraphernalia of independence and progress: a national assembly, trade unions, elections and political newspapers'.[28]

Britain's announcement of its withdrawal from the region in the East of Suez policy of 1968 calmed the protests somewhat. However, this period saw the various forces of political opposition amalgamate and form the Constitutive Committee for the General Federation of Workers, Craftsmen and Tradesmen in Bahrain (CC). Emulating the success of the NUC before it, the CC was a non-sectarian, organised labour movement. The CC considered its work to be apolitical and legal, to promote education and protect labour rights within the country. It worked at the grassroots levels without political affiliations. Working publically and pointing to existing legislation as the legal basis of their actions, the CC was a new complication for authorities with more experience of clandestine groups. In 1972, with escalating strike actions and the Bahrain Defence Force called out onto the streets, all members of the CC, except one who fled, found themselves imprisoned and the uprising was quashed.[29]

Bahrain's short-lived National Assembly between 1973 and 1975 proved too difficult for the government to control and, as such, the country returned to a state in which there was no legally sanctioned space for true oppositional politics. Following the Islamic Revolution in Iran in 1979 and the execution of the prominent Iraqi scholar Muhammad Baqir al-Sadr at the hands of Saddam Hussein, there were protests in Bahrain once again with the UK Ambassador in Bahrain claiming that it was more likely this execution that was the greatest fomenter of dissent.[30] The new movements that formed in the eighties were more Islamist in nature and filled the vacuum left by the crushing of the leftist opposition such as the NLF.[31] Bahrain's religious clerics, such as Abdulamir al-Jamri, and Issa Qassim who later became very influential, had their formative political worldview shaped by their direct experience of parliamentary democracy and their main demand, therefore, was the return of the 1973 constitution for the next 25 years. Apart from a radical group called the Islamic Front for the Liberation of Bahrain (IFLB), which was dedicated to the overthrow of the Al Khalifa regime and which was also accused of plotting a *coup d'état* in 1981, the mainstream opposition's core demand for the rest of the decade remained in the consistent call for the return of the 1973 constitution and parliament. Regarding the IFLB, the government was successful in 'weaken(ing) the group almost to the point of virtual disappearance from the political scene'.[32] The opposition as a whole, including groups like the Bahrain Freedom Movement, were driven underground or into exile.

The movement resurfaced in 1992 with what has come to be known as the 'elite's petition', or *aridhat al-nukhba*. The petition called for a reinstatement of the parliament, the release of political prisoners, and the return of those in exile, and its (280) signatories consisted of 'secular and religious activists from both Sunni and Shi'a backgrounds'.[33] The petition was received by the Amir but never commented upon. Instead, he implemented the appointed Shura Council. A coalition of religious and secular groups – namely, the Islamic Liberation Front and Bahrain Freedom Movement (the religionists) and the National Liberation Front and the Popular Front (the leftists) – issued a statement reiterating the demands of the elite's petition. Gaining momentum, another petition – the popular petition, or *al-'aridha al-sha'abiyya* – was to be presented to the Amir on Bahrain's National Day, demanding the restoration of the 1973 National Assembly and the inclusion of women in the democratic process.[34] Khalaf notes that 'most participants went out of their way to demonstrate the national foundation of the movement and its non-sectarian character'.[35] The response of the Secret Intelligence Service, led by British officer Ian Henderson, was emphatic at this point, leading to him receiving the nickname 'the butcher of Bahrain'.[36] Activists and religious clerics were arrested and exiled to London. Widespread torture of political detainees was documented by international human rights organisations, such as Amnesty International[37] and Human Rights Watch.[38]

## False hopes and the mirage of liberal democracy

Soon after King Hamad bin ʿIsa Al Khalifa came into power in 1998, a noticeable shift and new liberal discourse emerged in what the state calls, al-ʿahd al-islaahi (the reform era) that incorporates the modern lexicon of democracy; referendums, elections, constitution, parliament, ombudsman whilst at the same time, centralising powers into the hands of the Amir, who later changed his title to King. On 14 February 2001, 98 per cent voted in a national referendum in favour of the return of the 1973 constitution – in a true display of unity over core demands. The year that followed was critical in shaping the contours of the opposition that we see today. In the euphoria that followed, with the promise of a new democratic era, various groupings emerged as the bases of new political parties and this largely happened along sectarian lines. The largest society that was established was the Al Wefaq Islamic Society – led by another former exile, Shaykh ʿAli Salman – which was supposed to represent conservative Shiʿi citizens, who have now become known as the 'moderates' or the 'tolerated opposition'. Tens of other new societies were also established that year including those that represented Sunni Salafi (al-Asala) and Muslim Brotherhood (al-Minbar al-islami) groups. A year later, in 2002, the true nature of the ruler's promises emerged, when a unilaterally amended constitution was promulgated in what has been termed a 'constitutional coup'. Elections were announced, creating a fissure in the opposition over the decision to participate in or to boycott a disempowered parliament that falls far shorter of the version that existed in 1973.

Along with these 'reforms', the ruler had announced a general amnesty in 2001. Several exiled activists returned, including Abdulhadi al-Khawaja, who had by this point experience and knowledge of human rights activism in Europe. Al-Khawaja and Nabeel Rajab formed in 2002 what is today the most prominent human rights organisation in Bahrain, the Bahrain Center for Human Rights (BCHR). Rajab recalls that, in the preceding years, human rights involved mostly activist veterans from left-leaning political backgrounds, who had lost grassroots appeal amongst the majority conservative constituency over the previous two decades. Some of these leftist veterans went on to establish the Bahrain Human Rights Society. The nimble and savvy al-Khawaja returned from Denmark, where he had learnt his trade as a human rights activist, and joined Nabeel Rajab to establish the BCHR. In Rajab's own words, 'he [al-Khawaja] believed in empowering people, involving people, and training them. We had this aspect in common. Making people do human rights work instead of us doing it on their behalf.'[39]

BCHR's mission was to 'encourage and support individuals and groups to be proactive in the protection of their own and others' rights; and to struggle to promote democracy and human rights in accordance with international norms'. BCHR's version of human rights was conceived on the streets early on, at the grassroots level, and on the peripheries of society. Committees to deal with the unemployed, the tortured, migrant workers, and Guantanamo detainees were set up and many would then take on a life of their own, eventually spinning off. The NGOisation problem – conceived as the malaise of the modern apolitical or elite-based western-orientated and professionalised approach of human rights NGOs – has been discussed at length on global fora over the past decade. But here, we see an entirely different approach, the belief that the body is the site of resistance, that an activist's voice is the voice of the oppressed, and that human rights is an exercise in popular sovereignty.

From the early years, the BCHR was organising and leading protests and symbolic acts of civil disobedience, carrying out grassroots initiatives, and, in 2004, al-Khawaja publicly called for the resignation of the Prime Minister. The Americans, in various WikiLeaks cables, frequently refer to al-Khawaja as a 'Shiʿa rejectionist'.[40] Though his is a now widely accepted demand, at that time it was a red line and seen to be radical; now, this demand is seen to be 'moderate' relative to the demands for a complete overthrow of the absolute monarchy. Restrictive NGO laws were introduced and, although they carried on with their work, the BCHR offices were closed down in 2004. Other notable successes came with projects for migrant workers, rescuing housemaids, and a campaign for the release of the Bahraini detainees in Guantanamo Bay. BCHR's work on migrant workers was so successful that the government decided to take it over and establish the Migrant Workers' Protection Society[41], and, in the case of the Guantanamo detainees, the government retained the same lawyer that the BCHR had hired for the case.[42] In 2006, when a government whistleblower, Salah al-Bandar, published hundreds of leaked documents exposing the state's sectarianisation policy, no journalist was willing to touch the file, but the BCHR published it in full on their website as evidence of systematic discrimination against the Shiʿa. This, as well as symbolic acts of solidarity with victims of state violence and the establishment of a platform for a regional and international activist network, set the ground for the BCHR to become one of the most important players in the 2011 uprising, and shaped the nature and strength of activism that we see today.

Due to the emergence of the BCHR as one of the vanguards of a historical rights-based struggle and the modern efficacy of human rights discourse, political groups in Bahrain have started devoting more time and resources to human rights work, particularly after the uprising in 2011, and the number of new human rights NGOs has proliferated, with a broad-based grassroots movement behind it. Similarly, the government has engaged with human rights norms by signing various treaties and creating specialist roles and institutions. The appeal of this universal human rights discourse for activists, the political opposition, and even the government has been a defining aspect of the 2011 uprising as we shall discuss in what follows.

## From tactics to enshrining secular rights principles: the attraction of human rights and the proliferation of NGOs

> We realised as we were working that human rights was something new that could be used to achieve democracy in our region. We discovered an arena which was ignored by the Arab world for many years. Governments could distance Arab nations from the human rights movement around the world by labelling it as an anti-Islamic movement . . . The earliest issues we tackled were defending people in Guantanamo, Sunnis and supposed Islamists, and discrimination against the Shi'a. Two issues to do with religion. People realized by seeing us do this that what the government was trying to tell them was not correct. Human rights is not against Islam. – Nabeel Rajab, 2014[43]

Bahraini human rights veterans had managed to strategically carve a secular space within an increasingly conservative and sectarianised environment. Having carried the banner for cases across a divided spectrum, it became very difficult to discredit Rajab later. Older groups, such as the BHRS and the BCHR, were established just after the 2001 political opening. Since 2011, the country boasts at least eight independent NGOs: the Bahrain Human Rights Observatory

(BHRO), the Bahrain Human Rights Forum (BHRF) based in Beirut, the European Bahrain Organisation for Human Rights (EBOHR), Bahrain Rehabilitation and Anti-Violence Organisation (BRAVO), Manama Human Rights Observatory, the Bahrain Institute for Rights and Democracy (BIRD) based in London, and Americans for Democracy and Human Rights in Bahrain (ADHRB) based in Washington, DC. Other groups, including Bahrain Watch, a collective of researchers that focus on accountability and transparency. Political opposition parties, such as Al Wefaq, have also begun to use the language of human rights and have realigned their focus by dedicating several senior members to advocacy work in Washington, Geneva, and London to lobby for action at the international level for greater human rights accountability, for example by setting up the Bahrain Justice and Development Movement in London and Bahrain Salam for Human Rights.[44]

The state's strategy to securitise and sectarianise the problem of anti-regime protests is a dual attempt to return to the status quo ante and present the protesters as politically illegitimate by casting them as pawns of foreign powers. The human rights framework promotes a normative position that is 'universal', overcoming the rules of subordination and the sectarianised politics of divide and rule on the island. In its modern practised form, human rights tends to portray itself as 'anti-politics'[45] in defence of universal claims. It is locally and transnationally appealing and able to facilitate advocacy work done by exiled communities and those inside the country. It also breaks from the familiar religious, Islamist, and leftist ideological discourses of the past, which no doubt retain some salience among older generations. This framework also has the power to 'provide a minimal language in which radically different agendas (can) fuse'.[46] The case of Bahrain illustrates how human rights have provided a unifying framework for different groups in the opposition. By orientating the movement towards human rights advocacy and solidarity with victims of violations, street revolutionaries, human rights activists, and politicians now have a basic platform to work on together and reconcile differences. At the same time, however, this unifying framework has clear political boundaries. It has served to mute political criticisms of a deeper nature or demands for a more comprehensive form of justice. Political groups like Al Wefaq, which have always preferred a softer non-confrontational approach, can find the HR discourse convenient and accommodative of their belief that change within the system is possible.

As early adopters, human rights activists like Rajab and Maryam al-Khawaja were quick to exploit social media platforms to report on the situation, as shocking images emerged. Rajab with 260 thousand followers became an important source globally. With the all-too-common and frequent personal experiences with the judicial and prison systems and, the nature of a close-knit community, the majority were either arrested themselves, had a relative or a friend imprisoned, or were moved by an incident of some kind. Many instinctively, were propelled into the human rights activism and quickly learnt the language, the tools, the principles. Some have described their role as being an 'accidental activist', such as many of the doctors who were arrested and tortured for treating injured protesters.[47] Even if human rights campaigns have not stopped the government from engaging in gross violations of rights, this form of activism can certainly be transgressive and has certainly empowered the victims and the opposition through the transgressive act of exposure. Notwithstanding, the sense of self-emancipation experienced in the euphoria of mass protests can be a life-changing personal transformation. We also see the re-emergence of a network of local and foreign human rights NGOs to put pressure on the government to comply with the terms of ratified international agreements and the BICI[48] recommendations they have accepted. These transnational advocacy networks have been redefined as 'networks of activists, distinguishable largely by the centrality of principled ideas or values in motivating their formation'.[49]

Moreover, it is this advocacy revolution, largely amplified by social media, that has enabled the movement to gain an unprecedented voice and visibility, albeit not in the mainstream media, to make its own case to the world. Importantly, the pressure on the state as a signatory of human rights conventions is maintained by continually exposing the gap between its promises and practices. Without the advocacy revolution, it is unlikely that the plight of so many victims of abuse would have been known so widely within Bahrain or outside. The intra-communal solidarity and international solidarity received is an important empowerment tool in the psychological battle against the regime. As soon as someone is arrested, local and foreign human rights activists are contacted, and family, friends and local media groups begin to use social media to campaign for their release. They post details of the arrest, pictures, start petitions, and organise protests on the hundreds of social media accounts reflecting political organisation at the village-level – such as Karrana News Network or Duraz Prisoners or Muharraq News on Twitter. In this way, individuals' suffering becomes a collective problem and a basis for mobilisation.

Many human rights activists gained popular legitimacy through their direct and active engagement with the revolutionary protest movement, earning recognition partly due to the risk and sacrifices they were forced to take. Those that have gone beyond 'apolitical' human rights activism, beyond speaking out on arrests and torture, have found themselves in prison. Prominent activists were rounded up early on in March 2011, such as Abdulhadi al-Khawaja and Abduljalil al-Singace, and others but over the few years that followed, arrests continued on an adhoc basis, including Nabeel Rajab, Zaynab al-Khawaja and Yusuf al-Muhafda and many many others. Facing arbitrary and inconsistent sentences that could range from a few months to 10 years, to life imprisonment. Nabeel Rajab, Zaynab al-Khawaja and Yusuf al-Muhafda. For Bahraini activists, it is disheartening that there has been little international criticism regarding

- Spin..

**Roulette wheel:** The numbers on the wheel represent jail terms in years. The three Arabic words say 'death', 'life imprisonment', and '50 years'. The cartoon highlights the seemingly arbitrary nature of justice in Bahrain, where harsh sentences are given out without due process or a fair trial. The bored look of the judge also indicates the frequency with which these trials occur, as if the uprising has turned the legal system into a conveyor belt leading towards jail for political dissidents.

the imprisonment of these activists. Shunned by the 'international community' – read: 'Western powers' – few garner a belief of their sincerity and desire to uphold human rights. When the US State Department was asked about its position on Nabeel Rajab's imprisonment, for example, Michael Posner responded that, 'Rajab's case is a bit more complicated'.[50]

The political boundaries of the human rights sphere, were certainly being centested and it is sometimes a case of trial and error as to where the line is. In Bahrain, since the BICI, Al Wefaq, has focused on the implementation of the report's recommendations as a key demand, as well as the Geneva recommendations from the outcome of the Universal Periodic Review in 2012. The message, arguably, becomes almost indistinguishable from that of the government, that hasn't rejected these human rights demands at all, in fact it has accepted them and they are 'work-in-progress'. It has launched four 'dialogue' initiatives in 2011, 2013, 2014 with the tolerated opposition, which were set up to fail and simply to detract, delay and disrupt a process of reconciliation and reform. Today, there is no longer a 'tolerated' opposition, the opposition who wanted to initially work within the system, then to defy it when the uprising began by resigning from the parliament, and then accepted to join every dialogue attempt but refused to be capitulated. The leaders of all the main opposition groups across the political board are in jail including ʿAli Salman and Ibrahim Shareef. The regime has effectively jailed the side with which it claimed it sought dialogue and a negotiated settlement. All the red lines drawn by the regime and the opposition have been broken – the regime expects the opposition to surrender, but the more it gets knocked down, the more defiant it becomes. When Ebrahim Sharif was released very briefly in July 2014 after 4 years in prison, his first public speech was damning.

## A brief topography of opposition actors

Nabeel Rajab in an interview with the authors in the summer of 2014, said:

> the political groups and political demands are human rights issues. The political movement is also demanding equality, demanding justice, demanding human rights, demanding democracy. This is the same standard, the same criteria that we (the human rights movement) are fighting for. Later when you have a proper political system you will have political parties based on ideology, but it's not ideology now it's the legitimate demand for democracy. So it's very much combined.[51]

The blurring of the lines between the political movement and the human rights movement in Bahrain has certainly been a factor in the way in which the Bahraini government has dealt with the crisis. The difficulty of the human rights movement remaining 'apolitical' in an arena where political and human rights advocacy are united in challenging the perpetrators of abuse is evident. It is no surprise, therefore, that a great number of human rights activists have been imprisoned alongside the political opposition leaders on charges of terrorism; indeed, the only difference between the two is simply referential. It is worth briefly offering a topographic profile of some of the main oppositional human rights and political actors.

## The vanguard of human rights: BCHR

The strategic turning point for the BCHR appears to have been the decsion to close down the centre by the Minister of Labour and Social Affairs, Majeed al-Alawi in 2004. Upon deciding to continue their work, despite having their offices closed, Rajab remarked that they transformed from an organisation to a movement.[52]

As previously mentioned, the BCHR has worked on a variety of projects that included all segments of society, including migrant workers. The organisation is the recipient of a number of international human rights awards[53] and is well connected both regionally and transnationally, an aspect which has been of great importance in pressuring the Bahraini government on human rights issues.

Al-Khawaja is currently serving life in prison and Nabeel Rajab is also imprisoned, having served a two-year sentence and rearrested for daring to criticise the Saudi-lead war in Yemen at the start of it in April 2015. Many members have been arrested, imprisoned, and harassed. Currently, former Head of Monitoring, Sayed Yusuf al-Muhafda, lives in self-imposed exile due to threats towards himself and his family. Maryam al-Khawaja, who acted as a temporary president of the organisation, left in 2014 to focus on the Gulf Center for Human Rights. Through careful manoeuvring, flexible working arrangements, mass appeal, interchangeability of members inside and outside the country, the BCHR has managed to sustain the organisation; more importantly, its leadership, through personal integrity, rose up to face one of the most difficult crackdowns in the history of the country and confronted it head on.

## The registered opposition: Al-Jamiyaat al muʿavidha

Although political parties are banned, de facto parties exist in the form of political 'societies' that need to register and adhere to restrictive laws on organisation, fundraising and assembly (e.g., pre-approval for conferences, marches, etc.). Al Wefaq is the biggest political society in Bahrain[54] and represents the conservative Shiʿi constituency within the country. It is the biggest member of an alliance of smaller societies, generally referred to as al-jamiyaat al-muʿaridha (opposition societies), of mainly leftist political persuasion, such as Waʿad political society. The registered opposition having boycotted the first parliamentary elections in 2002, it then took part in 2006 and 2010 but then boycotted the most recent elections in Bahrain in 2014, despite enormous US and UK pressure for it to participate. The severe repression and lack of any political reforms, failure to achieve any of its demands lead its supporters to reject its participation. In 2010, Al Wefaq won eighteen seats in the forty-seat Lower House of parliament. After the events following the uprising of 2011, all eighteen MPs resigned to protest against the killing of protesters. Al Wefaq, Waʿad and their partners are referred to as 'moderates' for their willingness to engage and compromise with the regime rejecting the call for the removal of the regime at the height of the protests in 2011 and advocating for a constitutional monarchy. Al Wefaq has always maintained back door channels with the regime, engaging in at least four attempts at open and secret dialogue since 2011, seeking concessions that will allow at least the basic demands outlined in the Manama Document[55] to be fulfilled. However, its efforts have rather humiliatingly led to further capitulation – its leader is in jail and various other senior leaders such as Majid Milad, Khalil Marzoog are in and out of prison.

It continued to organise 'authorised' rallies on a weekly basis outside the capital, complying with police decisions on where and when to protest, despite several of the protest organisers getting arrested and accused of vandalism. Al Wefaq also respected the ban on protest in the capital, and continues to refer to the King as *sāhib al-jalāla*, 'His Highness'. Shaykh ʿAli Salman was convicted in June 2014 and sentenced to four years imprisonment for inciting hatred against the regime and denigrating a public body.[56] The charges refer to a speech in which Salman declared that the option of militarising the opposition was offered (without stating who from) and rejected. Al Wefaq's main partner is Waʿad, a liberal leftist party, whose president, Ibrahim Sharif, was imprisoned in 2011, having taken a much more active role in the uprising. Sharif's arrest was seen as retribution for years of work exposing corruption by the government. Sharif's short-lived experience with mass politics did not translate into increasing Waʿad's grassroots appeal, though Sharif himself remains a widely respected figure across the political spectrum who can potentially bridge sectarian differences but whom the state has stood and challenged directly for the past decade, by denying him a seat in parliament through vote manipulation and then imprisoning him.

## The street revolutionaries: Al-iʿitilaaf, the February 14 Youth Coalition

The 'February 14 Youth Coalition', which has emerged as a powerful underground anarchic actor, is a union of various groups that coalesced during the protests at the Pearl Roundabout in Manama during February and March 2011.[57] The group is decentralised, leaderless, and revolutionary in its demands, which are laid out in the Pearl Charter.[58] Its coordinators are unknown, but it relies on a network of affinity groups across Bahrain's small villages. In their own words, 'the first and foremost goal that revolutionaries are struggling for is the liberation of our land from Saudi occupation and the overthrow of the Al-Khalifa regime, which has lost its popular and constitutional legitimacy'.[59] The February 14 Youth Coalition has been a critical driving force behind the uprising and the continuation of the nightly protests and police clashes that can still be witnessed in villages. Protest banners adorned with the February 14 Youth Coalition logo can frequently be seen in the villages.

Whilst the group claims that 'the Coalition's relationship with other opposition groups is based on the principle of respect and considers them integral in the struggle',[60] it can be seen as a challenger to the traditional forces of opposition in Bahrain. Indeed, it represents a new generation of political activists, with new modes of operation and widespread support. Their revolutionary demands, however, do locate the group closer to the 'Alliance for a Republic' and others advocating the overthrowing of the current regime, rather than Al Wefaq. The Coalition's success is seen in its widespread popularity amongst the youth and its inclination towards action rather than rhetoric. In breeding a teen subculture based on street resistance to police incursions, especially checkpoints, balaclava-clad protesters have made police confrontation a daily pastime. Scores of members have died or are in jail. After the destruction of the Pearl Roundabout, the Coalition led several calls to return to the site, bringing the capital to a standstill. In one instance, a symbolic protest in the city centre shopping mall was met with such brutal police repression, that female protesters were piled up on the ground and then arrested. It has been creative in its modes of resistance, using word-of-mouth and twitter to rally crowds around on key dates such as February 14 (the uprising anniversary), March 14 (the Saudi intervention), August 14 (day of independence), December 17 (official national day). Since security is so high, and mobilisation is harder and harder, the Coalition creates ideas based on everyday activities that allow as many people to participate as possible. Things like a traffic go-slow, picnics, shop strikes, and the bank of Dignity, that called on people to withdraw their savings from certain banks on the same day.

## The veteran opposition: the Alliance for a Republic

On 7 March 2011, in the midst of the intensive political standoff by protestors at the Pearl roundabout and the government in increasing panic, Abdulhadi al-Khawaja resigned from his job at the Irish NGO Front Line Defenders. Up until that point, Khawaja, observed and interviewed by the authors at the time, had not openly played a role in the protests. Pressure on him to declare his position and to join the protestors grew. Earlier, veteran opposition leader Hassan Mushaima returned from exile in the UK on 26 February and gave a ground-shaking speech at the packed Pearl Roundabout, announcing the establishment of a new coalition comprising of Al-Haq, Wafa'a and the UK-based Baharain Freedom Movement. Al-Khawaja decided to join this 'Alliance for a Republic' which had 'adopted the choice of a complete downfall of the regime, and the establishment of a democratic republic in Bharain . . . We will work with the free people of this country, and the 14th February Youth and all others who believe in this popular, legitimate and revolutionary option . . . by all means of peaceful revolutionary tactics through a program of civil disobedience and resistence' (statement on March 7 2011). This, they believe, had become necessary in light of the 'oppressive and corrupt' rule of the Al Khalifa family over the course of a century.[61] This represented an escalation in demands as a result of the incredible outrange from the killing of protesters by government forces and the fast momentum that the uprising was gaining.

The first people to be arrested and disappeared for months after the Saudi-led incursion on March 17 were Hassan Mushaima, Abduljalil al-Singace, Shaykh ʿAbd al-Jalil al-Muqdad ʿAbd al-Wahab Husayn and Shaykh Saʿid al-Nuri. All were given life prison sentences in military trials and their horrific torture has been widely reported, including in the commissioned BICI report. The 'Bahrain 13', as they have come to be known, were accused of terrorism and the judge in his sentencing described terrorism as, 'all means of moral pressure, ruin, destruction, or the obstruction of facilities'. It is testament to the Bahrain 13, the majority of whom are over fifty and suffering from ailing health, that, having spent over four years in prison, they have not succumbed to the immense pressure to back down from their initial demands or to offer the apology needed for a royal pardon.

The grassroots movement around the Alliance appeared to take on a life of its own during this period and generally pushed aggressively for the escalation of protests, which reached a number of key politically strategic locations including the King's palace in Safriya in the West, the Royal Court in Riffa, and the Bahrain Financial Harbour just days before the Saudi 'invasion' and 'occupation'. Given the threats of violence, and presence of armed thugs, these protests saw up to 80,000 people take part. While protests were spilling inside-out from *al-dawār*, the registered opposition was organising parallel protests that spilled from the outside-in to *al-dawār*. The protest on 23 February in commemoration of those who had been slain on 17 February was the largest in the history of Bahrain, with estimates of at least 200,000 protesters.

The opposition movement, comprising all the aforementioned actors, reflects the splits we have seen in other countries in the region; between those who want reform, and those who want revolution, specifically here, advocating a constitutional monarchy and others a democratic republic. Remarkably, however, the opposition was united on the adherence to non-violent activism. But here, the term 'radical' as opposed to 'moderate', as the veterans and the registered opposition are often referred to, is a product of a very particular context in which the terms reflect extreme risk factors that fluctuated according to the precarious position of the state. During the very intense period of February–March 2011, all political red lines had been redrawn. The idea of a republican system was a radical one and it was intended to force Al Wefaq, at the time engaged in a secret dialogue with the Crown Prince, to push for more political concessions than it was willing to and to settle for nothing less than a genuine constitutional monarchy. The fear of conceding to anything less was spawned by the distrust of and sense of betrayal by the King over the 2002 backtracking on the National Charter a decade earlier. At the same time, however, there was a negative effect: the idea was immediately manipulated by the state as evidence that the opposition wanted an "Islamic" republic and used it as a *casus belli* for Saudi intervention. Regardless, it is believed that, behind the scenes, the state along with its Gulf allies had been preparing for a military incursion on the island for at least two weeks before the fateful day of 14 March 2011.

It is only after this point, with Al Wefaq forced to retreat, the Alliance essentially behind bars, and martial law declared, that Nabeel Rajab rose to take the mantle of the movement and the idea of the enshrined 'right to self-determination' emerged as a banner that united the goals of both factions. By introducing a new discourse and leading symbolic protests in the capital, protesters rallied around this secular and outspoken man. One of the pioneering users of Twitter, the savvy use of social media amplified his voice and became an important source of news. A new space was created where none was supposed to have existed and with it a new problem and challenge for the state.

## Upgrading authoritarianism

The use of strategies by authoritarian states to remain in power and retain legitimacy in the international system has been described as 'upgrading authoritarianism',[62] or 'liberalised autocracy'.[63] Heydemann argues that, in the contemporary era, authoritarian states have been 'upgraded' using a plethora of repertoires of legitimacy and survival strategies, which include appropriating and containing civil societies, managing political contestation (provoking or containing it), capturing the benefits of selective economic reforms, controlling new communications technologies, and diversifying international linkages.[64] During revolutionary times, this upgrading also becomes a necessary part of survival, or what Louër calls, 'coup-proofing strategies'.[65] Within this framing, the government veraciously used its usual tools of repression and co-option, including sectarianised repression, PR companies, Western arms purchases, surveillance, state media propaganda, and human rights discourse, amongst other things. Interestingly, however, we find its attempts at co-opting human rights itself a new example of this 'upgrading' process. Universal human rights is a normative, if contested, concept in contemporary global politics. States, particularly small states, must abide or ratify laws and conventions if they wish to retain legitimacy in the international system, even if opposed in practice. In Bahrain, this is complicated further owing to the nature of the state's strong historical and ongoing political ties with the British and the presence of several foreign military bases (British, American, and GCC). Bahrain is seen as a major Western ally in the region with the US Fifth Fleet stationed on the island, and has free trade agreements in place. The state is also a keen consumer of Western arms. This deep relationship with the West has meant that the government has been compelled to engage with human rights discourse in a way that other states like it on the periphery of the international system have not needed to. The need for a liberal political cover for essentially authoritarian rule has been the pinnacle strategy since the current ruler took the helm. The King's reform project was hailed as an example of George Bush's Greater Middle East Initiative. With Obama, Bahrain was mentioned in key speeches ("We have insisted publicly and privately that mass arrests and brute force are at odds with the universal rights of Bahrain's citizens, and will not make legitimate calls for reform go away", May 2011 speech). The British, however, have not just avoided criticism but consistently supported the regime throughout. In January 2015, on the same day that ʿAli Salman was put on trial and Nabeel Rajab sentenced to six months imprisonment for a tweet, the British Foreign Secretary stated, 'It is a country which is travelling in the right direction . . . It is making significant reform.'[66]

The King's establishment of the BICI to investigate violations is a manifestation of this attempt at co-opting human rights; the King, using it to place himself above the political fray, and his responsibility for any abuse was automatically absolved. The BICI has now become part of the state's 'ritual of celebration' and 23 November (the day it was published) has become an excuse for the regime to receive praise from its allies for having taken this 'unprecedented' initiative. Instead of restorative justice, this gloating is symptomatic of the hubris of power that it can afford to maintain, in fact, had you not realised, Bahrain is already a democracy, and prisoners are quite happy in five-star prisons, according to state media. At the lavish ceremony where the report was presented to the King, and in the presence of several NGOs and official dignitaries, none would dare utter a whisper of condemnation for the systemic and systematic practice of torture and extrajudicial killings outlined in the report. Although there was tacit acceptance of the report (for how could they reject a report that they had commissioned), in practice the state has done little to comply with the limited recommendations and this testifies to the extreme denial of responsibility for the violations documented in it. The regime has used the BICI to gain international respectability and build more institutions that offer the veneer of liberal reform, such as a police ombudsman's office. The BICI's greatest achievement is in confirming in consistent detail accounts of human rights abuses, but its recommendations fall far short of the necessary political overhaul required. It also offers no guidance on who should be held accountable or how this should happen. The report was left open-ended and has not been followed up with an action plan or a time frame for implementation.

The government has also set up a Ministry of Human Rights, alongside a National Institution of Human Rights (NIHR) and several GONGOs, which claim to be independent but are funded directly or indirectly by the Bahraini government, for example, Bahrain Human Rights Watch Society, Bahrain Monitor, and the Manama Centre for Human Rights. There have been UNHRC Periodic Reviews in 2012, which the Bahraini government voluntarily engaged with, and a member of the Bahraini regime has been voted onto the UN Human Rights Advisory Committee. Bahrain is also planning to be home of the Arab Court for Human Rights described by Cherif Bassiouni as 'little more than a "Potemkin tribunal" – a fake institution designed only to impress people'.[67] Others described it as an 'empty vessel'.[68]

Thus, the government is engaging with human rights, manufacturing a shadow of civil society within the state, and even hailing its own human rights record. This liberalising facade is a smokescreen and thwarts the efforts of genuine human rights organisations working locally and internationally.[69] A cadre of Western consultants and PR companies have been paid tens of millions in order to assist the state to this effect, whilst the UK government itself has given '£1.2 million worth of support to Bahrain's reform programme [in the 2014/2015] financial year' that 'is focused on strengthening human rights and the rule of law', increasing this to £2.1 million for 2015–2016.[70]

One basic constant remains: repression of dissent is enacted in most spheres of public and private life, but now it is done, according to British advice cited in the Introduction, in an 'acceptable' manner using an improved discourse, better surveillance technology, leaving less physical marks after torture and more importantly, with less journalists allowed in the country to cover anything that goes on.

## Is human rights advocacy enough? Where do we go from here?

Here is where the peculiar case of the Bahraini human rights movement can wade into the current critical debate on human rights that is raging in academic and activist fora. In December 2014, *The Guardian* published an article by Eric Posner called 'The case against human rights', arguing that, despite the moral achievement of human rights law, a radically different approach is now required.[71] He cites some basic facts: that 150 out of 193 countries continue to engage in torture and that the number of authoritarian countries has increased. It is no wonder that people living within those countries, especially in the Arab world, frequently make similar criticism of human rights. Indeed, the challenge of human rights remains not just on the polemical level, but also in the day-to-day decisions that activists face on the ground, in the position that an activist takes towards a regime, and the tactical approaches employed. According to the prevailing conception of human rights, activists are expected to disarticulate local politics from their discourse and actions, such as avoiding boycotts, and to engage with abusive authorities. Their statements continue to appeal to the very state many of its victims are trying to radically transform. The fear, therefore, is what Samuel Moyn warns of in *The Last Utopia*, that human rights discourse can de-politicise and oversimplify because it is framed in a way that evades any deep questioning of politics, including radical transforming strategies. Through the simultaneous need to both represent people as victims and appeal to the current regime to stop practices that victimise people, the paradoxical nature of human rights becomes evident and frustrating. In the case of Bahrain, as elsewhere, this tension has led to differences of opinion and approaches within the movement. By way of an example, Amnesty International, the OHCHR, and the ICRC, by accepting the terms and conditions set by the regime, have forged a bilateral cooperation that has served to change the discourse of state institutions like the NIHR and the Ombudsman's office in favour of the regime in some of their reports, albeit retaining some level of criticism. In some instances, as some of our interviewees have told us, iNGOs (international NGOs) have at times worked behind the scenes to pressure local groups like the BCHR to change course on certain campaigns, for example, the Wanted for Justice campaign. But, where these antagonise the regime, it also antagonises its loyalists along with it. The universality of the discourse has done little to allay the fears of Sunni counterparts, but for them, Nabeel Rajab refers to his record of defending the rights of all citizens, including Sunnis, those jailed in Guantanamo, and migrant workers. For that, at least, actions speak louder than words, and the universality of rights is extended not just to the majority protesting but to the other underrepresented groups.

Thus human rights discourse can be exploited to legitimise the rights-abusing state and its institutionally engineered human rights bodies, such as the NIHR, Ombudsman or Ministry of Human Rights, all appointed directly by the King without questioning their structures. The NIHR, for example, violates the Paris Principles on independence. This effectively reinforces the state and its biopolitical power, by not questioning the unfettered discretion over how to contend with protesters and prisoners. Hence, the template of activism set by international NGOs has become one of outlining how the regime is abusing human rights and then making a report in which they compile a set of 'recommendations' to the state. The state, the repeat offender, is asked to reform itself from being an abuser to a protector of human rights, including an expectation to overcome its own structured reliance on torture and abuse to maintain its rule. The asymmetric nature of the relationship between local NGOs and iNGOs is, although mostly symbiotic, at times tense.

However, it is how local activists and groups conceive of human rights and how they sit within the wider struggle, history, and beliefs of those they are defending that matters. It is here that human rights activism is capable of mobilising constituencies to become powerful enough to force the government to stop abuse. As a consequence, effective human rights activism is inevitably political. The critical issue here is not the engagement of human rights activists with politics, it is the response of the threatened state and its allies that justifies repression and punishment on the grounds that such human rights demands pose a threat to the state itself. As Eric Posner asks, 'is there any reason to believe that Human Rights Watch, or its donors, knows better than the people living in [X country] know how their governments should set priorities and implement policy?' Though the advocacy revolution gives individuals agency and empowers them, human rights activists argue that at least they provide moral support to the oppressed. However, rights language itself imposes limits upon aspirations for deep and meaningful political change in the way that political demands are compartmentalised into discrete rights claims – the right to a fair trial, the right to peaceful assembly, the right to free expression, and so on – that require a gradual piecemeal approach that is at odds with the substantial overhaul of an old and rotten order demanded by the now-active citizenry. The Bahraini state has gradually been reinforcing itself through human rights institutions that carry the banner of those rights, whilst continuing to operate as a sectarian state. Disappointment by vulnerable people sets in when human rights abuse becomes 'controlled' and 'limited' and normalised in the every day. Their everyday suffering and abuse turns into a spectacle of slow death.

To overcome this, the Bahraini opposition and human rights activists have settled on the wider, but more ambiguous, 'right to self-determination', which echoes the events of 1972 and 2001, where Bahrainis engaged in writing and voting on a constitutional settlement with the Al Khalifa. 'To have human rights, then, is to have a state, and to have a modern state is to have a nation emancipated from foreign domination and self-constituted as a realization of such Burkean qualities as local, distinct culture, language, and peculiar historical fate (among so many other possible features)',[72] or what we understand to be 'self-determination'.

Therein lies the state-based human rights paradox: human rights activists are both antagonistic and amiable to the state; antagonistic in their charge that the state and its allies are responsible for violations, but amiable in the way they appeal to the state and, in so doing, relegitimise it in its illiberal form. However, Bahrain's human rights activists appear much more savvy and conscious of this. Over the course of a decade, they have chartered a course of innovative action and agitation, even when it costs them positions, jobs, or awards in international organisations. When human rights activists call for the 'downfall' of an authoritarian regime and call for its replacement with a 'republican' system, as Abdulhadi al-Khawaja did, or when Rajab points out the security connection with the 'Islamic State', a clear flaw at odds with a major military offensive in the name of fighting terrorism, this antagonism is used as a justification for their arrest and incarceration.

Such activists find themselves in jail having not only dissented against the authority of the state, but having deviated from the accepted modern, practised, human rights approach itself. By leading protests, calling out the perpetrators, including the King, and pointing to truths that the 'tolerated' opposition diplomatically avoids, they have been excoriated by the regime as 'extremists', 'radicals', or 'hardliners' to justify their incarceration and to define political red lines and the boundaries of human rights. At the same time, the power of non-violent direct action post-2011 is directly linked to information tools and the increased visibility of protest actions. Nabeel Rajab now boasts over 250,000 followers on Twitter, which is the equivalent of half the Bahraini population. His popularity now extends beyond the small borders of the island and is greater than any Bahraini state official sharing the same social media addiction.

The case in Bahrain can be summarised as a situation where there is a contradictory force pulling between convention, pragmatism, and revolution. This affects the way that groups engage amongst themselves. For example, it is widely believed that Nabeel Rajab's revolutionary calls to protest in the capital city of Manama were embarrassing for political opposition groups, which refused to sustain the call for fear of reprisals. At the same time, however, these political opposition groups are investing large amounts of their energy into human rights advocacy and are thereby duplicating the work of under-resourced NGOs dedicated to this task rather than engaging in politics or pushing the street movement forward.

If the problem in Bahrain today is defined in terms of terrible human suffering owing to a lack of human rights and a surplus of abusive state power, then human rights advocacy is the best tactic against this problem. But, if it is diagnosed as the systematic disenfranchisement of the people from the prospects of self-governance and democracy, and a gross economic injustice through a monopolisation of the nation's wealth, 'the pragmatist, moral, and anti-political mantle of human rights discourse tends to eschew, even repel, rather than invite or address these questions'.[73] The political project in Bahrain, therefore, is fertile for demands for restorative justice, restitution for economic deprivation and a redistribution of wealth, and a definitive end to autocratic rule, institutionalised corruption, and demographic manipulation. Human rights violations are naturally the outcomes of the state's exertion of violence and power to protect its rule.

## New realms, new possibilities, new times

The old order is largely back in business. But something is fundamentally different: these are the old ways in new times, when the old order faces new political subjects and novel subjectivities; when the memories of sacrifice, the taste of triumph, and betrayal of aspirations are likely to turn quiet but lingering mass discontent into periodic social upheavals. These are uncharted political moments loaded with indefinite possibilities, in which meaningful social engagement would demand a creative fusion of the old and new ways of doing politics.[74]

Human rights discourse has been a tractable facilitator of a creative fusion of old and new ways of doing politics in the uprising currently raging in Bahrain. The reclaiming of the political sphere by protesters 'unsettled the foundation of the status quo, shaping a society that is fundamentally different'.[75] The idiom of human rights has helped provide people in Bahrain with moral resources and agency, and with a way to express themselves which has resonated locally as well as with the wider world. But authoritarianism has been upgraded and the ruling family has learnt to play the 'human rights game', engaging with the UNHRC and celebrating its 'track record' on human rights, thereby giving itself a liberal fig leaf for what is a fundamentally illiberal regime and thus enabling it to reinforce its position in the international community, whilst highlighting the hypocrisy of the latter.

However, as the struggle continues into its fifth year and fatigue and disillusionment set in, there is a risk that faith in this discourse will run its course. The counter-revolution has asymmetric strengths and is reinforcing its apparatus of control and coercion. Its British partner has succeeded to a limited degree in its 'advisory role' to encourage suppression in an 'acceptable' manner.

The principles of normative 'universal' notions of human rights are appealing, yet they are not universally accepted or applied. Whilst the idiom of human rights has proliferated within the current movement, forcing the regime to also adopt it, the regime cites its 'right to security' and continues to receive Western aid in the name of a 'reform programme' and the 'rule of law'.[76] 'The language of rights, untethered to specific legal interpretations, is too "spongy" to prevent governments from committing abuses and can easily be used to clothe illiberal agendas in words soothing to the western ear.'[77] This has produced a 'battle for discourse'. Human rights activists as well as the government are appealing to the same discourse in an attempt to further their own objectives and visions for the state.

The human rights movement in Bahrain has been internationalised and reinforced by the exiled and diaspora communities that can be found across the world. The local–global human rights movement now has some of the most well-known human rights activists in the world, winning numerous awards and representing the local human rights movement in the halls of power in major cities such as Washington, DC, London, and Geneva, where they keep knocking at the door of someone they hope will listen.

Human rights in the Arab world was first articulated by the Arab Organization for Human Rights in terms of freedom: freedom of thought, expression, and participation, as well as freedom from state violence, including murder and torture. Freedom was expressed as their ultimate goal. In the Declaration of the Tunis Conference of 1983, they made the following statement: '[f]reedom is a supreme value for all Arabs because they are deprived of it. The Arab people are deprived of freedom of thought and expression, of the right to participate in decision making; they are exposed to imprisonment, torture, and murder.'[78] What Bahrain's experience of the Arab uprisings have shown is the return to a human rights idiom based on a discourse of liberation, one that would produce a new social order based on egalitarianism and social justice. It can be used to find new spaces and new creative endeavours to sustain the resistance to authoritarian rule. Local activists conceive of human rights in their own ways that serve their local communities. Where it is routine, activists have found new anarchic tactics. Where they are expected to engage with a criminal state, they prefer civil disobedience. Where human rights is 'spongy', activists have found meaning.

## CHAPTER 5

# The many afterlives of Lulu

## The story of Bahrain's Pearl Roundabout[1]

## Amal Khalaf

*The pearl teeters; it rolls lazily to one side as the monument's six concrete legs start to fall apart. Between broken bones, the pieces of the pearl's cracked skull lie in sand and rubble.*

Squaring the circle is a problem handed down from the Ancient Greeks. It involves taking the curved line of a circle and attempting to draw a perfect square from it; a task that for centuries mathematicians were convinced they could figure out. In the nineteenth century, when the problem was proved unsolvable, the phrase to 'square the circle' came to signify an attempt at the impossible. But in 2011, within days of the most sustained and widely broadcasted protests in Bahrain's recent history, a circle was named a square. The once unassuming Pearl Roundabout or Dowar al Lulu, famous in the international media as the site of the Gulf's answer to the 'Arab Spring', became Bahrain's 'Pearl Square' or Midan al Lulu.

A month of mass protests later and the roundabout was razed to the ground. In its death, the Pearl Roundabout took on a life of its own, becoming the symbol of a protest movement; the star of tribute videos and video games, the logo for Internet TV channels and the subject of contested claims, rebuttals and comments wars. These manifestations of the roundabout – multifaceted, changing, and often contradictory – produce a haunting rhetorical effect, instigating debates fuelled by images of past and ongoing violence in Bahrain's history. In its afterlife, Lulu continues to act stubbornly in resistance to the state, despite the government's attempts to shape the monument's memory to serve its own interests, going so far as to tear the monument down and rename the ground on where it once stood. Today, Lulu is a powerful symbol for thousands of people recasting their ideals in the monument's image: a 'public space', or *midan* – Arabic for civic square, one that no longer exists as a physical 'thing', but rather, lives on as an image-memory.

## The birth of Lulu

The Pearl Roundabout was a central roundabout in Bahrain's capital Manama. At its centre stood a 300-foot tall monument, milky white and built in 1982 to commemorate the 3rd Gulf Cooperation Council (GCC) Summit, a meeting of Gulf States. The monument's six white, curved 'sails' represented each GCC member state: Bahrain, Kuwait, Oman, Qatar, Saudi Arabia, and the United Arab Emirates. A large cement pearl sat atop these sails in homage to the region's former pearl diving economy, which attracted the likes of Jacques Cartier to Bahrain's soil. But with the pearling industry in decline and tanker traffic drilling and dredging the region's seabeds, destroying them in the process; the GCC looked forward to a new era of economic development. The 1982 summit also launched the Gulf Investment Corporation, a $2.1 billion fund, and a military partnership between the GCC states: the creation of the Peninsula Shield Force or Dr'a al Jazeera. This treaty codified what is now the pillar of the GCC's military doctrine: that the security of all the members of the council relied on the notion of the GCC operating as an 'indivisible whole'.

To celebrate the end of the momentous summit, a cavalcade of cars took officials to the unveiling of a plaque commemorating the construction of the 25 km causeway linking Bahrain to the mainland Arabian Peninsula. King Fahd bin ʿAbd Al ʿAziz of Saudi Arabia and Shaykh ʿIsa bin Salman Al Khalifa, Emir of Bahrain, stepped forward to release the black drapes. Bahrain, at least in theory, was no longer an island. After its construction, Lulu became the chosen pearl in Bahrain's crown: the star of souvenir shops. It was, for a while at least, a symbol of Bahrain, sanctioned by the government, photographed by tourists and its image presented on neon shop signs.

Drive around Bahrain in January 2013 and there are symbols everywhere. As the 21st Gulf Cup (a biannual football tournament) was held at Bahrain's newly revamped Sheikh ʿIsa Sports City, the highways and streets are lined with flags and symbols of the Gulf Cooperation Council, marking a summit meeting held in Bahrain in December 2012. Yet, all over the island, behind trees covered in red and white fairy lights, royal crests, billboards of smiling leaders and flags of GCC countries, we see walls. And on these walls are many images and symbols that counter the state sponsored GCC branding campaigns, especially in villages and smaller side streets in Manama. You will see graffiti scrawled in Arabic and in English, some of which you can read if you happen to pass by before they have been painted over. Through layers of paint, these walls bear the traces of a conversation, an argument. Images and names of political prisoners, cries for help, or calls to fight. The most popular word you see written on the walls is *sumood* – perseverance – stencilled or scrawled alongside hastily drawn pictures of the former Pearl Roundabout.

## Roundabouts and amnesia

Monuments are often inscribed with a desire to inculcate a sense of shared experience and identity in society. As markers of a nation's history, the state imprints its self-image on the citizens through the erection of such memorials to key historical events and figures. These ideas and messages can often become overlooked, their original meanings forgotten over time. 'There is nothing in this world as invisible as a monument,' historian Robert Musil wrote. 'There is no doubt that they are erected to be seen . . . But at the same time they are impregnated with something that repels attention.'[2]

Like many GCC countries, Bahrain is inundated with roundabouts featuring monuments of pearls, fish, falcons, sails, and desert animals. Rather than featuring direct references to historical events or figures these monuments make up part of the visual language and urban inscription of national and regional identity in the Gulf. Key to this state-controlled image economy is the foregrounding of 'traditional Arab culture'. Emphasis is placed on the ruling family as representatives of the nation, which therefore privileges Sunni Muslim, male, and tribal identities. Concurrently, Bahrain's historical influences from the wider Arab world, the Indian subcontinent and Persia are downplayed or ignored and any histories of struggle are silenced. Instead, whitewashed concrete pearls, fish, falcons, Arabian horses, and the oryx are mediating national historiographies, as seen in the proliferation of official portraits of monarchs in public spaces and framed on the walls of most institutions in the region. Like the Pearl Roundabout, such symbols are used to construct an image of the state. As anthropologist Sulayman Khalaf describes:

> Ruling families and their allies have invented and made use of cultural traditions, nationalism, authenticity and 'traditional' values to identify themselves as the guardians of authentic Arab values and traditions, and bolster 'dynastic political structure'.[3]

Yet by the early 2000s, with its various paint jobs and facelifts, the Khaleeji-modern Pearl Roundabout became dwarfed by the rise of the high-rises constructed around it; the Bahrain Financial Harbour and the World Trade Centre, for example – glittering monuments of progress and national prestige. Bahrain, seemingly got bored of its overused tagline, 'Pearl of the Gulf', and moved on to 'Business

Friendly Bahrain'. These new, sparkling towers replaced the monument in an image conscious branding campaign, 'staging' Bahrain as a leading financial centre in the region,[4] a campaign that extended to the entry stamp at immigration and black cabs in London.[5]

Alongside the branding campaigns, the history of Bahrain's pearling industry became an integral part of the Ministry of Culture's remit. Cultural heritage became framed as a strategic positioning of Bahrain in the global imaginary. The rhetoric of Bahrain National Museum's 'Investing in Culture' campaign, for example, describes how cultural investment bolsters a 'process of forging cultural links and global communication'.[6] The government's investment in branding campaigns and strategies of self-representation internationally reflects the importance of controlling and maintaining an image of the country, bolstering the government's construction of a national identity that is itself intimately linked with Bahrain's position in the global sphere of international foreign investment. This experience of advanced neoliberalism in Bahrain has caused the widening of the gap between poorer citizens and those who have benefited from the island's position as the 'freest economy in the Middle East'.[7] But Bahrain's totalising mythos has been maintained by the suppression of dissent and a privatised urban infrastructure designed to sustain a facade of stability; of Bahrain as a business-friendly tourist hub.

Indeed, as opposition movements in Bahrain have been active for decades, so has the state's security apparatus, which often targets marginalised low-income areas and subjects dissenters to torture and detention.[8] These violent histories of struggle are ignored and often denied mention in state narratives. Bahrain's contested history is strictly controlled, requiring approval from the Ministry of Information[9] – many historical studies and publications have been banned and any counter-narratives silenced.[10] At the same time, increased privatisation has brought with it the shrinking of public and common land, including the disappearance of public beaches.

Large gatherings can only legally[11] happen within neighbourhoods and private spaces and Bahrainis have found it difficult to access public space in which to gather, let alone voice dissent.[12] As writer and architect Todd Reisz describes:

> roundabouts offered Bahrain an advantage: open space without extending those spaces for human use. An expanse of green parkland is isolated by an undying stream of traffic (. . .) roundabout circles are not places; they are voids. In other words, Bahrain might have green spaces, but there are few public spaces needing to be monitored.[13]

An example of this is in Manama's old souq, located in an area now referred to as being near the 'Fish Roundabout'. This rundown neighbourhood of the souq, near hardware shops and the three-star Caravan and Adhari Hotels, features a small fenced garden with a roundabout at one end with two intertwined fish. It was once home to the first municipality building in the region, built in 1923, and which hosted an elected, municipal council. Surrounding this building was a busy open boulevard flanked by markets, the *souq alaham* or meat market, cafes and small guesthouses. The market was, in all senses, a civic space with a thriving political life. It was here that, in the days of British rule, a series of labour protests and gatherings were held: a movement, which grew stronger in the 1970s during the rise and fall of the first National Assembly. Today, the Fish Roundabout – with a bench that is often empty and cars and scooters parked around it – makes for a quiet corner of Manama. No physical markers of its history remain; there are no traces of this place ever being a politicised public space.

   Thinking back to the events that took place around the Pearl Roundabout, spurred on by uprisings in other cities in the region,[14] this was a social alliance that had been – in part – summoned up via Facebook. On 14 February 2011,[15] tens of thousands of people joined in a demonstration resulting in the Pearl Roundabout's occupation.

As traffic stood still, the international media came to witness the Gulf's answer to the 'Arab Spring' and overnight, the government had lost control of its carefully constructed image of a 'Business Friendly' Bahrain, as news networks broadcast images of the Pearl Roundabout surrounded by protestors demanding reforms. A circle was named a square. The naming of the roundabout as Pearl Square or Midan al Lulu in the international media, though initially seen by many Bahrainis as a laughable and ignorant mistake, soon became appropriated by some protesters, who saw it as an underlining of the roundabout's new figuration as a 'civic square' or *midan*.

The unprecedented occupation of the 'square' became front-page news internationally as Manama was brought to a halt. Within days, there were attempts by the state to quell the growing protests with tear gas and other threats of force culminating in a violent crackdown on the roundabout at 3 am on 17 February 2011. Over four days, there were hundreds of injuries and seven civilian deaths. This harsh response surprised and radicalised many who had witnessed the events either first hand, in the international media, or through hundreds of shaky, panicked mobile phone videos posted on YouTube. Yet despite this heavy-handed repression, many defiantly returned to the roundabout, now a site of trauma and renamed Martyrs' Square or Midan al Shuhada by some.

As the battle over contested spaces continued, another battle was raging in the media, especially over the re-telling of the events of the 17 February crackdown on the roundabout. Overwhelmed by the unprecedented interest and reporting from the international media, international journalists were deported and none were let back in. The Ministry of Information and state TV began a campaign to discredit journalists and protesters using a tactical sectarian slant. While the international media spoke of pro-democracy protesters, the language of the state was of traitors and foreign agents. The roundabout was referred to by its official name: the GCC Roundabout or Dowar Majlis al Ta'awon. Days later, at the Al Fateh Mosque,[16] one kilometre away from the Pearl Roundabout, a counter-rally was organised by an umbrella group named 'The Gathering of National Unity'. Tens of thousands of citizens waved Bahraini flags, with posters of the King held high, and a cable of thanks was sent from the King to the organisers of the rally. Meanwhile, hundreds were arrested including doctors, nurses, bloggers, and journalists, and hundreds more lost jobs for being absent during the days of the protests.[17]

After a month of protests, martial law was declared. The Bahrain-Saudi causeway rumbled with the sounds of hundreds of tanks of the Dr'a al Jazeera or Peninsula Shield. For the last time, the roundabout was cleared by force, main roads leading up to the roundabout were sealed off and villages were kettled by armoured vehicles. Days later, in a spectacularly reactionary move, Bahrain's state TV replayed scenes that would within minutes circulate the digital mediasphere. As the country watched from their phones/homes/computer screens, the Pearl Monument exploded into a pile of bones over the ruins of an occupied 'square'.

Attempting to reset the political clock, the image of the Pearl Roundabout began to be officially erased from public view; the 500 fils coin, engraved with the image of the Pearl monument, was taken out of circulation and postcards featuring its image were removed from tourist shops in the souq and official government websites. In an edited report with subtitles by 'Feb14 TV', one of the hundreds of YouTube channels that have emerged out of Bahrain since 2011, we see the footage by Bahrain Television with another clip of a press conference a few days after the broadcast.[18] The video is one of the hundreds of the demolition of the Pearl Roundabout: an edit of the original footage of the demolition, aired by Bahrain state TV and followed by 'unseen clips', cut out of the state TV broadcast, of a tragic accident where a migrant labourer was killed during the hasty demolition. An abrupt wipe brings us to a press conference with Foreign Minister and prolific tweeter, Shaykh Khalid bin Ahmad

Al Khalifa, as the Foreign Minister explains how the monument was brought down because 'it was a bad memory'.

Such acts could be labelled as acts of *damnatio memoriae*, literally meaning 'condemnation of memory', a practice that included the destruction of images of a person deemed by government decree an enemy of the state in the Roman world. Such a decree meant that the name of the damned was conspicuously scratched out from inscriptions, his face chiselled from statues and the statues themselves often abused as if it were a real person, while frescoes would be painted over and coins bearing any image of the blacklisted were defaced, and any documents or writings destroyed. In demolishing the roundabout, it became clear to all who watched that this speechless stone monument, which had once bore witness to the Bahraini uprising and once symbolised state-sanctioned progress, had since become an enemy of the state. Its punishment was erasure.

## Lulu rising

With no monuments, roundabouts, or coins to bare its traces, the Pearl Roundabout was removed from state narrative by a government hoping to create a clean slate with which to rewrite sanctioned memories post-uprising. The Pearl Roundabout's traces were re-inscribed for the last time when the area was provocatively renamed the 'Al Farooq Junction',[19] a barricaded, inaccessible traffic intersection. Two years after its destruction, the site where Lulu once sat remains inaccessible: all the roads leading to the newly built junction are blocked with riot police vans and soldiers. There are also signs strictly prohibiting photography.

But though it no longer exists in physical form, the Pearl Roundabout rises from the rubble not only through graffiti or as the logo for the 'February 14 Coalition',[20] but also through the thousands of YouTube videos, channels, online images, and digital parodies circulating the Internet. As with many historical examples of iconoclasm, such as the well-documented removal of Saddam Hussein's statues in Iraq in 2003, the official destruction of images, monuments and symbols – it can be argued – guarantees the production of images. As Paul Virilio notes, the mechanical reproduction of images are like ghostly 'clones' and a production of 'the living dead'.[21] In the case of Lulu, we see the Pearl Roundabout as an object resurrected and once again destroyed, time and time again in the footage of its demolition. In these digital images, we come into contact with the Pearl Roundabout's life and death: its image resurrection and redispersal. Its inert material as an image can then be considered living, or at least 'undead' – an immortal activist, a martyr, or an enemy of the state, instilling itself in the memories of the Bahraini people and mingling daily with some sort of collective consciousness.

Given the potency of the monument as a contemporary symbol, it is near impossible to destroy its image once it has been posted online, no matter how hard one might try to destroy it. These Pearl clones have the potential to wreak social and political havoc when caught in a circuit of meaningful exchanges in online networks, thus producing new narratives and counter-memories. Like the 'mirror scene' in Sam Raimi's 1992 *Army of Darkness*,[22] where evil clones burst from the shattered pieces of mirror, the Pearl Roundabout might be positioned as the shattered mirror from which a multiplicity of spatially dispersed images emerge. Each image of the monument is presented on screens that are owned and viewed by individuals with their personal subjective relationship to the monument's image. In this, the Pearl Roundabout cannot be contained by a single point of view precisely because it means different things to different people.

As with objects, the image can act and function in multiple ways that shift continually across time and space, fluidly negotiating ever-changing subjectivities and realities. Today, a YouTube search for 'Pearl Roundabout' in Arabic yields 4,170 results and in English 1,720; a Google image search has 71,900 in Arabic and 299,000 results in English.[23] Bahrain, although the least-populated country in the region, was the subject of the greatest number of Twitter hashtags, with 2.8 million mentions at the end of 2011, while in Arabic it clocked 1.48 million hashtags.[24] Considering how Bahrain has been connected to the Internet since 1995 and rates of use were estimated at 77 per cent in 2011,[25] the popularity of the '#Bahrain' hashtag and the proliferation of hundreds of websites, blogs, social media pages, have created online digital archives, which can only confirm that the virtual world has become a site of counter-memory and discourse. Alongside the unprecedented wave of media about Bahrain reported by opposition, government supporters, and journalists, the Bahraini government was spending millions on international PR companies to counter a negative image.[26] The government was an early adopter of Twitter and YouTube at the start of the protests in 2011, populating news feeds and Twitter streams with one line of argument. The social media landscape of Bahrain is graphic, violent, and controversial, making the scramble for answers and information about the ongoing protests increasingly difficult.

In his essay 'Nietzsche, Genealogy, History',[27] Foucault describes how counter-memory splinters the monolithic, and ruptures the homogenous narratives imposed by the powerful. Counter-memory allows 'scratched over', eroded, and repressed archives, documents, and images to 'shine brightly' alongside those that correlate with the state-endorsed images that support homogenous narratives of power. Unlike its status as a monument, silent and invisible, the post-demolition image of the Pearl Roundabout is mutable, ever changing in circuits of meaningful exchange. It does not fix or ossify, but rather, as Roland Barthes has written on the photographic image, 'blocks memory, quickly becom[ing] a counter-memory',[28] precisely because it now exists as an image.

## The splintered image

*I remember the Lulu Roundabout as the tallest structure on the island. As a child, it seemed colossal and unapproachable; the car seemed to lean slightly as we circled its unusually large circumference. At its base were fountains and at night and on National Day and Eid, the monument would be lit up with colourful light shows. Seeing people on the manicured grass of the roundabout was rare, and those moments would often involve migrant labourers, on a Friday afternoon break, dangerously navigating traffic to get on the roundabout for that keepsake photo. I would peek out of my window dizzily, trying to look at the pearl, which seemed to vanish into the sky, fading from the field of vision, as we got closer.*

As the Bahraini uprising continues, two years after the Pearl Roundabout was violently erased, Lulu has taken on a mythical status. And as we circle the roundabout like lost satellites, we bear witness to the multiple manifestations of this politically charged monument both as a physical, exploding object, and as an explosion of digital files. A Google image search for the Pearl Roundabout only gives a glimpse of the vast production of discourses, truth-claims and narratives that the Pearl Roundabout generates. Photoshopped edits of the same recycled images of Lulu fill blog posts, articles, and online forums focused on the topic of the Bahraini uprising. These images and videos of the Pearl Roundabout are often memorials of their own to the roundabout and its occupation. The monument is often viewed nostalgically, such as in one 3D rendering of the monument with birds circling in a halo around its crown.[29] The use of 3D recreations of the monument are also common, reanimating the roundabout as a martyr, featured in video games and hero videos, such as 'Bahrain Revolution', which ends with the monument emerging from the sea and a lone protester saluting it. In 'Children of Bahrain and their memories',[30] we see another YouTube video that recreates a model of the roundabout and area surrounding it, built by children using rubber bullets and other weapons used by Bahraini security forces. Emotive, militaristic music is overlaid with images of this model and text blaming state violence for the violent memories of Bahrain's children.

The production, dissemination, and consumption of images of the Pearl Roundabout and the discourses generated around these images is inherently tied to the narration of events that surrounded it during the uprising, not to mention its role in the raging political and ideological battles that have since emerged. The monument, once used as part of the state's image economy, has been turned into a memorial for an uprising against the very state that created it. This is clear in the case of the many physical reappearances of Lulu in the streets of Bahrain. Through a practice of commemoration and reproduction, 'Lulu clones' appear at various events and happenings, from sit-ins, protests, and even religious festivals such as the annual Ashura marches. In a video from April 2011, filmed during the period when a state of emergency was declared in Bahrain and rallies and protests were banned, activists leave a reproduction of the monument on a street as riot police prod it gingerly. Another action in June 2011, several police re-enact the demolition of the monument[31] in an unwitting public performance at the Aaynali village roundabout as they try to remove it. Aside from becoming both an act of defiance,[32] these commemorations share a common function: they aim to reactivate something that was once alive.

In its reimaging and reinscribing as a digital object, we see the distinctions between virtual and real blur as the image of the Pearl Roundabout is infused with multiple writings, rewritings, claims, and memories by the state and citizens. A ubiquitous image, Lulu is the point of focus for the battles that have raged in the streets between citizens and state since 2011, but these discourses and narratives stretch far beyond the 2011 uprisings. They can be traced to descriptions of clashes between protesters and state security forces that have been going on in Bahrain since even before the March Intifada of 1965. Clashes and protests have long been described by the Bahraini government as *a ʿamāl shaghab*: acts of hooliganism or *a ʿamāl irhābiyya*, acts of terrorism, while opposition groups describe the conflict as an *intifāḍa sha ʿbiyya*, or popular uprising.

Online, these discourses manifest in blog posts and on social media in an argument between the state, government supporters, commentators, and those that oppose the government.

The fifty-second clip of the demolition of the Pearl Roundabout, originally aired by Bahrain state television following the destruction of the monument, has been used and reused in various and some-times oppositional narrations of the Bahraini uprising. YouTube user, 'mohammedalbuainain' produced a video[33] overlaying text on the demolition video adding photos of faces of opposition figures with 'we made fools out of them' stamped on their faces, and a 'he he he' on top of the video of the roundabout collapsing, ending with a request to follow him on Twitter at his user name @khalifa4ever, reflecting a view on the protests that echoes a video depicting the occupation as a carnival called 'The scandal of "Dowar al Shisha" (Shisha Roundabout)'. The video – with a soundtrack of a child laughing – contains images of the roundabout with shisha, haircuts, food, and even the appearance of Barney the Dinosaur, discrediting the protesters political motivations for the demonstrations. It ends with a text saying 'these people don't know the meaning of revolution or peace'.

In other videos,[34] such as 'Dowar al Mut'a', the mixed-gender occupation of the roundabout becomes the key point of contention, depicting the roundabout as a place of 'filth' and for *mut'a*, a temporary marriage custom permitted in Shi'a Islam.[35] Posted by 'BahrainShield', the film presents a montage of images taken after the 17 February crackdown and clearing of the roundabout. Sexually discrediting protesters is quite common among anti-opposition online comments as well as a strategy used by 'internet trolls' to discredit female activists, who have had a key role in the Bahraini uprising, often making up more than half the participants in marches and street protests.[36] On the flipside, those who supported the protests have also used this footage. It appears in 'We will return to Midan al-Shuhada' (Martyrs' Square)' by 'AlBahrainRevolution'.[37]

Dramatic music and heavy treatment of the original footage is edited alongside images of protests, riot police, and state violence ending dramatically with a fire-explosion wipe and the Pearl Roundabout as featured in the logo for the 'February 14 Media Network', one of the many networks of citizen journalists disseminating media on the Internet.

In this pattern of image reproduction, the Pearl Roundabout's surfaces, textures, and dimensions, are immersed in a pervasive cycle of images mimicking the thick layers of paint on the graffiti-covered walls of Bahrain. These digital images, such as the videos discussed above, play out a 'war of ideas' where surges of support are set in motion both on national and global networks through the viral spreading of images, leaving it difficult for the government to defend its own strategic narrative. Yet the distinctions between reality and fiction become as difficult to identify as the boundary between original image and copy, especially when thinking about the endless, tampered images of the Pearl Roundabout consistently presented as evidence or validation, rather than a marker of fictitious, alterable entities. These constant reappropriations invite us to rethink our relationship with the image and its existence in the digital universe, where images cannot be destroyed because they exist in code. Digital images act like a membrane: the shiny surface of media-skin. And the challenge when viewing such pictures is not unlike the experience of Alice stepping through the mirror in Lewis Carroll's *Through the Looking Glass*. To cross over and back is to try to get through the media surface, saturated with violent, affective images depicting a complicated and dark reality. Such actions might serve to connect such things as memory and architecture, or the sense of place and the experience of struggle in a transaction between both sides of the screen.

Jean Baudrillard once described the image as the site of the disappearance of meaning. After 9/11, he wondered to what extent certain photographs had become parodies of violence. The question was no longer about the truth or falsity of images, but about their impact. This suggests that images themselves have become an integral part of conflict, protest, revolution, and warfare. Today, Lulu has persisted in its presence as a symbol through the violence recalled in its image, from the martyrdom of protesters who died in the square and in the years that followed, to the violence upon the collective memories of Bahrain and the denials of its representation embedded in the roundabout's image. In this, Bahrain has a new monument with which to view its past and present violence: a monument that reclaims space for multiple histories and narratives to come together, from a censored homogeneous state narrative to a symbol for an active, politicised, and heterogeneous society. Thinking back to the Pearl Roundabout as I gazed at it from the car window as a child, to the images of it today, it seems the roundabout – this digital monument – has become a vanishing point of reality. The image itself has become violent.[38]

CHAPTER 6

# *Tn Tn Ttn* and torture in Bahrain

## Puncturing the spectacle of the 'Arab Spring'

## John Horne

> I spent the whole morning till two o'clock interrogating the
> prisoners, at first they couldn't speak but I beat a few of them till
> they did speak. It was all very barbarous and illegal but on some
> occasions one has to behave illegally.
> – Sir Charles Belgrave, British advisor to the
> Ruler of Bahrain, 27 May 1932[1]

ʿAli ʿIsa Ibrahim Saqr was pronounced dead on 9 April 2011,
aged thirty-one. He was killed as a consequence of severe torture,
whilst being held by Bahrain's Ministry of Interior. Bahrain state
television later aired a filmed confession Saqr had made under
torture, seemingly failing to realise that the same person seen
confessing on screen had just emerged dead.[2] Authorities initially
claimed he died from injuries sustained whilst resisting officers.
When Nabeel Rajab, President of the Bahrain Center for Human
Rights (BCHR), published photographs of Saqr's body showing
extensive marks of torture, he was summoned for questioning by
a military prosecutor.[3] At a press conference, the Government
Health Minister confidently accused Rajab of photoshopping the
pictures, before a BBC reporter, Frank Gardner, interrupted to say
that he'd seen the injuries on the body himself.[4] Gardner, reported

that 'his wounds were quite simply horrific. Beaten black and blue, his lacerated back resembled a bloody zebra; he appeared to have been whipped with heavy cables, his ankles and wrists manacled'.[5] The Bahrain Independent Commission of Inquiry (BICI) found that Saqr had been tortured to death. The two officers who were eventually charged with his killing, however, had their sentences reduced to two years on appeal, with the court arguing that the police had been 'preserving the life of detainees'.[6]

The images of ʿAli Saqr's bruised and battered body were widely circulated on social media by Bahrainis seeking accountability and justice. They offered just one example of the brutal treatment being meted out by security forces in response to the pro-democracy uprising. Four other Bahrainis were tortured to death between April and May 2011, during the period of martial law. A cruel pattern began of people being 'disappeared' then returned to their families from official custody, dead: Karim Fakhrawi, a respected businessman and co-founder of Bahrain's only independent newspaper; Zakariyya al-ʿAshiri, a blogger; Jabar al-ʿAlaywat, an elderly gentleman. Photographs and videos of their tortured bodies spread with cumulative outrage across Bahrain. Their brutal, senseless killings and the collective shock they triggered acted as a central site of humiliation and indignity, inflaming the anger of protesters and cementing hatred towards the regime. The routine denials and absurd and blatantly untrue reasons given – sickle cell anaemia or kidney failure – served only to add further indignity and insult.[7] By contrast, these images – and the wider repression they represented – triggered relatively little interest or reaction in the West.

Torture has been a central tactic of Bahrain's security apparatus, currently and historically, in its decades-long quest to curtail calls for democracy, socio-economic equality and fundamental human rights.[8] The multiple stories of torture at the hands of the regime are embedded within the collective conscious and lived experience of many Bahrainis, forming something of a folklore of repression and dissent. As a consequence, individual stories like ʿAli Saqr's are felt collectively, resonating deeply across large sections of Bahrain's citizenry. Such stories cannot be distanced, because they stoke the scars felt within families and villages. 'To some spectators, the tortured body, purged of the evil at the moment of death, became pure and almost sacred, as the sheer stubbornness of life in the bodies that refused to die became a counterpoint to royal might. The condemned sometimes became popular heroes, symbols of the injustices of the sovereign.'⁹ The torturers themselves – and those who instructed, authorised, and hold responsibility for their deeds – have acted, and continue to act, relatively safely in the knowledge that they will not be held accountable, locally or internationally.¹⁰

This chapter is concerned with how torture in Bahrain has been seen by – and screened from – the international community across the course of the Arab uprisings. As well as discussing the transgressive act of exposure in resistance to epistemic violence, this chapter focuses on the ethics and political responsibility of the Western spectator. Whilst the Bahraini government has worked tirelessly to control the visual frame through which it is encountered in Western, mainstream, English-speaking media, Bahraini activists have turned to social media platforms to urgently communicate the brutality of the state that governs them and the complicity of Western states in perpetuating this. As the opening epigraph suggests, there is a long history of Western, especially British, complicity in supporting and sustaining the repressive structures that enable torture in Bahrain to persist with impunity.

Edward Said had argued that 'the representation of other societies and peoples involved an act of power by which images of them were in a sense created by the Western spectator who constructed them as peoples and societies to be ruled and dominated, not as objects to be understood passively, objectively or academically'.¹¹ Accordingly, a key concern throughout what follows is the role of imagery in fostering internal solidarity and the position of the Arab and Western observer when encountering such imagery.¹² Equally, I consider the external mediation of the Bahrain Uprising and the impact of the circulation of actual images of torture by activists in seeking intercommunal and external solidarity. When untethered from their domestic resonance, graphic imagery may only evoke a limited response. As such, I turn to *Tn Tn Ttn* (2012), a short film made by unknown Bahraini activists, in order to see how Bahraini activists, whether intentionally or inadvertently, undermined the mediated 'spectacle' of the so-called 'Arab Spring'.

## *Tn Tn Ttn*: a short film

*Tn Tn Ttn* dramatises the arrest, torture, and killing of a citizen (figured by an air horn, or what is also known as a *vuvuzela*) who will not stop honking 'Tn Tn Ttn', the coded revolutionary rhythm meaning 'Down With [King] Hamad'. 'Tn Tn Ttn' lends itself to easy expression through horns, drums, and everyday objects, deriving as it does from the syllabic rhythm of the Arabic slogan; two stressed syllables followed by two quick successive and unstressed syllables: *yas-qut Ha-mad*. Along with other expressions that question the inviolability of Bahrain's ruler, publicly uttering 'yasqut Hamad' is considered a criminal offence by the regime, under the constitutional and legal rubric of 'insulting the King'. This particular revolutionary slogan is the most popularly used in street protests until today.

The rhythm, and its multiple modes of expression, is foundational to the creative forms of protest that emerged across the course of the uprising. This creative resistance includes sculptures, such as a throne for King Hamad made from tear gas canisters; satirical videos parodying the police made by a group called Baharna Drama; a 'Flame Race' held during the 2013 Formula One Grand Prix; and countless artistic reworkings of the demolished Pearl Roundabout in cartoons, graffiti, logos of grassroots village protest groups.[13] The film *Tn Tn Ttn* sits alongside these as an aesthetic call for solidarity, understanding and the fulfilment of a political demand, and channelling indignation towards the central figure at the apex of power. The video was circulated under its Arabic title on 13 February 2012, the day before the first anniversary of the 2011 uprising when renewed mass protests were planned. Its distribution to a local audience, as most grassroots activist visual works appear to do in the first instance, was thus a means of advocating a radical message to motivate and reinstate hope to compatriots for the overthrow of the regime.[14]

It was uploaded again on 15 February 2012, with an English title and description, facilitating its spread to the West and non-Arabic-speaking audiences. Furthermore, as I will argue below, the film creates a continual appeal to the spectator to look beyond the tortured body and recognise not just the structures that oppress it, but their complicity in sustaining them. In this chapter, I will consider the ways by which the regime has sought to control the visual domain through which it is encountered by the West, restricting the *visibility* of torture and silencing protesters' demands. This, as we shall see, is facilitated in part by the marginalisation of Bahrain's recent uprising and subsequent crackdown within international coverage, both regional and mainstream, of the wider regional turmoil and the manner in which it was framed.

## The 'visual rush' and the problematic 'spectacle' of the Arab uprisings

Before analysing *Tn Tn Ttn*, it is important to view the film within the context of the Arab uprisings. The impact of the spectacle on mediating events in Bahrain transformed the Pearl Uprising into little more than a tragic miniseries on television or computer screens around the world. Indeed, this serial was part of the so-called 'Arab Spring', a spectacle par excellence.

Western media settled on the term 'Arab Spring' to encompass the uprisings in a readily understood manner and it quickly took on common currency amongst commentators and academics.

The term has been deeply contentious and is increasingly rejected. When soliciting contributions for a collection on the uprisings, Ahmed Shihab-Eldin and Maytha Alhassen found that their initial call for a book entitled *Youth Voices from the Arab Spring* 'fell on deaf ears', as their 'prospective contributors . . . had no idea what [they] were talking about'. Locally, they note, 'the terms most widely used . . . were *thawra* (revolution) and *ḥarakat al-thawrat* (revolutionary movements)'.[15] Indeed, 'Arab Spring' was imported into discourse by Marc Lynch[16] and imposed on events from its previous usage by neo-conservative commentators after the US invasion of Iraq and who, by 2005, were suggesting that President Bush's actions were ushering in an 'Arab Spring'.[17] Equally, as Rami Khouri suggested in 2011, the term's 'popularity . . . in the West mirrors some subtle Orientalism at work, lumping Arabs into a single mass of people who all think and behave the same way'.[18]

Central to such an 'act of power', in the sense of Edward Said, is rendering the structures of power invisible as such, sustaining the notion of the West (and its citizen-spectators) as benevolent observers. Khouri would add that the 'Arab Spring' may also be popular in the West because it 'conveniently removes the element of culpability and foreign complicity in the dark, bitter and endless "winter" that we endured for three generations of incompetent Arab police and family-mafia states'.[19] 'Arab Spring', then, can be understood as a containing and troubling framework through which complex and locally specific events were bracketed and mediated into a simplistic, celebratory, and often romanticised narrative. Furthermore, as Sheyma Buali argues, this 'narrative of euphoria overshadowed the reality of the betrayal, brutality and deaths that also occurred'.[20] Although the death of street vendor Mohamed Bouazizi in Tunisia did generate the wider understanding that 'The Arab Spring martyr is a needless victim in the larger fight for the universal values of dignity and human rights, who then transcends victimisation to become associated with agency'.[21]

For many, myself included, the Arab uprisings unfolded on a screen or, often, several screens: television, computer, and mobile device. Lina Khatib has referred to this as the 'visual rush' of the Arab uprisings,[22] emphasising the role of the rapid circulation of imagery across multiple platforms. Images, of protest, police brutality, armed conflict, and, occasionally, celebration captured by journalists and local citizens alike were watched by Western spectators in homes and on phones. Indeed, in their analysis of how protests were consumed, Aday *et al.* find that 'the vast majority of attention' given to it 'came from outside of the MENA region'.[23]

Yet, despite the complexity of the Arab uprisings, much of what happened was subsumed by this deluge of images and pictures, most which were selected and consumed in the West via media structures defined by national and corporate politics that did little to unsettle the assumption of the Western observer as a 'benevolent spectator'. This is particularly true of violence, which is both highly selective and highly sanitised in mainstream media. Indeed, for Douglas Kellner, the uprisings formed a 'media spectacle', which he defines as 'media constructs that present events which disrupt ordinary and habitual flows of information, and that become popular stories which capture the attention of the media and the public'.[24] In describing how the actualities of uprisings were encountered and consumed from afar, Kellner and Khatib both draw on Guy Debord's notion of the 'spectacle', which he described as 'a social relation between people that is mediated by images'.[25] However, in disagreement with Kellner particularly, I do not consider the spectacle as a potential site of 'reversal, and even revolution',[26,27] but rather precisely the totalising entity that Debord describes, particularly in his later writing. Here, the spectacle – the confluence of media, advertising, television, cinema, and so forth – is always ultimately the product of capital, tethered to state and corporate power, which functions to distract and nullify civic agency. As a consequence,

citizens 'can never lastingly free themselves from the crushing presence of media discourse and of the various forces organised to relay
it'.[28] Even though Bahrain's uprising was more image-heavy than
previous periods of dissent, the dominant discourse represented by
the spectacle of the 'Arab Spring' marginalised the pro-democratic
aims of Bahrainis, mostly due to Western powers' strategic concerns
with their Bahraini ally. For this reason, disrupting the 'spectacle'
itself became an act of resistance.

In this sense, then, the 'visual rush' consumed by the Western
spectator and contained through the 'Arab Spring' framework can
(and should) be demarcated as a mediated event, separate from the
complex, multifaceted events within and across different countries
in the Middle East–North African region (MENA). By mediated,
I mean both the process of turning events into images and narratives
that were watched, alongside the deeper act of mediation via
existing cultural, historical, and ideological codes. In suggesting
this, however, I am conscious not to demarcate the real from the
imaginary or the representation from the reality. That is, I am not
claiming, in the manner of Baudrillard,[29] that the Arab uprisings
'did not take place' simply because they were experienced for many
on screens, filtered and simplified as the 'Arab Spring'. Indeed,
doing so would risk privileging and centring the Western observer
in relation to the majority world. Rather, following Sarah Kember
and Joanna Zylinska,[30] I'm treating mediation as a productive
process, shaping events rather than simply representing them.
Put simply, the extensive presence of Western media in Tahrir
Square, Cairo, during the eighteen days of protest that led to the
overthrow of President Mubarak should be seen as contributing
to and amplifying the demonstrators' demands. Or, put another
way, the comparative absence of mainstream Western media from
Bahrain weakened the appeals of the pro-democracy protesters and
enabled the government crackdown to occur with little international
censure, or even public awareness.

In the case of Bahrain, one consequence of mediation on Western perception was the entrenching of a sectarian framework. Reporters routinely transformed popular discontent into a narrative of 'Shiʿa majority versus ruling Sunni minority', echoing the regime's current (and historic) attempts to control the situation by sewing sectarian division. Also largely lost were the decades-long demands for democracy and socio-economic justice advocated in uprisings stretching back nearly a century, with Western coverage typically treating the 2011 uprising as the 'year zero' of popular discontent there.[31] Indeed, as Debord argues, 'Spectacular domination's first priority was to eradicate historical knowledge in general'.[32] Thus we have two competing problems with regard to Bahrain. First, events in Bahrain became part of the spectacle of the so-called 'Arab Spring' and the little coverage Bahrain received put forward an idea of a political imbroglio that suited Western strategic interests, and not those of pro-democracy protesters, with little historical context. Second, the absence of Western media weakened the resonance of the Bahrain uprising with the international community, diminishing external forms of solidarity and pressure.

Within this, of course, Arab media played a central role in how Bahrain's uprising was mediated to spectators in the region. This was typically destructive, not just in how the democratic struggle was communicated and framed, but also in how it fostered regional fragmentation along sectarian lines. Qatar-based Al Jazeera Arabic opted to largely ignore events in Bahrain, in stark contrast to their reporting in Egypt, Libya, and Syria. Journalist Ali Hashem resigned from the station in protest at their bias, alleging that their decision to 'cover up the situation in Bahrain' was 'a political one taken by people outside the TV centre'.[33] Conversely, Saudi-based Al Arabiya reported events directly in line with the Bahraini (and Saudi) government. As Hashem observes, 'Al Arabiya produced several documentaries on the unrest in Bahrain; they all carried one message: the regime (Bahrain) is facing an Iranian conspiracy'.[34]

Sustained regional coverage of the uprising and crackdown came from Hezbollah's Al-Manar television, Iranian state media, such as Press TV, and Shi'a stations in Iraq. As Lamis Andoni notes, this 'polarised coverage only served to further confuse public opinion, nurturing the sectarian beast'.[35] Faced with a relentless stream of fabricated stories in the state media,[36] an antagonistic Arab media split between Saudi and Iranian sponsored outlets, and a Western media showing minimal interest, there was very little opportunity in the face of these corporate media structures to influence the field of representability.

## Controlling the 'field of representability' of the national self-image

Mainstream Western mediation of the 'Arab Spring' contributed towards the event becoming a 'spectacle', setting new challenges for activists, who had to disrupt what Judith Butler calls the 'field of representability'. For Butler, 'we cannot understand the field of representability simply by examining its explicit contents, since it is constituted fundamentally by what is left out, maintained outside the frame within which representations appear'.[37] As such, framing is 'structured by the instrumentalizing of certain versions of reality', whilst 'de-realizing and de-legitimating alternate versions'.[38] The Bahraini government worked hard to control the 'field of representability' through which it was encountered – its national self-image, a framing buttressed by Western states' keenness to keep democratic challenges to a strategic ally away from their public's gaze.

The Bahraini government has aggressively challenged what little coverage there was, claiming that Western media is complicit in spreading lies and falsehoods through their albeit infrequent reporting on repression there. Bahrain has even said that they would sue *The Independent* newspaper, accusing them of 'orchestrating a defamatory and premeditated media campaign'.[39] They coupled this with the enhanced projection of Bahrain as a 'business-friendly' modern state and a tourist haven,[40] an image that has been carefully cultivated since 2002 following the uprising in the nineties and the subsequent limited parliamentary reform. This saw a decade of praise from the West, with George Bush saying that Bahrain was 'on the forefront of providing hope for people through democracy' and Cherie Blair calling it a 'beacon of democracy'.[41] Images of torture and extrajudicial killing that emerged after 2011 are the absolute antithesis of this, puncturing the liberal facade. As such, the imagery generated from 2011 onwards was especially formative in constructing Western perceptions of Bahrain. The visual plane thus became a critical site of contestation, with both state and opposition actors vying to influence Western citizens and governments amidst the wider 'visual rush' of the Arab uprisings.

As a means of limiting global criticism whilst repressing a pro-democracy movement, the Bahraini regime worked hard to restrict the flow of images from the country. It achieved this in part by denying entry to international media and targeting Bahraini photographers on the ground, including arresting award-winning photojournalists Mazen Mahdi and Mohammed Alshaikh. It coupled this tactic with the projection of a fake, apolitical, and ahistorical spectacle for observers (domestic, Arab, and Western) in order to conceal the actuality on the ground. This projection was reinforced by Western unfamiliarity and lack of history with Bahrain, particularly the socio-political and historical context. Furthermore, local media is heavily controlled by the government, at one point closing down the only independent *Al-Wasat* newspaper and prohibiting the opposition from owning media outlets.[42] As such, the regime sought to efface the agency of its citizens by mediating the 'social relation' between them and the West. Where protesters did enter the frame, they were, in the spectacle of the 'Arab Spring', typically (and falsely) bracketed as bearing sectarian-based demands (for example, the BBC in June 2011 emphasised that 'mostly Shi'a' demonstrators were seeking 'more rights for the country's Shi'a majority in the Sunni-ruled kingdom').[43]

A central and ongoing tactic was to restrict and inhibit access. Due to its small size, the Bahraini authorities are able to easily police their borders and maritime territory. The two main ports of entry are the airport and the causeway connecting Bahrain to Saudi Arabia. Since February 2011, over 240 journalists, NGO employees, academics, and other outside observers have been denied access to Bahrain, whether by being refused entry at the airport or by being denied a visa in advance.[44] This problem was particularly acute at the height of the 2011 crackdown and during subsequent flashpoints, such as the one-year anniversary of the 2011 uprising or the 2012 Formula One race. When in the country, foreign journalists were subjected to assault, arrest, and even deportation by the security forces. For example, a CBS journalist described how in March 2011 'the riot police . . . just saw a camera and started firing'.[45] Restrictions on access and reporting have been the case even when the media has the express consent of the government. For example, in 2013, after many months trying to negotiate a visa, a BBC crew was allowed to enter Bahrain. However, they had their camera impounded at the airport, were detained twice, and were constantly followed by secret police.[46] As a consequence of all this, some news organisations simply gave up trying to visit the country and their reporting on Bahrain dwindled, compounding the constructed spectacle of Bahrain's uprising within the 'Arab Spring'.

Even when international media was able to report from inside the country, Bahrain's government found other ways to control how it was seen. Former CNN journalist Amber Lyon and a three-person crew spent eight days in Bahrain in late March 2011, under extremely difficult circumstances, filming what would become a one-hour documentary entitled *iRevolution: Online Warriors of the Arab Spring*. The award-winning documentary that resulted cost CNN over $100,000 to produce. Amber Lyon gave several interviews on CNN discussing her experience in making it. The content is very powerful and often shocking, being one of the rare examples of a full documentary crew working in Bahrain since the start of the uprising. However, CNN, to date, has only aired the documentary once and never showed it on CNN International. In September 2012, frustrated by the failure to air the film, Lyon became a whistle-blower, leaking internal emails and other inside knowledge to *The Guardian*, claiming that CNN had bowed to external pressure from the Bahraini government. One email sent in April 2011 by a 'senior producer' at CNN states, 'We are dealing with blowback from Bahrain govt on how we violated our mission, etc.'[47]

Other media organisations encountered similar 'blowback'. For example, the Bahraini government hired UK law firm Carter-Ruck to attack *The Independent* for its coverage of Bahrain, particularly concerning the arrest and torture of medics (Press Complaints Commission, 2011).[48] Similarly, in January 2012, British PR firm Dragon Associates made legal threats against *The Guardian* after they published an article about abuse and torture carried out in 2011 at the Bahrain International Circuit, where the annual Formula One race is held.[49] *The Guardian* was forced to remove the article from its website for nearly three weeks whilst tickets for the 2012 race were on sale. The race is a central event in the government's calendar, with the Crown Prince especially invested in it commercially. The fact that it now takes place on a site where torture took place points to the matrix of repression and denial that underlies the purported normalcy projected by the regime to the outside world.

Dragon Associates was one of many Western PR firms who worked for the Bahraini government following the 2011 uprising and subsequent crackdown. As Bahrain Watch has documented, between February 2011 and April 2014, the Bahraini government spent or allocated over $50 million on US- and UK-based PR firms.[50] The precise work undertaken by these companies remains largely opaque, although they engaged in both producing propaganda materials and trying to shape and influence the Western coverage.

Cloud Media Entertainment was paid to produce a fifty-minute documentary. *Turning Points: One Month That Changed a Nation* (2012) utilises temporal manipulation and omission to put forth 'a strongly pro-government narrative of events in February and March 2011, arguing that the Bahrain revolution should not be seen in the context of the Arab Spring'. The documentary echoes the government line that Bahrain is unique in the region because its current ruler has been committed to political and human rights reforms for years. Pro-democracy protesters are thus framed as saboteurs of the King's progressive path, motivated by a sectarian

**Man with glasses:** This cartoon represents how the world views Bahrain through distorted lenses. A man, representing the state, can be seen plastering the lenses with banners carrying buzzwords that shape the narrative and discourse. In an attempt to diminish international support for Bahrain's protest movement, the government has used PR and propaganda to depict opposition forces as sectarian, Iran-sponsored terrorists, rather than as a peaceful pro-democracy movement. Credit to: Ali al-Bazzaz.

agenda that is orchestrated by Iran. Such a false narrative has nevertheless resonated in the West, particularly because of concerns over Iranian intentions in the region.

American company Qorvis created several anonymous websites, issued dozens of pro-government press releases, arranged meetings between Bahraini officials and US journalists, and placed letters and op-eds in various media outlets. Two of Qorvis's websites – Explore Bahrain and Bahrain Stories – use a large amount of photography to enhance their appeal.[51] Explore Bahrain presents itself as something of a neutral guide to Bahrain, posting articles on a range of subjects. The photographs chosen to highlight each section and article are vibrant and seductive, emphasising Bahrain's modernity and attractiveness to both business and tourists and describing Bahrain as a beautiful, peaceful country, where real estate, business, banking, and culture is thriving. These images evoke the neoliberal project that drives the contemporary Bahraini state, conjuring a spectacle that conceals corruption, the theft of public land, and the repressive apparatus that keeps dissent suppressed.[52] Never mind that the island barely has any accessible natural shores, where only 3 per cent remain in public property.

Through these PR firms, the Bahraini government has worked to project a spectacle of capital flow, culture, and commerce as a means of aligning Bahrain with free market principles enshrined in the Free Trade Agreement with the United States. Indeed, a key stratagem appears to be the creation of cognitive dissonance in Western observers. By promulgating aesthetically pleasant imagery of thriving business, natural beauty, and sporting and cultural prowess to spectators perhaps unfamiliar with the country, doubts can be sown over the reports of torture, extrajudicial killings, and other human rights abuses. Indeed, these marketing images create a fantasy that seeks submission and passivity in the way they are used to override and conceal the unpleasantness of reality, a reality that may demand responsibility and accountability.

## Puncturing the 'field of representability' with state violence

Content circulated by activists through social media platforms like Twitter, Facebook, and YouTube offered the possibility of puncturing the 'field of representability' that governed Western coverage of the uprisings. Citizens could, for example, opt to directly seek out tweets made on the '#Bahrain' hashtag (one of the most widely used in 2011 in the Arab world), rather than depend on the mainstream media's filtering and framing of online content to make sense of the 'visual rush'. As a consequence of the democratisation of image production through social media, however, the Bahraini regime also sought to silence activity online, arresting people even for simply 'liking' something on Facebook.

I want to briefly discuss the circulation by Bahraini activists of actual imagery of torture, and the short film *Tn Tn Ttn* mentioned above, to consider their ability to not simply break through the 'field of representability', but foster both solidarity and the recognition of complicity of the Western spectator.[53]

With international media largely absent and Western states unwilling to support the pro-democracy demonstrations, social media offered, at least, a space for expression, to get messages out, despite the risks involved in being arrested for simply tweeting. The text, pictures, and videos that have been circulated cover the spectrum of protest, politics, and repression. Perhaps the most striking, in terms of urgency and suffering, are the steady stream of photographs of torture victims, particularly the five men who were killed by torture in April and May 2011. Bahraini activists have tried to harness the potential potency of such images to demonstrate the barbarism of the state and seek solidarity with the international community in their struggle against it. However, as we have seen, such awareness and support has not been especially forthcoming. Torture has persisted in Bahrain in the three years since the BICI report found it to be a 'systematic practice' of the security forces,[54] documented in reports by numerous local and international NGOs. It continues, in part, because of an entrenched culture of impunity and denial, and an absence of international censure.

In April 2012, former Assistant Commissioner for Britain's Metropolitan Police John Yates, who had been hired as an advisor to Bahrain's Ministry of Interior, was asked about reports that torture was occurring in secret detention sites. Yates dismissed these accusations, saying flippantly, 'But that would be on YouTube'.[55] However, actual torture – that is, the act of torture – is rarely captured on camera. In the case of Bahrain, there exists footage of brutal police beatings in public, but little from behind closed doors other than photographic evidence of the graphic aftermath.

In one unprecedented case, on 11 June 2013, a policeman uploaded a video of a shirtless detainee, clearly under duress and with a visible injury on his shoulder, giving a coerced confession in a police station. Elaine Scarry has called torture a 'world shattering' experience from the perspective of the victim. She argues that, 'torture systematically prevents the prisoner from being the agent of anything', with the interrogation being a means through which the regime forces the prisoner to 'speak their words'.[56] In the video, the young man was forced to do precisely this, claiming that opposition and religious leaders had threatened to kill him unless he attacked the security forces. In speaking the words of the regime, his agency (and body) are stripped as he is made to parrot their paranoid fantasies. The video was swiftly removed, but opposition activists had saved a copy and republished it, eventually forcing the Ministry of Interior to respond. The Chief of Police later told the BBC that he was 'outraged' by what had happened and that the policeman involved was being investigated.[57] However, the policeman responsible was ultimately found 'not guilty' of forcing the prisoner to confess and successfully won an appeal, which overturned his six-month sentence for uploading the footage.[58]

Images of torture have the capacity to shock. That the government even responded to this incident was likely a consequence of its visibility and the fact that the source was the policeman himself. Similar incidents persist on a daily basis, documented only in written testimonies and reports. Susan Sontag,[59] amongst others, has argued that shock can be a means of provoking a moral response from Western spectators through forcing them to encounter the actual suffering of distant individuals. Such images of real suffering puncture established fields of representability, unsettling the security of the subject position through which the Western spectator typically encounters the world. Simply put, the suggestion is that people are so shocked by what they see that they are moved to action. However, as Butler argues, 'we have to remember that graphic depictions can sometimes do no more than sensationalize events'.[60]

Indeed, the failure of the international community to act in response to not just the reports, but the visceral images of torture, suggests that, whilst they might have briefly shocked Western citizens and embarrassed allies, little tangible action followed. Moreover, the Western spectator is often encouraged to feel pity or compassion towards the suffering individual, rather than solidarity towards them or complicity in sustaining their pain. Furthermore, such images alone can never represent the experience of torture. Indeed, whilst they offer essential evidence of its existence, they risk reducing the act to the physical injuries it can leave, ignoring not just psychological torture, but also the use of stress positions, sleep deprivation, humiliation, and other forms of torture which do not leave visible marks, let alone the additional suffering of the victim's family and loved ones. Equally absent are the local and global structures that facilitate, enable, and condone Bahrain's repressive security apparatus.

Here I must point out that the very same images have a strong and abiding resonance for many Bahrainis, where any additional context is unnecessary: they are markers of a lived and shared experience, providing visible proof of state brutality. Moreover, in the case of those killed, visual documentation plays a central role in their memorialisation as martyrs. As Buckner and Khatib argue, the martyr is 'both a symbol and narrative framework used to galvanise opposition to state regimes'. In Bahrain, the circulation of such photographs can mobilise thousands to attend a funeral where only a few hundred would otherwise attend. Buckner and Khatib suggest that the Arab uprisings have ushered in a 'new model of the Arab martyr'. This involves 'the production of martyrs' images from the state to the citizen' and a 'transition from portrayals of victimisation to empowerment and agency'.[61] This citizen-led empowered mode of representation, however, can potentially be lost as the images travel outside national and regional borders, as I have argued earlier.

## Puncturing the 'field of representability' with creative resistance

The spectator's exposure to real suffering has, with caveats, been advanced as a necessary ethical act.[62] Imagery of torture, I argue, challenges such assumptions. Although photographs of torture are a transgressive act of exposure that resonates deeply among large sections of the Bahraini population, hardening opposition to the regime and strengthening communal bonds, untethered from their local, social, and historical contexts, even the individuals depicted could become reduced to object status. This is not, however, to argue that such pictures and videos cannot puncture the spectacle, revealing the reality it seeks to conceal. Rather, I contend that the ethical act is not one of *witnessing* the suffering body alone, but rather *recognising* the structures that oppress it and the demand of justice. Such a stance should be *unsettling*, as it seeks to foster empathy and solidarity through the spectator's recognition of the deeper realities concealed. Physical representation is necessary, especially when the state seeks to keep the fact of torture invisible, but I suggest that symbolic representations, particularly in unsettling the structures of complicity that govern the spectacle, are just as transgressive. In particular, creative resistance through the use of artistic representations infused with concrete politics and authentic domestic demands can not only bridge distance, but also force the spectator to draw closer between. As such, I conclude by returning to the short film I described at the start – *Tn Tn Ttn* – a film released the day before the first anniversary of the uprising and one which achieves some of these aims.

In the film, the horn wakes up and begins its day by heading outside to gleefully honk its heart out. A security officer, figured by a Spiderman toy, begins shooting at the horn in a failed attempt to silence it. Angered, the officer pursues the horn, before violently arresting it and taking it to jail. Imprisoned, the horn is tortured through suspension, beating, and simulated drowning. No matter what, it never stops honking. Unable to stop this simple sound of 'Tn Tn Ttn', the officer takes a gun and shoots the horn dead. Three other horns then arrive and carry their friend away. The security officer is nowhere to be seen, but the chair on which the horn was suspended comes crashing to the ground. Symbolically, at least, the throne has been overturned.

*Tn Tn Ttn* is, on its surface, very accessible. At a fundamental narrative level, the story is easy to grasp and there is no dialogue or words spoken. Geographical representational barriers are also collapsed. Whilst it is clearly set in Bahrain, there is a universality to the story. It is almost like a fable, suggesting that repressive means ultimately never succeed. The use of inanimate objects limits the spectator's emotional engagement and amplifies the films symbolism. The casting of Spiderman against type – obviously he is a hero in Western popular culture – is a form of *détournement*,[63] used to establish a geopolitical undercurrent to the film, symbolising opposition anger at the perceived Western support for the authorities in Bahrain and referencing their long complicity in facilitating torture and impunity. However, much of this symbolism – like the meaning of 'Tn Tn Ttn'– requires the spectator to have some local knowledge to interpret it. This isn't simply imagery of torture which can be slotted into, say, a human rights discourse. As such, the horn is not seeking appeals to the state to stop torture, but soliciting solidarity against the state.

The collapse of the chair at the end of the film clearly represents the fall of the throne and thus, the success of the demand: 'Down With [King] Hamad'. Equally, the chair's use as a prop from which the horn is suspended whilst being beaten cements a link between the throne and the structures of torture. However, the ending also subverts what might be expected, particularly if this were a Western film: there is no retribution. After the horn has been shot, there is a cut to a Bahraini flag and three new horns appear and enter the torture room. Spiderman has disappeared and the chair falls by itself. Street noises are then heard. A title announcing 'The End' comes on screen before the film cuts to a wide shot of Pearl Roundabout during the period when it was occupied by pro-democracy protesters.

The film is strikingly amateur throughout. Several sequences are rendered spatially and temporally confusing, not through intent but rather lack of resources. The figures are 'animated' by people moving them along, which limits the scope of establishing shots and often results in a somewhat odd framing. As a consequence, the spectator's subject position is unsettled. Like the torturer, they are denied a position of mastery: the film, rather than its viewer, retains agency. All this, however, conveys a sense of the personal, which extends into both the popular and the political, given the anonymity of the makers. When the film was first released, many wanted to know who made it. However, the necessity of their anonymity is precisely the point. Furthermore, whilst being entirely engaging, the film is the antithesis of the glossy PR materials made for the Bahraini government, which seek to seduce the Western (consumer/investor) spectator.

The final shot echoes the brief opening sequence. The film begins with a rapid sequence of shots to the tune of 'Tn Tn Ttn' that cuts between Pearl Roundabout and title cards saying '2012'. As Amal Khalaf has said of Pearl Roundabout, after it was demolished it became a 'powerful symbol for thousands of people recasting their ideals in the monument's image'.[64] '2012' clearly refers to the aspiration that it will be the year those ideals will be realised. Without prior familiarity with the tune and the symbol, such a reading is far from obvious to anybody outside Bahrain. By the film's end, however, even if Pearl Roundabout itself remains unfamiliar, it has been endowed with heightened meaning by the preceding events.

*Tn Tn Ttn* thus portrays a paranoid and violent response to a peaceful articulation of political demands. The film works to communicate torture in Bahrain to the outside world, wedded to a revolutionary rhetoric that will not be silenced. The horn retains agency throughout, never once allowing its torturer to force it to 'speak their words'. Instead, its constant refrain fosters a continual appeal to the spectator to recognise not only the innate desire for liberation but also the local and international structures denying them. Moreover, *Tn Tn Ttn* helps reveal how vulnerable to exposure repressive ideology can be and challenges the national self-image that seeks to protect itself from international intervention. Rather than trying to puncture the 'field of representability' with real images, the film playfully unsettles and undermines the spectacle in order to forge new social relations. As such, it shifts the Western spectator's focus away from witnessing the suffering body to adopting a stance of solidarity towards it, and against the structures that oppress it. The challenge faced by those who seek to end torture and abolish the culture of impunity in Bahrain is to creatively break through the 'field of representability' in a manner that instils recognition and responsibility. For the Western spectator, this will necessarily be unsettling as it must highlight their complicity, but therein lies the path to genuine solidarity.[65]

# PART THREE

# Suppressing dissent in an acceptable manner

Modes of repression, colonial legacies, and institutional violence

## CHAPTER 7

# On the side of decency and democracy

## The history of British–Bahraini relations and transnational contestation

### Zoe Holman

> The occasional presence of a warship in Bahrain harbour would do much to keep our prestige alive among a set of people who are only too apt to forget that the British Empire exists and does take an interest in Bahrain affairs.[1] – Major Dickson, Political Agent Bahrain, March 1920

> Your security is our security. Your prosperity is our prosperity. Your stability is our stability.[2] – Philip Hammond, UK Foreign Secretary, December 2014

A photograph on the British government website shows the British ambassador in Manama posing with members of Bahrain's government against a backdrop of Union Jack- emblazoned Rolls-Royces, Morris Minors, and a gleaming double-decker bus. The lurid tableau was assembled to promote the island's inaugural 'Great British Week' held in January 2014. Patronised by King Hamad and attended by the Duke of York, the event aimed 'to emphasise the friendship and strong bilateral relationship' between the two kingdoms through a range of cultural and business activities.[3] Throughout the week, the red 'Boris bus' toured the streets of the capital promoting local investment by UK companies, including BAE Systems, Ernst & Young, and Standard Chartered, while families played rugby and celebrated with ice cream and bunting at the British Club and Rugby Club. Elsewhere in the capital, billboards proclaimed 'Welcome. You are GREAT Britain', as Bahrain commenced official preparations for festivities to mark the 2016 bicentenary of bilateral relations between the nations. Indeed, since it established formal dealings with the Al Khalifa royal family in the draft 'treaty of friendship' in 1816,[4] Britain has given Bahrain's rulers much to celebrate. Over the past two centuries, the UK's enduring diplomatic, political, and security support has amounted to backing which remains unrivalled by any Western power. It came as no surprise then when, in December 2014, Philip Hammond announced that Britain is to expand its base as a return to its 'East of Suez' policy, giving the UK a permanent presence in the Gulf for the first time since its official withdrawal in 1971.

More recent years have seen an erstwhile imperial protection and tutelage reproduced in London's unequivocal support for the Bahraini regime since the resurgence of opposition protest in 2011; a 'long friendship' reaffirmed. Where the King himself in 2012 lauded the supporter who had 'stood head and shoulders above others', so too the UK has been recognised by scholars, activists, and British officials themselves as being Bahrain's closest non-Arab ally throughout the three-year-old conflict.[5] Yet, where abiding UK support has been central to the regime's capacity to stifle dissent on home soil and stave off criticism internationally, so too has Britain provided a key site for its opposition to enact contentious politics on the global stage. The consistent and expanding presence of Bahraini exiles and opposition activists in the UK – the largest Bahraini opposition community in the West – has enabled dissidents since independence to challenge the iniquities of the Bahraini regime outside the evermore repressive strictures of the island. Facilitated by the mechanisms of democratic civil society not available in Bahrain, activists in the UK have re-established and reified Bahrain's opposition movement, an 'international front' through which to counter the regime and the neocolonial safeguards of its British exponent.[6]

This chapter will detail key features of this unique British–Bahraini relationship and its implications both for those officials in Britain attempting to downplay the atrocities of the regime and for the opposition activists attempting to denounce them. In doing so, it will document the perspectives of Bahraini opposition exiles and opposition expatriates in Britain whose own activities trace a historical and evolving dynamic of struggle and estrangement in both countries.

## Bahrain's long 'friendship' with Britain

When questioned in a House of Commons debate during the spring of 2011 regarding what would become known as Bahrain's 'Bloody Thursday' and Britain's role in the repression then being meted out against protesters in Manama, Foreign Secretary William Hague responded by evoking Britain's lengthy affinity with the Al Khalifas. 'We have had a long friendship for the past 40 years with Bahrain, and it is felt strongly in that country', he explained.[7] It was thus necessary, Hague proposed, to impress upon its rulers the importance of conceding to popular demands through 'appropriate' reform, while respecting cultural differences in governing styles:

> Britain is of course on the side of decency and democracy everywhere in the world, including in the Middle East and the Gulf states . . . Among the leadership in Bahrain, there is the appetite and determination to carry out those reforms. There is no doubt about the sincerity of the King of Bahrain and the leaders of the country about that. We will therefore continue to give our advice and to deplore situations where violence arises and lives are lost.[8]

However sincere the Secretary's own belief that such reform would transpire, his statement accurately reflected a long-standing paradigm of British–Bahraini relations: a pattern of governing violation, perfunctory British pressure, and cosmetic reform that had endured since before nominal independence in 1971.

Bahrain was drawn into Britain's informal empire alongside other Gulf states during the imperial climax of the early nineteenth century, when *Pax Brittanica* emanated from its colonial headquarters in India. With the waters of the Persian Gulf then beset by naval feuds – so-called 'piracy' by London – local rulers who denounced this instability were allied as signatories to a truce with Britain in 1820, affording imperial protection in exchange for cooperation in combating piracy.[9] Among the heads of these 'Trucial States' was the recently established shaykhdom on the island of Bahrain, conquered by the Al Khalifa tribe from the ruling Persians in 1782. Henceforth, a series of contracts laid out the respective rights and obligations of the British Crown vis-à-vis Bahrain's rulers, its territories, and citizens. These included stipulations that 'the British government has the right to establish an agent or broker at Bahrain' and 'the Ruler of Bahrain must always be at peace with the British Government'.[10] Britain's entry into the Gulf amid these insecure circumstances thereby assumed all the resonances of colonial pacification and protection, a narrative of responsibility and benevolent authority in the region which was sustained into the twentieth century.[11] Bahrain's independence was further stymied by subsequent treaties. By 1861, the signing of the 'Perpetual Truce of Peace and Friendship' had turned Bahrain into an informal protectorate of Britain. 'In exchange for control over Bahrain's foreign policy, Britain was now bound to protect the Bahraini government from external aggression.'[12] Indeed, the strategic and symbolic significance of the region to the British Empire was confirmed by its envoys of the time. In a visiting speech to the Trucial chiefs in 1903, Viceroy of India, Lord Curzon, described the hybrid of interest and paternalism that characterised Britain's engagement in their territories:

We were here before any other Power, in modern times, had shown its face in these waters. We found strife and we have created order. It was our commerce as well as your security that was threatened and called for protection . . . We saved you from extinction at the hands of your neighbours . . . We have not seized or held your territory. We have not destroyed your independence, but have preserved it . . . We shall not wipe out the most unselfish page in history. The peace of these waters must still be maintained; your independence will continue to be upheld.[13]

Britain's determination to retain this position was confirmed the same year by the Secretary of State for Foreign Affairs, who told the House of Lords, *that* 'we should regard the establishment of a naval base or a fortified port in the Gulf by any other power as a very grave menace to British interests, and we should certainly resist it by all means at our disposal'.[14]

These tenets in effect informed Britain's relations with Bahrain's rulers henceforth, with the post-war decline of British influence in Persia heightening the imperative to protect oil supplies and strategic allegiances in Bahrain. However, attempts to administer de facto British rule through the designated 'Political Agent' also revealed the inherent difficulties of a system which sought to simultaneously exert influence, extract interest, and create a semblance of independence in Bahrain. The vagaries – and, at times, elasticity – surrounding Bahrain's protected status quickly manifested in conflicts over the terms of British involvement in its internal affairs. Encroaching British jurisdiction on matters including Bahrain's judicial system, parliament, and relations with other Arab shaykhs inspired resentment among the Al Khalifa and their tribal allies, and in turn antagonism toward the British Agent. Relations strained by such interference became visibly fraught by disputes over the treatment of Bahrain's indigenous inhabitants, the Baharna majority population, whose grievances were increasingly difficult to ignore for both Britain and the Al Khalifa monarchy. As noted in a 1921 correspondence by the Agent, abuses 'too numerous to quote' by Bahrain's governing classes against the Baharna were then customary.[15] Among them, British authorities noted the illegal seizure of property, political murder, detention without trial, discriminatory taxation, and wrongful imprisonment.[16] Although the Agent on occasion intervened to protect victims at their request, Baharna unrest around the injustices saw pressure mount for more determined British action against misrule. Envoys were petitioned directly by political groups and communities. In particular, organisations were keen to impress on British officials their duty of protection towards the subjects of Bahrain's monarchy, as well as its reigning heads.[17] As was observed by one Foreign Office representative in response to an aggrieved Baharna campaign in 1921:

> It is obviously not desirable to make the Agency into a Court
> of Appeal against decisions of the Shaikh, but on the other
> hand . . . Bahrain subjects are afraid to take the law into their
> own hands as the Shaikh is under our protection, and they urge
> with some reason that we ought to prevent the Shaikh from
> abusing his authority.[18]

UK officials of the time likewise questioned Britain's habitual strategy of appeasing the Shaykh in such instances of abuse. As was noted in a despatch to the Foreign Office from Manama, 'the policy adopted by His Majesty's Government . . . that "the amelioration of the internal Government should be brought by indirect and pacific means through the increase of influence with the Shaykh by gaining his confidence and trust" has not proved a success'.[19] Nonetheless, any immediate shift in tactic that might aggravate hostility with the Shaykh, and thus threaten Britain's position in Bahrain, was ruled out. According to an official directive from the Colonial Office, Britain was 'not prepared to consider drastic action against Bahrain misrule' until all more benign means of coercion had been eliminated. Officials were instead instructed to 'impress your personal influence on the Shaikh and his family and restore prestige of Agency'.[20] Representatives were, however, also encouraged to draw the Shaykh's attention to the conditionality of British endorsement, namely, that 'if misrule leads to uprising the Government will find it difficult to render him any support whatsoever'.[21]

The following decades thus saw British authorities attempting to placate both Bahrain's marginalised Baharna population and its testy rulers, who were, according to officials, oblivious to the fact that they were 'sitting on a volcano' of popular hostility.[22] In the face of persisting violations by the Al Khalifa monarchy, a precarious path was pursued, which sought to neither alienate 'influential opinion on the island' with any suggestion of diminishing Sunni privilege nor give the suggestion to international observers that Britain was 'acquiescing to misrule in Bahrain'.[23] Yet the cosmetic ministrations of reform under the British 'advisor' Sir Charles Belgrave did little to remedy the problems of divisive Al Khalifa governance. Alienated from the flow of oil revenues from the 1930s and the Sunni beneficiaries of British patronage, Bahrain's Baharna majority, as well as Bahraini nationalists, became in equal parts resentful of their local oppressors and opportunistic imperial custodians. In addition, ongoing British protection over Bahrain undermined growing calls for independence, particularly prominent among Bahraini youth educated abroad, exacerbating popular hostility towards the imperial authority.[24] (As the Lebanese nationalist intellectual Ameen Rihani wrote scathingly in 1930, 'security and peace, England has brought to the Arabs of the Gulf . . . But what is it costing the Arabs? The Gulf should be renamed: it is neither Persian nor Arabian, it is British.'[25]) Accordingly, popular campaigns for justice became increasingly anti-British and anti-colonial in tenor. Belgrave himself dismissed protest leaders as opportunists appealing to the 'illiterate element in the population', but opposition soon manifested in mass strikes and demonstrations explicitly calling for the Advisor's departure.

(During the foment of 1954, Belgrave himself characterised protest slogans as 'anti-British, anti-Shaykh and anti-me' to BBC journalists covering the events.[26]) Similarly, a 1956 stopover in Manama by the Foreign Secretary, Selwyn Lloyd, saw the Minister's car stoned by protesters insisting on Belgrave's removal. Reports from officials in Manama and surrounding villages meanwhile related the daily dawn patrol by officers to erase 'subversive' nationalist slogans that appeared across towns overnight.[27] The ensuing alarm about preserving British authority in Bahrain (and, by extension, in the Gulf) permeated the highest levels in London and soon saw Prime Minister Anthony Eden himself advocate a military incursion on the island to restore order. (As he proposed, the solution might 'show them we are still alive and kicking'.[28]) The dilemma was aptly characterised by Lloyd, who, while acknowledging the plausibility of weighing in on behalf of the Al Khalifas, advised against armed measures. As the Foreign Secretary explained, 'it would be likely to lead to a popular uprising in favour of reform and before long, British troops would be shooting down people whose claims are in accord with our own proclaimed beliefs and practices'.[29]

However, the arrest of the three popular opposition leaders, 'Abd al-Rahman al-Bakir, 'Abd al-'Aziz al-Shamlan and 'Abd al-'Ali 'Aliwat in 1956 provided a timely opportunity for Britain to cooperate with the Shaykh to combat disorder through a more discreet betrayal of its espoused principles. The activists, of mixed ethnic and Bahraini origins, were all members of the Committee of National Union, a nationalist democratic organisation with an anti-colonial and anti-sectarian political charter.[30] British officials agreed via a court decision to transport the so-called 'Nasser-inspired forces' to the remote South Atlantic island of St Helena on the pretext that they had participated in a plot to assassinate both Belgrave and the Shaykh.[31] The joint action was met with some objection from commentators and politicians in Britain, as reflected in newspaper columns expressing concern for the possible mistreatment of the prisoners (as well as their peers detained in Bahrain). Such grievances were dismissed by the Advisor as 'ill-informed', yet 'Abd al-Rahman al-Bakir appealed 'to the Supreme Court of St. Helena and to the Judicial Committee of the British Privy Council for a writ of habeas corpus'. After a successful action, the three exiles were released from St Helena and Britain's relationship with Bahrain temporarily soured. Belgrave was retired on the grounds of illness in 1957 and British involvement in local security and intelligence was enhanced with the desired stabilising effect.[32]

Yet awareness of the growing tide of Arab Nationalism, narrowly averted in Bahrain, culminated the following decade in Britain's resolve to withdraw from its territories 'East of Suez'. Despite warnings that the move could open a power vacuum in the region, it was decided by the Labour government of 1967 that Britain's future strategic and political interests in the Gulf would be best served by a timely withdrawal. (As one official noted, to leave amid an atmosphere of political amity was calculably preferable to 'outstaying our welcome'.[33]) A far-sighted decision to depart in 1971 was thus attended by rigorous efforts to 'tidy up' Britain's future in Bahrain in advance of withdrawal.[34] Chief among the associated tasks was that of securing a stable long-term political environment on the island by insulating its monarchy against the more palpable, immediate threats of popular revolt and international criticism. As one Agency official noted in a 1966 letter to the FCO:

> We must clearly not be deceived by improvements into thinking
> that everything in the garden is lovely . . . There may be
> no tension at the moment . . . but no significant political or
> social action has been taken by the ruler to remove the deep-
> rooted causes of discontent and frustration among the mass
> of the educated and semi-educated population. If he signed
> and implemented the admin reform . . . this would be quite a
> different matter.[35]

British authorities were nonetheless reluctant to push more forcefully for reform, lest such unwelcome pressure give 'the boat of Anglo-Bahraini relations a rock'.[36] Likewise, envoys feared that any more substantial intervention could undermine the object of their pre-departure designs, namely, 'the appearance of autonomy and independence of British influence which the Bahrain Public Security Department and State Police should be anxious to preserve'.[37] Al Khalifa misgovernment was thus countenanced by more clandestine forms of British cooperation in domestic security, a strategy which nonetheless reflected one of its most flagrant incursions into Bahrain's internal politics. It was subsequently through Colonel Ian Henderson's system of covert surveillance that British interests in Bahrain were safeguarded. Where dissidents demanding modern political reform had been formerly exported off-shore, 'subversive groups' and other would-be agitators could now be intercepted locally by what became in effect an 'anti-terrorist' force.[38] So productive was the alliance between Henderson's security apparatus and the ruling monarchs that his services were retained for a further thirty years after independence: a new marker of the symbiosis which had characterised British–Bahraini relations since 1820.[39] The defence of *Pax Britannica* in the Gulf had proved mutually beneficial and its core tenets would be sustained long after Britain's formal departure and concurrent military withdrawal in 1971. (The latter was particularly undesirable for Bahrain's rulers who, increasingly anxious about aggression from Iran,[40] offered economic incentives against withdrawal.)

Britain's departure from the Gulf was paralleled by the ascent of American hegemony, as signified by the establishment of a US base in Bahrain in 1947 that subsumed UK naval bases after their withdrawal. Despite claims by the Americans that theirs was only a 'show-the-flag' operation, documentation testifies that they intentionally overrode eviction notices issued by representatives of the newly formed state.[41] Thus in 'post-independent' Bahrain, the spectre of British influence continued to be felt in the presence of UK diplomatic staff, business advisors, private mercenaries, expatriates, and civil servant classes across Bahrain's police force, hospitals, and ministries. Indeed, such was the prominence and persistence of the British–Bahraini affinity after independence that, when asked in 1999 how Britain's withdrawal from the Gulf had altered the region, a long-serving British advisor to the Emir of Bahrain replied, 'British withdrawal? What withdrawal? We're still here!'[42]

## Outside Bahrain but inside the people: Bahrain's opposition abroad

The persistence of repressive misrule in Bahrain over its post-independence decades saw the country's dissidents forced abroad in ever greater numbers. Since the establishment of the Trucial Agreement, Bahrainis had travelled to Britain for health, tourism, and education purposes (all current office-holding members of the Al Khalifa family undertook university or military training in England, including the current ruler). Many subsequently resettled in England to capitalise on economic or vocational opportunities, forming the UK base of a community of supporters and beneficiaries of the Bahraini ruling class. However, this presence was equalled by a parallel class of exiles and expatriate activists which took shape in Britain.[43] Contrary to common perceptions of the Gulf as being devoid of civil-society activity, this sphere has always been vibrant in Bahrain (as Bahrainis commonly joke, every ideological or intellectual current in the Arab world has been represented in Bahrain, even if by just one person).[44] Likewise, this mobility and diversity has been reflected in the civil-society activities of its diaspora.[45]

Regarding post-1965 exile, Claire Beaugrand notes, 'From this time on, two different waves of exile took place: the Marxist and Arab nationalist movements of the 1960–1970s, when Bahrain was still under British protection, and the Shiite [sic] Islamist currents of the

1980–1990s'.[46] Bahrain's principal waves of exile were engendered by crackdowns on the burgeoning communist and Arab Nationalist campaigns in the years prior to and following independence. The majority of these activists were members of the underground labour movement or student unions and found refuge in Yemen, or in Ba'athist pre-Saddam Iraq and Syria, owing to the then sympathetic, pro-communist policies that granted asylum to any Gulf dissidents. The eighties saw a second wave of predominantly Shi'a Islamist opposition activists exiled from Bahrain to the West. With the wane of the communist movement and simultaneous upsurge in Islamist sentiment around the Iranian Revolution of 1979, opposition protest in Bahrain was imbued with some features of Shi'a Islamism. The region-wide Islamist revival in Bahrain manifested in two main political strands: the Shiraziyyin, who supported more radical forms of confrontation with the Bahraini regime, including armed opposition; and the affiliates of the Dawa Party, who remained committed to progressive action through legal channels and whose MPs constituted part of the parliamentary 'Religious Bloc' during Bahrain's brief democratic interlude of 1973–75.[47] The latter group, members of which continued to leave Bahrain for Europe and North America throughout the 1980s, formed the backbone of the opposition community in London. There, a number a key exiles established the Bahrain Freedom Movement (BFM) and, later its main mouthpiece, the Voice of Bahrain website. Throughout the 1980s and 1990s, the London dissident cohort was joined by Islamist exiles and expatriates from a range of political and religious allegiances, among them the prominent Shi'a cleric Shaykh 'Ali Salman of Al Wefaq, who was granted asylum in Britain following uprisings in 1995. The persistent, transnational nature of opposition protest (and its suppression) after 1975 also meant that many politicised Bahrainis and their families who had emigrated temporarily for study or work found themselves unable to return and exiled.

Despite often diverging ideological positions, these London-based Bahraini oppositions were able to cohere into a relatively unified front around key claims and political agendas. Where revolutionary leftists affirmed their commitment to a reformist programme, Islamists too endorsed the tenets and practices of liberal democracy over any notion of implementing religious law. (This general trend towards opposition alignment has been countered by some notable exceptions, most prominently the Shiʻa cleric Shaykh ʻIsa Qassim, among those who concurrently diverged from moderate reformism towards greater ideological zealotry.) The British-based opposition thus consolidated four central demands: the restoration of the 1973 Constitution, the election of a national parliament, the lifting of the governing 1975 State Security Law, and the release of political detainees with an amnesty for political prisoners and exiles. Similarly, exiled opposition forces successfully adopted the language and means of their Western host countries in support of these localised political ends. They emphasised human rights, and other, violations made by the Bahraini state through organised demonstrations, petitions, newsletters, and other bilingual media. Campaigns were fortified early on by effective links to human rights and other NGOs, including Amnesty International, Human Rights Watch, and the International Labour Organisation, who generated publicity and thereby pressure on the Bahraini regime. Collaborative working relationships were also established between exiles and elements within British government, including a number of MPs and Lords, most prominent among them Lord Avebury, a determined public critic of the Bahraini regime and its Westminster alliance. This coalescent, transnational campaign of the 1990s was thereby situated by its advocates, the exiled opposition at the helm, within a broader global discourse of human rights. Such a strategy reflected what Asef Bayat has recently deemed a more general 'post-Islamist' ethos to political movements in the region, one which has characterised Bahrain's opposition movement.[48]

Likewise, such a framework for opposition demands aligned with the central tenets of progressive internationalism being articulated with reformulations of a so-called 'ethical foreign policy' by Blair's New Labour of the time.

The cohesion among different facets of the Bahraini opposition in Britain thus contrasted markedly in relations with their regime-aligned counterparts, the majority of them Sunni, and often students on government-sponsored scholarships. The two camps' respective political activities gave rise to occasional interaction, often with hostile connotations, outside of which there appeared to be a self-enforcing divide. As one UK-based activist explained, 'we don't talk to the pro-government side. We know who they are, they know who we are and we know where each other lives, but we don't talk'. Similarly, another young activist noted the distinction between his more varied social sphere in Bahrain and the more stark ideological divides of the Bahraini diaspora in Britain; as he explained, 'when I was in Bahrain, I maintained good relations with Sunni friends, though many of them were regime supporters. But in London it's different – I have no personal communication with any of them'.

The threat posed to the regime by more radical forms of contestation from abroad was confirmed by the regime's transnational repression of diaspora figures, as underscored in the initial period of purported reform post-2002. Many of those exiles who had been accused of 'terrorist' activities by the monarchy in the decades after independence found the same charges being mounted against them under the new constitution. Naming on official lists of terror cells, *in absentia* trials for plotting to overthrow the government, and the threat of Interpol arrest warrants became fixtures of their demonisation and denunciation by local authorities in Bahrain. Some also encountered physical intimidation in England, with the London home of the BFM founder Saeed Shehabi attacked by arsonists in 2009 in what was interpreted as a political threat. The ongoing use of such trademark tools of authoritarianism across borders cemented opposition perceptions of regime illegitimacy and in turn their commitment to undermining the government's repression through a transnational strategy. Shortly after another terror-related charge by the regime in 2010, Saeed Shehabi explained to a London press conference:

> [Since 1975] we suffered immensely under the state security court and state security law. Then in 2000 this man came and promised he would create a Plato's republic in Bahrain. But now we can only see a hell on earth . . . I was implicated in 1980, 1984, 1988, 1996, 2007, 2009 and this time . . . We know they have been recruiting agents inside and outside, some in this room. For years we know that they are planning to undermine our cause.[49]

This long-reach of the Bahraini regime, ever vigilant to police its subjects and defend its interests abroad, in many respects fortified the connection between exiles and oppositional politics inside Bahrain. The issuing of active legal charges and threats across borders gave added currency to opposition activities, reifying the place of exiled activists on the expanding stage of Bahraini national politics. Similarly, the presence of family members in Bahrain, combined with the island's small population, enabled activists in London to retain close ties to local politics via regular communication and coordination with those active on the ground. Such channels were strengthened by the movement of opposition figures between Britain and Bahrain in the form of exiles who chose to return to the country following the amnesty of 2001–2002, among them Abdulhadi al-Khawaja, who repatriated from Denmark after twelve years of activism abroad. As such, the UK-based Bahraini opposition was 'outside the country', but 'inside the people'.[50] Contrary to the experience of some other diaspora communities, exile in many respects enhanced the local profile of Bahrain's opposition abroad, now able to seize the instruments of democratic civil society to adopt a more vocal and visible international stance against the regime. So too, assistance rendered to new exiles by those already established in Britain helped to cement London as a base for the Bahraini opposition abroad during the decades post-independence. As the prominent young Europe-based activist and daughter of Abdulhadi al-Khawaja, Maryam explained:

> We've had a Bahraini opposition living and operating from
> London for a long time. They've played a strong role in
> advocacy and in helping those who need to get out, which
> is why most Bahrainis come to London. Like the rest of the
> country, the diaspora is tiny, but it has a strong connection with
> those inside Bahrain.[51]

When pro-democracy campaigners turned out at Pearl Roundabout in Manama and Bahrain's London embassy in Belgravia for the scheduled 'Day of Rage' protests in February 2011, their demands came not only with a sense of continuity across time, but also across borders. The date of the protests was elected to coincide with the anniversary of the referendum for the National Action Charter (NAC) on 14 February 2001 and to highlight that its democratic 'guarantees' remained unrealised. Inside Bahrain, both established opposition figures and younger activists emerged in a movement that would later call itself the February 14 Youth Coalition. Protesters turned out across the country to denounce the failed accord and demand a new constitution. As the then President of the Bahrain Youth Society for Human Rights explained, 'we have been in revolt for more than a century . . . This uprising marks the death of the national charter a decade later'. Diaspora activists too, were acutely aware that, although inspired by events in Egypt and Tunisia, the campaign which surfaced in Bahrain from February 2011 was not a nascent product of the so-called 'Arab Spring'. As one young British-Bahraini activist explained in June 2014, 'in terms of uprisings, this is nothing new to Bahrain. Every decade there is an uprising just like this one – these have been our demands since the British left in 1971. So now we are just trying to get back that broken promise'.

Many of Bahrain's veteran dissidents, inside the country and abroad, were therefore at the forefront of the uprising which resurfaced from February 2011, reiterating their unmet demands of old within a new, vastly augmented protest movement. Links between the diaspora opposition and that inside Bahrain were likewise fortified by the renewed indictment of exiled figures alongside local leaders. In what Bahrainis refer to as 'the case of icons', a group of twenty-one opposition figures, including politicians, rights activists, bloggers, clerics and exiles, some already detained in Bahrain, were named by authorities from March 2011 in relation to their role in the unrest. The group included Abdulhadi al-Khawaja and secular liberals like Ibrahim Sharif, as well as the Haq and Al Wefaq leaders, Abduljalil al-Singace and Hassan Mushaima. Following a series of arrests, the group were tried (some *in absentia*) and convicted of 'setting up terror groups to topple the royal regime and change the constitution'.[52] While the seven exiles among them were beyond the reach of physical harm, the detention and mistreatment of the remaining thirteen prisoners,[53] routinely subjected to torture and injustices, became a pivotal rallying point for the Bahraini uprising but garnered little international attention.

The alacritous local repression of the movement by Bahrain's security forces meant that the axis of visible opposition began to shift away from Bahrain. Newly exiled and settled diaspora activists with the means to give expression to rebellion became coordinators, advocates, and media spokespeople for those stifled by the crackdown inside the country. Many young Bahrainis assumed roles at the forefront of the transnational campaign, providing information and publicity to activists on the ground as violence escalated. As one young woman described of her early experiences of the uprising from abroad:

At the time of the massacre on February 17 at Pearl Roundabout, Bahraini TV was airing a cooking programme. It was so sad to see intelligent people unable to express what was going on in their minds and on their streets. The revolution was still there, inside people, but it had been gagged. I felt a responsibility on my part to continue what they started because I am lucky enough to be in England. Of course I have received numerous death threats, or people calling me a 'dirty Iranian agent', but here I have the luxury of freedom.

Counter to official goals, attempts to eliminate the influence of opposition icons inside Bahrain also served to propagate dissident activity amongst a new generation of Bahrainis. By providing a mouthpiece for imprisoned or otherwise silenced political leaders, the mobilisation of media-astute young Bahrainis reflected a continuation of their forerunners' long-standing campaign. Yet their activism also elaborated on these demands, with the new youth movement manifesting a programme that was often more dynamic and more radical than that of prior uprisings. One London-based activist and the son of a Bahrain 13 leader described the shifting dynamics of opposition leadership since the seminal 'Day of Rage' in 2011:

Now there are many new youth leaders who are able to mobilise in ways that parties like Al Wefaq could not do, for example, the February 14 Movement. They have a huge amount of belief and faith and ability to get people out on the street . . . It is necessary to continue our protest with new leaders, especially with old ones like my father in prison.

Other new activists recounted becoming politicised by the ongoing, but increasingly visible social inequities of present-day Bahrain, where the ruling regime authorities continue to buttress their minority rule through judicial discrimination and demo-graphic engineering projects including the mass 'naturalisation' of immigrants from Sunni Muslim countries. One young, British-educated activist, Sayed Alwedaei, now a refugee in London, described how he was drawn into opposition activism after returning to Bahrain:

> It is amazing how the demands the political leaders expressed in the 1950s are the very same demands the people have right now, but before I was not fully aware of these political injustices. It is only when you go home to Bahrain and everywhere you see these people who don't even speak Arabic – working in banks and hospitals and government offices – who are simply mercenaries. Only when you see how the regime is actually trying to change the demography of the country by naturalising citizens, do you really understand.

## Bahraini activism in the UK

The presence of this new wave of activist exiles from 2011 vastly expanded the opposition base in London, where campaigns were coordinated from the hub of the Bahraini community centre in Euston, the de facto 'embassy for the revolution'. The *Financial Times* reports that about 185 Bahrainis have applied for UK asylum since February 2011. Home Office data show that 102 applications have since been granted.[54] The transnational Bahraini uprising which was reanimated with the so-called 'Arab Spring' thus reflected the grievances of decades of political dissent, overlaid with the fresh claims and resolve of a new generation of regime opponents. As one young British-Bahraini recounted of the changes she had witnessed in the diaspora since 2011, 'there is a new scene happening now that is not about the old guard. Before, political activism was something my father and his friends did. But now it is inclusive of a much wider spectrum. The fuel has completely changed'.

The importance of Bahraini external opposition has been underscored by numerous acts of protest by activists abroad and in particular in Britain – acts which, if performed in Bahrain, may result in torture, lengthy prison sentences, or even death. In May 2013, Sayed Alwadei, a Bahraini granted asylum after being tortured by the authorities, disrupted the prestigious Royal Windsor Horse Show when he approached Queen Elizabeth II and the King of Bahrain, who were both sitting in the VIP stand. Bearing a large Bahraini flag, Alwadei was reportedly able to deliver the following message to the Queen: 'Your Majesty, stop supporting the dictator of Bahrain. Our people [have] been killed in Bahrain. Release our prisoners.'[55] Although arguably a mere simple publicity stunt to some, the symbolism of the British Queen seated alongside King Hamad cut deep with many activists. As one new asylum seeker noted shortly after the Al Khalifas' visit to Royal Windsor in May 2013:

> To me, one of the worst, the most insulting images, I ever saw was the torturer King Hamad and his brother sitting in the VIP section at Windsor. There are people who are oppressed and tortured in Bahrain, I am one of them, and the UK government is granting me protection from an oppressive regime. And yet we also receive this oppressor at the highest levels and greet them as VIP. This is the saddest part of the story.[56]

Various other opposition protests abroad have drawn headlines, including when Ali Mushaima and Moosa Satrawi, two UK-based Bahraini opposition activists, mounted the rooftop of the Bahraini Embassy in London. Here, they draped from the roof images of Abdulhadi al-Khawaja, an incarcerated Bahraini activist who spent over 100 days on hunger strike, and Hassan Mushaima, the General Secretary of Haq, a banned political society in Bahrain. According to the BBC, Moosa Satrawi stated: 'I'm not going down until I hear Mr al-Khawaja call me or Mr Mushaima . . . Otherwise I will jump from the roof'.[57] The protest was widely covered by the media and, although both activists received suspended prison sentences, an equivalent stunt in Bahrain might have resulted in a far worse punishment.

While Bahrain's opposition abroad may enjoy more lenient treatment at the hands of the British authorities, the claws of the Bahraini government are exceedingly long. In 2011, a number of Bahraini students studying at British universities lost their government scholarships after taking part in protests in the UK.[58] Several of these students also reported that their parents were being harassed back in Bahrain. Arab activist Amin al-Wasila commented on how it was difficult to feel safe protesting in the UK, stating that 'it seems very strange that every time something happens here in Britain there is a repercussion there'. Again, the darker side of social media emerged here with some students revealing that they suspected their pictures had been taken by 'Bahrain or Saudi "spies" alerted to the event on Facebook'.[59]

As well as engaging in street protests, activists have also been turning to other British institutions in order to lobby against the Bahraini regime. In October 2014, the quashing by the UK High Court of a decision to grant Prince Nasser immunity from prosecution for torture in Bahrain – including of an activist later granted asylum in Britain – afforded a hopeful indicator of this potential. Furthermore, simultaneous UK government findings that a complaint by human rights activists against companies participating in Bahrain's Formula One Grand Prix 'merit[ed] further examination' served as a vindication of efforts by the opposition abroad.[60] Such gains also reflect their growing traction in Western media and among civil society, developments which are themselves testament to the progressive capacities of diaspora politics more broadly.[61] In this vein, Abdulhadi Khalaf, a leftist politician and former lecturer of sociology at the University of Lund in Sweden, explains that 'exiles are privileged as they are less exposed to the pressures and ramifications of the day-to-day confrontations that leaders in the country face'.[62]

## 'A right way to frame things': contesting British-Bahraini relations

Yet, while the resurgent protests of 2011 saw the opposition abroad respond to events with an evolving catalogue of new strategies and influences, the same could not be said of British policymakers in their host country. Rather, the dominant approach in London from 2011 served to confirm Britain's role as ally and guardian of Bahrain's ruling elite. As has been widely noted, the success of transnational and/or diaspora movements depends to a large extent on how its aims and ideas are received in the political milieu of its host state.[63] The British government's continued resistance to any bona fide endorsement of protesters' demands that might disturb Bahrain's iniquitous ruling status quo thus drew UK policymakers directly into the ambit of the opposition campaign: a transnational challenge to local and foreign sources of repression that echoed former struggles against malign imperial interference.

London's unwavering official support for the Bahraini regime was made readily apparent within days of the February 2011 protests. The first challenge raised to William Hague in the House of Commons on the subject – in the words of MP Denis MacShane, whether the policy of 'turning a blind eye to the repression and corruption of the regimes in this region may be coming to an end?' – characterised British policy towards Bahrain henceforth. While emphasising a shared British–Bahraini determination for reform, Hague also stressed the need for 'a right way to frame those things – with a deeper understanding of what is happening in those societies'. Sensitivity to the political context in Bahrain, he claimed, entailed recognition of the unique tensions there, in particular those exacerbated by Iran. So too, it was necessary to acknowledge that each country has a 'different pace of reforms'. According to the Foreign Secretary, diplomacy proceeding from this understanding would produce the most effective outcomes in Bahrain.

This reform framework was simultaneously being peddled before Western audiences by Bahrain's royal family, sheathed in a fitting vocabulary of political tolerance and openness. In a rare Western media interview on CNN on 20 February, Crown Prince Salman, who was then charged with leading the political dialogue, lamented in his flawless English the loss of life and apparent divisive sectarianism of the previous weeks. Comparing the violence at Pearl Roundabout with the conflict in Northern Ireland, he told reporters, 'this is our tragedy . . . and we almost lost our soul'. Accordingly, he offered assurances of a return to 'normal' through a process of dialogue with all Bahrainis.

Despite stark indicators of continuing repression by the security forces, British authorities appeared contented by the cosmetic reformist offerings from the regime over the coming months. David Cameron subsequently addressed Gulf leaders in the Kuwaiti parliament with an air of confidence on events in Bahrain during a defence-trade tour of the region. The Prime Minister's treatise, which came only a fortnight after 'Bloody Thursday', did not airbrush the spectre of violence in Bahrain, but rather endorsed Salman's pledges of a new and restrained approach. As, he explained,

> Using force cannot resolve grievances, only multiply and deepen them. We condemned the violence in Bahrain, and welcome the fact that the military has now been withdrawn from the streets and His Royal Highness the Crown Prince has embarked on a broad national dialogue.[64]

UK officials' adherence to such a line, even as GCC tanks crossed the causeway into Bahrain several weeks later in the most flagrant display of force, served as a more precise yardstick of London's support. Indeed, the full extent of British cooperation in the Saudi-led crackdown has since come to light, with gradual revelations of UK assistance in the form of military provisions to train Saudi Arabian National Guard recruits by the British Armed Forces.[65]

To many Bahraini observers, the event signified an all too familiar pattern of Western complicity. Maryam al-Khawaja, whose father was arrested within weeks of the Saudi invasion and later handed a life sentence, characterised opposition sentiment in her account of Britain's response:

> The way it worked in the beginning was that there was *some* kind of attempt by the UK government to a minor degree to *try* and pretend that they *sort of* cared about human rights and democracy in Bahrain. But of course this was totally messed up when the Saudis came in. That the British are actually playing a role in this is something that is understood by a lot of Bahrainis – the UK has been one of the leading forces in helping this regime stay in power. And this is not something that started in 2011, it is something that goes back way beyond that.

Yet where British officials had on some past occasions intervened to temper extreme instances of violence or injustice by the Al Khalifas prior to independence – or, as one former ambassador recently described, 'when the regime got too firm with the stick' – it now appeared that Bahrain was largely beyond reprimand in Britain. This was confirmed for many by Cameron's reception of the Crown Prince in May 2011, as the crackdown continued unguarded. (Salman had diplomatically declined to attend the royal wedding the previous month on the grounds of the unrest, after his invite provoked criticism in the British press.) His visit to Downing Street was likewise met with protest and official outcry in Britain, including from MP Denis MacShane, who deplored the Prime Minister for 'rolling out the red carpet for . . . the real-life, real-time crushing of the human spirit'.[66]

Nonetheless, government representatives persevered in their attempts to project that reform was afoot in Bahrain, a task facilitated by the convening of the Bahrain Independent Commission of Inquiry (BICI) several months later in November 2011. A novel initiative for any government in the region, the BICI was varnished by slick publicity and its efficacy was readily apparent. A lavish ceremony was held at the King's palace and the report was handed over by the Chief Commissioner to the King in a red velvet box. The Foreign Office fluidly seized its recommendations as evidence of progress in Bahraini governance and security apparatus (despite continuing evidence to the contrary from diaspora activists and UK-based NGOs such as Human Rights Watch[67]). Over the following year, UK officials continued to issue favourable appraisals of the reform programme. As Foreign Minister Alistair Burt commented in February 2012, 'we welcome the steady progress on . . . the Commission's recommendations, and efforts to ensure that Bahrain's policing meets international standards and has at its centre a respect for human rights'.[68] Bahraini activists were quick to criticise how the BICI report was used for whitewashing human rights abuses. As Sayed Alwedaei noted:

> Bassiouni is the best PR game the Bahraini regime could play, and Britain has been the report's biggest advocate. It has allowed them to say 'Bahrain is the only regime who has taken such measures'. It has documented what we all know and all agree on: that there is systematic torture. But we don't need an investigation to show us this: what we need is for is the person responsible for the killing to be named.

Conversely however, British energies continued to be channelled into efforts to dilute the appearance of regime culpability. Within weeks of the release of the BICI findings, the former Assistant Metropolitan Police Commissioner, John Yates, was hired as an advisor to the Bahrain Ministry of Interior (MoI) to assist in reforming the 'culture of impunity' that had reportedly led to security forces' actions in 2011. (Yates subsequently accompanied the Bahraini Minister of the Interior to London for meetings with the Director General of MI5, and other officials, from whom he was reportedly 'keen to learn'.) Invariably, Britain's Bahraini opposition noted the historical parallels of these developments, with Yates personifying a long tradition of British assistance to secure internal stability under the rubric of reform. Moreover, revelations about Yates's liaison with the Bahraini MoI from as early as February 2011 raised questions around his role in facilitating surveillance of Bahraini dissidents in Britain, especially those being tried *in absentia*. Furthermore, Bahrainis saw similarities between Yates and the former security advisor, Ian Henderson (the so-called 'Butcher of Bahrain'), who had so efficiently orchestrated the repression of dissent. As one activist, who had been detained by the regime before being granted asylum in Britain, noted of Yates's deployment:

> Just like under Henderson, since Yates arrived, arrests and violations have actually gotten worse. But this time they have taught the police in Bahrain how to keep your violations and crimes hidden. You can do the same things, but there will be no more of those stupid, messy crimes the regime committed in public in early 2011. Now it is all about the 'intelligent' crackdown.

Where dissent in Bahrain could not entirely be erased, PR resources seconded from the UK underscored Britain's interest in containing the more unpalatable aspects the crackdown. As John Horne discusses in his chapter, this PR discourse often referred to thinly veiled, or often direct, references to the age-old threat of Shiʿa extremism from Iran, which once more became justification for the employment of appropriately harsh counter-extremist measures by the regime. Such propaganda devices had become well worn for their dissident targets in Britain over the decades prior to 2011. As Saeed Shehabi noted wearily of his recurrent indictment as a terror suspect in the national press at the time:

> terrorism did not exist in Bahrain and it does not exist. It is only in the minds of the royal family. Terrorism is when you speak

your mind and oppose the regime . . . I have been implicated
in every single 'terror' cell since 2001, with people I have never
met, and never heard of. I am always the mastermind of the plot,
named at the top of some fictional organisational structure, of
course aligned with Hezbollah and supported by Iran, and always
with all the headlines 'MoI has uncovered cell'.

Not only did this language, as noted by the BICI itself, serve to
conflate internal dissent with terrorism, it also recast opposition
to the regime along sectarian lines in what many regarded as a far
more damaging false paradigm of political contest in Bahrain. From
their inception, the mass demonstrations at Pearl Roundabout
and across Manama were attended by aggrieved Bahrainis of
Shiʿa, Sunni, and other denominational backgrounds. Although
the rekindled uprising, like the Bahraini political opposition
itself, drew its base from the country's subordinated Shiʿa majority, protesters were conscientious to establish a unified, cross-sect
campaign, an ethos which echoed that of Bahrain's progressive
political movements since prior to independence. Anti-sectarian
sentiment was reflected in the common chant 'no Sunni, no Shiʿa',
and banners reading 'we are one'. Members of the diaspora too,
were emphatic that the opposition campaign was inspired by a
democratic, not ideological, spirit. As Hussein explained, 'the tension is not between Shiʿa and Sunni in Bahrain. It is more about
a divide between those who call for democracy and change and
those who cannot imagine any change'. Similarly, another young
activist noted that:

There are two categories in the opposition in Bahrain: the
political parties that were in the parliament, and then all the
other leaders who have called for reform and who are behind bars –
the 'extremists'. But British policymakers will not see people
representing that group, people like me, because they consider
us radicals – radical because we want change, because we want
people to be held to account for their promises.

This account characterised the experience of the newer generation of Bahraini dissidents abroad who had assumed the legacy and demands of political detainees in Bahrain and encountered similar resistance in London. Speaking during the near-fatal 110-day hunger strike by her father in 2012, Maryam al-Khawaja described the support lent to her campaigns by individual lords and MPs in Britain. However, despite engaging with high-ranking representatives in the United States, Maryam was not granted a single meeting with either Hague or Burt. (Her mother, Khadija al-Musawi, did eventually meet with the Foreign Minister shortly before he left office in 2013 in what was perceived as a perfunctory meeting to detract from this record.) As she noted, 'it has been a lot more difficult in the UK where they are not at all happy to hear about the human-rights situation in Bahrain . . . In the US, through constant lobbying and contact with officials we were actually able to stop an arms sale. In the UK you can barely make a difference; we have not even succeeded in stopping Alistair Burt or Sayeeda Warsi making patently untrue and illogical statements!' (al-Khawaja was referring to the former Conservative parliamentarian's incendiary comments in which she claimed that 'the UK has not received any specific evidence of the use of torture to extract confessions'.[69] The comment, made in 2014, stands in stark contrast to the evidence of the BICI report, which documents systematic torture in Bahrain during 2011).

Unlike David Cameron, Obama ventured to make a number of critical statements about the practices of the ruling family, including the allegation that 'real dialogue' was not possible while the majority of the opposition remained 'in jail'.[70] British policy, by contrast, was seen to have regressed from mild criticism of ruling violence to galvanised support for the Al Khalifas over the course of the uprising. To the surprise of a number of activists, Britain had thus emerged as a more vocal apologist for Bahrain. As a young London-based refugee explained of his observations in 2013:

We are walking backwards. Since 2011, King Hamad has not once visited the US, but he has been to the UK more than three times. This is his favourite Western country, where he is welcomed and invited to meet the PM, where he knows he will be received as an ally and given the cover and the legitimacy which he seeks from the government. And to be honest, I think they are doing a good job.

Indeed, activists were unanimous in their descriptions of the magnitude of British influence in Bahrain, as well as its historic antecedence. However, many also noted that their sustained criticism of UK policy on this basis had enabled a more reductive distortion of opposition demands by some observers. Rather than any form of armed intervention in the genre of the Libya campaign, opposition members were emphatic that their requests to Bahrain's Western allies amounted to no more than that governments refrain from obstructing their campaign – that is, a call for non-interference. Fatima, who participated in the mass demonstrations at the Royal Palace, described the feeling:

> To be so close to a break-through and see an entire foreign army crossing the bridge, you feel not only that you are fighting the royal family, but the rest of the world. We were never asking for intervention – for tanks, guns and removal of Bahraini regime, or for some imperial power to come and save us. We are saying stop conferring the legitimacy that you have been providing cost-free for the past one hundred years, every time Bahrainis have risen up. We are saying that as powers you, Britain and the US, are standing in our way.

Accordingly, Britain has emerged as a key international actor and determinant in the 'repressive potential' of the Bahraini regime in the eyes of the opposition.[71] Just as imperial protection was lent to the fledgling rulers of the country over the nineteenth and early twentieth centuries, Britain now buttressed a regime that would otherwise be unable to sustain itself, either internally or as an independent actor in the international arena, without recourse to foreign support.[72] Attempts by UK policymakers to shield the regime, and indeed downplay its own leverage, have since manifested in Britain's own political forums, for example, with the 2012 official inquiry by the Foreign Affairs Committee into UK relations with Saudi Arabia and Bahrain.[73] Among other foreign-policy goals, the enquiry sought to investigate how the government balanced UK interests in defence, commerce, energy security, counter-terrorism, and human rights in the two kingdoms and how it might best encourage 'democratic and liberalising reforms'. Yet leaders of Britain's Bahraini opposition readily observed that, although many among them had provided lengthy written submissions, only one activist and an exiled former MP were selected to testify, the only Bahraini witnesses in proceedings.

Such calculated manoeuvring by UK policymakers has become emblematic of Britain's response to the democratic demands put forth by Bahrain's opposition, and thereby the sense of umbrage felt by many. Likewise, the paradoxical practice of granting asylum to so many victims of the Bahraini regime while simultaneously lending support to their persecutors was seen as further evidence of British duplicity. Indeed, many more recent arrivals to the UK perceived their asylum status there as tacit vindication of their political claims – a back-handed, bureaucratic acknowledgement of the violence so rigorously airbrushed from Britain's broader public discourse on Bahrain. Thus, indictments of British hypocrisy were manifold among those who had experienced first hand the effects of its policy in both Bahrain and the UK.

## Conclusion

Britain's ostensibly immovable support for Bahrain had, by the third anniversary of the 2011 uprising, been enshrined as fact for the opposition, in equal parts a testament to the power of geopolitics and the whims of Western democratic discourse as applied in the region. Indeed, for many Bahraini activists and exiles, themselves fluent in the argot of human rights and democracy, Britain's wilful blindness to their cause served as a reminder of a broader tradition of selective Western support for progressive politics in the region. Through the official discourse of policymakers and its undercurrents of implicit 'culture talk', nominated actors continued to be branded as legitimate 'progressive allies', 'reformers', or 'pro-democracy campaigners', and others were 'sectarian', 'extremist' or 'Islamist' suspects, or undeserving of Western support.[74] These practices have not gone unnoticed among Bahrain's opposition (or other democratic actors from the region), as was noted by Nabeel Rajab in mid-2014, who said that he and his family were treated 'like criminals' when they were detained in London's Heathrow Airport.[75]

Incidents like these galvanise Bahrain's rulers' conviction of Britain's enduring support. Invited to address guests at the inauguration of the Endurance Ride at Windsor in June 2013, King Hamad happily proclaimed to attendees that the British–Bahraini relationship was as strong as it had ever been, if not stronger. He explained:

> I see the cooperation and friendship we have met here as symbolising the relationship between our two countries. The first Treaty of Friendship was signed in 1820 . . . and it remained until replaced by a new one in 1971 on Britain's withdrawal from the Gulf – a unilateral decision of which my father said – 'Why? No one asked you to go!' In fact for all practical and strategic purposes the British presence has not changed and it remains such that we believe we shall never be without it.

The apparently decisive nature of Britain's backing and the continuity of the colonial legacy has thus more recently seen the transnational opposition turn towards other institutions and platforms as potential avenues to change. With Bahraini dissidents being stripped of citizenship and compelled abroad in ever greater numbers,[76] it remains clear that any enduring broader solution to the conflict must come from within the country itself.[77] Reiterating this sentiment, Abdulhadi Khalaf has argued that 'exiles are not, and cannot be, effective leaders although they can contribute greatly as leading figures, or just front figures, in various capacities'.[78] However, against the weight of Bahrain's historic and enduring international ally in repression, 'Great' Britain, alternate transnational allegiances, international solidarities, and democratic partnerships will be crucial to stimulating progress within its borders.

## CHAPTER 8

# Rotten apples or rotten orchards

## Police deviance, brutality, and unaccountability in Bahrain

## Marc Owen Jones

> *Halqawanīn ma ḥada yaṭabaqhā ʿalaykum, ila ʿalāqatnā*
> *wayākum, w-ila yaṭabaq ʿalaykum yaṭabaq ʿalayna iḥna, jisud*
> *wāḥad.*
>
> These laws cannot be applied to you. No one can touch this
> bond. Whoever applies these laws against you is applying them
> against us. We are one body.
>
> – Shaykh Khalifa bin Salman Al Khalifa, the Prime
> Minister of Bahrain to Mubarak bin Huwail,
> a man accused, but exonerated of torture

In December 2011, a video[1] emerged on YouTube of a group of
wounded young men, groaning and lying among puddles of blood
on a grey, hard, and barren concrete floor. Some were piled on top
of one another, all were clearly shaken and afraid. While those whose
hands were not bound by cable ties busied themselves with freeing
their fellow victims, others crawled low on the ground, attempting to
make sense of their hideous circumstances. Somewhat eerily, there
was no sign of any assailants and the hushed tones of the young man
filming the video lent it a conspiratorial tone. When the video went
viral, many dismissed it as a fabrication, a cynical attempt by the
opposition to gain sympathy and media coverage from international
observers. Others claimed this was clearly the work of Bahrain's

'No to foreign interference in our affairs'

**Jar:** Each jar represents the foreign governments (US, UK, Saudi Arabia) that are closest to the regime, represented by the man in the middle carrying a banner that reads 'no to foreign intervention in our affairs'. The regime frequently complains of foreign interference by human rights NGOs and the UN, yet it always neglects to mention that its continued existence is very much dependent on Saudi/British/American political and military assistance. Credit to: Ali al-Bazzaz.

security services, whose reputation for brutality is already well established. However, the latter were soon vindicated in their belief when, throughout the day, six different videos emerged. Shot from different people's mobile devices, these videos showed a group of about twenty police savagely beating the group of young men on a rooftop of a house in the mostly Shiʿa village of Shakhura.[2]

Although police brutality had been documented many times before, the Shakhura incident was startling. It was difficult to take out of context and, thanks to social media, never before in Bahrain had such an incident been so unequivocally verified. Even the Ministry of Interior, which frequently responded to threats of police brutality with claims that the security services were merely reacting to threats to the lives and safety of their personnel, were unable to explain it away using the usual PR script.[3] The fact the young men had their hands bound, and that they had not even been arrested, emphasised the gratuitous and punitive nature of the actions. The number of police involved also emphasised it was not simply the deviance of a single officer, but the collective deviance of a number of recruits. This, coupled with the countless videos depicting police brutality, highlighted a culture of permissibility in the security forces, one in which violence and vandalism were not simply the result of individual or even collective negligence, but of state policy. Indeed, as of May 2014, the Bahrain Center for Human Rights has reported that ninety-eight people have been killed as a result of excessive police force since 14 February 2011.[4] While the empirical difficulty of proving that this was deliberate state policy precludes us from simply asserting this without equivocation, the consistency with the documented pattern of frequently reported cases lends support to such claims. The combination of different forms of evidence, including videos, photos, NGO reports, and diplomatic cables also underscores the fact that the deviant behaviour of Bahrain's security services is not a recent anomaly, one brought about by unforeseen circumstances beyond the control of the authorities, but the consequence of a security force shaped by Bahrain's colonial and tribal histories. This chapter will therefore shed light on why police deviance in Bahrain is a systemic problem.

Moreover, Shakhura illustrates a policing and political culture shaped by the tenacity of tribal and colonial rule, which has resulted in the 'violation of established boundaries dictating acceptable police behaviour'.[5] This 'deviance' includes acts of misconduct that can involve the transgression of criminal and civil laws, as well as international laws and governmental and departmental policies. Here, police deviance[6] can be defined as acts of excessive force, brutality, and misconduct, and the 'failure to perform law enforcement duties'.[7] While there is a tendency to chalk police deviance up to the work of a couple of 'rotten apples' – that is to say, rogue officers operating with individualistic motives, but whose actions are not reflective of the police institution as a whole – this is not adequate in the case of Bahrain. A more generous analysis would suggest that police deviance in Bahrain was the result of what O'Connor describes as 'rotten barrels',[8] namely, groups of police acting together but whose misconduct is also not representative of the police institution in general. However, given the habitual nature of police deviance in Bahrain, the concept of a 'rotten orchard' seems more appropriate. This metaphor, originally suggested by Maurice Punch, illustrates that deviance is not merely the fault of individuals or groups, but the result of systemic problems that either encourage, reward, or necessitate police deviance. In Punch's definition, systems refer to formal structures such as 'the police organization, the criminal justice system, and the broader socio-political context'.[9] Even the BICI report focused on systematic torture, and not systemic deviance. The distinction is important, as the definition of 'systematic' implies that a practice is 'habitual, widespread and deliberate', but that it does not occur with the direct intention or will of the government. 'Systemic', on the other hand, implies that such practices are condoned, or at least tacitly accepted, by those in power. Furthermore, 'systemic deviance' refers to how the very structure of the state and its institutions facilitate the emergence of deviance.

As the 'rotten apple' theory tends to discount the more complex organisational structures that explain police deviance, it has become a convenient political tool that tends to detract attention from deeper issues and the Bahraini government has been quick to attribute deviance to the work of rogue officers acting alone. Indeed, the necessity of using the 'rotten apple' excuse becomes more useful the more endemic the systemic deviance, for it detracts from exposing problems that go to the very heart of the establishment. Thus, Bahrain's extensive systemic deviance is more likely to be covered up, for its exposure threatens the current order and contradicts what is arguably the *raison d'être* of the law-enforcement institution: the maintenance of the existing regime. In the case of Bahrain, the police are the 'strong-arm of a non-representative government', whose modus operandi is to protect the hegemony of the Al Khalifa regime.[10]

In order to expose systemic deviance, one must critically examine the relationship between politics, society, and the police. As Strobl states, 'the Bahraini police are influenced by a variety of identifiable and overlapping influences: kinship networks, colonial administration, global capitalism, and international police professionalism, to name a few'.[11] However, while the colonial and postcolonial development of policing is highly influenced by the political power struggle between a Sunni government ruling a Shiʿa majority, this does not explain the nuances of the occurrences of police deviance. It is, therefore, important to examine the historically rooted structures of subordination that have led to this police deviance.

## The absence of consent: the emergence of colonial, tribal, and ethnic policing in Bahrain

Although Bahrain was only ever an informal protectorate and not a British colony, policing evolved, as did many colonial forces in the region, as a 'complex mixture of paramilitary, civil and tribal organizations; of civil and tribal courts administering different law'.[12] Policing also 'had little to do with serving the community and everything to do with upholding the authority' of the post-colonial state'.[13] As a result, the security services have always struggled to gain the consent of those being policed. This lack of public approval stems from the fact that the primary function of the security forces has not been to serve the citizenry, but to defend the interests of the ruling family and its external protectors: the British, the Saudis, and the Americans. Subsequently, the security services have gained the reputation of being 'agents of arbitrary "traditional" rule' and colonial domination.[14] The role of the security forces as defenders of private, colonial, and Al Khalifa interests became more salient with the creation of the state police in the 1920s. The British official Charles Belgrave, who was both financial advisor to the Ruler and the Commandant of the Police, symbolised this blurring of the roles between the police as a tool of public service and as a tool protecting the wealth and position of the ruling family. As late as 1965, the British superintendent of the police, Benn,[15] was being given a supplementary financial emolument 'paid for privily' out of the personal pocket of the Prime Minister, Khalifa bin Salman Al Khalifa.[16] This had become 'embarrassingly widely known', a fact that no doubt underlined accusations that the British were mercenary enforcers of Al Khalifa hegemony.[17]

Unsurprisingly, public anger at the security forces' impartiality has long been an issue. A group of Bahrainis complained about this problem as early as the 1940s, stating how Bahraini houses could be raided without warrants whereas police required a warrant from the Political Agent if they wished to raid the house of a foreigner. Over the years, this arbitrary rule was consolidated into vague and broad security laws, including the Emergency Law of 1956, the Public Security Decree of 1965, the State Security of Law of 1974 (which lasted until 2001), and the National Safety Law of 2011. These had the effect of suspending basic rights while giving the state considerable scope to suppress any element of dissent and allowed the ruling elites to manage dissent with minimal recourse to bureaucratic or legal obstruction. In Bahrain, a 'state of exception . . . has . . . now become the rule'[18] and legitimate political activity has been criminalised so that 'increasingly numerous sections of residents [are] deprived of political rights'.[19]

The weakening of political consensus spawned by growing popular discontent with the judiciary, the police, corruption, and colonialism resulted in repeated unrest through the latter half of the twentieth century. However, 'where the consensual foundations of political identity weaken, the coercive methods for maintaining political dominance become increasingly the only inhibitor of radical political changes'.[20] As the government was loath to make any reforms that threatened the Al Khalifa monopoly and power, their primary response was to strengthen Bahrain's coercive apparatus. This in turn led to the establishment of a militant security force that could be capable of quelling widespread dissent, a disposition that frequently resulted in civilian deaths and injuries. In 1954, an incompetent and ill-trained force opened fire in the Manama market, killing three Shi'a who were protesting at the incarceration of their co-religionists in an altercation with a group of Sunnis in Sitra. In addition to this, a perennial lack of resources and the absence of political will meant that recommendations to improve police training in tactics such as 'mob dispersal' following the 1954 incident fell by the wayside. Accordingly, few lessons were learned and, despite requests for 'something less lethal than rifles' to be used in 1954,[21] the police opened fire in the Manama market two years later, killing five civilians and injuring seventeen.

This administrative apathy was compounded by British foreign policy concerns. Bernard Burrows, the Political Agent at the time, argued that the criticism of the police in the 1954 inquiry resulted in a severe lowering of their morale over a long period and that the 'diminution of it [police morale] would bring nearer the possibility of intervention by British forces'.[22] In this respect, there were compelling political pressures that indicate that the outcome of the inquiry should not be too critical of the police. Indeed, Bernard Burrows was adamant that statements from the British 'should not (repeat not) criticise the police'.[23] Thus police accountability and reform was tempered by Britain's desire to limit the possibilities of having to put British boots on the ground. As a consequence, the Bahraini police force had to evolve to be both an adequate military deterrent as well as a police force. In 1965, eight more civilians were killed as police opened fire on protesters with Greener Guns.[24] While the British eventually attempted to address this militancy by having Peter Edward Turnbull author an extensive report – which recommended significant police reform, including a severe reduction in numbers – the Al Khalifa were sensitive on issues of security and chose to ignore the Turnbull report and increase the size of the police instead.[25,26] In fact, the police force almost doubled between 1965 and 1970, increasing from 1012 personnel to 2012.[27] Diminishing British influence leading up to and following independence meant that ruling family policies advocating securitisation measures could continue relatively untempered.

## The Al Khalifa and the post-independence police state

This 'security inflation' grew worse following Bahrain's independence from Britain in 1971 as the removal of formal British protection led to the bolstering of the security apparatus to fill the perceived security deficit. This also included the creation of the Bahrain Defence Force, a small army designed to give the illusion of sovereignty. However, the British were anxious that increasing Al Khalifa control of the police would only result in Bahrain becoming an actual police state. In 1974, Robert Tesh, the British ambassador to Bahrain, stated that:

> Bahrain was never a police state in the sense that its ears cocked for the dreaded knock on the door at 3 a.m. It was however true that if you worked actively against the al Khalifa you had to do it in secret and were likely to be invited by the Special Branch to spend a day or two with them and sent away with a warning; and if you were a top organiser of subterranean opposition you would find yourself on Jidda [sic] Island at the Amir's pleasure.[28]

This fear reflected broader tensions between the British and the Al Khalifas, who both wanted to maintain stability in what was becoming both an important finance centre and hub for British expatriates. To make matters more complicated, ruling family rivalries between King Hamad bin ʿIsa Al Khalifa and Shaykh Khalifa bin Salman Al Khalifa (Prime Minister) spawned an arms race between the Interior Minister and the Bahraini army. As a result, the police increased in size and were better equipped in order to deal with the potential threat to power posed by the army. A British cable reveals that the biggest threat to Bahrain's stability was the army itself:

> The greatest danger is still the Bahrain Defence Force, against which the Special Branch efficiency offers almost the only protection. The Cabinet claim to recognise the danger and they have allowed no increase in the Defence Force while ensuring a considerable expansion of the police; but the menace remains.[29]

This increase in the strength of the security services was coupled with a decrease in British operational influence in the police. Jim Bell and Ian Henderson, who previously had regular contact with the Prime Minister, now rarely ever saw him.[30] However, Tesh's earlier fears of Bahrain becoming a police state seemed to have been well founded following the reassertion of Al Khalifa influence over the security forces, which contributed to the anti-Shiʿa crackdown that accompanied the Iranian Revolution of 1979. Control of the police force and army had now fallen into the hands of hardliners and there was little to moderate it. This, combined with a quasi-militant police force, allowed the government to quash labour unrest in the 1970s with brutality and ease. The role of the British was reduced, although there was still a considerable number of officers working in Bahrain. In 1982, there were seventeen British personnel in both the intelligence and police sectors. Indeed, Ian Henderson made it quite clear that the Al Khalifa family could not continue without British support and he generally 'took a gloomy view of the Al Khalifa to survive'.[31] In the unredacted part of a

document from 1977, Henderson is reported to have stated that if
the British officers were to leave, the 'effect on the efficiency of the
security apparatus generally would be severe'.[32] David Tatham adds
that 'he [Henderson] and Mr Bell were trying to keep up standards
but a general sloppiness was creeping in'.[33] The necessity of British
support for maintaining Al Khalifa hegemony is a recurring theme
in diplomatic correspondence since the 1920s. While 'Henderson
retired in 1998, he stayed on as special advisor to the Minister of
the Interior, and his previous position was filled by another British
ex-serviceman Colonel Thomas Bryan'.[34] Other British officers to
have recently held command positions in Bahrain include Alistair
McNutt,[35] who retired from his job as a colonel in the Ministry of
the Interior in 2002. The latest British policeman to have courted
controversy in Bahrain was former Assistant Commissioner of the
Metropolitan Police, John Yates, who was drafted in in 2011 to help
reform the Bahraini police. This shift of the British role to being
an advisory rather than operational one, could be either one of
simple semantics, or reflect genuine diminishing British influence
in internal security as post-independence sovereignty shifted to the
Al Khalifa regime and its Saudi protectors.

## The institutionalisation of deviance and sectarian policing

British suspicion of communist and leftist forces diminished
and was less significant upon independence and, as a result of Al
Khalifa/Saudi ascendency, Bahrain's Shiʻa citizens soon began
to face the more overtly harsh treatment mirrored by their Saudi
co-religionists. This mistreatment manifested itself in the form of
deviance by the state security forces. Roger Tomkys noted in 1982
that the more brutal torturers were 'invariably Bahraini' and that
'the encouragement they get from some members of the Al Khalifa is
to be more rather than less tough in their methods'.[36] The historic

animosity felt by the ruling elite towards the Shiʿa Baharna stemmed from what Abdulhadi Khalaf describes as the 'Al Khalifa legacy of conquest'. Indeed, unlike in the neighbouring shaykhdoms such as Qatar and Kuwait, where the ruling families assimilated more into the local population, forming a more cohesive political entity, the Al Khalifa continue to 'jealously guard their identity/image as "settler-rulers"'.[37] This legacy of conquest has often had brutal consequences for the country's indigenous Baharna. Writing in 1829, Major Wilson noted that 'the enormities practised by the Uttoobees [sic] towards the original inhabitants of Bahrein [sic] far exceed what I have ever heard of tyranny in any part of the world'.[38] While British reforms came to temper Al Khalifa oppression of the indigenous Shiʿa Baharna, which had been rife before the 1920s, the Al Khalifa continued to exhibit their own colonial prejudice to both Shiʿa and the indigenous Baharna. In one case in 1932, when Shaykh Muhammad bin ʿAbd al-Rahman bin ʿAbd al-Wahab Al Khalifa (a member of the Ruling Family) became a Shiʿa, sectarian tensions in Bahrain came to a head as members of the ruling family took to the market to publicly ridicule both him and the Shiʿa sect in general.[39] In addition to inflaming ethnic tensions, this demonstrated a religio-tribal sense of superiority amongst the Al Khalifa.

This prejudice against the Baharna and the wider Shiʿa population had ramifications for the security services. In 1953, a British official commented that among the various deficiencies in the police, a major problem was that they were mostly Sunnis, who 'naturally enough, felt the best way to restore order was to hit a Shiite [sic]'.[40] Indeed, Bahrain's security forces have almost always been exclusively drawn from the Sunni sect, while Shiʿa citizens require a certificate of good behaviour to join the police.[41] The importance of privilege in determining employment in the police undoubtedly affected its ability to function impartially and efficiently.[42] While the ruling family's increasingly pervasive control in the country led to a greater degree of repression, the Iranian Revolution certainly gave the government a pretext for their punitive policies. Indeed, the current Prime Minister himself has demonstrated signs of the historic Al Khalifa ethnocentrism and bigotry in dealing with the country's Shiʿa problem. In 1981, although the religious festival of Ashura had passed peacefully, the Prime Minister encouraged and ordered the arrest of 650 Shiʿa.[43] This was in addition to the 200 people who had been arrested beforehand. The Prime Minister's reason for moving against the Shiʿa was reportedly to demonstrate to them that the 'Bahrain Government were true Arabs'. Even Ian Henderson, the so-called 'Butcher of Bahrain' disagreed with the decision to order this crackdown, as it would 'probably have the opposite effect from that desired'.[44] The reassertion of Al Khalifa hawkishness towards the Baharna and the country's Shiʿa community was also demonstrated when Ian Henderson reported that 'Bahraini authorities acting for Shaikh Hamad or the Prime Minister'[45] had deported 'about 300 people . . . all of them of Bahraini passport holders'.[46] Henderson worried that such deportations, which 'had no legal basis', 'undermined any chance of reconciliation between the Shia [sic] community and the present regime in Bahrain'.[47]

More recently, in 2007, when the Bahraini religious scholar Shaykh al-Najati complained of discrimination against Shiʿa in the security forces, the King's brother and head of Bahrain's National Guard, Shaykh Muhammad bin ʿIsa Al Khalifa reportedly said that he (Najati) should be grateful that he did not dismiss all the Sunnis married to Shiʿa.[48] Yet while this discrimination against the recruitment of Shiʿa is often attributed to the Iranian Revolution, the reality is more complicated, and the Shiʿa had long been excluded from the police force in Bahrain. Charles Belgrave, for example, did not like to recruit Baharna because their 'physique and eyesight are not on the whole as good as that of the Arabs and men of African origin'.[49] This suggests something of the 'significance of imperial prejudices about the attributes of different races and cultures'.[50] However, Persians were soon eschewed, mainly due to Ibn Saud's animosity towards Persia, exposing the historically rooted Saudi

Arabian encroachment in dictating Bahrain's internal security policy. Despite this discrimination against the Baharna, recruitment policy often reflected the political goals of the dominant hegemonic order. In the 1920s, when the British were attempting to combat Khalifa agitation against British-led reforms, the administration exploited religious differences in order implement control policies. To this effect, a Shiʿa Baharna named Hajji Salman became the highest ranking native policeman. Upon his death, his family even tried to get his son to take his place, despite his lack of qualifications. While the British perceived this as a sense of entitlement, it was no doubt due to the fact that many Shiʿa in Bahrain felt that one of their Baharna brethren would be a bulwark against Al Khalifa oppression, which had been rife until the British-led reforms in the 1920s. Indeed, despite the presence of Hajji Salman in the early days, and some other notable high-ranking Shiʿa officers, the recruitment into the security forces in Bahrain was the result of a balancing act, an attempt to control recalcitrant Al Khalifa while also not overly antagonising them. Unsurprisingly, the faction of the Al Khalifa which opposed the British-led reforms directed attacks against the police in the early days as a means of limiting their influence. In the present era, there are some Shiʿa in the police yet, as Ibrahim Sharif notes, these are confined to the lower ranks. In many cases, they often work as informants, or 'undercover in the villages',[51] to provide valuable intelligence to the security forces. The continued discrimination almost alludes to a culture of revenge, one that was fuelled by a beneficial, yet humiliating political contract with the British, whose protection, in the eyes of the Al Khalifa, had made the Baharna uppity and entitled.

## The quality of recruits: from villains to mercenaries

Recruitment into the police has always been a sensitive issue and there has been a struggle to both enlist 'suitable' local personnel and depoliticise the recruiting process. In the 1920s and 1930s, the British attempted to ameliorate ruling family hostility towards the security services by co-opting a number of the Al Khalifa into joining the police. Unfortunately, it was difficult to expect impartiality from the Al Khalifa who had, until recently, been feudal lords with unlimited rights over the local population. For this reason, the police force was frequently populated by unpleasant, villainous, and unpopular characters. Disliked by the majority of the population, many of the recruits were also drawn from the country's *fidawiyya*, the notorious henchman and enforcers used by the Al Khalifa to extract tax, intimidate the populace, and uphold their feudal rule. Until the British-led reforms of the 1920s, these *fidawiyya* spent much of their time harassing and extorting the indigenous population. In the 1920s, the Amir of Manama, whose role was 'Governor and Chief of Police combined',[52] was described as 'one of the worst characters in Bahrain'.[53] Similarly, the Amir of Muharraq was described by Charles Belgrave as a 'fat useless one eyed rascal who never [did] any work'.[54] In 1956, a British officer in the Bahraini police turned whistle-blower, Major William Oscar Little, described the Director of Police and Public Security, Shaykh Khalifa bin Muhammad, 'not only as a debauchee and a drunkard, but a leading crook, with a finger in every nefarious and profitable racket, from drug smuggling to the slave transit traffic and procurement of girls'.[55] Shaykh Khalifa's replacement, Muhammad bin Salman Al Khalifa, was reportedly of no better character. As the ruler's son, he enjoyed considerable immunity and in 1954 he and a group of Bedouin, broke into a Baharna's house and beat up the occupant for no reason. All this, according to Belgrave, was on the orders of the ruler, who had been sending his sons out with the Bedouin in cars.[56] In order to spare the ruler embarrassment, Charles Belgrave went round to persuade the victim not to make a complaint.[57] Notwithstanding the frequent Orientalist references to people in the region in general, British officials seemed to reserve their most

scathing remarks for the Al Khalifa. In 1923, Lieutenant Colonel
A. P. Trevor wrote in his diary:

> Selman bin Hamad has all the worst qualities of the Al Khalifa
> family. He is totally uneducated, vain, lazy, and inclined to
> oppress and tyrannize over anyone who is powerless to resist.
> Selman is absolutely unfit to succeed is father as ruler.[58]

The employment in the security forces of characters who were
'inclined to oppress' and discriminate, particularly in the higher
ranks, has contributed to the systemic institutionalisation of deviance,
embedding it within the policing culture in Bahrain.

## Mercenaries, ancillaries, and *baltajiyya*

Another factor in the growth of systemic deviance is the Bahraini
government's reliance on foreigners in the police forces. 'The running
joke in Bahrain is that you can expect to be arrested by a Pakistani,
interrogated by a Jordanian, tortured by a Yemeni, and judged by
an Egyptian, but at least you can expect your fellow prisoners to be
Bahraini.'[59] This reliance on mercenaries stemmed from the British
idea that Bahrainis made bad police because they were too lazy, not
amenable to discipline, or preferred fishing. Furthermore, the British
made frequent references to the fact that Bahrainis might not be relied
upon to police other Bahrainis. However, there were also geopolitical
considerations. In the first half of the twentieth century, the presence
of Persian police excited historical animosity between the Al Khalifa,
Al Saud, and Persia. Given the tensions between the 'Persians' and
'Najdis',[60] which resulted in riots in which a number of Persians were
killed, the British caved to Saudi pressure and a less politically contentious police force was sought from India and Oman, thus ending
any chance of Shi'a or 'Persian' ascendency in the security services.

Most recruits were drawn from different corners of the British
Empire, a fact that was said by some Bahrainis to 'harden their

[the police's] hearts',[61] engendering a more contentious disposition to their presence and reducing police sympathy towards the policed. Further shifting geopolitical configurations changed the nature of this recruiting policy, yet they always brought with them questions of police legitimacy. Following India's independence, the British had to look elsewhere for recruits. In the 1950s, soldiers from Iraq and tribal militias from Saudi Arabia[62] (al-Hasa) were brought in to help keep order.[63] These troops were acceptable to both the Al Khalifas and the British, but not the citizens, who protested as early as the 1930s at the predominance of foreigners in the police. Despite this, 'the British tradition of recruiting strangers to police strangers continued into the 1960s when the British commandant (Winder) of the police went to Pakistan to recruit ex-servicemen'.[64] In 1965, only 25 per cent of the 921 strong police force were Bahraini, with the majority being from Yemen.[65] Following independence, increasing Saudi hegemony in Bahrain meant that the recruiting policy shifted slightly, especially in the newly established military. In 1974, 300 'kindred tribesmen' from Saudi Arabia were brought in to join the Bahrain Defence Force, highlighting the increasing encroachment of Saudi interests in Bahrain.

In 2013, Pakistan's Foreign Minister Naila Chohan said that 10,000 Pakistanis were serving in Bahrain's 'defence services'.[66] In addition to this, many of Bahrain's security forces were recruited from Yemen, Syria, Jordan, and other countries in the Arab world. In April 2014, the *Bahrain Mirror* published leaked documents showing that there were at least 499 Jordanian citizens working in the Bahraini security sector.[67] Other reports suggest that there may be as many as 2,500 former members of the Jordanian security services working in Bahrain.[68] In addition to this, at least 4,000 Saudi and Emirati military and security personnel entered Bahrain in 2011 to augment the Bahraini forces.[69] These Emirati police remained until at least March 2014.[70] In 2011, Bahrain's Interior Minister, Shaykh Rashid Al Khalifa, even stated that, because of Bahrain's small size, Bahrainis could not be trusted to police other

Bahrainis.[71] Despite these large numbers, part of the benefit for the Al Khalifa regime is their expendability. Mercenaries brought from abroad are expendable and can be sacked with minimal political fallout. This was demonstrated recently when two curious reports emerged about two large contingents of soldiers being deported back to Pakistan on charges of indiscipline.[72] The use of foreigners, termed *al-murtazaqa* (mercenaries) by many Bahrainis, is provocative on a number of levels. Not only does it raise issues of employment by depriving Bahrainis of many state-sector jobs, thus promoting antagonism along political and economic lines, but it also means that a non-native police force is tasked with policing a native citizenry, an issue that erodes the legitimacy of the police.

Although Bahrain's security services have evolved considerably since their inception in the 1920s, a number of characteristics have contributed to this tendency towards deviance. One is the unclear distinction between different legal and extra-legal control agents such as vigilantes, which has been exacerbated by the government's ambiguous attitude towards law enforcement tactics. The evolution of the *fidawiyya* into the police services, and the traditional role played by Bedouin loyal to the ruling tribes in quashing dissent, have blurred the lines between those legitimately able to carry out state violence and those whose sanction to commit violence in defence of the ruling tribe is unofficial, but tacitly accepted. The role of these ancillaries is well documented and, during times of increased political unrest, the ruler either used or threatened to use his 'irregular forces' (Bedouin).[73] In 1938, a young political group, the Shabab al-Watani, claimed they were beaten by a government agent and a 'number of bedouins' after protesting outside the British Agency.[74] In 1954, the police and the 'Ruler's Bedouin' were patrolling the communal disturbances of that time.[75] The same occurred in 1956, when the lack of suitable recruits meant that Charles Belgrave deemed such ancillaries necessary,[76] even though they had not received any formal police training. This did not go unnoticed and the Higher Executive Committee protested against the 'provocative attitude of the Bedouin police auxiliaries'.[77] In addition to these loyal Bedouin, the police were often supported by *nawatir*, armed watchmen whose job was to guard buildings or sensitive areas. These *nawatir* were often used to put down dissent, even though they had inferior training and were thus more likely to engage in acts of deviance. In 1965, there were 500 *nawatir* who helped quash the March uprising.[78]

The trend of using auxiliary forces has continued more recently and came into sharp relief when Ahmad Ismail, a citizen journalist, was shot and killed by people in an unmarked car.[79] Over the last few months, numerous reports have also emerged that cases of civilian *baltajiyya* (thugs) attacking citizens were common, a notable example being the attack on Bahrain University. Dr Mike Diboll, a witness to the affair, described how thugs and naturalised Bahraini citizens were vandalising property and attacking and threatening Bahraini students:[80]

> On 13 March 2011 I witnessed a serious on-campus disturbance at the UoB, which began when a peaceful pro-democracy demonstration was attacked by a gang of 'loyalist' vigilantes who had arrived on campus equipped with pickaxe handles, iron bars, swords, spears and machetes; these were supported by Ministry of the Interior Police.[81]

When policing was not being conducted by foreign trained mercenaries, foreign powers have sought, in various ways, to protect the Bahraini government. In 2011, the GCCPS, consisting mostly of Saudi troops, arrived to help quash the unrest. In 1981, following an alleged coup attempt by the Islamic Front for the Liberation of Bahrain, the Bahrainis requested that the US dock a warship in the harbour in order to act as a deterrent.[82] The idea was to deck the ship out in Bahraini flags and to tell the press that its presence was part of a 'routine movement'.[83] During the unrest in 1956, the British put Royal Marines in Bahrain to help put down the unrest. While these more formal engagements are recent, in the nineteenth and twentieth centuries the Al Khalifa often relied on Bedouin from the Arabian hinterland to fight off threats, something the British put a stop to. However, Bahraini independence caused a reassertion of Saudi hegemony and thus the recent incursion by Saudi troops follows a long tradition of intervention from the 'mainland'.

## Brutal redux: policing the Bahrain Uprising of 2011

While the tactics used by the state security forces and the government are multidimensional and multilayered, the militarisation of the Bahraini security services is both a defining characteristic of repression in Bahrain and also an increasingly inevitable response to a political strategy designed to increase animosity between the state and its citizens. Indeed, the security forces frequently use 'military style deployment of large police and army formations, numerous detentions and arrests as well as use of water cannons, mounted police and dogs, tear gas, and rubber bullets'.[84] These confrontations often deteriorate into what seem like 'police-riots', a term used to describe 'unrestrained and indiscriminate police violence' against protesters and property.[85] As discussed, this inclination towards violence has been facilitated by a number of factors, including poor training, sectarianism, use of mercenaries, ambiguous role definitions, inappropriate equipment, and a lack of accountability. In addition to this, recent evidence suggests that paramilitarisation may have been a result of the training. It emerged in 2012 that the Special Security Forces Command (Elite Riot Squad) had been trained by the US military and served Bahrain's UN obligations in Afghanistan by providing 'base security'.[86] Added to this was the arrival of John Timoney, the former chief of the Miami police who, according to Matthew Cassel brought with him the notoriously brutal 'Miami model'.[87] Couched within the progressive terms of 'police reform', the Miami model seemed to add 'expert' legitimacy to a form of policing that Jeremy Scahill simply describes as 'paramilitary soldiering'.[88]

However, this reform may simply have added a veneer of credibility to a form of policing likely to result in deviance. From the very opening days of the uprising, activists were quick to document police brutality and many videos shot from mobile phones showed gratuitous acts of police violence. Videos of groups of police and individual officers brutalising civilians were common. In 2011 in Bahrain, police were documented stamping on protesters' heads, kicking them in the face, slapping them in front of their children, hitting them with batons, and kicking them when they lay defenceless on the ground.[89] Like the Shakhura video, other videos emerged of dangerous and reckless police tactics, such as driving at speed among civilians to disperse them.[90] In several incidents, civilians were killed or injured after being hit by speeding police vehicles, including sixteen-year-old ʿAli Yusuf al-Sitrawi, who died after he was struck by a police jeep.[91] In 2011, journalist Fahad Desmukh collated a large number of videos of police officers vandalising cars and property. A lot of the footage shows police using non-standard weapons. At least seven videos emerged of riot officers throwing Molotov cocktails at civilians,[92] while other videos showed riot police throwing metal construction rebars at protesters. In one incident, a young woman called Zahra Muhammad Salah was killed when one of these rebars pierced her forehead, entering her brain.[93] A grisly video emerged and the government-controlled press quickly claimed she had been killed by protesters throwing rebars. However, the truth of what happened is far from clear. Other graphic images burned themselves into the psyche of Bahrain's population, such as that of Ahmed Farhan being carried by a grief-stricken friend, his open skull vacated of brain matter by a close-range shotgun wound to the head.

The sheer extent of brutality, both in public and in private, has highlighted a continued tendency in the security services to resort to draconian means of violence, one that has increased post-independence. Groups of police patrolling the streets and administering retributive punishment ad hoc, and the state-acknowledged destruction of Shi'a religious structures documented in the BICI report, have also prompted accusations of collective punishment, an occurrence no doubt facilitated by the fact that Bahrain's villages are often inhabited by either Shi'i or Sunni majorities. While this sectarian topography is a hangover from Bahrain's feudal days, in which Sunni landowners ruled over Shi'a tenants, continuing government discrimination has resulted in the emergence of a rural Shi'a underclass. Roger Tomkys noted in 1982 that such discrimination was 'likely, perhaps certain' to continue as long as the Al Khalifa remained in power.[94] Shi'a religious figures such as Shaykh al-Najati have argued that the Governate of Muharraq banned sales of land to Shi'a in 2007.[95] The emergence of other social engineering projects, as revealed in the Al Bandar report, has also highlighted the state attempts to marginalise the country's Shi'a, both politically and geographically. The exact extent of state engineering of urban policy to reflect sectarian differences is unclear, but it does explain how riot police can launch dozens of tear gas canisters into whole villages without having to be too concerned about angering non-Shi'a, Sunni, or expatriate residents. Furthermore, videos and eyewitness reports show riot police throwing and firing tear gas canisters into people's homes and even removing air-conditioning covers and window sealants, a move that facilitates the spread of tear gas.[96] The frequency of this evidence has led the NGO Physicians for Human Rights to accuse the Bahraini authorities of 'weaponising' tear gas, an outcome that is symptomatic of a state policy that has led to the ghettoisation and subsequent gassing of Shi'a villages, whose populations are dehumanised to the extent that the threshold of tolerance for collateral damage is increased. As of 2013, Physicians for Human Rights reported that up to thirty-nine people had died[97] as a result of tear gas or tear gas related complications.[98]

## State unaccountability and impunity

While this collective punishment points at a systemic problem that derives from institutionalised and socialised anti-Shiʿa discrimination, police deviance has also been severely compounded by a culture of impunity. While 'court and administrative decisions exonerating legal control agents are to be expected in any polity',[99] this problem is particularly acute in Bahrain. Failure to prosecute those policeman who have acted egregiously has contributed to an absence in public confidence in the police, as well as the judicial system. This was noted above in the uprisings of 1956 and 1965, where no measures were taken to prosecute the police. In fact, Amnesty International has noted that not one member of the SIS or CID has been brought to justice for engaging in acts of torture prior to 1995.[100] The same appears to be true of police accused of using excessive force. In 2002, the state legitimised impunity through Royal Decree 56, which granted an amnesty to all those accused of crimes that took place before 2001. This meant that the likes of Colonel Adil Falayfil, an SIS officer accused of torture in the 1990s, evaded prosecution without consequence. On other occasions, the government has chosen to remove or shuffle ministers or officials following controversial events. In 2004, for example, Bahrain's Interior Minister since 1974, Muhammad bin Khalifa Al Khalifa, was dismissed from his post following clashes between police and Shiʿa protesters in Manama.[101] In 2011, following the release of the BICI report, the head of Bahrain's National Security Agency (NSA), Shaykh Khalifa bin Abdullah Al Khalifa, was dismissed from the NSA but rewarded with the post of Secretary General of Bahrain's Supreme Defence Council.[102]

Generally speaking, when prosecutions against police do occur, they seem to be little more than attempts to appease the concerns of local opposition and international actors.[103] As a result, the Bahraini government has been quick to underscore its prosecution of police officers accused of unlawful killing, torture, or mistreatment. However, it has been loath to convict them. A distinct pattern of legal wrangling has emerged, one that obscures the lack of accountability, and it is this impunity that functions as a 'feature of power which serves as key source for state crimes'.[104] While these prosecutions routinely begin with charges directed at several police officers, the number of defendants is often whittled down. The number of officers actually taken to trial is also small compared with the overall amount of suspected cases of police abuse, many of which are documented in the BICI report. This phenomenon is demonstrated in the much-publicised case of former France 24 journalist Naziha Saeed. In her initial testimony, Saeed claimed she was abused by at least four officers, but only one, Sara Muhammad ʿIsa al-Musa, was ultimately prosecuted. Despite witness testimonies and three medical reports that corroborated the torture Saeed had suffered, al-Musa was exonerated and an appeals court upheld the acquittal. Saeed had therefore exhausted all legal means of complaint.[105] The same is true of ʿAli ʿIsa Ibrahim Saqr, who died in custody after being tortured. Five security officers were accused of involvement in his killing, but only two were convicted.[106]

The state uses a long and drawn out legal process to obscure the lack of accountability. Legal procedures that initially incriminate but ultimately repeal or commute the sentences of security officials are common. For example, the two policemen who tortured and killed ʿAli Saqr were originally sentenced to ten years in jail, but this was later reduced to two years.[107] The two officers accused of shooting Fadhil al-Matruq in February 2011 were acquitted. The five policemen accused of beating blogger Zakariyya al-ʿAshiri to death in custody were also acquitted.[108] The policemen who tortured and killed civilian Karim Fakhrawi were sentenced to seven years for manslaughter, but had their sentences reduced to three after appeal.[109] The police officer accused of killing and shooting civilian ʿAli ʿAbdulhadi Mushaymaʿ was first sentenced to seven years for manslaughter, but this was reduced to three following an appeal.[110] The police officer who shot Hani ʿAbd al-ʿAziz Jumʿa was also sentenced to seven years for manslaughter, reduced to six months on appeal. ʿAli al-Shayba, an officer accused of permanently disabling a man by shooting him in the leg, first had his five year sentence reduced to three, and then six months on account of his ill health.[111]

It is also unclear whether these verdicts are final or still subject to another appeal. Both Amnesty International[112] and the BCHR[113] have reported that convicted officers remain on duty. This is particularly problematic, as it means potentially unfit police officers remain on duty while their cases are resolved.[114] Moreover, it is unclear whether convicted security officers actually serve time in prison. In a report detailing the human rights situation in Bahrain, the US State Department said they did not know whether 'courts enforced any of the sentences and if security officers were actually in prison following sentencing'.[115] Crucially, the depth of this impunity is highlighted in the opening quote of this chapter, where Bahrain's Prime Minister offers protection from justice to those who aid the preservation of the regime, a shocking incident that garnered little media attention.

In many other cases in which civilians were reportedly killed by the state, the police and other members of the security forces have simply been acquitted, or the case has been explained away. Between 2011 and 2012, forty-five cases where the police were suspected of being involved in the killing of civilian were dismissed due to lack of evidence.[116] The Ministry of Interior (MoI) frequently defends security officers facing prosecution by saying that they were simply acting in self-defence, thus implying the victim was endangering the lives of the police. In cases where security officers are actually convicted of killing or torture, they are only ever charged with 'manslaughter', absolving them of malicious intent in committing these crimes. In some cases, the government even refuses to accept that deaths warrant suspicion,[117] such as in the case of a sixty-one-year-old man found dead, stuffed in a plastic bag in a car park. The BICI deemed his death to be suspicious, but the authorities concluded there was no sign of criminal activity or malicious behaviour surrounding his death.

There are also issues surrounding who is prosecuted. Given the government's reliance on foreign mercenaries, many of those prosecuted are low-ranking officers from countries such as Yemen and Pakistan.[118] The Bahraini authorities claim that the highest ranking official to have been prosecuted is a lieutenant colonel, though it is unclear what charges he faced. By and large, high-ranking officers and members of the ruling family seem to have evaded prosecution, even though one human rights report accused at least four members of the ruling family of involvement in torture.[119] One royal, Nura bint Ibrahim Al Khalifa, was acquitted of torturing two doctors and twenty-one-year-old student Ayat al-Qurmazi. Even King Hamad's son, Nasir bin Hamad Al Khalifa, has been accused of torturing detainees and has had his diplomatic immunity in the UK lifted. As we can see, the tactic of selectively holding only low-level security officers accountable represents an attempt to paint police deviance as the work of a couple of 'rotten apples', rogue officers operating with individualistic motives but whose actions are not reflective of any shortcomings of either the police or the political system as a whole.

## The role of society

In addition to discriminatory institutional structures, antagonistic recruiting policies, sectarianism, and a lack of accountability, deviance perpetrated by the state security forces is also legitimised by many of those who support the regime. This is especially true in times of crisis, where police behaviour and tactics become increasingly responsive to the desires of Bahrain's loyalist community, whose mostly Sunni identity has been sharpened on account of the government's instrumentalisation of sectarian rhetoric. The fact that the state's monopoly of violence is concentrated in the hands of one sect becomes particularly problematic during times of political unrest, as such unrest usually prompts the regime to 'play the sectarian card' in order to mobilise support along sectarian lines. This reflects an important conundrum for not only is state violence carried out by a predominantly Sunni-staffed security force operating on behalf of a predominantly Sunni government, but violence against the security forces is usually carried out by members of Bahrain's disenfranchised Shiʿa community. The nature of this violence, which has become sectarian by virtue of the state's discriminatory approach to recruiting its police force, has a mobilising effect. The problem with this mobilisation is that the police force, to many loyalists, are then perceived to be heroic warriors defending Bahrain against an encroaching Shiʿa threat. The extent to which the regime is successful in mobilising religious sectarianism is such that high levels of police deviance are tolerated by those on whom the regime's legitimacy is traditionally based. In other words, the perceived threat of a Shiʿa theocratic takeover leads to increased demands for protection, which legitimise police behaviour that might otherwise be considered deviant.

Such a phenomenon is not unique to Bahrain and it is common for residents in places with endemic crime problems to adopt a 'tough on crime' mentality. In such environments, there is more tolerance for what might otherwise be termed police deviance. In this way, 'police abuse does not stem simply from police authority alone, but also from a larger belief system shared by citizens in which brutality is acceptable as long as it is directed against "bad people"'.[120] The problem with this argument is that it attempts to confer legitimacy on deviant policing by invoking an element of consent. In actual fact, the fear that allows people to exercise greater tolerance towards police deviance is an artificial construct, born out of the regime's ability to exaggerate the sectarian threat. Indeed, this exaggeration of a sectarian threat plays into Federico Ferrara's notion of 'Hobbes's dilemma', wherein regimes suspend social order in order to make residents face a choice between dictatorship and anarchy. Inevitably, many choose the former.[121]

Given that the tolerance for police deviance comes from the constituency on whom the ruling family's legitimacy is based, failure to be 'tough on crime' can result in a loss of political support. Indeed, the past year has shown that police deviance is actually a form of political currency, necessary in appeasing important allies within the political camp. Escalating violence has repeatedly resulted in pro-government groups and parliamentarians calling for the police to be armed with more effective weapons. In one instance, a strongly worded article in pro-government newspaper *Al-Watan* demanded that police be armed and better protected.[122] Two days later the Minister of Interior announced that police were to be given new armour, guns that fire rubber bullets, as well as gas and sound bombs. Similarly, foreign embassies, such as that of Pakistan, which maintain large workforces in Bahrain, are under pressure to protect their citizens.[123] In January 2012, Pakistanis complained to their embassies that they needed more weapons and protection to help combat protesters. One officer reportedly stated, 'We need weapons or at least something that would help us in self-protection.'[124]

The role of society in demanding more protection, firepower, and aggressive policing may facilitate human rights abuses. In 2011, fears of a growing 'garrisons state' were compounded by the decision of the infamous Colonel Adil Falayfil to form a 'militia'[125] consisting of retired military and security personnel to advise the government on issues of security.[126] Similarly, societal pressure to shield police from justice has negative consequences for accountability. This was aptly demonstrated when hundreds of pro-regime supporters formed a society to defend the interests of police accused of committing crimes during the unrest.[127] They argued that the police were being victimised for simply doing their job. Indeed, the state's decision to overturn the death penalty of two protesters convicted of killing two policemen prompted widespread anger among many Sunni pro-regime supporters, who stated in no uncertain terms that their loyalty should not be taken for granted.[128] In light of this, leniency towards those perceived by loyalists as traitors and terrorists only becomes acceptable if leniency is shown towards the police who engage in deviance. Indeed, the government even refers to those policemen killed in the unrest as 'duty martyrs',[129] a term they do not use to refer to civilians killed by the police, and itself a *détournement* of the rhetoric of revolutionaries across the Arab world. It is unsurprising then, that in 2012, Amendment 221 of Law No. 33 imposed stringent sentences on those who attacked or injured members of the security forces, even if it was done unintentionally. Even though these military security officers have been the direct targets of militant protest groups, these attacks are described as 'terrorism', a general term used to invoke broad-brush anti-terrorism legislation that authorises, among other things, the prosecution of parents of protesters and the owners of cars if seen in protest areas, amongst others.

Societal support for the security services and the government have also manifested themselves in the form of pro-government rallies held by groups like Al Fateh Youth Union and the National Unity Gathering.[130] While these expressions of solidarity with the security services are peaceful, they sometimes regress into vigilantism. In one instance, hundreds of people gathered at a large roundabout to protest against what the Ministry of Interior described as a 'terrorist bomb blast' in the village of Eker. After destroying the cars of two civilians, the mob then ransacked and looted a local supermarket owned by a businessman accused of giving food to protesters at the Pearl Roundabout. Despite the nature of this violence, the Ministry of Interior refused to call the group vandals, rioters, or terrorists, terms they use liberally when describing the acts of political activists. Instead, it used the term 'group'. More revealingly, the CCTV footage that emerged following the store's looting actually shows police standing idly by as the store is ransacked. One policeman even smashes a window whilst another helps himself to a bottle of water. The attack on the store was one of fifty-four that had occurred in a twelve-month period on the same chain of stores (Jawad). The motivation was down to the fact that it was owned by a Shi'a businessman.[131] On other occasions, members of the security forces have been accused of dressing as civilians and going into areas to provoke trouble and stir up animosity.[132] In other instances, police have turned a blind eye to government supporters throwing Molotov cocktails at civilians.[133,134] This kind of leniency is rarely shown towards demonstrators. This remarkable tolerance towards acts of criminality carried out by pro-government supporters and police illustrates that failure to enforce the law, itself a form of deviance, is important in maintaining the support of Bahrain's loyalist community.

## Asymmetric policing and systemic police deviance

The problem with letting the sectarian genie out of the bag is that the perceived threat of a Shi'a takeover has become so intense that many of those traditionally loyal to the regime see any compromise with the opposition as a threat to national security. Thus, the idea of any form of political compromise is compounded by the need to appease loyalists, who are increasingly advocating a more punitive approach to policing and justice. It has also aggravated religious polarisation that has contributed to the radicalisation of Sunnis who have left Bahrain to join the Islamic State (ISIS), including at least one policeman. This problem is particularly acute in the relatively homogeneous security services, which human rights activist Nabeel Rajab described as an 'ideological incubator' for ISIS.[135] However, the government's paranoia about isolating its Sunni loyalist core, along with the fact that patrimonial ties frequently link these jihadis with influential Bahrainis, means that Bahrain is not committing the same resources to tackling Salafi obscurantism[136] as it is to the so-called 'Shiʿa threat', even though it made a big show of removing citizenship from some Bahrainis accused of involvement with ISIS in February 2015. Nonetheless, it is important to not get carried away by implying simply sectarian arguments. Sectarianism has been instrumentalised and deployed in such a way as to ensure survival strategies of the regime. While sectarianism is exploited, and social distrust exists, this tends to manifest itself more notably during times of political mobilisation. Bahrain's faultlines are exposed by the regime and the state-controlled media, which perpetuate fears of an impending Iranian style theocracy.

Although it's hard to quantify the exact relationship between police deviance and political pressure, continued political support for policing strategies that 'facilitate human rights abuses' remain a serious impediment to police reform.[137] The likelihood of police deviance increases in a 'country whose unelected government does not enjoy major popular support, for retaining the reigns of power necessitates a disproportionate use of violence and fear, one that replaces "rule of law" with "rule by law"'.[138] In other words, law is used as a weapon of social control rather than a consensual means of resolving disputes. Furthermore, the government's legitimacy deficit periodically places unsustainable strains on conventional procedures of justice, which must be subverted by both the police and judiciary in order to ensure the rule of the Al Khalifa regime remains intact. In other words, cyclical systematic abuses arise when systemic problems are not addressed.

Given that the regime's continued rule is highly dependent on support from specific, predominantly Sunni groups, it is impossible to apply the law equally, for doing so runs the risk of angering those on whom their legitimacy is derived. The problem here though is that it creates a 'rule of law imbalance', one in which excessive measures must be taken against one group (who are predominantly Shi'a) and concessions given to another (who are predominantly Sunni). This asymmetry in policing and justice is indicative of systemic deviance for it demonstrates how responsive the country's legal institutions are to Bahrain's loyalist community. In this respect, as long as the modus operandi of Bahrain's police force is to protect Sunni hegemony in Bahrain, meaningful police reform is impossible. Even the regime's attempts to introduce community policing will not address the nepotism and discrimination that characterises the upper echelons of the police and judiciary. Only through an empowered representative government will Bahrainis have the capacity to influence the sectarian based discrimination that pervades, sustains, and preserves the current hegemonic order. Unfortunately, on account of the opposition's boycott of the 2014 parliamentary and municipal elections, even Bahrain's toothless and generally pro-government elected house is able to quickly ratify draconian anti-terror legislation that is not conducive to easing police deviance.

Police deviance in Bahrain can largely be explained as the inevitable consequence of a political system that deliberately exacerbates tensions between different groups in society. This is done by excluding groups from both decision-making processes and institutions, while privileging members of other groups at the expense of Bahrain's citizens. It may also be part explained by a policing culture that allows impunity, which in no part is due to the ideological 'settler' mentality of the Al Khalifa. Combined with a 'legacy of conquest',[139] this has resulted in the police force becoming an institution that predominantly protects the private interests of a ruling elite. Although these trends were set in motion following the British reforms of the 1920s, deviance became more acute following independence, and there will be little to temper increasing Saudi influences and elite hardliners in Bahrain.

There is little political will to create a police force or regulatory body sufficiently independent or accountable that could result in a decline in police deviance. The newly appointed Ombudsman, put in place to make sure the security services abide by the country's laws and police code of conduct, has already been accused of being window dressing to give the illusion of human rights reform.[140] Thus, to an extent, 'the mandate to prevent radical changes in the distribution of power and privilege is incompatible with the idea of a legally or ethically limited effort to do so',[141] especially when the legal system claims to protect basic rights. In Bahrain, the legal and justice system has essentially been the prerogative of the elites, irrespective of reform, and this has been compounded by Bahrain's precarious sovereignty.

## CHAPTER 9

# Social media, surveillance, and cyberpolitics in the Bahrain Uprising

Marc Owen Jones

> Sami Abd al-Aziz Hassan was the leader of the 'Yokogawa Labor Union of Bahrain', a trade union at the Middle East division of Japanese engineering firm Yokogawa. He was sacked from his job in early 2013 after he was identified as the author of anonymous Tweets exposing alleged labor law violations by his employer. His Twitter account was targeted with IP spy links sent publicly via Twitter mentions.[1] – Report by Bahrain Watch

Irrespective of political stance, both government supporters and activists turned to social media and the Internet to follow the Bahrain Uprising that began in 2011. The number of Twitter users in Bahrain shot up,[2] and dozens of Facebook groups materialised, the majority of which were posting updates, information, and photos related to unfolding events. Bahrainis, both activists and spectators, were actively becoming more networked. Indeed, media coverage of the 'Arab Spring' tended to popularise the social media aspect of the struggle, with many news outlets focusing on the role of Twitter and Facebook in the revolutions. Much of their discourse subscribed to the position of a 'technological utopia', viewing social media and the Internet as a positive force that democratises information, reinvigorates citizens' political engagement, encourages freedom of expression, and brings people together.[3] Others were somewhat cynical, arguing that social media was merely a tool and was not necessarily integral to the efficacy of the revolutions as whole. Few, however, fully assumed the 'technological dystopian' or 'neo-Luddite' position, which posits that technological developments such as the Internet simply serve to 'confound the problems of space, access and interaction by alienating people from each other and even themselves'.[4] In addition to fears that technology may actually work against integration, the dystopian position describes the fear that Web 2.0 technologies may be used as part of the 'informational-control continuum' and thus shape media content through 'propaganda, psychological operations, information intervention, and strategic public diplomacy'.[5] The dystopian potential of technology has recently been examined by Evgeny Morozov, who highlights the failure of cyber-utopians to predict how authoritarian regimes would use the Internet as a tool for propaganda, surveillance, and censorship.[6] Indeed, the post-Snowden era has highlighted the extent of web surveillance by governments.

Having said that, the Internet cannot be reduced to a simple dystopian versus utopian binary. Instead, one must acknowledge that it can work simultaneously as a tool of both empowerment and control, depending on who is using it and what objectives they are seeking to achieve. As Rebecca MacKinnon states:

> People, governments, companies, and all kinds of groups are using the Internet to achieve all kinds of ends, including political ones . . . Pitched battles are currently under way over not only who controls its [the internet's] future, but also over its very nature, which in turn will determine whom it most empowers in the long run – and who will be shut out.[7]

Examining the nature of these 'pitched battles' on a case-by-case basis is a useful endeavour, as temporal and contextual factors influence the manner in which the Internet and social media are used. Given that the uprising in Bahrain has not succeeded in achieving regime change, it makes sense to focus on how hegemonic forces have utilised social media to subjugate both dissent and dissenters in the months following 14 February 2011. This chapter therefore focuses more on the dystopian potential of technology and looks at how social media, and in particular Twitter and Facebook, has assisted the Bahraini government and those representing the hegemonic order in maintaining their position of dominance. In particular, it examines how the Al Khalifa regime has used social media for the purposes of surveillance, censorship, and propaganda.

## The growth of web activism and control in Bahrain

Ever since the Internet arrived in Bahrain, it has been used by political activists as a space for resistance. Forums such as Bahrain Online were used to post photos of rallies and acts of government oppression carried out by the state security apparatus. More importantly, as has been charted in the introduction to this book, it was also used for political discussion and organisation.[8] Since the start of the protests, all of these forums have assumed either a pro- or anti-government identity. In a very real sense, Bahraini cyberspace has become segregated. This segregation is not formalised, yet the nature of interactions in Bahrain's forums is very much based on political and social loyalties, and as such there are often implicit expectations of what one should and should not say. Twitter, for example, is a different format, and its functionality made it an extremely useful tool in the Arab uprisings. The surge of users generated by protests on the street resulted in a proliferation of interactions online, the basis of which was often the political context that inspired the user to join. Unlike forums however, Twitter is not a closed community. As a result, interactions between those of opposing opinions and political allegiances are not restricted. On the contrary, they are common.

In Bahrain, the resulting interactions were often characterised by volatility, hostility, and aggression. Despite these aspects, Twitter is perhaps the most effective place for activists and Bahrainis to communicate in real time with both local and global actors who might be outside their immediate networks.

This is especially important in light of the state's tight control of the national media, which increased during the 2011 crackdown. Indeed, the regime temporarily closed down *Al-Wasat*, which was the only Bahraini newspaper that was remotely critical of the regime. Its editor, Mansoor al-Jamri, was charged by the general prosecutor for publishing false information that 'harmed public safety and national interests'.[9] Opposition figures have also been excluded from the state media, which creates 'frustration . . . and results in these groups resorting to other media outlets such as social media'.[10] This inability to seek representation through official media outlets inevitably increases the importance of digital spaces and social media. This was especially apparent following the declaration of the National Safety Law in Bahrain on 15 March 2011.[11] The law, which was the precursor to a broader crackdown, saw the destruction of important political and religious structures, as well as a clampdown on public gatherings of any sort. Yet, given Bahrain's history, the law was nothing exceptional, as the Internet in Bahrain has always been the target of government legislation and regulation. Cybercafes in Bahrain are strictly regulated: subversive websites are blocked and live streaming/chat services are blocked. In short, anything that may be deemed to violate Articles 19 and 20 of the country's press rules, which include 'instigating hatred of the political regime, encroaching on the state's official religion, breaching ethics, encroaching on religions and jeopardizing public peace or raising issues whose publication is prohibited by the provisions of this law',[12] can be subjected to government censure and censorship. In 2012, Reporters Without Borders designated Bahrain an 'enemy of the internet' due to its imprisonment of bloggers, restricting of net access, and filtering of content.[13]

Just as physical places posed a threat to the regime and so were destroyed, so too do digital spaces, which are new frontiers for activism and are the locations from which people can challenge the homogenising power of authoritarianism. In order to counter the threat embodied by these digital spaces, the Bahraini government and those representing the hegemonic order are employing tactics to control them. These tactics are numerous, yet can generally be seen under the umbrella of 'surveillance', for they are all attempts to instil normative and acceptable repertoires of behaviour through both observation and creating a fear of observation.

## Surveillance and sousveillance

Surveillance is the process by which organisations and governments observe individuals or groups of individuals. It is an asymmetric process that affords power to the observer but not to the observed, and is therefore a process by which the surveillant asserts his domination over the surveilled. The means by which an organisation conducts surveillance are multifaceted, yet technological developments have facilitated the speed and efficacy of the process, allowing for more efficient and pervasive observation. Indeed, the rise of what Jan van Dijk first termed the 'network society'[14] has given both organisations and the state unprecedented opportunities to carry out surveillance. As David Lyon argues, the information society is also the surveillance society.[15]

The historical role of technology in surveillance is perhaps most famously illustrated by Jeremy Bentham's Panopticon, a building whose geometry allowed a prison guard to watch the inmates without them knowing. Timothy Mitchell describes the Panopticon as the 'institution in which the use of coercion and commands to control a population was replaced by the partitioning of space, the isolation of individuals, and their systematic yet unseen surveillance'.[16] Mitchell's work on Egypt draws heavily on the work of Michel Foucault, who outlined the importance of the power differential within the context of the 'unseen'. Ben and Marthalee Barton summarise Foucault's argument, stating that the 'asymmetry of seeing-without-being-seen is, in fact, the very essence of power' and the 'power to dominate rests on the differential possession of knowledge'.[17] As well as stressing the importance of asymmetry, Foucault states that, '[the] major effect of the Panopticon is to induce in the inmate a state of conscious and permanent visibility that assures the automatic functioning of power'.[18]

In other words, it is not just being watched that is enough to induce obedience to authority, but rather the *possibility* of being watched. An example of such an apparatus could be seen in Saddam Hussein's Iraq, where a mosque with an unusually high minaret was built in order to keep track of the Shiʿa in Karbala.[19] The Hassan Mosque, itself a modern-day Panopticon, functioned alongside a highly repressive state intelligence apparatus (*mukhabarāt*). Likewise, in the Bahrain, the *mukhabarāt* have been integral to the functioning of Bahrain's intelligence system. Ian Henderson, the British head of security in Bahrain in the latter part of the twentieth century, instituted pseudo-gangs (pseudo-gangs were co-opted members of political groups who would be used as undercover police informants) to infiltrate opposition networks. Although it had been perceived as a 'liberal' state by regional standards in the decade prior to the 2011 uprising with fewer restrictions on internet access,[20] it still suffers from many of the same repressive measures that serve to limit both dissent and political mobilisation. Even before 14 February, Bahrain had blocked websites deemed to be politically controversial and arrested on a number of occasions bloggers such as Ali Abdulemam.[21]

This censorship indicates the threat that new technologies pose to regimes around the world. They must therefore adopt new methods of observation, ones that preferably permit coercion with minimal resort to violence. While such observation was traditionally carried out by the naked eye, 'surveillance techniques have increasingly become embedded in technology'.[22] Oscar Gandy[23] and Mark Poster[24] argue that the growth of information technology and databases has led to an asymmetrical monitoring of behaviour. This surveillance allows particular organisations, whether they be corporate or bureaucratic, to 'not only commodify the personal information of those observed, but also use such information to inform practices of social control and discrimination'.[25] Facebook and Twitter are therefore a potential opportunity for organisations to extract information which can be used to further the agenda of the particular institutional body collecting the data.

So, just as the Panopticon allowed the asymmetric observation of a prison's inmates, the modern-day neo-panopticon can be seen as the use of observational technologies to discourage certain forms of behaviour in a wide range of places, from malls to high streets, to forums and social media.[26] While the essence of this surveillance is based on the fact it is asymmetrical, the use of new technologies by individuals to observe those in authority represents a sort of inverse panopticon, one where citizens can challenge the government monopoly on information.[27] This idea is described as 'sousveillance', 'from the French words for "sous" (below) and "veiller" to watch'.[28] 'Sousveillance', itself a form of 'reflectionism', is a term invented by Steve Mann to describe the process of using technologies to confront organisations by documenting their actions or the consequences of their actions.[29] In other words, it gives those being observed by the hegemonic power the ability to become the observer and the power to resist the authority of the state. However, Mann also discusses the idea of 'personal sousveillance', which is the use of technology such as social media to document one's own day-to-day experience. An example of this might include Bahraini activists who photographed themselves at the Pearl Roundabout, or those who documented their experience with the judicial system.

Yet, as William Marczak *et al.* note, 'targeted surveillance of individuals conducted by nation-states poses an exceptionally challenging security problem, given the great imbalance of resources and expertise between the victims and the attackers'.[30] Indeed, such seemingly banal 'personal sousveillance' can be reappropriated by the regime and its supporters and used as part of its own surveillance apparatus. This is nowhere more evident than in Bahrain, where the regime initially used the increasing polarisation of society to encourage citizens to use social media as a tool of peer-to-peer, vigilante sous/surveillance, before employing commercially available digital surveillance technology like Finfisher for data gathering. In addition to the regime encouraging this behaviour, or turning a blind eye to it, loyalists and supporters of the regime could use social media to encourage vigilantism.

## Social media, surveillance, and counter-revolutionary vigilante sousveillance

### Government spying

The rise of new technologies posed new challenges for the government, which turned to novel tactics to uncover activists using social media. An investigation by the advocacy and transparency group Bahrain Watch revealed that at least eleven activists were put in jail in 2012–13 for writing anonymous tweets referring to King Hamad as a 'dictator' (*taghiyya*) or 'fallen one' (*saqit*) in Arabic. The tactics, most likely orchestrated by the Ministry of Interior's Cyber Crime Unit, were crude: malicious links generated from freely available online services were sent out by government-operated accounts to those engaging in 'subversive' activity; if the target clicked on the malicious links then that would reveal to the attacker the victim's IP address. According to Bahrain Watch:

> When an individual connects to the internet on his computer or phone, they are temporarily assigned an IP address by the phone company or internet provider whose service they are using (e.g., Batelco, Zain, Menatelecom, etc.). Bahraini law requires

that every time an IP address is assigned, the internet service provider must record the name of the subscriber of the internet connection, as well as the date and time. This information must be preserved for at least one year, and the security forces must be able to directly access this information at any time. [31]

In addition to this 'IP spying' technique being used on Twitter, malicious links were also sent out from accounts and numbers 'through Facebook, e-mail, and likely via other services including YouTube, InstaMessage, and mobile messaging services including BlackBerry Messenger and WhatsApp'.[32] Some activists, who were later arrested, were sent malicious links from trusted accounts that appear to have been hacked by government agents.[33] The breadth of those accounts targeted with malicious links is staggering. So far, the government has used this tactic to target 'journalists, labor unions, human rights groups, activists, licensed opposition groups . . . whistleblowers, Sunni groups, vigilantes, and even residents opposed to the seizure of their homes to build a government housing project'.[34] Even parody accounts, such as that of '@Sheikh-KhalifaPM', an account that pokes fun at the Prime Minister, were targeted. Ever irreverent, @SheikhKhalifaPM responded by saying 'Bloody typical..hot young women only get in touch with me when they want something from me..like maybe my IP address'.[35]

Similarly, the Ministry of Interior was found to be using FinSpy, malware developed by UK-based Gamma International. Finspy can secretly take remote control of a computer, copy its files, activate the microphone, take screenshots, intercept Skype calls, and log every keystroke.[36] Finspy was often sent to activists via malicious files disguised as email attachments the target might find interesting. In one example, FinSpy was attached to an email that appeared to come from the bona fide Al Jazeera journalist Melissa Chan before being sent to activists.[37] Bahrain Watch's investigation also revealed that the Bahraini government used FinSpy to infect the country's most prominent lawyers, activists, and politicians.

This included Ibrahim Sharif, the head of the country's liberal Waʿad party, Mohammed al-Tajir, a leading human rights lawyer, Hadi al-Musawi, head of the human rights department of Al Wefaq, Bahrain's largest opposition society, and Hassan Mushaima, an incarcerated opposition leader deemed by Amnesty International to be a prisoner of conscience.[38] Saeed Shehabi was also among three Bahraini exiles granted asylum in the UK to have their computers targeted, illustrating how Bahrain's repressive reach extends well beyond its borders as a form of transnational repression. Other people were also targeted in Belgium and Germany.[39]

The authorities have also taken advantage of vulnerabilities in the social media app Zello, which allows people to use their phones like walkie-talkies. Bahrain Watch expressed concern that fifteen activists were arrested after they were lured to a false meeting posted by police, who posted the message through the account of a compromised member. Following this, police even posted messages via the app saying that they were coming to get the activists 'one by one'.[40]

## Trolling

Broadly speaking, trolling can be defined as a form of aggressive Internet communication, where people using anonymous accounts engage in abusive behaviour towards other users. It is a form of what MacKinnon calls 'cyber-harassment' and can vary in severity, ranging from provocative comments to outright bullying. Trolling in Bahrain 'usually comes from anonymous accounts, and its severity can range from death threats and threats of rape, to spiteful comments and personal abuse'.[41] For example, one Twitter user feared for the safety of her child when an anonymous troll started tweeting about how he (the troll) knew where the child went to school. He even named the school and gave details of its layout and location. Another activist reported how trolls created five parody accounts, all of which were dedicated to ridiculing her. In an attempt to rectify this, the victim had to send to Twitter on each occasion proof of identity to get rid of the anonymous accounts. Tiring of this, Twitter eventually suggested she just tweet under a separate or anonymous identity, essentially admitting defeat at the hands of the troll(s).

Bahrain's Twitter trolls have acquired such a reputation that they have prompted many international journalists or activists reporting on Bahrain to write/blog about them, including Jillian York,[42] David Goodman,[43] and Brian Dooley.[44] Following the release of the BICI report on 23 November 2011, Al Jazeera reporter Gregg Carlstrom tweeted: 'Bahrain has by far the hardest-working Twitter trolls of any country I've reported on'. Global Voices editor for the Middle East and North Africa Amira Al Hussaini tweeted: 'Yawn: cyberbullying = censorship! Welcome to the new era of freedom in #Bahrain'. A number of people told me how trolling stopped them from tweeting politics, with one user stating: 'Don't know how long, Marc, my heart is heavy. Even my moderate views get attacked by trolls'.

Few people who engage in trolling have accounts that reveal their true identity and it is precisely this anonymity that makes many people suspicious. There are perhaps thousands of anonymous accounts, all of which have very few followers, and usually have an avatar that symbolises their support for the regime (such as a picture of a member of the royal family). Despite the fact that the regime enjoys some degree of legitimacy in Bahrain, there is a belief that many of these accounts are created by the security forces or PR companies to bully activists and give the illusion of widespread support for the government.[45] Given that the US military is developing software that will allow it to 'secretly manipulate social media sites by using fake online personas to influence internet conversations and spread pro-American propaganda',[46] it comes as no surprise that the private sector might seek to profit from it. Indeed, it was revealed that BGR Gabara, a British PR firm reportedly working for the Bahraini government, planned to organise a 'Twitter campaign' on behalf of Kazakh children.[47]

A number of studies noted unusual patterns of tweeting prior to bouts of government repression. One group of bloggers noted that a 'large group of organized troll accounts were created by the government. They then flooded twitter with a disinformation campaign. Once violence broke out the Troll Army vanished'.[48] While there is no evidence that the above is the regime, or companies operating on the regime's behalf, it is certainly an unusual pattern of tweeting. A report by Freedom House adds, 'hundreds of accounts suddenly emerged to collectively harass and intimidate online activists, commentators, and journalists who voiced support for protests and human rights'.[49]

What these findings illustrate is that trolling can result in people changing their tweeting habits. A number of people interviewed said how they were less likely to tweet anything against the regime after being trolled. Others changed their Twitter privacy settings so that their tweets would not be seen by the global public. This demonstrates how hegemonic forces can use social media to influence the flow of anti-government rhetoric, thus contributing to the state's censorship apparatus. Dissuading people from tweeting also creates an informational vacuum, one that can then be filled with pro-regime propaganda/PR. Even some expatriates interviewed living in Bahrain stopped blogging anything critical following discussions with their families about the possible implications.

## Name and shame

Perhaps one of the most pernicious things to come out of the uprising is the 'Haraqhum' Twitter account. Haraqhum, which literally means 'the one that burns them', is a self-proclaimed 'defender of Bahrain' and spends its days disclosing information about 'traitors' in Bahrain. This includes posting photos of people seen at anti-government rallies, circling their faces, disclosing their addresses, their places of work, and their phone numbers. Unfortunately, the account has achieved such notoriety that it was singled out in the BICI report. It did, however, spawn several spin-offs such as 'Mnarfezhum'. An example of its impact was revealed to me by one informant who said, 'My friend she left the country after her husband who works in a bank became a target of this 7araghum [sic]. I don't think she'll ever come back.' The climate of fear that existed when this message was sent should not be underestimated, for it was a time when thousands of Bahrainis were being fired from work for taking in part in strikes, even though the strikes were 'within the permissible bounds of the law' (BICI, 2011: 420).[50] Haraqhum also set the tone for sectarian discourse on social media and frequently deployed anti-Shiʿa terminology such as *majūsi*, *rawāfiḍ*, *safawi*, and *walad al-mutʿa*.[51] This discourse has now become far more commonplace in the region, especially with the rise of ISIS. An investigation by Bahrain Watch also revealed that the government might have been running extremist accounts on Facebook or Twitter to both incite sectarianism and launch IP attacks on activists and prominent tweets.[52]

While many have tried to unveil Haraqhum's identity, no one has been successful. It is believed to be a number of people taking it in turns to manage the account. However, it was later revealed that the Mnarfezhum Twitter account was run by a member of the ruling family, Mohammed bin Saqr Al Khalifa. This open secret was confirmed when he entered the Ministry of Finance brandishing a gun.[53] Of course, no charges were made, again implying that impunity is indicative of normalisation of the kind of harmful sectarian discourse employed by those close to, and allied to, the Al Khalifa regime. Haraqhum and Mnafezhum have become an institution in themselves in Bahrain, with people using them to report suspected 'traitors' and also to find information about these 'traitors'. One such example was provided by someone whose father used to have a high position in a Bahraini company. He was contacted by someone who had information about a potential 'traitor' working in the company: 'this guy sends a message to my Dad pasted from Haraqhum about an [insert company name] employee . . . He was sending it to my dad because my dad is still well connected, so can make things happen . . . So he was telling my dad "Do the needful" (i.e. get him fired)'.

Prior to Haraqhum, there were other examples of people with anonymous Twitter accounts receiving messages disclosing their name and identity (for example, imagine you had gone to great lengths to protect your identity on Twitter and then someone you don't know contacts you and tells you your name, phone number, and address). On describing Haraqhum, the BICI report stated:

> In some cases, a photograph of a protester was posted with a comment asking for the name of the person, and other Twitter users then posted the requested information. Witnesses reported to the Commission that persons who had been named or identified by Harghum [sic] would then avoid sleeping at their home address for fear of an attack. Harghum [sic] also allegedly advertised a MoI hotline, which people could call in order to report on persons engaged in anti-government activity.[54] The Harghum [sic] Twitter account targeted anti-government protesters and even disclosed their whereabouts and personal details. Harghum [sic] openly harassed, threatened and defamed certain individuals, and in some cases placed them in immediate danger. The Commission considers such harassment to be a violation of a person's right to privacy while also amounting to hate speech and incitement to violence.[55]

As of December 2014, the government has done nothing about the account, even though the Commission stated that Haraqhum 'produced material that international law requires to be prohibited and which is in fact prohibited under Bahrain law'.[56] It is interesting to note that similar 'name and shame' groups existed on Facebook, yet it is easier to have Facebook remove these groups.[57] Twitter, on the other hand, makes it hard to remove such groups unless they are reported for spam. What this has led to is many pro-government supporters leading campaigns where they get people to report human rights activists such as Nabeel Rajab and Maryam al-Khawaja for spam. Despite Facebook's more sympathetic policy in getting rid of such groups, it was reportedly used to identify the workplace and home of twenty-year-old poet Ayat al-Qurmezi, who had angered authorities by reading out a poem that criticised King Hamad. Visitors to this Facebook page were told to write the 'traitor's name and workplace'. Soon afterwards masked men arrested her.

## *'Passive' observation and offline factors*

In anticipation of the protests, the Bahraini government created a number of Twitter accounts, most notably one for the Ministry of Interior (MoI), the body responsible for Bahrain's security forces. While the MoI's account tended to publish news without interacting with other people, this did not stop people from interacting with the MoI. Between the months of February and April, it was common for pro-regime supporters to use Twitter to 'report' people they thought were traitors to the MoI. The following tweet is an example of this: '@hussainm89 Dear @moi_bahrain can you please arrest this MOFO Hussain Mirza born 1989, he is a traitor'. Although it is doubtful that the ministry takes such complaints seriously, the impact that the potential threat of surveillance has is very real, as someone once made clear: 'Be careful, Marc. Don't argue a lot. A lot of people from MoI on Twitter. And if you mention the King, justice, etc., you might be unable to enter the country. Just be careful plz'.

Offline factors refer to a number of pressures that do not necessarily occur online, but still work to increase censorship by discouraging people from using social media (the phrase self-censorship is problematic, as it implies that there is no stimulus that causes the censorship, shifting the responsibility from the hegemonic order to the individual). In March 2011, a photo of 'web terrorists' was circulated on Twitter. This included Manaf al-Muhandis, Mahmud Yusif and Muhammad Masqati, all prominent Twitter users or bloggers who were subsequently arrested.[58] They were all detained for varying lengths of time and none of them tweeted anything controversial or very political for a considerable time following their release. Prominent blogger Ali Abdulemam, who went into hiding for over two years, was sentenced *in absentia* to fifteen years in prison for 'spreading false information and trying to subvert the regime'. However, he managed to escape the island in 2013, fleeing to Britain.[59] In addition to this, blogger Zakariyya al-ʿAshiri was tortured to death in prison on 9 April 2011, as was Karim Fakhrawi, a Bahraini book publisher who was killed by security services after he went to a police station to make a complaint. As a result of the above arrests, important representatives of the activist community disappeared, further diminishing the visibility of credible online activism and also prompting much fear among other online activists, who were far more reluctant to tweet anything critical of the regime. The death of Zakariyya also resulted in Reporters Without Borders putting Bahrain on a list of 'enemies of the internet'.[60] Other offline factors include family pressure not to use social media (particularly Twitter) and widespread fear that the government is able to hack accounts and access personal information. One informant stated: 'I used to tweet but then when some of my friends got arrested my father sat me down and gave me a looong [sic] talk, guilting me into deleting all my tweets.'

### The 'unknown'

Other perhaps more sinister elements faced by activists are the clandestine operations undertaken by companies such as Olton, a UK-based intelligence gathering/PR firm that has a contract with the Bahrain Economic Development Board. One activist told me:

> There's this British company called Olton. I don't know exactly what they do except that they employ Bahrainis loyal to the regime to do something with social media. The person recruiting them is ex-UK military.

Despite the government of Bahrain's Tender Board's description of Olton's work being 'to develop an electronic system to track international media', one of their employees is known to have worked for the MoI, the body responsible for Bahrain's security forces.[61] Furthermore, Olton was at the IDEX Arms Fair in Abu Dhabi, where the company was reported to be marketing its 'web-trawling' software as something that could head off unrest in the Middle East. It would do this through monitoring social media in order to identify ringleaders.[62] Fears that Twitter and Facebook were being monitored were further exacerbated after at least forty-seven students were dismissed from Bahrain Polytechnic for 'participating in unlicensed gatherings and marches'. This was 'based on evidence mostly obtained from social media pages like Facebook'.[63] Some were dismissed for simply 'liking' an anti-government post on Facebook.[64] Many reported that they were dismissed after authorities showed them printouts of their Facebook pages.

## Propaganda and disinformation

Blurring this line between propaganda, PR, 'data-mining' and intelligence-gathering was 'Liliane Khalil', a hoax journalist who used blogs, Twitter, and email to build up a convincing online persona. Although she had claimed to be the US editor of a pro-government blog called 'Bahrain Independent', an investigation revealed that she was a hoax.[65] Although Liliane Khalil's actual identity remains unknown, there is evidence that links her to Task Consultancy, a Bahraini company that was paid by the Bahraini government to formulate a PR plan.[66] Liliane Khalil also interviewed a number of activists on the understanding that she wanted to hear 'their side of the story'. However, several of those interviewed reported that she passed on their personal information to a pro-regime Twitter user, who then broadcast it on Twitter stating that the interviewees were traitors.

Similarly, the government has hacked or taken over accounts used by activists and then utilised them to disseminate pro-government propaganda. YouTube videos were edited and taken out of context in order to demonise protesters. Conspiratorial recordings became popular and were often propagated by government officials. In one case, a video showing protests allegedly waving Bahraini flags with twelve-point flags instead of five was widely circulated,[67] its significance lying in the fact the twelve points signify the twelve Shiʿa Imams, and thus the flag waving suggests a seditious Shiʿa conspiracy.[68] Even though the flags in the video did not even contain twelve-point flags, Sameera Rajab, at the time an Upper House legislator, went on Al Jazeera to claim that this was evidence of a conspiracy. However, it was pointed out the flag she held only had ten points.[69] In another example, a video was circulated on YouTube allegedly showing people applying make-up to children in an attempt to suggest that activists were faking their injuries and that the government was attacking children. It transpired that the video was an edited video from Nazareth, Israel, showing children being made up for an event. Despite this, the video shortly received over 17,000 hits, not including mirrored copies.[70] As I said in 2011:

> [T]he presence of such disinformation is very harmful in times of conflict, for it is also a time when people are feeling vulnerable, defensive and afraid. I have even seen Trolls termed 'e-thugs' in recent days, perhaps not surprising since the term 'thug' has now become an important part of the Middle Eastern protest lexicon. The trolls are exploiting both our need for information, which surely increases in times of crisis, and also the dearth of credible information on the issues. This lack of credible official information compounds the issue, and as the government continues to remain absent, the scramble for answers is both desperate and blind.[71]

## The anti-social movement surveillance state

For activists, using social media as a tool for activism or representation is fraught with danger. The tactics adopted by the dominant power in Bahrain contributed to a climate of fear and distrust, one that disrupted social media space by assimilating it as part of the regime's surveillance apparatus. Trolling, for example, is not only a form of social control that exercises its power through intimidation, but also serves as a reminder that one's behaviour is always being watched and that any potential dissent will never be without fear of observation. Even the mere presence of an MoI Twitter account was enough to regulate some people's behaviour by reminding them that they were being monitored. The incarceration of key online activists also reminded Bahrainis of the potential costs of utilising social media for dissent and thus asserted that the transgression of a certain set of normative behaviours (in this case acquiescence) would not be tolerated. These, combined with different surveillance tactics such as IP spying and the phishing of activist accounts, also lead to insecurity and distrust intended to 'undermine the necessary bonds of trust on a social network that make it work'. [72]

The impact in Bahrain of trolling and naming and shaming illustrates the dangers of these forms of 'cyber-vigilantism', which will only become more detrimental as social cohesion in Bahrain is further eroded. Accounts like Haraqhum and the type of spin-offs it has generated are a particular worry, for it became a quasi-official institution endorsed by some supporters of the regime that gave it tacit support of its utility as a method of social control. Just as plain-clothes thugs operate alongside the police in suppressing protests, accounts like Haraqhum worked alongside the regime's intelligence-gathering apparatus, appropriating citizens' 'personal sousveillance' and using it to persecute, vilify, and threaten. Although Haraqhum's identity still remains unknown, the opaque way in which the regime has so far conducted the crackdown, and the blurring of lines between law enforcement and state-endorsed vigilantism, has heightened the suspicions of activists, many of whom believe that Haraqhum actually operates with MoI approval. Whether or not this is the case is in many ways irrelevant. This is because perception plays a fundamental role in surveillance, for what we perceive and not what is actual form the underlying mechanism of the panopticon, which seeks not only to watch, but to make people *believe* they are being watched.

Another alarming trend is the clandestine role played by predominantly western PR and security firms, many of which are 'exploiting the burgeoning but unregulated surveillance market'.[73] Bahrain also enlists the services of companies like Nokia Siemens, whose SMS monitoring technology was used by the state's security apparatus to intercept the communications of suspected dissidents.[74] Olton, the British company offering expertise in social media, and now acquired by Protection Group International, sold a 'reputation management' service. This aimed to promote 'positive' online commentary while 'mitigating the negative'.[75] The fact it is also an 'intelligence-gathering' company has serious implications for freedom of speech. As I have stated elsewhere:

> The threat posed by unscrupulous PR companies to freedom of speech should not be underestimated. It is bad enough that they distort the public sphere in exchange for money, yet it is the rise of companies like Olton that is the most alarming, for when does intelligence gathering become evidence gathering? Furthermore, when does 'reputation management' involve facilitating the silencing of those narratives that oppose the desired rhetoric of the paying client?[76]

The recent revelation that British PR firm Bell Pottinger was offering to help companies hijack citizen petitions in order to influence European Union law raises questions about a similar incident that occurred in Bahrain last year.[77] This involved the circulation of a petition on Twitter that claimed to be a proposal listing the demands of Bahrain's youth for an upcoming reconciliation initiative called the National Dialogue. Over a thousand people signed it, though many of the signatories were anonymous, sockpuppet accounts. The following day the National Unity Gathering (Bahrain's new pro-government political party) used the petition as a basis for determining what Bahraini youth wanted (unsurprisingly, they did not want political change, just security).[78] The notion that anonymous online accounts might be rubber-stamping policies in order to give them a veneer of democratic legitimacy illustrates the ease with which social media can be used to manufacture consent. Although this might seem like the stuff of Orwellian fantasy, one must not underestimate the dangers of a growing, global surveillance industry, one that capitalises on the desire of authoritarian regimes around the world to monitor, control, and suppress dissent.

Fighting the spread of surveillance technology like FinSpy is costly and time consuming. The rights group Privacy International launched a legal case against Her Majesty's Revenue and Customs (HMRC) in the UK over its refusal to provide 'details about potentially unlawful exports of spyware tools made by Gamma International'.[79] In May 2014, the British High Court ruled in favour of Privacy International and stated that HMRC's refusal to release information was 'unlawful'.[80] Privacy International along with Bahrain Watch filed a criminal complaint with the UK National Cyber Crime Unit, 'asking them to investigate the targeting of three UK-based Bahrainis with Gamma International's FinFisher computer spyware'.[81] In December 2014, the Organisation for Economic Co-operation and Development (OECD) ruled that Gamma International had breached the human rights of the activists it had targeted.[82]

## Concluding remarks

Through the aforementioned methods, government agents and loyalists alike are able to preserve the status quo through extending the means by which they conduct surveillance. Such methods are attempts to impose normative forms of behaviour in spaces that allow for the performance of identities that challenge the hegemonic order. These spaces, which include Shiʿa religious structures, the Pearl Roundabout, and social media, all represent what Foucault described as 'heterotopias',[83] that is, places that challenge 'safe space' and allow for the flourishing of resistance identities that challenge the structures of power. This capacity of social media to function as a space of resistance did not go uncontested in Bahrain and hegemonic forces also used it to enhance and 'mobilise identities to facilitate the extraction of resources from the society to confront the external (and in Bahrain's case, internal) threat'.[84] So, while social media allows activists to 'overcome the powerlessness of their solitary despair . . . and fight the powers that be by identifying the networks that are',[85] it also allows the state to resist change (Castells, 2009: 431). Furthermore, Bahrain illustrates how it is not simply faceless authoritarian regimes that resist political change, but corporations and citizens too, especially those who benefit both economically and socially from maintaining the status quo. Indeed, just as those advocating political change can use social media to create networks of resistance, those representing the hegemonic order can mobilise their own networks of domination. Cybertechnology therefore becomes another space where structures are violently reproduced.

Perhaps one of the saddest aspects of all this is how information shared amid a climate of optimism, such as photos of peaceful protesters at the Pearl Roundabout, was reappropriated by the likes of Haraqhum and reframed within a context of treachery, terrorism, and betrayal. Such abuses of social media not only remind Bahrainis of the potential costs of sharing information publicly but also demonstrate how trust is an increasingly scarce commodity. The nature of this breakdown of trust was nowhere more evident than on Facebook and numerous interviewees shared stories of how they purged their 'friend lists' through both anger at their newly developed political outlook and through fear that that person might gain access to potentially 'incriminating' photos or information. The erosion of trust is itself a crucial part of the effects of surveillance, for the inability to trust others promotes increased isolation of the individual, which can unravel social cohesion and discourage the formation of strong activist networks that advocate social justice.

Although it must be emphasised that these negative effects are very real, they by no means undermine the importance of social media as a tool for sousveillance. It is an instrument of both empowerment and control, yet the extent to which it functions as either depends very much on the cultural, geopolitical, technological, and temporal context in which it is being used. The role of social media is ambivalent and although it has been an incredibly positive force in Bahrain, documenting its successes would necessitate a separate article. Unfortunately, the government's claims of reform since 2011 have been rendered hollow by a lacklustre implementation of the BICI report recommendations. New media laws appear to legitimise even tighter state control over the media; an 'independent regulator',[86] the Supreme Council for Media and Communication,[87] has been created following watered-down recommendations in the BICI report, which is questionable in itself considering that all members are essentially appointed by the King.[88]

As it stands, pro-democracy activists still face a great many obstacles when it comes to finding spaces from which to represent themselves. The brutal daily crackdowns in the villages, the destruction of the Pearl Roundabout, and the demolition of mosques all represent attempts to control space and render it ahistorical, conformist, and safe. For the regime, these are all spaces of crisis, transformation and change, or heterotopias. Social media are no different and can also be regulated and controlled. As the struggle for democracy continues in urban space, so does it in cyberspace. In many ways, the battle is *for* cyberspace, for it is a battle between the principles of empowerment and control, the continuation of which underlines the argument that social media are tools for both emancipation and repression. At the moment, the message from the regime is clear: you will be punished or imprisoned if you tweet against us and, if you are anonymous, we can find you.

This chapter is an updated version of the following article, used with kind permission from the University of Westminster: M.O. Jones, 'Social media, surveillance, and social control in the Bahrain Uprising', *Westminster Papers in Communication and Culture: The Role of Social Media in the Arab Uprisings, Past and Present*, 9/2 (April 2013).

# Notes

## FOREWORD

1. See, for example, J. Beinin and F. Vairel (eds), *Social Movements, Mobilization, and Contestation in the Middle East and North Africa*, Stanford University Press, Stanford, 2013; S.E. Nepstad, 'Mutiny and nonviolence in the Arab Spring: exploring military defections and loyalty in Egypt, Bahrain, and Syria', *Journal of Peace Research*, 50/3 (2013); K.C. Ulrichsen, 'Bahrain's aborted revolution', London School of Economics, 2012, www.lse.ac.uk/IDEAS/publications/reports/pdf/SR011/FINAL_LSE_IDEAS__BahrainsAbortedRevolution_Ulrichsen.pdf

2. See, for example, Bahrain Online, 'Is central organization at the Pearl Roundabout better than in the villages' [web forum discussion], 11 February 2011, http://bahrainonline.org/showthread.php?t=259768

3. Abdulwahab Hussain and Hassan Mushaima are among several leading members of the 1992–99 uprising who have been pushed to the sidelines by their former comrades following disagreement on how to deal with King Hamad's failure to implement political reforms. Hussain and Mushaima founded al-Wafa'a Party and the Haq Movement respectively. Both underground movements have advocated more confrontational opposition activities. Both were arrested after Saudi military incursion on 15 March 2011. Later that year, they were sentenced to life imprisonment.

4. The King consolidated his position as the ultimate power in the country. His positions include being head of state, commander of the armed forces, and head of the executive and judicial branches of government. The King can amend the constitution and can appoint: the Prime Minister, members of the Upper House, the Shura Council, as well as judges, including members of the Constitutional Court.

5. The end of the boycott led to a serious split within the opposition into two factions: the participators and the boycotters. The latter included leading members of Al Wefaq and other organisations, who resigned protesting the newly adopted 'conciliatory' line towards the regime.

6. Officially recognised opposition organisations seemed more apprehensive towards 'irresponsible attempts to disrupt the status quo by unruly groups'. Al Wefaq, in particular, has repeatedly pointed out the benefits of its non-confrontational strategy. The organisation has consolidated its position as the leading opposition and the regime's main Shi'a interlocutor. The parliamentary elections of 2006 gave Al Wefaq 17 of the 40 contested seats and validated, in the eyes of its own constituency, the prudence of its conciliatory strategy towards the regime. In October 2010, they won 18 of the 40 contested parliamentary seats in what it described as 'fair and free parliamentary elections'. *Al-Wasat*, 'The Prime Minister sends a cable of good wishes to the General Secretary of Al Wefaq on the occasion of their success in the parliamentary and municipal election', 4 November 2014, www.alwasatnews.com/2981/news/read/496462/1.html

7. Ordinarily, a radical flank comprises individuals and/or networks who share the general grievances, platforms and/or objectives of an organised collective action, but doubt the efficiency of its leadership, pace, tactics, demands, and/or rhetoric. See, for example, W.A. Gamson, *The Strategy of Social Protest*, Wadsworth, Belmont, CA, 1990; J.B. Braithwaite, 'Rethinking radical flank theory: South Africa', RegNet Research Paper No. 2014/23, http://ssrn.com/abstract=237744

8. Contingent accelerators refer to events and/or actors that define and precipitate political opportunities to mobilise for collective action through emerging, unplanned, emotional climates. See, for example, J.-P. Reed, 'Emotions in context: Revolutionary accelerators, hope, moral outrage, and other emotions in the making of Nicaragua's revolution', *Theory and Society*, 33/6 (2004); J. Foran, *Taking Power: On the Origins of Third World Revolution*, Cambridge University Press, Cambridge, 2006.

9. *Gulf Daily News*, 'Chaotic scenes outside hospital', 18 February 2011, www.gulf-daily-news.com/NewsDetails.aspx?storyid=299770

10. *Al-Wasat*, 'Crown Prince orders military off Bahrain streets', 19 February 2011, www.alwasatnews.com/3088/news/read/528052/1.html; *Gulf Daily News*, 'Crown Prince urges restraint', 19 February 2011, www.gulf-daily-news.com/NewsDetails.aspx?storyid=299817

11. See A. Khalaf, 'Unfinished business: contentious politics and state-building in Bahrain', Research Reports in Sociology, Department of Sociology, University of Lund, 2000, p. 1.

INTRODUCTION

1. F.G. Gause and S.L. Yom, 'Resilient royals: how Arab monarchies hang on', *Journal of Democracy*, 23, 74–88, 15 October 2012, p. 118.

2. Bahrain Online, 'Let's choose a specific day to begin the popular revolution in Bahrain' [web forum discussion], 26 January 2011, http://bahrainonline.org/showthread.php?t=258985&page=2

3. CNN iReport, 'A statement by Bahraini Youth for Freedom', 11 February 2011, http://ireport.cnn.com/docs/DOC-554209

4. Bahrain Online, 'Sites and possibilities of peaceful protest on Bahrain's Day of Rage on 14 February' [web forum discussion], 31 January 2011, www.bahrainonline.org/showthread.php?t=259208

5. Bahrain Online, 'Positives and negatives of the two sites Pearl Roundabout and . . .' [web forum discussion], 5 February 2011, www.bahrainonline.org/showthread.php?t=259492; Bahrain Online, 'Positives and negatives of King Faisal Corniche', 6 February 2011, www.bahrainonline.org/showthread.php?t=259544; Bahrain Online, 'Positives and negatives of the site Marina Club', 7 February 2011, http://bahrainonline.org/showthread.php?t=259563

6. F.S. Hasso, 'Sectarian/gendered police and rupture in Bahrain's Pearl Revolution', in F.S. Hasso and Z. Salime (eds), *Borders, Bodies, and Intimate Politics in the Arab Revolutions* (forthcoming).

7. R. Fisk, 'I saw these brave doctors trying to save lives – these charges are a pack of lies', *The Independent*, 14 June 2011, www.independent. co.uk/voices/commentators/fisk/robert-fisk-i-saw-these-brave-doctors-trying-to-save-lives-ndash-these-charges-are-a-pack-of-lies-2297100. html

8. *The Daily Show with Jon Stewart*, 'America's freedom packages' [online video], 21 March 2011, http://thedailyshow.cc.com/videos/6x58a1/america-s-freedom-packages

9. Bahrain Center for Human Rights, 'Individuals killed by government's excessive use of force since 14 February 2011', 22 May 2014, www.bahrainrights. org/en/node/3864

10. Al Jazeera, 'Bahrain launches probe into prisoner death', 10 November 2014, www.aljazeera.com/humanrights/2014/11/bahrain-launches-probe-into-prisoner-death-20141110103437335342.html

11. M.C. Bassiouni *et al.*, 'Report of the Bahrain Independent Commission of Inquiry' [BICI Report], 23 November 2011, BICI, Manama, p. 420, www.bici.org.bh/BICIreportEN.pdf

12. Ibid.

13. Ibid., p. 366.

14. S. Yasin, 'Bahrain: where a Facebook "like" gets you expelled', Index on Censorship, 14 October 2011, www.indexoncensorship.org/2011/10/bahrain-where-a-facebook-like-gets-you-expelled/

15. M. E. Matar, 'Fighting for democracy while supporting autocracy', LobeLog Foreign Policy, 9 October 2014, www.lobelog.com/bahrain-isis-democracy/

16. J. Gengler, 'The most dangerous men in Bahrain', *Religion and Politics in Bahrain* [blog], http://bahrainipolitics.blogspot.se/2011/06/most-dangerous-men-in-bahrain.html

17. Ibid.

18. O. AlShehabi, 'Bahrain's fate', *Jacobin*, January 2014, www.jacobinmag.com/2014/01/bahrains-fate/

19. F. Khuri, *Tribe and State in Bahrain: The Transition of Social and Political Authority in an Arab State*, University of Chicago Press, Chicago, 1981, pp. 194–95.

20. Hasso, 'Sectarian/gendered police'.

21. A. Robinson, 'An A to Z of theory: Alain Badiou: the event', *Ceasefire*, 15 December 2014, https://ceasefiremagazine.co.uk/alain-badiou-event/

22. A. Badiou, quoted in 'Badiou on the revolutions in Egypt and Tunisia' (translated extracts by Anindya Bhattacharyya), bato20.com [blog], 11 March 2011, http://bato20.com/2011/03/11/badiou-on-the-revolutions-in-egypt-and-tunisia/

23. A. Bayat, 'Revolution and despair', *Mada Masr*, 25 January 2015, www.madamasr.com/opinion/revolution-and-despair

24. A. Bayat, 'Revolution in bad times', *New Left Review*, March–April 2013, http://newleftreview.org/II/80/asef-bayat-revolution-in-bad-times

25. Ibid.

26. A. Khalaf, 'Contentious politics in Bahrain: from ethnic to national and vice versa', Paper to the Fourth Nordic Conference on Middle Eastern Studies: The Middle East in a Globalizing World, 13–16 August 1998, Oslo, http://org.uib.no/smi/pao/khalaf.html

27. A. Shehabi and T.C. Jones, 'Bahrain's revolutionaries', *Foreign Policy*, 2 January 2012, http://foreignpolicy.com/2012/01/02/bahrains-revolutionaries/

28. Ibid.

29. M.O. Jones, 'Bahrain video feature: celebrating creative resistance', *EA Worldview*, 21 January 2012, www.enduringamerica.com/home/2012/1/21/bahrain-video-feature-celebrating-creative-resistance-owen-j.html

30. Ibid.

31. Hasso, 'Sectarian/gendered police'.

32. RUSI in Foreign Affairs Committee, 'Bilateral relations with Bahrain', in *The UK's Relations with Saudi Arabia and Bahrain* (HC 2013–14, 88), Ch. 4, www.publications.parliament.uk/pa/cm201314/cmselect/cmfaff/88/8808.htm

33. Ibid.
34. A. Khalaf, 'Arab reform brief: the outcome of a ten-year process of political reform in Bahrain', Arab Reform Initiative, December 2008, www.arab-reform.net/sites/default/files/ARB.23_Abdulhadi_Khalaf_ENG.pdf
35. A. Khalaf, Opening remarks, 'Bahrain: 30 years of unconstitutional rule', Parliamentary Human Rights Group, House of Lords, 25 August 2005, http://jaddwilliam2.blogspot.co.uk/2005/08/royal-dream.html
36. Khalaf, 'Contentious politics in Bahrain'.
37. Khuri, *Tribe and State*, p. 236.
38. A. Shehabi, 'Inviolable sheikhs and radical subjects: Bahrain's recurring sovereignty crisis', *Arab Studies Journal* (forthcoming).
39. C. O'Murchu and S. Kerr, 'Bahrain land deals highlight alchemy of making money from sand', *Financial Times*, 10 December 2014.
40. H.V. Mapp, *Leave Well Alone!*, Prittle Brook Publishers, Southend, 1994.
41. M.O. Jones, 'A right royal robbery: how the Al Khalifa took a quarter of Bahrain's wealth', *Marc Owen Jones* [blog], 16 August 2012, https://marcowenjones.wordpress.com/2012/08/16/a-right-royal-robbery-how-the-al-khalifas-have-taken-a-third-of-bahrains-wealth/
42. T. Sellin, *Culture, Conflict and Crime*, Social Science Research Council, New Jersey, 1938.
43. Unpublished survey of around 600 top three positions across ministries and public agencies.
44. A. Pollack, 'Underlying the uprisings', *International Socialist Review*, Issue 93, http://isreview.org/issue/93/underlying-uprisings
45. A. Hanieh, *Lineages of Revolt: Issues of Contemporary Capitalism in the Middle East*, Haymarket Books, Chicago, 2013.
46. 'Under the terms of the Abu Safa Field Co-operation Treaty, signed in 1958, Bahrain receives a 50% share (150,000 bpd) of the oil produced from neighbouring Saudi Arabia's offshore Abu Safa oilfield. Bahrain imports and refines a further 230,000 bpd from Saudi Arabia's state-owned oil company, Saudi Aramco, via its major oil pipeline, AB-1.' (From 'Oil and gas regulation in Bahrain: overview', Practical Law: A Thomson Reuters Legal Solution, 2014, http://uk.practicallaw.com/0-525-3563#null)
47. J. McDougall, 'The British and French empires in the Arab world: some problems of colonial state-formation and its legacy', in S.N. Cummings and R. Hinnebusch (eds) *Sovereignty After Empire: Comparing the Middle East and Central Asia*, Edinburgh University Press, Edinburgh, 2011, p. 50, www.jstor.org/stable/10.3366/j.ctt1r1xmt
48. E. Nakhleh, *Bahrain: Political Development in a Modernizing Society*, Lexington Books, New York, 2011, p. 111.
49. WikiLeaks, 'Bahrain security decree' [diplomatic cable], 22 June 1975, https://search.wikileaks.org/plusd/cables/1975MANAMA00716_b.html

50. A. Austin Holmes, 'The base that replaced the British Empire: de-democratization and the American Navy in Bahrain', *Journal of Arabian Studies: Arabia, the Gulf, and the Red Sea*, 4/1 (2014), pp. 20–37.

51. WikiLeaks, 'Bahraini political developments: foreign minister's comments' [diplomatic cable], 11 September 1975, https://search.wikileaks.org/plusd/cables/1975MANAMA01057_b.html

52. WikiLeaks, 'Bahraini political situation' [diplomatic cable], 21 September 1975, https://search.wikileaks.org/plusd/cables/1975MANAMA01086_b.html

53. Austin Holmes, 'De-democratization'.

54. T.C. Jones, 'Time to disband the Bahrain-based U.S. Fifth Fleet', *The Atlantic*, 10 June 2011, www.theatlantic.com/international/archive/2011/06/time-to-disband-the-bahrain-based-us-fifth-fleet/240243/

55. D. Della Porta, A. Peterson, and H. Reiter (eds), *The Policing of Transnational Protest*. Ashgate, Aldershot and Burlington, 2006.

56. *Mahmood's Den* [blog], '"Just Bahraini" not welcome at checkpoints', 19 March 2011, http://mahmood.tv/2011/03/19/just-bahraini-not-welcome-at-checkpoints//

57. YouTube, 'Bahrain: the regime sends its mercenaries to spread hatred of the Shia, describing revolutionaries as "children of muta'a"' [online video], 12 July 2013, www.youtube.com/watch?v=VmpldioCjqk

58. O. AlShehabi, 'Divide and rule in Bahrain and the elusive pursuit for a united front: the experience of the constitutive committee and the 1972 uprising', *Historical Materialism*, 21/1 (2013), pp. 94–127.

59. A. Hammond, 'Tense Bahrain under spotlight again over uprisings', Reuters, 2 February 2012, http://uk.reuters.com/article/2012/02/02/uk-bahrain-bassiouni-return-idUKTRE8110S720120202

60. J. Gengler, 'Bahrain's Sunni awakening', *Middle East Report Online*, 17 January 2012, www.merip.org/mero/mero011712

61. T.C. Jones, 'Theorizing the Arabian Peninsula roundtable: thinking globally about Arabia', *Jadaliyya*, 22 April 2013, www.jadaliyya.com/pages/index/11294/theorizing-the-arabian-peninsula-roundtable_thinki

62. Khalaf, 'Contentious politics in Bahrain'.

63. Ibid.

64. T. Matthiesen, *Sectarian Gulf: Bahrain, Saudi Arabia and the Arab Spring That Wasn't*, Stanford University Press, Stanford, 2013; F. Wehrey, *Sectarian Politics in the Gulf: From the Iraq War to the Arab Uprisings*, Columbia University Press, New York, 2014; L.G. Potter (ed.), *Sectarian Politics in the Persian Gulf*, C Hurst & Co Publishers Ltd, London, 2013.

65. S. Hertog, *Princes, Brokers, and Bureaucrats: Oil and the State in Saudi Arabia*, reprint edition, Cornell University Press, Ithaca, 2011.

66. Gengler, 'Bahrain's Sunni awakening'.
67. Bahrain News Agency, 'Bahrain will always remain an oasis of peace and security, says HRH Premier', 21 April 2011, www.bna.bh/portal/en/news/453767?date=2011-05-3
68. A. Shehabi, 'Bahrain's flashy crony capitalism cannot last', *The Guardian*, 20 May 2012, www.theguardian.com/commentisfree/2012/may/20/bahrain-flashy-crony-capitalism
69. A. Bayat, 'Revolution in bad times'.
70. Hanieh, *Lineages of Revolt*.
71. A. Bayat, 'Revolution in bad times'.
72. D.M. Mertens, 'Philosophy in mixed methods teaching', *International Journal of Multiple Research Approaches*, 4/1 (2010), pp. 9–18.
73. Hasso, 'Sectarian/gendered police'; A. Khalaf, O. AlShehabi, and A. Hanieh (eds), *Transit States: Labour, Migration & Citizenship in the Gulf*, Pluto Press, London (forthcoming).

CHAPTER 1

1. Case No. 11 (Examined by forensic team); Date of statement: 3 August 2011; Statement: At approximately 01:50 on 17 March 2011, a group of masked men surrounded the witness's home. Accompanying the men were a number of armed policemen and a national security officer who was unarmed and dressed in civilian clothing. They did not have an arrest warrant. They handcuffed and blindfolded the detainee and placed him in a civilian car. They took him to an unknown location where he was photographed and examined by a doctor. He was then transferred to Dry Dock Detention Centre and was verbally abused on the way. At 05:00 the detainee arrived at Dry Dock Detention Centre. He was made to stand while he was insulted and he heard sectarian insults directed at the Shia detainees around him. He was told that he was at a location outside Bahrain. He was told to renounce his political views and 'put his hands in the King's hands'. The detainee told the officers that he would do that but without renouncing his demands for constitutional reform. He was then taken back to his cell. Cold water was poured on his mattress, pillows and blanket while the air conditioner was running. Sleep was impossible in the cold and dampness. Later, a group of masked men entered his cell and took turns slapping, punching and kicking him. They insulted him and told him to praise the King and the Prime Minister. They also made the detainee insult himself and at one point he felt someone place a finger in his anus. He was frequently forced to stand for long periods with his hands in the air. The same cycle of torture continued for a week, during which time they beat him two

or three times per day, often with a hose, and poured cold water on him and his mattress. He was interrogated while blindfolded and was told to write down everything he knew about the 14 February movement. On the 13th day of his detention, officers at the Military Prosecution wanted to conduct his investigation without a lawyer present but the detainee refused. He was appointed a lawyer and submitted his statements, informing the military prosecutor that he had been beaten the previous day. The Prosecutor assured him that no more beatings would occur but the beatings continued nonetheless. His torturers at the prison told him that he would be beaten further if he complained again about the treatment. On 10 June, the detainee was moved from solitary confinement to a wing where he was permitted to interact with other detainees. (M.C. Bassiouni *et al.*, 'Report of the Bahrain Independent Commission of Inquiry' [BICI Report], 23 November 2011, BICI, Manama, p. 441, www.bici.org.bh/BICIreportEN.pdf)

2. Ibrahim Sharif al-Sayed at the Court of Appeal, Bahrain, 5 June 2012.
3. Bassiouni *et al.*, 'Report of the BICI', p. 162.
4. An Arabic term used to describe paramilitary militias loyal to the ruling Al Khalifa family.
5. Literally translated as 'one fifth', this refers to a tax traditionally paid by many Shiʿa.
6. Literally, the 'guardianship of the Islamic jurists', this refers to a system of governance in Shiʿa Islam in which a clerical figure should have limited or absolute authority on matters of governance. A system of absolute *wilāyat al-faqīh* exists in Iran.

### CHAPTER 2

1. An extract from ʿAli Al Jallawi's memoir *Allah baʿda al-ʿashira*. This translation was first published in August 2011 by Words Without Borders (www.wordswithoutborders.org) and reprinted here with permission.
2. A *ghutra* is a piece of cloth traditionally worn on the head by men in the Persian Gulf and other parts of the Arab world.
3. Known for his eloquence, Zamakhshari was a medieval Muslim scholar who subscribed to the Muʿtazila theological doctrine.

### CHAPTER 3

1. This chapter first appeared as a series of blogs on T. Mitchell, *My Interesting Life* [blog], 4–9 December 2011, https://tonydmitchell.wordpress.com/2011/12/04/hello-world/

CHAPTER 4

1. Tahiyya Lulu is the pen name of the writer of *The Guardian* article.
2. T. Lulu, 'In Bahrain, first they came for the athletes', *The Guardian*, 22 April 2011, www.theguardian.com/commentisfree/2011/apr/22/bahrain-counter-revolution-televised-athletes
3. W. Brown, '"The most we can hope for . . .": human rights and the politics of fatalism', *South Atlantic Quarterly*, 103/2–3 (2004), pp. 451–63.
4. N. Guilhot, *The Democracy Makers: Human Rights and the Politics of Global Order*, Columbia University Press, Chichester, 2005, p. 8.
5. H. Arendt, *The Origins of Totalitarianism*, new edition, Harcourt Brace, Orlando, 1958, p.302.
6. D. McAdam, 'Conceptual origins, current problems and future directions', in D. McAdam, J.D. McCarthy, and M.N. Zald (eds) *Comparative Perspectives on Social Movements: Political Opportunities, Mobilizing Structures, and Cultural Framings*, Cambridge University Press, Cambridge, 1996, pp. 23–40.
7. For a critique of civil society and democratisation theory, and an explanation of stable autocracy, please see F. Cavatorta (ed.), *Civil Society Activism under Authoritarian Rule: A Comparative Perspective*, Routledge, Oxford, 2013.
8. F.S. Hasso, 'Sectarian/gendered police and rupture in Bahrain's Pearl Revolution', in F.S. Hasso and Z. Salime (eds), *Borders, Bodies, and Intimate Politics in the Arab Revolutions.* (forthcoming).
9. Campaign Against the Arms Trade, 'Saudi Arabia uses UK-made armoured vehicles in Bahrain crackdown on democracy protestors', 16 March 2011, www.caat.org.uk/media/press-releases/2011-03-16
10. Bahrain Center for Human Rights, 'Individuals killed by government's excessive use of force since 14 February 2011', 22 May 2014, www.bahrainrights.org/en/node/3864
11. T. Risse and K. Sikkink, 'The socialization of international human rights norms into domestic practices', in T. Risse, S. Ropp, and K. Sikkink (eds) *The Power of Human Rights: International Norms and Domestic Politics*, Cambridge University Press, Cambridge, 1999, pp. 1–38.
12. Note that whilst we acknowledge the concept of 'transnational advocacy networks', we feel that there are issues with Snow *et al.*'s concept of 'framing'. For the concept of 'framing', see D. Snow, E.B. Rochford Jr, S.K. Worden, and R.D. Benford, 'Frame alignment processes, micromobilization and movement participation', *American Sociological Review*, 51 (1986), pp. 456–81; D.A. Snow and R.D. Benford, 'Ideology,

frame resonance, and participant mobilisation', in B. Klandermans, H. Kriesi, and S. Tarrow (eds) *From Structure to Action: Social Movements Participation Across Cultures*, JAI Press, Greenwich, CT, 1988, pp. 197–217. For a critique of the concept of framing, see M.W. Steinberg, 'Tilting the frame: considerations on collective action framing from a discursive turn', *Theory and Society*, 27/6 (1998), pp. 845–72; J.M. Jasper, *The Art of Moral Protest: Culture, Biography, and Creativity in Social Movements*, University of Chicago Press, Chicago, 1997, Ch. 4.

13. L.S.G. Bhatia and A. Shehabi, Unpublished interview with Nabeel Rajab [audio recording], 12 August 2014, London.

14. WikiLeaks cable, 22 May 2006, https://wikileaks.org/cable/2006/05/06 MANAMA891.html

15. Human Rights Watch, '"Interfere, restrict, control": restraints on freedom of association in Bahrain', June 2013, www.hrw.org/sites/default/files/reports/bahrain0613webwcover.pdf

16. F. Ragazzi, 'Governing diasporas', *International Political Sociology*, 3 (2009), p. 386.

17. 'Administration report of the Bahrain Agency for the year 1955', in *Persian Gulf Administration Reports 1873–1957*, Cambridge Archive Editions, Cambridge University Press, Cambridge, 1989, p. 390.

18. N. Fuccaro, *Histories of City and State in the Persian Gulf*, Cambridge University Press, Cambridge, 2009, p. 158.

19. 'Graffiti and anonymous notices started to appear on the walls of Manama. One of their favourite targets was the Bahraini court, the highest judicial authority in the country, which they considered the symbol of Bahrain's flawed legal system under Belgrave, the British advisor to the ruler, and the Al Khalifa. Leaflets circulated inciting popular militancy against the government. They ordered the 'noble Arab nation' to go on strike and to boycott cinemas and modern amenities in order to devote its energy to the struggle against the corruption of the government and the despotism of the advisor.' Fuccaro, *Histories of City and State*, p. 175.

20. Fuccaro, *Histories of City and State*, p. 176.

21. The National Union Committee (NUC) can be read similarly as the Higher Executive Committee (HEC).

22. C. Belgrave, *Personal Column*, Hutchinson, London, 1960, p. 239.

23. The NUC established the Co-operative Compensation Fund, an insurance scheme for local taxi drivers. Previously British companies held a monopoly over insurance in Bahrain.

24. A. Khalaf, 'Labor movements in Bahrain', *Middle East Report*, 132 (1985), pp. 24–9.

25. A. Khalaf, 'Contentious politics in Bahrain: from ethnic to national and vice versa', Paper to the Fourth Nordic Conference on Middle Eastern

Studies: The Middle East in a Globalizing World, 13–16 August 1998, Oslo, http://org.uib.no/smi/pao/khalaf.html

26. O. AlShehabi, 'Divide and rule in Bahrain and the elusive pursuit for a united front: the experience of the constitutive committee and the 1972 uprising', *Historical Materialism*, 21/1 (2013), pp. 94–127.

27. Khalaf, 'Labor movements in Bahrain'.

28. The National Archives, 'Annual review of Bahrain affairs, 1965', in Political Agent Bahrain to Political Resident Bahrain, 2 January 1966, FO 371/185327 PRO.

29. AlShehabi, 'Divide and rule', p. 121.

30. The National Archives, 'Bahrain review', 1980, FCO 08/3894.

31. M.O. Jones, 'Bahrain's prime minister and his role in the anti-Shia crackdown of the 1980s', *Marc Owen Jones* [blog], 8 April 2013, http://marcowenjones.wordpress.com/2013/04/08/bahrains-prime-minister-and-his-role-in-the-anti-shia-crackdown-of-the-1980s/

32. The National Archives, 'Bahrain review', 1980, FCO 08/3894, pp. 612–13.

33. L. Louër, 'Sectarianism and coup-proofing strategies in Bahrain', *Journal of Strategic Studies*, 36/2 (2013), p. 247.

34. Excerpt from the petition: 'We are facing crises with dwindling opportunities and exits, the ever-worsening unemployment situation, the mounting inflation, the losses to the business sector, the problems generated by the nationality (citizenship) decrees and the prevention of many of our children from returning to their homeland. In addition, there are the laws which were enacted during the absence of the parliament which restrict the freedom of citizens and contradict the Constitution. This was accompanied by lack of freedom of expression and opinion and the total subordination of the press to the executive power. These problems, your Highness, have forced us as citizens to demand the restoration of the National Assembly, and the involvement of women in the democratic process'.

35. A. Khalaf, 'Contentious politics in Bahrain'.

36. *The Telegraph*, 'Ian Henderson – Obituary', 22 April 2013, www.telegraph.co.uk/news/obituaries/10011292/Ian-Henderson.html

37. Amnesty International reported that, 'violations included the arbitrary arrest and prolonged administrative and incommunicado detention without charge or trial of suspected political opponents; the torture and ill-treatment of detainees, particularly during pre-trial detention, in order to extract "confessions"; grossly unfair trials before the State Security Court; and the forcible exile from the country of Bahraini nationals'. Amnesty International, 'Bahrain: a human rights crisis', 1995, www.amnesty.org/en/library/asset/MDE11/016/1995/en/915a01e3-eb32-11dd-92ac-295bdf97101f/mde110161995en.html

38. Human Rights Watch, 'Routine abuse, routine denial: civil rights and the political crisis in Bahrain', June 1997, http://pantheon.hrw.org/reports/1997/bahrain/

39. Bhatia and Shehabi, Unpublished interview: Nabeel Rajab.

40. *The Telegraph*, 'New human rights NGO aligned with government', 18 February 2011, www.telegraph.co.uk/news/wikileaks-files/bahrain-wikileaks-cables/8334631/NEW-HUMAN-RIGHTS-NGO-ALIGNED-WITH-GOVERNMENT.html

41. WikiLeaks, 'Migrant workers' rights NGO approved by GOB', 2005, www.wikileaks.ch/cable/2005/01/05MANAMA15.html

42. Bhatia and Shehabi, Unpublished interview: Nabeel Rajab.

43. Ibid.

44. Bahrain Human Rights Society (BHRS): www.bhrs.org; Bahrain Center for Human Rights (BCHR): www.bahrainrights.org; Bahrain Human Rights Forum (BHRF): www.bfhr.org; European Bahrain Organisation for Human Rights (EBOHR): www.ebohr.org; Bahrain Institute for Rights and Democracy (BIRD): www.birdbh.org; Americans for Democracy and Human Rights in Bahrain (ADHRB): www.adhrb.org; Bahrain Watch: www.bahrainwatch.org; Bahrain Justice and Development Movement (BJDM): www.bahrainjdm.org; Bahrain Salam for Human Rights: www.bahrainsalam.org.

45. Brown, 'The most we can hope for', p. 453.

46. S. Moyn, *The Last Utopia: Human Rights in History*, Belknap, London, 2010, p. 146.

47. For a Human Rights Watch interview with Dr. Nada Dhaif, a dentist initially sentenced to fifteen years in prison but acquitted on appeal, describing how she became and 'accidental activist', go here: Human Rights Watch, 'Bahrain: Nada Dhaif, accidental activist', 2012, www.hrw.org/audio/2012/04/13/bahrain-nada-dhaif-accidental-activist

48. The Commission was asked to determine whether the events of February and March 2011 (and thereafter) involved violations of international human rights law and norms, and to make the recommendations that it deemed appropriate. M.C. Bassiouni *et al.*, 'Report of the Bahrain Independent Commission of Inquiry' [BICI Report], 23 November 2011, BICI, Manama, www.bici.org.bh/BICIreportEN.pdf

49. M. Keck and K. Sikkink, *Activists Beyond Borders: Advocacy Networks in International Politics*, Cornell University Press, Ithaca, 1998, p. 1.

50. 'Implementation of the Bahrain Independent Commission of Inquiry Report', Hearing before the Tom Lantos Human Rights Commission, House of Representatives, 112th Congress, Second Session, 1 August 2012, http://tlhrc.house.gov/docs/transcripts/2012_08_01_Bahrain/08_01_12_Bahrain.pdf

51. Bhatia and Shehabi, Unpublished interview: Nabeel Rajab.

52. Ibid.
53. Awards include: The Rafto Prize, 2013; The Stieg Larsson Prize, 2012; The Baldwin Medal of Liberty, 2012; The Martin Ennals Award, Final Nominee, 2012; The Index on Censorship Advocacy Award, 2012; The Silbury Prize, 2011; Ion Ratiu Democracy Award, 2011.
54. WikiLeaks, 'A field guide to Bahraini political parties', 4 September 2008, https://wikileaks.org/plusd/cables/08MANAMA592_a.html
55. Manama Document, 'Bahrain's road to freedom and democracy: a joint document by opposition political societies', 12 October 2011, http://alwefaq.net/cms/2011/10/12/5934/
56. *The Guardian*, 'Bahrain opposition leader Ali Salman sentenced to four years in jail', 16 June 2015, www.theguardian.com/world/2015/jun/16/bahrain-opposition-leader-ali-salman-sentenced-to-four-years-in-jail
57. These groups included: The February 14 Youth, The February 14 Media Centre, The February 14 Liberals, The February 14 Scholars, The February 14 Martyrs, The Youth of Martyrs' Square.
58. February 14 Youth Coalition, 'Pearl Charter', 2011, https://docs.google.com/file/d/0B4hFNWHWtbDGZGQyODM2N2MtMGM2ZC00NmJjL WE3MWQtMDQyZTNkMDk3YWYy/edit
59. T.C. Jones, 'Bahrain's revolutionaries speak: an exclusive interview with Bahrain's Coalition of February 14th Youth', *Jadaliyya*, 22 March 2012, www.jadaliyya.com/pages/index/4777/bahrains-revolutionaries-speak_an-exclusive-interv
60. Ibid.
61. Bassiouni *et al.*, 'Report of the BICI', pp. 115–16.
62. S. Heydemann, 'Upgrading authoritarianism in the Arab world', Analysis Paper 13, The Saban Center for Middle East Policy at The Brookings Institution, October 2007.
63. Daniel Brumberg, 'Transforming the Arab world's protection-racket politics', *Journal of Democracy*, 24/3 (2013), pp. 88–103.
64. Heydemann, 'Upgrading authoritarianism'.
65. Louër, 'Sectarianism and coup-proofing'.
66. R. Spencer, 'Philip Hammond praises improvements in Bahrain's human rights records', *The Telegraph*, 20 January 2015, http://www.telegraph.co.uk/news/worldnews/middleeast/bahrain/11358765/Philip-Hammond-praises-improvements-in-Bahrains-human-rights-record.html
67. 'Bassiouni: new Arab court for human rights is fake "Potemkin tribunal"', International Bar Association, 1 October 2014, www.ibanet.org/Article/Detail.aspx?ArticleUid=c64f9646-15a5-4624-8c07-bae9d9ac42df
68. Human Rights Watch, 'Proposed Arab court of Human Rights: an empty vessel without substantial changes to the draft statute', 6 June 2014, www.

hrw.org/news/2014/06/06/proposed-arab-court-human-rights-empty-
vessel-without-substantial-changes-draft-stat

69. This dilemma of distinguishing between the public and private spheres
    is noted in K. Mikirova, K. Mueller, and J. Schuhmann, 'The influence
    of civil society activism on regional governance structures in the Russian
    Federation: cross regional and policy comparisons', in F. Cavatorta
    (ed.), *Civil Society Activism under Authoritarian Rule: A Comparative
    Perspective*, Routledge, Oxford, 2013, pp. 111–34. In their analysis of the
    influence of civil society activism on regional governance structures in
    Russia, they show that what constitutes 'genuine civil society' is at times
    difficult to ascertain in a context where independent actors co-exist with
    state sponsored actors in a shared public sphere.

70. Bahrain: Written Question – 220679, Ann Clywd to the Secretary of
    State, Foreign and Commonwealth Office, 14 January 2015, www.they-
    workforyou.com/wrans/?id=2015-01-14.220679.h&s=Bahrain

71. E. Posner, 'The case against human rights', *The Guardian*, 4 December 2014,
    www.theguardian.com/news/2014/dec/04/-sp-case-against-human-rights

72. B. Gregg, 'State-based human rights', Paper presented at the annual
    meeting of the Midwest Political Science Association, Palmer House
    Hotel, Chicago, 12 April 2007, p. 2.

73. Brown, 'The most we can hope for', p. 460.

74. A. Bayat, 'Revolution and despair', *Mada Masr*, 25 January 2015, www.
    madamasr.com/opinion/revolution-and-despair

75. Ibid.

76. Bahrain: Written Question.

77. Posner, 'The case against human rights'.

78. Declaration of the Tunis Conference Concerning Democratic Freedoms
    in the Arab World, supra note 1, cited in J. Crystal, 'Human rights in the
    Arab world', *Human Rights Quarterly*, 16/3 (1994), pp. 435–54.

## CHAPTER 5

1. This was first published on *Ibraaz*; it has been reproduced here
   with permission, and with very minor edits made for style consistency.
   A.Khalaf, 'The many afterlives of Lulu: the story of Bahrain's Pearl
   Roundabout', *Ibraaz*, 28 February 2013, www.ibraaz.org/essays/56

2. R. Musil, *Monuments, Posthumous Papers of a Living Author,* trans.
   P. Worsman, Eridanos Press, Boston, 1987, p. 61.

3. S. Khalaf, 'Poetics and politics of newly invented traditions in the Gulf:
   camel racing in the United Arab Emirates', *Ethnology*, 39/3 (2000),
   p. 243.

4. See Bahrain's aptly named website: http://staging.bahrain.com/home.aspx

5. See Sheyma Buali's series of photographs in 'Gulf ads on black cabs', *Visual Urban Cultural* [blog], 10 June 2010, http://humanette.blogspot. co.uk/2010/06/gulf-ads-on-black-cabs.html

6. See: A. Khalaf, 'The Many Afterlives of Lulu: The Story of Bahrain's Pearl Roundabout', 28 February 2013, http://www.ibraaz.org/essays/56#_ftn5

7. *USA Today*, 'The freest economy in the Middle East', United World supplement, 2 July 2008, www.unitedworld-usa.com/pdf/bahrain.pdf

8. For a brief history of political struggle in Bahrain see: O. Al-Shehabi, 'Political movements in Bahrain: past, present and future', *Jadaliyya*, 14 February 2012, www.jadaliyya.com/pages/index/4363/political-movements-in-bahrain_past-present-and-fu; and A. Khalaf, 'Contentious politics in Bahrain: from ethnic to national and vice versa', Paper to the Fourth Nordic Conference on Middle Eastern Studies: The Middle East in a Globalizing World, 13–16 August 1998, Oslo, http://org.uib.no/smi/pao/ khalaf.html

9. For the latest list of banned books in Bahrain, see N. Mohan, 'Banned books from Bahrain', *Sampsonia Way*, 6 June 2012, www.sampsoniaway. org/blog/2012/06/06/banned-books-from-bahrain/

10. For information on significant banned books, such as the diaries of Charles Belgrave, British advisor to the Bahraini ruling family (1926–1957), considered one of the most significant historical collections documenting a major stage in the history of Bahrain, and the Bahraini government-funded study by anthropologist Fuad I. Khuri, see Bahrain Center for Human Rights, 'Banning one of the most significant historic books in the history of Bahrain', 25 May 2010, www.bahrainrights.org/en/node/3105 and F. Khuri, *Tribe and State in Bahrain: The Transition of Social and Political Authority in an Arab State*, University of Chicago Press, Chicago, 1981.

11. On 30 October, Bahrain's government placed a blanket ban on all protests and gatherings. See I. Black, 'Bahrain bans all opposition rallies', *The Guardian*, 30 October 2012, www.guardian.co.uk/world/2012/oct/30/ bahrain-opposition-protests-ban

12. For more on privatisation and prestige projects, see 'Bahrain's flashy crony capitalism cannot last', *The Guardian*, 20 May 2012, www. theguardian.com/commentisfree/2012/may/20/bahrain-flashy-crony-capitalism, and Jones, M.O., 'Sexing up a city: neoliberalism, public space and protest in Bahrain', *Marc Owen Jones* [blog], 4 March 2011, www.marcowenjones.hostbyet2.com/?p=107

13. T. Reisz, 'Bahrain: a roundabout way to signify nothing', *World Post*, 4 May 2011, www.huffingtonpost.com/todd-reisz/bahrain-roundabout_ b_844276.html

14. Tahrir Square, or Midan Tahrir, is also a roundabout, but one with a long history of protest and one seen as a symbol of liberation, and in a part of

the city with a pedestrian culture. For more information, see N. Al Sayyad, 'Cairo's roundabout revolution', *New York Times*, 13 April 2011, www.nytimes.com/2011/04/14/opinion/14alsayyad.html?pagewanted=all&_r=0

15. The demonstration was held to mark the tenth anniversary of the National Action Charter.

16. Jane Kinninmont writes: 'People of various religious and political persuasions attended the first rally, held in the largest mosque in Bahrain. The mosque is Sunni and the term "Al Fateh" – the Conqueror – is a reference to the first Al Khalifa ruler of Bahrain. TGONU reportedly includes Shia, Christian and Jewish members, though probably very few'. J. Kinninmont, *Bahrain: Beyond the Impasse,* Chatham House, London, 2012, p. 8.

17. See Al Jazeera, '"Mass sackings" in Bahrain crackdown', 14 May 2011, http://english.aljazeera.net/news/middleeast/2011/05/2011514104251715508.html, and *The Guardian*, 'Bahrain oil company fires almost 300 over anti-government protests', 11 May 2011, www.guardian.co.uk/world/2011/may/11/bahrain-oil-company-fires-300-protests

18. YouTube, 'Scenes the world has never seen about the destruction of Lulu' [online video], 16 July 2011, https://www.youtube.com/watch?v=jpzrH-Tcxaw&feature=youtu.be

19. A reference to ʿUmar ibn al-Khattab, a historical figure and one of the most powerful caliphs in Islamic history, and a figure remembered differently among various Islamic sects. Viewed negatively in Shiʿa literature, the naming of the junction as 'Al Farooq' is seen as a sectarian dig at the largely Shiʿa population.

20. For more information about the February 14 Youth Coalition, see T.C. Jones, 'Bahrain's revolutionaries speak: an exclusive interview with Bahrain's Coalition of February 14th Youth', *Jadaliyya*, 22 March 2012, www.jadaliyya.com/pages/index/4777/bahrains-revolutionaries-speak_an-exclusive-interv

21. '[W]e will see industrial production of a personality split, an instantaneous cloning of living man, the technological recreation of our most ancient myths: the myth of the double, of an electroergonomic double whose presence is spectral - another way of saying a ghost or the living dead.' P. Virilio, *Open Sky*, Verso, New York, 1997, p. 40.

22. Reference via Sophia Al Maria.

23. Zawya, 'Rise of Arab social media', 24 July 2012, www.zawya.com/story/Rise_of_Arab_social_media-ZAWYA20120724051637// [link removed].

24. S. Kelly, S. Cook and M. Truong (eds), *Freedom on The Net 2012: A Global Assessment of Internet and Digital Media*, Freedom House, New York, 2012, p. 66.

25. Ibid.

26. The Bahraini government was reported as having spent more than $32 million in PR fees since February 2011. For more information, see Bahrain Watch, 'Bahrain government hires 18 Western companies to improve image after unrest', 23 August 2012, https://bahrainwatch.org/press/press-release-8.php

27. Foucault, M., 'Nietzsche, Genealogy, History', in D. Bouchard (ed.), *Language, Counter Memory, Practice: Selected Essays and Interviews*, Cornell University Press, New York, 1977.

28. R. Barthes, *Camera Lucida: Reflections on Photography*, Hill and Wang, New York, 1982, p. 91.

29. YouTube, 'We Will Back To Pearl Roundabout – Imaginary 3D Scene' [online video], 4 September 2011, https://www.youtube.com/watch?v=2xXc0pHIRnM&list=PL12772150445D19C2

30. YouTube, 'Children of Bahrain and there memories' [online video], 19 September 2011, https://www.youtube.com/watch?v=qy0Onzvxu7U&list=PLTOgz3bT-TwV7tg-KYDDJFYFR1DkDmler

31. YouTube 'Mercenaries destroy statue of Lulu in the village of A'ali' [online video], 1 June 2011, https://www.youtube.com/watch?v=Fjsf6HuH91Q&list=PLTOgz3bT-TwV7tg-KYDDJFYFR1DkDmler&index=45&feature=plpp video

32. For more information on this kind of resistance, see Jones, M.O., 'Creative resistance in Bahrain', *Marc Owen Jones* [blog], 19 January 2012, www.marcowenjones.hostbyet2.com/?p=512#comment-2356

33. YouTube, 'Lulu Roundabout' [online video], 10 March 2012.

34. YouTube, 'Bahrain Shield: Clear pictures of Bahrain's "Mut'a Roundabout" published for the first time' [online video], 7 June 2011, https://www.youtube.com/watch?v=A1h5LZzcd9l&list=PLTOgz3bT-TwV7tg-KYDDJFYFR1DkDmler&index=14&feature=plpp video

35. For more information on mut'a marriage, see V.J. Cornell and V. G. Henry-Blakemore (eds.), *Voices of Islam Volume III: Voices of Life: Family, Home and Society*, Praeger Publishers, Westport, 2007, pp. 66–68.

36. For more on this homophobia, read E. Kilbride, '"Too gay to represent #Bahrain": homophobia and nationalism in the wake of a revolution', *Muftah*, 15 December 2012, http://muftah.org/homophobia-and-nationalism-in-bahrain/

37. YouTube, 'Bahrain Revolution: Return to the Martyrs' Square' [online video], 23 January 2012, https://www.youtube.com/watch?v=BFqaMDoovJE

38. J. Baudrillard, *The Conspiracy of Art*, Semiotext(e)/MIT Press, New York, 2005, p. 207.

CHAPTER 6

1. C. Belgrave cited in M.O. Jones, 'Methods of a mild Spanish Inquisition: British torture in Bahrain before Ian Henderson', *Marc Owen Jones* [blog], 29 May 2013, https://marcowenjones.wordpress.com/2013/05/29/methods-of-a-mild-spanish-inquisition-british-torture-in-bahrain-before-ian-henderson/

2. This broadcast is available online: www.youtube.com/watch?v=koDTy7qBJtc

3. M. Tran, 'Bahrain accuses human rights leader of faking pictures of beating', *The Guardian*, 11 April 2011, www.theguardian.com/world/2011/apr/11/bahrain-human-rights-activist-accused

4. The video of the encounter can be viewed here: www.youtube.com/watch?v=3jBqUMYto90 A graphic video showing Saqr's injuries is online here: http://youtu.be/Xjixs_02QHc

5. F. Gardner, 'Bahrain's security clampdown divides kingdom', BBC News, 14 April 2011, www.bbc.co.uk/news/world-middle-east-13088600

6. Human Rights Watch, 'Criminalizing dissent, entrenching impunity: persistent failures of the Bahraini justice system since the BICI Report', May 2014, p. 48, www.hrw.org/sites/default/files/reports/bahrain0514_forUpload.pdf

7. Bahrain state media fabricated a lot of news from 2011 onwards. This included reported false statements purportedly made by senior international figures and organisations. For more, see the Bahrain Watch project 'Fabri-Gate': https://bahrainwatch.org/media/

8. See, for example, United Nations, 'Report of the Special Rapporteur, Mr. Nigel S. Rodley, submitted pursuant to Commission on Human Rights resolution 1995/37 B', E/CN.4/1997/7, 1997; Human Rights Watch, 'Torture redux: the revival of physical coercion during interrogations in Bahrain', 2010, www.hrw.org/sites/default/files/reports/bahrain0210webwcover_0.pdf;

   M.C. Bassiouni *et al.*, 'Report of the Bahrain Independent Commission of Inquiry' [BICI Report], 23 November 2011, BICI, Manama, www.bici.org.bh/BICIreportEN.pdf;

   REDRESS and IRCT, 'Bahrain: Fundamental Reform or Torture Without End?', April 2013, www.redress.org/downloads/country-reports/Fundamentalreform.pdf

9. T. Blom Hansen and F. Stepputat, *Sovereign Bodies: Citizens, Migrants, and States in the Postcolonial World*, Princeton University Press, Princeton, 2009, p. 11.

10. We have yet to see how far the police complaint against Nasser bin Hamad, son of the King, will go in the UK.

11. E. Said, *Covering Islam: How the Media and the Experts Determine How We See the Rest of the World*, Routledge & Kegan Paul, London (original English typescript), 1981, cited in L. Khatib, *Filming the Modern Middle East: Politics in the Cinemas of Hollywood and the Arab World*, I.B. Tauris, London, 2006, p. 7.

12. In this chapter, 'Western observer' refers to the consumers of most mainstream, English-speaking media.

13. For more on this, see A. Khalaf, 'The many afterlives of Lulu: the story of Bahrain's Pearl Roundabout', *Ibraaz*, 28 February 2013, www.ibraaz.org/essays/56;
Jones, M.O., 'Satire, social media and revolutionary cultural production in the Bahrain Uprising' [online video], 2014, http://youtu.be/D8EC6EgiaAE

14. The film can be viewed here: www.youtube.com/watch?v=ZPW1FgcttaU. It was uploaded on 13 February 2012, with the Arabic title: 'Film yasqut Hamad 2012 tin tin tytin' ('Hamad did not fall, 2012 Tn Tn Ttn'). Two days later, another account uploaded it with the English title 'Bahrain Tin Tin Tytin Movie 2012' (www.youtube.com/watch?v=YC1jIqJuedI).

15. M. Alhassen and A. Shihab-Eldin, *Demanding Dignity: Young Voices from the Front Lines of the Arab Revolutions*, White Cloud Press, Oregon, 2012, p. 247.

16. M. Lynch, 'Obama's "Arab Spring"?', *Foreign Policy*, 6 January 2011, http://lynch.foreignpolicy.com/posts/2011/01/06/obamas_arab_spring

17. For example, J. Jacoby, 'The Arab Spring', *Boston Globe*, 10 March 2005, www.boston.com/news/globe/editorial_opinion/oped/articles/2005/03/10/the_arab_spring/; C. Krauthammer, 'Three Cheers for the Bush Doctrine', *Time*, 7 March 2005, www.time.com/time/magazine/article/0,9171,1034732,00.html

18. R. Khouri, 'Arab Spring or revolution', *The Globe and Mail*, 18 August 2011, www.theglobeandmail.com/globe-debate/arab-spring-or-revolution/article626345/. Several authors have argued that the coverage of the uprisings carried forward Orientalist framings; for example, P. Jahshan, 'The 2011 Arab uprisings and the persistence of orientalism', *The Arab World Geographer*, 14/2 (2011), pp. 122–27; R. El-Mahdi, 'Orientalising the Egyptian Uprising', *Jadaliyya*, 11 April 2011, www.jadaliyya.com/pages/index/1214/orientalising-the-egyptian-uprising; M. Esseghaier, '"Tweeting out a tyrant": social media and the Tunisian Revolution', *Wi: Journal of Mobile Media*, 7/1 (2012), http://wi.mobilities.ca/tweeting-out-a-tyrant-social-media-and-the-tunisian-revolution/

19. Khouri, 'Arab Spring or revolution'.

20. S. Buali, 'Digital, aesthetic, ephemeral: the shifting narrative of uprising', *Ibraaz*, 2 November 2012, www.ibraaz.org/essays/48

21. E. Buckner and L. Khatib, 'The martyrs' revolutions: the role of martyrs in the Arab Spring', *British Journal of Middle Eastern Studies*, No. 0 (3 June 2014): 1, doi:10.1080/13530194.2014.918802

22. L. Khatib, *Image Politics in the Middle East: The Role of the Visual in Political Struggle*, I.B. Tauris, London, 2013, pp. 117–67.

23. S. Aday, *et al.*, 'Watching from afar: media consumption patterns around the Arab Spring', *American Behavioral Scientist*, 20/10, p. 1.

24. D. Kellner, *Media Spectacle and Insurrection, 2011: From the Arab Uprisings to Occupy Everywhere*, Bloomsbury, New York, 2012, p. viii.

25. G. Debord, *Society of the Spectacle,* trans. K Knabb, Rebel Press, London, 2000, p. 7.

26. D. Kellner, *Media Spectacle*, p. xvii.

27. Khatib suggests a distinction between spectacle as deployed by states and spectacle used 'as a form of critique' by 'opposing political actors' (*Image Politics*, p. 117).

28. G. Debord, *Comments on the Society of the Spectacle*, trans. M Imrie, Verso, London, 1998, p. 19.

29. J. Baudrillard, *The Gulf War Did Not Take Place*, trans. P Patton, Indiana University Press, Bloomington, 1995.

30. S. Kember and J. Zylinksa, *Life after New Media: Mediation as a Vital Process*, MIT Press, Cambridge, MA, 2012.

31. This is even true of the supportive documentary *We Are The Giant* (2014), which devotes around half of its running time to the current uprising in Bahrain, yet fails to locate it historically.

32. G. Debord, *Society of the Spectacle*, p. 13.

33. A. Hashem, 'The Arab spring has shaken Arab TV's credibility', *The Guardian*, 3 April 2012, www.theguardian.com/commentisfree/2012/apr/03/arab-spring-arab-tv-credibility

34. A. Hashem, 'The Bahrain Blackout in Arab Media', *Al-Monitor*, 13 January 2013, www.al-monitor.com/pulse/iw/originals/2013/01/bahrain-arab-spring-protests.html

35. L. Andoni, 'Bahrain's contribution to the Arab Spring', Al Jazeera English, 30 August 2011, www.aljazeera.com/indepth/opinion/2011/08/2011830147330 1296.html

36. See Media Watch project on www.bahrainwatch.org

37. J. Butler, *Frames of War: When Is Life Grievable?*, Verso, London, 2010, p. 73.

38. Ibid., p. xiii.

39. B. Quinn, 'Bahrain to sue newspaper over articles', *The Guardian*, 15 June 2011.

40. Artist Andrew Brück, for instance, was hired by British PR firm M&C Saatchi to help design the 'Business Friendly Bahrain' brand. A selection

of his work is online here: http://andrewbruck.com/Branding-a-country-Business-Friendly-Bahrain

41. White House, 'President Bush arrives in Bahrain', 12 January 2008, http://georgewbush-whitehouse.archives.gov/news/releases/2008/01/20080112-5.html; *Gulf News*, 'Reforms made Bahrain beacon of democracy', 8 January 2003, http://gulfnews.com/news/uae/general/reforms-made-bahrain-beacon-of-democracy-1.344082

42. Freedom House, 'Freedom of the Press 2013: Bahrain', 2013, www.freedomhouse.org/report/freedom-press/2013/bahrain

43. BBC News, 'Bahrain unrest: eight Shia activists sentenced to life', 22 June 2011, www.bbc.co.uk/news/world-middle-east-13872206

44. See Bahrain Watch's project 'Access Denied': https://bahrainwatch.org/access/. *Passim.*

45. CBS News, 'Bahrain clashes: "Riot police showed no mercy"', 17 March 2011, www.cbsnews.com/news/bahrain-clashes-riot-police-showed-no-mercy/

46. Journalist Bill Law discusses the problems in the BBC documentary that resulted, *Bahrain: Policing Protest.*

47. G. Greenwald, 'Why didn't CNN's international arm air its own documentary on Bahrain's Arab Spring repression?', *The Guardian*, 4 September 2012, www.theguardian.com/world/2012/sep/04/cnn-international-documentary-bahrain-arab-spring-repression

48. Press Complaints Commission, 14 December 2012, http://www.pcc.org.uk/case/resolved.html?article=NzU0MQ==

49. M. Cassel, 'Suppressing the narrative in Bahrain', Al Jazeera English, 16 February 2012, www.aljazeera.com/indepth/features/2012/02/201229153055296176.html

50. See Bahrain Watch's project 'PR Watch': https://bahrainwatch.org/pr/. *Passim.*

51. The websites are http://explorebahrain.org and http://bahrainstories.com respectively.

52. A. Shehabi, 'Bahrain's flashy crony capitalism cannot last', *The Guardian*, 20 May 2012, www.theguardian.com/commentisfree/2012/may/20/bahrain-flashy-crony-capitalism

53. The 2013 REDRESS and IRCT joint report on torture in Bahrain notes that there has been a failure to address 'past violations or the wider structural factors which enable [torture]'. The 'wider structural factors' enabling torture to persist to the present stretch beyond Bahrain's borders and towards the Western states which provide political support and diplomatic cover instead of sanctioning or condemning the regime, in the way it does for Russia or China, for example.

54. M.C. Bassiouni *et al.*, 'Report of the Bahrain Independent Commission of Inquiry' [BICI Report], 23 November 2011, BICI, Manama, p. 417, www.bici.org.bh/BICIreportEN.pdf

55. P. Weaver, 'Bahrain unable to guarantee safety for Formula One says former Met officer', *The Guardian*, 18 April 2012, www.theguardian.com/world/2012/apr/18/bahrain-formula-one-yates-safety

56. E. Scarry, *The Body in Pain: The Making and Unmaking of the World*, Oxford University Press, New York, 1985, p. 36.

57. J. Horne, 'Who provides the Ministry of Interior with CCTV?', Bahrain Watch, 26 August 2013, https://bahrainwatch.org/blog/2013/08/26/who-provides-the-ministry-of-interior-with-cctv/

58. N. Zahra, 'Confession leak officer spared jail', *Gulf Daily News*, 27 June 2014, www.gulf-daily-news.com/NewsDetails.aspx?storyid=379886

59. S. Sontag, *Regarding the Pain of Others*, Penguin, London, 2003.

60. Butler, *Frames of War*, p. xiv.

61. Buckner and Khatib, 'The martyrs' revolutions', p. 369 and p. 384.

62. For example: L. Chouliaraki, *The Spectatorship of Suffering*, SAGE, London, 2006; Sontag, *Regarding the Pain of Others*.

63. *Détournement* is a strategy developed by Guy Debord to challenge the spectacle by appropriating its own elements.

64. Khalaf, 'Many afterlives'.

65. Versions of this chapter were presented at 'New Media, New Politics?: (post-)Revolutions in Theory and Practice?' (University of Westminster, 26 April 2013) and 'Media Politics, Political Media' (Charles University, Prague, 20–22 June 2013). I am particularly grateful to the editors of this volume, as well as to Michele Aaron and Dima Saber, for their invaluable comments on this chapter.

CHAPTER 7

1. M. Abdulla al-Tajir, *Bahrain, 1920–1945: Britain, the Shaikh, and the Administration*, Routledge, London, 1987, pp. 4–5.

2. M. Burke, 'Philip Hammond: UK military base in Bahrain to "tackle the security threats"', *The Telegraph*, 6 December 2014, www.telegraph.co.uk/news/worldnews/middleeast/bahrain/11277304/Philip-Hammond-UK-military-base-in-Bahrain-to-tackle-the-security-threats.html

3. British Embassy Manama, 'British Embassy in Bahrain launches Great British Week', Gov.uk, 6 November 2013, www.gov.uk/government/world-location-news/british-embassy-in-bahrain-launches-great-british-week-2014

4. H. Al-Baharna, *Legal Status of the Arabian Gulf States: A Study of Their Treaty Relations and Their International Problems*, Manchester University Press, Manchester, 1968, p. 32.

5. Foreign Affairs Committee, 'Bilateral relations with Bahrain', in *The UK's Relations with Saudi Arabia and Bahrain* (HC 2013-14, 88),

Ch. 4, www.publications.parliament.uk/pa/cm201314/cmselect/cmfaff/88/8808.htm

6. C. Beaugrand, 'The Return of the Bahraini Exiles (2001–2006)', Mapping Middle Eastern and North African Diasporas, BRISMES Annual Conference, Leeds, UK, July 2008.

7. HC Deb 17 Feb 2011, Col. 1140W.

8. Ibid., Col. 1136W.

9. Al-Baharna, *Legal Status*, p. 30.

10. Others: 'the British government has the right to intervene in cases of piracy and acts of aggression committed by or against Bahrainis at sea'; 'the British government must permit Bahrainis to visit and trade in ports in India'. Cited in J. Onley, *The Arabian Frontier of the British Raj. Merchants, Rulers and British in the Nineteenth-Century Gulf*, Oxford University Press, Oxford, 2007, p. 282

11. G. Nash, *From Empire to Orient: Travellers to the Middle East 1830–1924*, I.B. Tauris, London, 2005, p. 131.

12. M.O. Jones, 'The history of British Involvement in Bahrain's internal security', openDemocracy, 8 August 2013, www.opendemocracy.net/opensecurity/marc-owen-jones/history-of-british-involvement-in-bahrains-internal-security

13. G. N. Curzon, *Lord Curzon in India: Being a Selection from his Speeches as Viceroy & Governor-General of India, 1898–1905*, MacMillan, London, 1906.

14. HL Deb 15 May 1903, cited in Sir A.W. Ward and G.P. Gooch, *The Cambridge History of British Foreign Policy 1783–1919: Vol. 1, 1783–1815*, Cambridge University Press, Cambridge, 1922, pp. 320–21.

15. Cited in Al-Tajir, *Bahrain 1920–1945*, p. 30.

16. For more information on these abuses, please see Marc Owen Jones's blog: 'Oppression of Bahrain subjects by the ruling family in Bahrain in the early 1900s: the full list', *Marc Owen Jones* [blog], 31 December 2012, http://marcowenjones.wordpress.com/2012/12/31/oppression-of-bahrain-subjects-by-the-ruling-family-in-bahrain-in-the-early-1900s-the-full-list/

17. See submissions in Al-Tajir, *Bahrain 1920–1945*, p. 31.

18. Cited in Al-Tajir, *Bahrain 1920–1945*, p. 34.

19. Ibid., p. 34.

20. Ibid.

21. Ibid.

22. Major Daly, cited in Al-Tajir, *Bahrain 1920–1945*, p. 36.

23. Ibid.

24. A *New York Times* correspondent, cited in Y. Oron (ed.), *Middle East Record*, Vol. 2, Israel Centre for Scientific Translations, Tel Aviv, 1961, p. 457.

25. A.F. Rihani, *Around the Coasts of Arabia,* Constable, London, 1930, p. 300.

26. Woodrow Wyatt's report for BBC's *Panorama,* 'Special Advisers in Bahrain', 1960.

27. 'Intelligence Digest, England, 1961', cited in Oron, *Middle East Record,* p. 457.

28. Cited in S.C. Smith, *Britain's Revival and Fall in the Gulf: Kuwait, Bahrain, Qatar, and the Trucial States, 1950–71,* RoutledgeCurzon, London, 2004, p. 10.

29. Ibid., p. 11.

30. A. Austin Holmes, 'The base that replaced the British Empire: de-democratization and the American Navy in Bahrain', *Journal of Arabian Studies: Arabia, the Gulf, and the Red Sea,* 4/1 (2014), p. 21.

31. M. Joyce, 'The Bahraini Three on St Helena', *Middle East Journal,* 54/4 (2000), pp. 613–23.

32. Ibid., p. 613.

33. Cited in Smith, *Britain's Revival and Fall,* p. 36.

34. Ibid.

35. 'British Political Agency: Letter from Tony Parsons to Michael Weir, Foreign and Commonwealth Office', in A. Burdett (ed.), *Records of Bahrain,* Cambridge University Press, Cambridge, 2006, p. 90.

36. A. Burdett (ed.), *Records of Bahrain,* Cambridge University Press, Cambridge, 2006.

37. Ibid.

38. A. Curtis, 'If you take my advice – I'd repress them', BBC Blogs, 11 May 2012, www.bbc.co.uk/blogs/adamcurtis/posts/if_you_take_my_advice_-_id_rep

39. M. Willis, 'Britain in Bahrain in 2011', *RUSI Journal,* 157/5, pp. 62–71 (October 2012).

40. Cited in Smith, *Britain's Revival and Fall,* p. 77.

41. Austin Holmes, 'De-democratization', p. 21.

42. Cited in J. Onley, *The Arabian Frontier,* p. 24.

43. Prior to Britain's collaboration in the removal of Committee dissidents to St Helena in 1953, leaders of protests against unequal working conditions in Bahrain had been banished to India as early as 1938.

44. Kinninmont, J., and Sirri, O., 'Bahrain: civil society and political imagination', Research Paper: Middle East and North Africa Programme, October 2014, Chatham House, London.

45. Diaspora is defined by context, but in this case it means a group of Bahrainis living outside their homeland, and who have largely been coerced into leaving. It would be interesting to explore, in diaspora studies, how protest forms part of their identifying with institutions that reassert communal identity and 'Bahraininess'.

46. C. Beaugrand, 'In and out moves of the Bahraini opposition: how years of political exile led to the opening of an international front during the 2011 crisis in Bahrain', in A. Khalaf, O. AlShehabi and A. Hanieh (eds), *Transit States: Labour, Migration & Citizenship in the Gulf*, Pluto Press, London, 2014, pp. 289–322.

47. Ibid.

48. 'A conscious attempt to conceptualise and strategize the rationale and modalities of transcending Islamism in social, political and intellectual domains', http://bahrainipolitics.blogspot.co.uk/2011/04/where-are-all-islamists-in-bahrain.html

49. Bahrain Center for Human Rights, 'Bahrain's slide to the abyss and the need to defend its people' [press conference], 10 September 2010, London, www.bahrainrights.org/en/node/3343

50. A. Addis, 'Imagining the homeland from afar: community and people-hood in the age of the diaspora', *Vanderbilt Journal of Transnational Law*, 45 (2012), pp. 963–1041.

51. Unless otherwise indicated, all quotes from activists are taken from unpublished interviews conducted in London during my PhD field-work.

52. Amnesty International, 'Urgent action: Verdict expected for 13 opposi-tion activists', 7 August 2012, http://www.amnestyusa.org/sites/default/files/uaa13911_3.pdf

53. The term 'Bahrain 13' was coined by Amnesty International and later adopted by media sources.

54. S. Kerr, 'UAE stops using former British officers as military trainers', *Financial Times*, 22 May 2014, www.ft.com/cms/s/0/53cc2584-e1ab-11e3-9999-00144feabdc0.html?siteedition=uk#axzz3LRhlPTrV

55. ITN Source, 'UK: Bahraini activist disrupts UK horse show attended by Queen Elizabeth II', 14 May 2013, www.itnsource.com/shotlist/RTV/2013/05/14/RTV010198882/RTV010198882-120?v=2

56. Z. Holman, private interview with Sayed Alwadei, 4 June 2013, London.

57. BBC News, 'Bahraini Embassy roof protester threatens to jump', 16 April 2012, www.bbc.com/news/uk-england-london-17734116

58. S. al-Bahraini, 'If you're a Bahraini, protesting in the UK can have "grave consequences"', *The Guardian*, 20 April 2011, www.theguardian.com/commentisfree/2011/apr/20/bahrain-student-protest-threats

59. R. Booth and J. Sheffer, 'Bahrain regime accused of harassing UK-based students', *The Guardian*, 16 April 2011, www.theguardian.com/world/2011/apr/15/bahrain-regime-uk-students

60. D. Roan, 'Bahrain F1 Grand Prix rights complaint "merits examination"', BBC News, 24 October 2014, www.bbc.com/news/uk-politics-29762156

61. The potential of this international alliance was underscored by mobili-sation around the 'Stop the Arms' campaign against exports to Bahrain

from 2011. After sustained campaigning by activists and NGOs based in Bahrain and internationally, the South Korean government agreed to halt shipments of tear gas canisters and tear gas grenades to Bahrain by the country's Dae Kwang Chemical Corporation. www.amnesty.org.au/armstrade/comments/33682/

62. M.O. Jones, email interview with Abdulhadi Khalaf, 13 December 2014.

63. M.S. Laguerre, *Diaspora, Politics and Globalization*, Palgrave Macmillan, New York, 2006, p. xi.

64. D. Cameron, 'Prime Minister's speech to the National Assembly Kuwait', Gov.uk, 22 February 2011, www.gov.uk/government/speeches/prime-ministers-speech-to-the-national-assembly-kuwait

65. J. Doward, 'UK training Saudi forces used to crush Arab spring', *The Guardian*, 29 May 2011, www.theguardian.com/world/2011/may/28/uk-training-saudi-troops

66. N. Watt, 'Anger as Cameron invites Bahrain crown prince to No 10', *The Guardian*, 20 May 2011, www.theguardian.com/uk/2011/may/20/cameron-row-bahrain-prince-visit

67. Human Rights Watch, 'World report 2011: Bahrain', 2011, www.hrw.org/world-report-2011/world-report-2011-bahrain

68. HC Deb 22 February 2012, Vol. 540, Col. 800W, www.publications.parliament.uk/pa/cm201212/cmhansrd/cm120222/text/120222w0001.htm

69. REDRESS, Letter to The Rt Hon. Baroness Warsi, 10 April 2014, www.redress.org/downloads/publications/10%20April%202014%20Letter%20to%20Baroness%20Warsi.pdf

70. B. Dooley, 'Seven helpful things the new ambassador to Bahrain can do', *World Post*, 16 December 2014, www.huffingtonpost.com/brian-dooley/seven-helpful-things-the_b_6336304.html

71. V. Boudreau, 'Precarious regimes and match-up problems in the explanation of repressive policy', in C. Davenport, H. Johnston, and C. Mueller (eds), *Repression and Mobilization*, University of Minnesota Press, Minneapolis, 2005, p. 37.

72. See E. Nakhleh, *Bahrain: Political Development in a Modernizing Society*, Lexington Books, New York, 2011.

73. Foreign Affairs Committee, 'Bilateral relations with Bahrain', in *The UK's Relations with Saudi Arabia and Bahrain* (HC 2013–14, 88), Ch. 4, www.publications.parliament.uk/pa/cm201314/cmselect/cmfaff/88/8808.htm

74. See M. Mamdani, 'Good Muslim, bad Muslim: a political perspective on culture and terrorism', *American Anthropologist*, 104/3 (2005), p. 767.

75. Z. Holman, telephone interview with Nabeel Rajab, 31 August 2014, London.

76. RTT News, 'Bahrain court orders deportation of 10 people stripped of nationality', 10 October 2014, www.rttnews.com/2405849/bahraincourt-orders-deportation-of-10-people-stripped-of-nationality.aspx?type=gn&utm_source=google&utm_campaign=sitemap

77. Kinninmont and Sirri, 'Bahrain: Civil Society'.

78. M.O. Jones, email interview with Abdulhadi Khalaf, 13 December 2014.

## CHAPTER 8

1. YouTube, 'The regime carry out a massacre in the village of al-Shakura in Bahrain' [online video], 14 April 2014, www.youtube.com/watch?v=-ZA91Jm4qVM

2. M.O. Jones, 'Police brutality from five different angles', *Marc Owen Jones* [blog], 16 December 2011, www.marcowenjones.hostbyet2.com/?p=446

3. Jones, M.O., 'Bahrain government flaunt their inadequacy in BICI follow up report', *Marc Owen Jones* [blog], 21 November 2012, http://marcowenjones.wordpress.com/2012/11/21/government-flaunt-their-inadequacy-in-bici-follow-up-report/

4. Bahrain Center for Human Rights, 'Individuals killed by government's excessive use of force since 14 February 2011', 22 May 2014, www.bahrainrights.org/en/node/3864

5. S.K. Ivkovic, 'Police (mis)behavior: a cross-cultural study of corruption seriousness', *Policing*, 28/3 (2005), pp. 546–66, paraphrased by N.W. Pino and L.M. Johnson, 'Police deviance and community relations in Trinidad and Tobago', *Policing: An International Journal of Police Strategies & Management*, 34/3 (2011), p. 454.

6. Police misconduct involves violations of formally written normative rules, traditional operating procedures, regulations and procedures of both the police and other public service agencies, and the criminal and civil laws . . . The second element in the typology, 'abuse of authority', can be defined as any action by a police officer – without regard to motive, intent, or malice – that tends to injure, insult, trespass upon human dignity, manifest feelings of inferiority, or violate an inherent legal right of a member of the police constituency in the course of performing 'police work'. Abuse of authority involves three areas of police deviance: physical abuse, psychological abuse, and legal abuse.

7. W.A. Geller, 'Police misconduct: scope of the problems and remedies', *ACJS Today*, 6–8 February 1984.

8. T.R. O'Connor, 'Police deviance and ethics', MegaLinks in Criminal Justice, 2005, http://faculty.ncwc.edu/toconnor/205/205lect11.htm

9. M. Punch, 'Rotten orchards: "pestilence", police misconduct and system failure', *Policing and Society*, 13/2 (2003), p. 172.

10. S. Strobl, 'From colonial policing to community policing in Bahrain: the historical persistence of sectarianism', *International Journal of Comparative and Applied Criminal Justice*, 35/1 (2011), p. 19.

11. Ibid., p. 33.

12. D. H. Johnson, 'From military to tribal police: policing the Upper Nile province of the Sudan', in D.M. Anderson and D. Killingray (eds), *Policing the Empire: Government, Authority and Control, 1830-1940*, Manchester University Press, Manchester, 1991, p. 151.

13. D. Killingray, 'Guarding the extending frontier: policing the Gold Coast, 1865-1913', in D.M. Anderson and D. Killingray (eds), *Policing the Empire: Government, Authority and Control, 1830-1940*, Manchester University Press, Manchester, 1991, p. 123.

14. D.M. Anderson and D. Killingray (eds), 'An orderly retreat? Policing the end of empire', in *Policing and Decolonisation: Politics, Nationalism, and the Police, 1917-65*, Manchester University Press, Manchester, 1992, p. 4.

15. According to Charles Belgrave, Benn was a 'CID man and quite competent' (C. Belgrave, 23 November 1956, Papers of Charles Dalrymple-Belgrave: Transcripts of Diaries, 1926-1957, Library of the University of Exeter).

16. The National Archives, J.P. Tripp to A.D. Parsons, 14 February 1965, FO 371/179788.

17. The National Archives, A.D. Parsons to T.F. Brenchley, 18 December 1965, FO 371/179788.

18. G. Agamben, *State of Exception*, University of Chicago Press, Chicago, 2005, p. 9.

19. G. Agamben, *Means Without End: Notes on Politics,* University of Minnesota Press, Minneapolis, 2000, p. 132.

20. A. Turk, 'Organizational deviance and political policing', *Criminology*, 19/2 (1981), p. 244.

21. The National Archives, 'Commission of inquiry report', 10 July 1954, FO 371/109813.

22. The National Archives, B.A.B. Burrows, No. 207 Bahrain to Foreign Office, 12 March 1956, FO 371/120544.

23. The National Archives, B.A.B. Burrows, No. 204 Bahrain to Foreign Office, 12 March 1956, FO 371/120544.

24. Commonly used by many British colonial police forces, the Greener Gun was a 14 gauge shotgun designed by British gunmaker W.W. Greener.

25. The National Archive, J.P. Tripp to M.S. Weir, 5 April 1965, FO 371/179788.

26. The National Archives, M.S. Weir, 7 October 1965, FO 371/179788.

27. These figures are taken from the statistics provided in the annual reports of Bahrain between 1924 and 1970.

28. The National Archives, R.M. Tesh, 'Internal political situation', 9 April 1974, FCP 8/2180.

29. The National Archives, A. Sterling, 'Bahrain: annual review for 1971', FCO 8/1823.

30. The National Archives, R.M. Tesh to I.T.M. Lucas, 'Internal political situation in Bahrain', 1 March 1975, FCO 8/2415.

31. Ibid.

32. D.E. Tatham, 'Internal security in Bahrain', 1977, FCO document, www.whatdotheyknow.com/request/164213/response/531538/attach/3/FOI%200544%2013%20releasable%20material%2020200614.pdf

33. Ibid.

34. M.O. Jones, 'The history of British involvement in Bahrain's internal security', openDemocracy, 8 August_2013, www.opendemocracy.net/opensecurity/marc-owen-jones/history-of-british-involvement-inbahrains-internal-security; F. Abrams, 'Strange ethics that makes friends with a state that tortures children', *The Independent,* 7 December 1998, www.independent.co.uk/news/strange-ethics-that-makes-friends-with-a-state-that-tortures-children-1189778.html

35. S. Baby, 'Tribute as top officer mourned', *Gulf Daily News,* 14 July 2005, www.gulf-daily-news.com/newsdetails.aspx?storyid=117021

36. The National Archives, W.R. Tomkys, 'Police brutality in Bahrain', 16 February 1982, FCO 8/4332.

37. A. Khalaf, 'Contentious politics in Bahrain: from ethnic to national and vice versa', Paper to the Fourth Nordic Conference on Middle Eastern Studies: The Middle East in a Globalizing World, 13–16 August 1998, Oslo, http://org.uib.no/smi/pao/khalaf.html

38. Major Wilson, 'Selections from the Records of the Bombay Government' [107] (149/733), British Library: India Office Records and Private Papers, IOR/R/15/1/732 in Qatar Digital Library, www.qdl.qa/en/archive/81055/vdc_100022870191.0x000096

39. C. Belgrave to Colonel Loch, 'Government of Bahrain', 28 January 1935, in P. Tuson, A. Burdett and E. Quick (eds), *Records of Bahrain 1820–1960,* 8 vols, Archive Editions, Slough, Vol. 5, 1993, p. 82.

40. J.W. Wall to B.A.B. Burrows, 5 October 1953, in P. Tuson, A. Burdett and E. Quick (eds), *Records of Bahrain 1820–1960,* 8 vols, Archive Editions, Slough, Vol. 7, 1993, p. 22.

41. Strobl, 'Colonial policing', p. 30.

42. A. Shehabi, 'Bahrain's sovereign hypocrisy', *Foreign Policy,* 9 August 2014, http://foreignpolicy.com/2013/08/14/bahrains-sovereign-hypocrisy/

43. The National Archives, K. Passmore, 'Internal political situation', 3 December 1980, FCO 8/3489.

44. M.O. Jones, 'Bahrain's prime minister and his role in the anti-Shia crackdown of the 1980s', *Marc Owen Jones* [blog], 8 April 2013, http://marcowenjones.wordpress.com/2013/04/08/bahrains-prime-minister-and-his-role-in-the-anti-shia-crackdown-of-the-1980s/

45. The National Archives, W.R. Tomkys, 'Deportations', 10 February 1982, FCO 8/4332.

46. Ibid.

47. Ibid.

48. W. Monroe, 'Prominent shias paint gloomy picture of shia outlook in Bahrain' [diplomatic cable], 9 April 2007, WikiLeaks, https://search.wikileaks.org/plusd/cables/07MANAMA328_a.html

49. C. Belgrave, 'Annual report for year 1357 (1938–1939)', *The Bahrain Government Annual Reports 1924–1956*, Vol. 2, Archive Editions, Gerrards Cross, 1986, p. 14.

50. D.M. Anderson and D. Killingray (eds), 'Consent, coercion and colonial control: policing the empire, 1830–1940', in *Policing the Empire: Government, Authority and Control, 1830–1940*, Manchester University Press, Manchester, 1991, p. 7.

51. Monroe, 'Prominent shias'.

52. C. Belgrave, 'The Bahrain municipality', in P. Tuson, A. Burdett and E. Quick (eds), *Records of Bahrain 1820–1960*, 8 vols, Archive Editions, Slough, Vol. 3, 1993, p. 651.

53. C.K. Daly, 'Note on the political situation in Bahrain November 1921', 6 January 1922, in P. Tuson, A. Burdett and E. Quick (eds), *Records of Bahrain 1820–1960*, 8 vols, Archive Editions, Slough, Vol. 3, 1993, p. 669.

54. C. Belgrave, 9 October 1929, in Papers of Charles Dalrymple-Belgrave: Transcripts of Diaries, 1926–1957, Library of the University of Exeter.

55. The National Archives, W.O. Little, 'Report by Major Little', in Pamphlet on Bahrain, Part IV, p. 4, 1957, FO 371/126918.

56. C. Belgrave, 5 December 1954, in Papers of Charles Dalrymple-Belgrave: Transcripts of Diaries, 1926–1957, Library of the University of Exeter.

57. Ibid.

58. M.O. Jones, 'Attitudes of British officials to the Al Khalifa family between 1920 and 1954', *Marc Owen Jones* [blog], 23 May 2013, https://marcowenjones.wordpress.com/2013/05/23/attitudes-of-british-officials-to-the-al-khalifa-family-between-1920-and-1954/

59. N. Kafai and A. Shehabi, 'The struggle for information: revelations on mercenaries, sectarian agitation, and demographic engineering in Bahrain', *Jadaliyya*, 29 May 2014, www.jadaliyya.com/pages/index/17912/the-struggle-for-information_revelations-on-mercen

60. Arabs from the 'Najd' region of Saudi Arabia. Before the creation of Saudi Arabia, this term was often used to describe Arabs from this region.

61. F. Khuri, *Tribe and State in Bahrain: The Transition of Social and Political Authority in an Arab State*, University of Chicago Press, Chicago, 1981, p. 123.

62. Ibid., p. 122.

63. Ibid., p. 207.

64. Jones, 'History of British involvement'.

65. As this time, the police totalled 921 personnel. Of these, 285 were from Yemen, 234 from Bahrain, 97 were 'Muscatis', 64 from Pakistan, 47 'Yaafis', 22 Baluchis, 16 Mahri, 7 Iraqis, and 149 from elsewhere, including Europe. (The National Archives, J.P. Tripp to A.D. Parsons, 14 February 1965, FO 371/179788.)

66. P. Muhammad, 'Foreign relations: tit-for-tat proposed over visa rejections', *The Express Tribune*, 1 April 2014, http://tribune.com.pk/story/689833/foreign-relations-tit-for-tat-proposed-over-visa-rejections/

67. *Bahrain Mirror*, '*Bahrain Mirror* publishes important document regarding Jordanian police: 499 policemen are costing Bahrain 1.8 million dollar per month', 3 April 2014, http://bmirror14feb2011.no-ip.org/news/14724.html

68. *Bahrain Mirror*, 'CNN: 2500 former Jordanian military personnel also working in Bahrain', 3 April 2014, http://bmirror14feb2011.no-ip.org/news/14762.html

69. J. Lessware, 'State of emergency declared in Bahrain', *The National*, 16 March 2011, www.thenational.ae/news/world/middle-east/state-of-emergency-declared-in-bahrain

70. *The National*, 'Emirati officer dies in Bahrain bomb explosion', 3 March 2014, www.thenational.ae/world/emirati-officer-dies-in-bahrain-bomb-explosion

71. YouTube, 'Interview with Shaykh Rashid Al Khalifa' [online video], 20 October 2011, www.youtube.com/watch?v=zTdOVFaWfoA

72. Terminal X, 'Bahrain deports 500 Pakistani security soldiers over "indiscipline"', 11 May 2014, www.terminalx.org/2014/05/bahrain-deports-500-pakistani-security-soldiers-over-indiscipline.html, and *The Express Tribune*, 'Broken promises: Bahrain deports 450 Pakistanis after alleged torture', 14 March 2013, http://tribune.com.pk/story/520669/broken-promises-bahrain-deports-450-pakistanis-after-alleged-torture/

73. J.W. Wall to FO, 25 October 1954, No. 781, in P. Tuson, A. Burdett and E. Quick (eds), *Records of Bahrain 1820–1960*, 8 vols, Archive Editions, Slough, Vol. 7, 1993, p. 73.

74. Al-Shabab al-Watani, 1938, in P. Tuson, A. Burdett and E. Quick (eds), *Records of Bahrain 1820–1960*, 8 vols, Archive Editions, Slough, Vol. 5, p. 130.

75. J.W. Wall to FO, 5 December 1954, No. 781, in P. Tuson, A. Burdett and E. Quick (eds), *Records of Bahrain 1820–1960*, 8 vols, Archive Editions, Slough, 1993, p. 86.

76. Ibid., Vol. 7, p. 87.

77. Ibid.

78. The National Archives, 'A review of the structure and organization of the Bahraini State Police Force', 1965, FO 371/179788.

79. Reuters, 'Bahraini protester dies after being shot at demonstration', 31 March 2012, http://in.reuters.com/article/2012/03/31/bahrain-death-idINDEE82U05S20120331

80. Foreign Affairs Committee, 'Written evidence from Dr Mike Diboll', in *The UK's Relations with Saudi Arabia and Bahrain* (HC 2013–14, 88), p. 55, www.publications.parliament.uk/pa/cm201314/cmselect/cmfaff/88/88vw25.htm

81. Ibid.

82. The National Archives, W.R. Tomkys, Telegram No. 223, 14 December 1981, FCO 8/3893.

83. Ibid.

84. A. Juska and C. Woolfson, 'Policing political protest in Lithuania', *Crime, Law and Social Change*, 57 (2012), p. 405.

85. Summary of report submitted by Daniel Walker, Director of the Chicago Study Team, to the National Commission on the Causes and Prevention of Violence, introduction by Max Frankel, E.P. Dutton, New York, 1968, www.fjc.gov/history/home.nsf/page/tu_chicago7_doc_13.html

86. M.O. Jones, 'Some of Bahrain's police are being trained by the US military – but how?', *Marc Owen Jones* [blog] 7 February 2012, http://marcowenjones.wordpress.com/2012/02/07/are-bahrains-police-being-trained-by-the-us-military/

87. M. Cassel, 'Even Bahrain's use of "Miami model" policing will not stop the uprising', *The Guardian*, 3 December 2011, www.theguardian.com/commentisfree/2011/dec/03/bahrain-miami-model-policing

88. J. Scahill, 'The Miami model', Democracy Now! on Information Clearing House, 24 November, www.informationclearinghouse.info/article5286.htm

89. M.O. Jones, 'Media distortion and lack of police accountability: the death of Mahmood al-Jaziri', Bahrain Watch, 22 March 2013, https://bahrainwatch.org/blog/2013/03/22/media-distortion-lack-of-police-accountability-the-death-of-mahmood-al-jaziri/

90. M. Kareem, 'Bahrain: are police cars running over protesters on purpose?', *Global Voices*, 12 November 2011, http://globalvoicesonline.org/2011/11/12/bahrain-are-police-cars-running-over-protesters-on-purpose/

91. Bahrain Center for Human Rights, 'Bahraini youth dies after being run over by police car', 19 November 2011, http://bahrainrights.hopto.org/en/node/4843

92. M.O. Jones, 'For the record: police in Bahrain throw Molotov cocktails', *Marc Owen Jones* [blog], 18 March 2012, http://marcowenjones.wordpress.com/2012/03/18/for-the-record-police-in-bahrain-throw-molotov-cocktails/

93. M.O. Jones, 'Bahrain special: the steel rods of the police', *EA Worldview*, 16 January 2012, www.enduringamerica.com/home/2012/1/16/bahrain-special-the-steel-rods-of-the-police.html

94. The National Archives, W.R. Tomkys, 'Political development in Bahrain', 18 September 1982.

95. W. Monroe, 'Prominent shias'.

96. Physicians for Human Rights, 'Weaponizing tear gas: Bahrain's unprecedented use of toxic chemical agents against civilians', August 2012, https://s3.amazonaws.com/PHR_Reports/Bahrain-TearGas-Aug2012-small.pdf

97. At least ten of those killed suffered from tear gas exposure at home.

98. Physicians for Human Rights, 'Tear-gas related deaths in Bahrain', 2012, http://physiciansforhumanrights.org/issues/persecution-of-health-workers/bahrain/bahrain-tear-gas-deaths.html

99. A. Turk, *Political Criminality: The Defiance and Defense of Authority*, Sage Publications, Beverly Hills, 1982, p. 147.

100. Amnesty International, 'Bahrain: a human rights crisis', November 1995, p. 9, http://refworld.org/docid/3ae6a9984.html

101. A. Ehteshami and S. Wright, *Reform in the Middle East Oil Monarchies*, Ithaca Press, Reading, 2011, p. 88.

102. Al Jazeera, 'Bahrain replaces national security chief', 29 November 2011, www.aljazeera.com/news/middleeast/2011/11/2011112942546281189.html

103. M.O. Jones, 'Bahrain's state unaccountability', *Muftah*, 17 April 2014, http://muftah.org/bahrains-state-unaccountability/#.VMEoj0esXbA

104. M. Welch, *Crimes of Power & States of Impunity: The U.S. Response to Terror*, Rutgers University Press, New Brunswick, 2009, p. 20.

105. Human Rights Watch, 'Criminalizing dissent, entrenching impunity: persistent failures of the Bahraini justice system since the BICI Report', May 2014, www.hrw.org/sites/default/files/reports/bahrain0514_forUpload.pdf

106. US Department of State, 'Bahrain 2013 Human Rights Report', 2013, www.state.gov/documents/organization/220560.pdf

107. Bahrain News Agency, 'SIU investigates various cases, Chief Public Prosecutor says', 9 October 2013, www.bna.bh/portal/en/news/583581

108. US Dept of State, 'Bahrain 2013'.
109. Ibid.
110. Ibid.
111. US Dept of State, 'Bahrain 2013'.
112. Amnesty International, 'Bahrain: reform shelved, repression unleashed', November 2012, http://amnesty.org/en/library/asset/MDE11/062/2012/en/fe6b00f5-989e-496b-8560-072b14b09152/mde110622012en.pdf
113. Bahrain Center for Human Rights, 'Show trial for the policemen accused of torturing two detainees to death, including an online journalist', 13 January 2012, www.bahrainrights.org/en/node/4966
114. Amnesty International, 'Bahrain: reform shelved'.
115. US Dept of State, 'Bahrain 2013'.
116. BICI Follow-up Team, 'BICI Follow-Up Report', November 2012, http://iaa.bh/downloads/bici_nov2012_en.pdf
117. Ibid.
118. Amnesty International, 'Bahrain: reform shelved'.
119. Russia Today, 'Royal treatment: Bahrain princess and princes accused of torturing activists', 25 January 2013, http://rt.com/news/princess-torture-bahrain-detention-665/
120. N.W. Pino and L.M. Johnson, 'Police deviance and community relations in Trinidad and Tobago', *Policing: An International Journal of Police Strategies & Management,* 34/3 (2011), p. 459.
121. F. Ferrara, 'Why regimes create disorder: Hobbes's dilemma during a Rangoon summer', *Journal of Conflict Resolution,* 47 (2003), p. 302.
122. H. Yusuf, Citizens: we must arm the security forces to protect them against terrorists', *Al-Watan,* 2012, www.alwatannews.net/en/post.aspx?id=V6TTTavrPTp4L7unyAVu5mdPf3KB7f0kW+p+iKqni4g=
123. H. Al-Alawi, 'Pakistanis in police seek protection', *Gulf Daily News,* 26 January 2012, available at: www.thefreelibrary.com/Pakistanis+in+police+seek+protection.-a0278035980
124. Ibid.
125. J. Gengler, 'A Gulf NATO?: what the new U.S.-GCC security partnership means for Bahrain', *Religion and Politics in Bahrain* [blog], 31 October 2011, http://bahrainipolitics.blogspot.co.uk/2011_10_01_archive.html
126. S. Singh Grewal, 'Ex-servicemen to form society', *Gulf Daily News,* 30 October 2011, http://gulf-daily-news.com/NewsDetails.aspx?storyid=316591
127. *Gulf Daily News,* 'Group formed to help policemen', 2 January 2012, www.thefreelibrary.com/Group+formed+to+help+policemen.-a0276117481
128. J. Gengler, 'Bahrain's Sunni awakening', *Middle East Report Online,* 17 January 2012, www.merip.org/mero/mero011712

129. Bahrain News Agency, 'UAE martyr of duty honoured', 23 July 2014, www.bna.bh/portal/en/news/627084

130. S. Singh Grewal, 'Rally to honour security forces', *Gulf Daily News*, 29 December 2011, www.gulf-daily-news.com/NewsDetails.aspx?storyid=320555

131. Since 2011, groups have either targeted or boycotted chains depending on the sect of their owner.

132. Sabla Oman, 'Youth of Manama attacked by thugs manage to arrest them' [web forum discussion], 15 March 2011, http://avb.s-oman.net/showthread.php?t=1101114&s=3c7a4c0f488fcf7eb259b55d6f654ab6

133. YouTube, 'Thugs throw Molotovs at people of Dar al-Kulayb' [online video], 6 January 2012, www.youtube.com/watch?v=pimFQQfGO4w

134. YouTube, 'Dar al-Kulayb: militas throw Molotovs at the people' [online video], 6 January 2012, www.youtube.com/watch?v=mvOaUaaW_zo

135. @NABEELRAJAB, 'Many #Bahrain men who joined #terrorism & #ISIS came from security institutions and those institutions were the first ideological incubator' [Twitter post], 28 September 2014, https://twitter.com/nabeelrajab/status/516179409720852480

136. A. Shehabi, 'Why is Bahrain outsourcing extremism?', *Foreign Policy*, 29 October 2014, www.foreignpolicy.com/articles/2014/10/29/why_is_bahrain_outsourcing_extremism_isis_democracy

137. Pino and Johnson, 'Police deviance'.

138. M.O. Jones, 'Bahrain special: the steel rods of the police', *EA Worldview*, 16 January 2012, www.enduringamerica.com/home/2012/1/16/bahrain-special-the-steel-rods-of-the-police.html

139. A. Khalaf, 'Arab reform brief: the outcome of a ten-year process of political reform in Bahrain', Arab Reform Initiative, December 2008, www.arab-reform.net/sites/default/files/ARB.23_Abdulhadi_Khalaf_ENG.pdf

140. Bahrain Center for Human Rights, 'Bahrain: Ministry of Interior Ombudsman does not prevent or investigate human rights violations', 14 October 2013, http://bahrainrights.org/en/node/6449

141. A. Turk, 'Organizational deviance and political policing', *Criminology*, 19/2 (1981), p. 241.

## CHAPTER 9

1. Bahrain Watch, 'The IP spy files: how Bahrain's government silences anonymous online dissent', August 2013, https://bahrainwatch.org/ipspy/ip-spy-files.pdf

2. *Al-Wasat*, 'The number of Bahrainis using Twitter has increased by 80% during recent events', 6 June 2011, www.alwasatnews.com/3194/news/read/564689/1.html (Arabic).

3.  M. Castells, *The Rise of the Network Society*, Blackwell, Oxford, 1996; L.K. Grossman, *The Electronic Republic. Reshaping Democracy in the Information Age*, Viking, New York, 1995; H. Rheingold, *The Virtual Community: Homesteading on the Electronic Frontier*, HarperCollins, New York, 1993; D. Saco, *Cybering Democracy: Public Space and the Internet*, University of Minnesota Press, Minneapolis, 2002.

4.  Saco, *Cybering Democracy*, p. xv.

5.  V. Bakir, *Sousveillance, Media and Strategic Political Communication: Iraq, USA, UK*, Continuum, London, 2010, p. 8.

6.  E. Morozov, *The Dark Side of Internet Freedom: The Net Delusion*, Public Affairs, New York, 2011.

7.  R. Mackinnon, *Consent of the Networked: The Worldwide Struggle for Internet Freedom*, Basic Books, New York, 2002 (Kindle edition), p. 27.

8.  F. Desmukh, 'The internet in Bahrain: breaking the monopoly of information', *Foreign Policy*, 21 September 2010, http://mideast.foreignpolicy.com/posts/2010/09/21/bahrain_government_vs_the_internet

9.  Trade Arabia, '*Al-Wasat* journalists to stand trial in Bahrain', 12 April 2011, www.tradearabia.com/news/MEDIA_196756.html

10. M.C. Bassiouni *et al.*, 'Report of the Bahrain Independent Commission of Inquiry' [BICI Report], 23 November 2011, BICI, Manama, www.bici.org.bh/BICIreportEN.pdf, p. 422.

11. Bahrain News Agency, 'HM King Hamad declares state of national safety', 15 March 2011, www.bna.bh/portal/en/news/449960

12. Information Affairs Authority, 'Press rules and regulations', 2002, www.iaa.bh/policiesPressrules.aspx

13. BBC News, 'Bahrain and Belarus named "enemies of the internet"', 13 March 2012, www.bbc.co.uk/news/technology-17350225

14. J.A.G.M. van Dijk, *De Netwerkmaatschappij, Sociale aspecten van nieuwe media*, first, second and third editions, Bohn Stafleu van Loghum, Houten, Netherlands, and Zaventem, Belgium, 1991/1993/1997.

15. D. Lyon, *Surveillance Society: Monitoring in Everyday Life*, Open University Press, Buckingham, 2001.

16. T. Mitchell, *Colonising Egypt*, University of California Press, Berkeley, 1991, p. x.

17. B.F. Barton and M. Barton, 'Modes of power in technical and professional visuals', *Journal of Business and Technical Communication*, 7/1 (1993), pp. 138–62.

18. M. Foucault, *Discipline and Punish: The Birth of the Prison*, trans. A. Sheridan, Pantheon, New York, 1977, p. 201.

19. Bakir, *Sousveillance*, p. 17.

20. A. Hofheinz, 'Arab internet usage: popular trends and public impact', in N. Sakr (ed.), *Arab Media and Political Renewal: Community, Legitimacy and Public Life*, I.B. Tauris, London, 2007, p. 60.

21. Desmukh, 'The internet in Bahrain'.

22. S. Mann, J. Nolan and B. Wellman, 'Sousveillance: inventing and using wearable computing devices for data collection in surveillance environments', *Surveillance & Society*, 1/3 (2003), pp. 331–55.

23. O.H. Gandy Jr, *The Panoptic Sort: A Political Economy of Personal Information*, Westview Press, Boulder, 1993.

24. M. Poster, *The Mode of Information: Poststructuralism and Social Construct*, University of Chicago Press, Chicago, 1990.

25. L. Humphreys, 'Who's watching whom? A study of interactive technology and surveillance', *Journal of Communication,* 61 (2011), p. 5765–95.

26. Mann *et al.*, 'Sousveillance', p. 332.

27. Ibid., p. 333.

28. Ibid., p. 332.

29. S. Mann, '"Reflectionism" and "diffusionism": new tactics for deconstructing the video surveillance superhighway', *Leonardo*, 31/2 (1998), pp. 93–102.

30. W. Marczak, J. Scott-Railton, V. Paxson, and M. Marquis-Boire, 'When governments hack opponents: a look at actors and technology', 23rd USENIX Security Symposium, 20–22 August 2014, San Diego, www.icir. org/vern/papers/govhack.usesec14.pdf

31. Bahrain Watch, 'The IP spy files'.

32. Ibid.

33. Ibid.

34. Ibid.

35. @SheikhKhalifaPM, 'Bloody typical..hot young women only get in touch with me when they want something from me..like maybe my IP address' [Twitter post], 18 September 2014, https://twitter.com/SheikhKhalifaPM/ status/512492182381400064

36. V. Silver, 'Gamma says no spyware sold to Bahrain: may be stolen copy', Bloomberg, 27 July 2012, www.bloomberg.com/news/2012-07-27/gamma-says-no-spyware-sold-to-bahrain-may-be-stolen-copy.html

37. W. Marczak and M. Marquis-Boire, 'From Bahrain with love: FinFisher's spy kit exposed?', Citizenlab, 25 July 2012, https://citizenlab.org/2012/07/ from-bahrain-with-love-finfishers-spy-kit-exposed/

38. F. Desmukh, 'Bahrain government hacked lawyers and activists with UK spyware', Bahrain Watch blog, 7 August 2014, https://bahrain-watch.org/blog/2014/08/07/uk-spyware-used-to-hack-bahrain-lawyers-activists/

39. European Center for Constitutional and Human Rights, 'Gamma/ FinFisher: no investigation into German-British software company', 12 December 2014, www.ecchr.de/surveillance-technology/articles/human-rights-organisations-file-oecd-complaints-against-surveillance-firms-gamma-international-and-trovicor.html

40. W. Marczak, 'Bahrain Watch issues urgent advice for activists to stop using @Zello due to security flaw', Bahrain Watch blog, 7 September 2014, https://bahrainwatch.org/blog/2014/09/07/bahrain-watch-issues-urgent-advice-for-activists-to-stop-using-zello-due-to-security-flaw/

41. M.O. Jones, 'Bahrain activists' trouble with trolls', Index on Censorship Uncut, 15 May 2012, http://uncut.indexoncensorship.org/2012/05/bahrain-marc-owen-jones-twitter-trolls/

42. York, J. 'Twitter trolling as propaganda tactic: Bahrain and Syria', *Jilliancyork*, 11 November 2011, http://jilliancyork.com/2011/10/12/twitter-trolling-as-propagandatactic-bahrain-and-syria/

43. Goodman, J.D. '"Twitter trolls" haunt discussions of Bahrain online', *The Lede*, 11 October 2011, http://thelede.blogs.nytimes.com/2011/10/11/twitter-trollshaunt-discussions-

44. Dooley, B. '"Troll" attacks on #Bahrain tweets show depth of government attempts to silence dissent', *Huffington Post*, 18 November 2011, http://www.huffingtonpost.com/brian-dooley/troll-attacks-on-bahrain_b_1099642.html

45. T. Halvorssen, 'PR mercenaries their dictator masters, and the human rights stain', *World Post*, 19 May 2011, www.huffingtonpost.com/thor-halvorssen/pr-mercenaries-their-dict_b_863716.html?

46. N. Fielding and I. Cobain, 'Revealed: US spy operation that manipulates social media', *The Guardian,* 12 March 2011, www.theguardian.com/technology/2011/mar/17/us-spy-operation-social-networks

47. M. Newman and O. Wright, 'Kazakhstan: PR firm's plan to target Sting after gig boycott', *The Independent*, 8 December 2011, www.independent.co.uk/news/uk/politics/kazakhstan-pr-firms-plan-to-target-sting-after-gig-boycott-video-6273824.html

48. Web 3.0 Lab, 'Bahrain's troll army', 17 February 2011, http://web3lab.blogspot.co.uk/2011/02/bahrains-troll-army.html

49. Freedom House, 'Freedom on the Net 2012: Bahrain', 2012, www.freedomhouse.org/sites/default/files/Bahrain%202012_0.pdf

50. M.C. Bassiouni et al., 'Report of the Bahrain Independent Commission of Inquiry' [BICI Report], 23 November 2011, BICI, Manama, p. 420, www.bici.org.bh/BICIreportEN.pdf

51. For more information on sectarian rhetoric in Bahrain, see M.O. Jones, 'Here's looking at YouTube', Masters dissertation, Durham University, 2010, https://marcowenjones.files.wordpress.com/2012/02/dissertations1.pdf

52. B. Marczak, 'Is Bahrain's government running extremist accounts?', Bahrain Watch blog, 5 August 2013, https://bahrainwatch.org/blog/2013/08/05/is-bahrains-government-running-extremist-accounts/

53. M.O. Jones, 'Member of Bahrain ruling family walks into ministry and threatens to shoot an employee', *Marc Owen Jones* [blog], 5 January 2013, https://marcowenjones.wordpress.com/2013/01/05/member-of-bahrain-ruling-family-walks-into-ministry-and-threatens-to-shoot-an-employee/

54. Bassiouni *et al.*, 'Report of the BICI', p. 391.

55. Ibid., p. 401, para. 1637.

56. Ibid., p. 401, para. 1639.

57. S.S. Al-Qassemi, 'McCarthyist rhetoric sweeps Gulf social media', *Huffington Post*, 25 April 2011, www.huffingtonpost.com/sultan-sooudalqassemi/mccarthyism-sweeps-gulf-s_b_853397.html; S. Dixon and agencies, 'Facebook "used to hunt down Bahrain dissidents"', *The Telegraph*, 4 August 2011, www.telegraph.co.uk/expat/expatnews/8681230/Facebook-used-to-hunt-down-Bahrain-dissidents.html; A. Hammond, 'Bahrain media play role in tension after protests', Reuters, 5 May 2011, http://in.reuters.com/article/2011/05/05/idINIndia-56790720110505

58. Reporters Without Borders, 'Bahraini and Syrian authorities try to impose news blackout', 4 April 2011, http://en.rsf.org/bahraini-and-syrianauthorities-04-04-2011,39946.html

59. Freedom House, 'Freedom on the Net 2013: Bahrain', 2013, www.freedomhouse.org/sites/default/files/resources/FOTN%202013_Bahrain.pdf

60. BBC News, 'Bahrain and Belarus named "enemies of the internet"', 13 March 2012, www.bbc.co.uk/news/technology-17350225

61. F. Desmukh, 'British intelligence gathering firm assists Bahraini regime amidst crackdown' [blog], 2011, http://chanad.posterous.com/british-intelligencegathering-firm-assists-b

62. Ibid.

63. S. Yasin, 'Bahrain: where a Facebook "like" gets you expelled', Index on Censorship, 14 October 2011, www.indexoncensorship.org/2011/10/bahrain-where-a-facebook-like-gets-you-expelled/

64. Ibid.

65. M.O. Jones, 'The hunt for #LilianeKhalil', Al Jazeera English, 4 August 2011, www.youtube.com/watch?v=TgCp15kVggI

66. F. Desmukh, 'An epilogue for Liliane Khalil' [blog], 2011, http://chanad.posterous.com/an-epilogue-for-liliane-khalil

67. F. Desmukh, 'Myths and lies in the Bahrain infowars' [blog], 11 April 2011, http://revolutionbahrain2.blogspot.se/2011/04/myths-and-lies-in-bahrain-infowars.html

68. H. Ibish, 'The Bahrain Uprising: towards confrontation or accommodation', A Henry Jackson Society Strategic Briefing, 2011, www.henryjacksonsociety.org/cms/harriercollectionitems/Bahrain1c.pdf

69. Bahrain Watch, 'Fabrigate', September 2014, https://bahrainwatch.org/media/#!sameerarajab

70. Desmukh, 'Myths and lies'.

71. M.O. Jones in J.D. Goodman, '"Twitter Trolls" haunt discussions of Bahrain online', *The Lede* [*New York Times* blog], 11 October 2011, http://thelede.blogs.nytimes.com/2011/10/11/twitter-trolls-haunt-discussions-of-bahrain-online/

72. Web 3.0 Lab, 'Bahrain's troll army'.

73. J. Doward and B. Lewis, 'UK exporting surveillance technology to repressive nations', *The Guardian*, 7 April 2012, www.guardian.co.uk/world/2012/apr/07/surveillance-technology-repressive-regimes

74. V. Silver and B. Elgin, 'Torture in Bahrain becomes routine with help from Nokia Siemens', Bloomberg, 22 August 2011, www.bloomberg.com/news/2011-08-22/torture-in-bahrain-becomes-routine-with-help-from-nokia-siemens-networking.html

75. Olton website, www.olton.co.uk/services/reputation-management

76. M.O. Jones, 'Bahrain's PR machine threatens free speech', Index on Censorship, 14 February 2012, http://www.indexoncensorship.org/2012/02/bahrains-pr-machine-threatens-free-speech/

77. K. Rawlinson, 'Revealed: lobbyists' plans to hijack "people's petitions"', *The Independent*, 10 April 2012, www.independent.co.uk/news/uk/home-news/revealed-lobbyists-plans-to-hijack-peoples-petitions-7628058.html

78. *Gulf Daily News*, 'Security is top wish of young', 15 June 2011, www.gulf-daily-news.com/NewsDetails.aspx?storyid=307981

79. G. Morgan, 'HMRC faces High Court challenge over spy software sales', V3.co.uk, 16 April 2013, www.v3.co.uk/v3-uk/news/2261787/hmrc-faces-high-court-challenge-over-spy-software-sales

80. D. Neal, 'Court rules HMRC must end FinFisher spy software stonewalling', V3.co.uk, 13 May 2014, www.v3.co.uk/v3-uk/news/2344407/court-rules-hmrc-must-end-finfisher-spy-software-stonewalling

81. Y. al-Saraf, 'Bahrain Watch welcomes partner Privacy International's legal action on government surveillance', Bahrain Watch blog, 14 October 2014, https://bahrainwatch.org/blog/2014/10/14/bahrain-watch-welcomes-partner-privacy-internationals-legal-action-on-government-surveillance/

82. 'Privacy International & Gamma International UK Ltd: Final statement after examination of complaint', December 2014, www.gov.uk/government/uploads/system/uploads/attachment_data/file/402462/BIS-15-93-Final_statement_after_examination_of_complaint_Privacy_International_and_Gamma_International_UK_Ltd.pdf

83. M. Foucault and J. Miskowiec, 'Of other spaces', *Diacritics*, 16/1 (1986), pp. 22–27.

84. S. Saideman, 'Conclusion: thinking theoretically about identity and foreign policy', in S. Telhami and M. Barnett (eds), *Identity and Foreign Policy in the Middle East*, Cornell University Press, Ithaca, NY, 2002.

85. Castells, M. (2009) *Communication Power*. Oxford: Oxford University Press.

86. Information Affairs Authority, 'Summary of BICI report', November 2012, http://iaa.bh/downloads/BICI_Executive_Summary.pdf

87. BICI Follow-up Team, 'BICI Follow-Up Report', November 2012, http://iaa.bh/downloads/bici_nov2012_en.pdf

88. POMED in their report on the implementation of the BICI speak of a seven-member 'Higher Media Board', containing four people appointed by the King, with the other three being appointed by the Prime Minister, the President of the Shura Council, and the President of the Council of Ministers (Project on Middle East Democracy, 'One year later: assessing Bahrain's implementation of the BICI report', November 2012, http://pomed.org/wp-content/uploads/2013/12/One-Year-Later-Assessing-Bahrains-Implementation-of-the-BICI-Report.pdf). However, the Bahraini government's report speaks of a nine-member 'Supreme Council for Media and Communication', consisting of nine members appointed by royal order (BICI Follow-up Team, 'BICI Follow-Up Report').

# Bibliography

Abrams, F., 'Strange ethics that makes friends with a state that tortures children', *The Independent,* 7 December 1998, www.independent.co.uk/news/strange-ethics-that-makes-friends-with-a-state-that-tortures-children-1189778.html

Aday, S., Farrell, H., Freelon, D., Lynch, M., Sides, J., and Dewar, M., 'Watching from afar: media consumption patterns around the Arab Spring', *American Behavioral Scientist,* 20/10, pp. 1–21.

Addis, A., 'Imagining the homeland from afar: community and peoplehood in the age of the diaspora', *Vanderbilt Journal of Transnational Law,* 45 (2012), pp. 963–1041.

'Administration report of the Bahrain Agency for the year 1955', in *Persian Gulf Administration Reports 1873–1957,* Cambridge Archive Editions, Cambridge University Press, Cambridge, 1989.

Agamben, G., *Means Without End: Notes on Politics,* University of Minnesota Press, Minneapolis, 2000.

Agamben, G., *State of Exception,* University of Chicago Press, Chicago, 2005.

Al-Alawi, H., 'Pakistanis in police seek protection', *Gulf Daily News,* 26 January 2012, available at: www.thefreelibrary.com/Pakistanis+in+police+seek+protection.-a0278035980

Al-Baharna, H., *Legal Status of the Arabian Gulf States: A Study of Their Treaty Relations and Their International Problems,* Manchester University Press, Manchester, 1968.

al-Bahraini, S., 'If you're a Bahraini, protesting in the UK can have "grave consequences"', *The Guardian,* 20 April 2011, www.theguardian.com/commentisfree/2011/apr/20/bahrain-student-protest-threats

Alhassen, M., and Shihab-Eldin, A., *Demanding Dignity: Young Voices from the Front Lines of the Arab Revolutions,* White Cloud Press, Oregon, 2012.

Al Jazeera, '"Mass sackings" in Bahrain crackdown', 14 May 2011, http://english. aljazeera.net/news/middleeast/2011/05/2011514104251715508.html

Al Jazeera, 'Bahrain replaces national security chief', 29 November 2011, www. aljazeera.com/news/middleeast/2011/11/2011112942546281189.html

Al Jazeera, 'Bahrain launches probe into prisoner death', 10 November 2014, www. aljazeera.com/humanrights/2014/11/bahrain-launches-probe-into-prisoner-death-20141110103437335342.html

Al-Qassemi, S.S., 'McCarthyist rhetoric sweeps Gulf social media', *Huffington Post*, 25 April 2011, www.huffingtonpost.com/sultan-sooudalqassemi/mccarthyism-sweeps-gulf-s_b_853397.html

al-Saraf, Y., 'Bahrain Watch welcomes partner Privacy International's legal action on government surveillance', Bahrain Watch blog, 14 October 2014, https:// bahrainwatch.org/blog/2014/10/14/bahrain-watch-welcomes-partner-privacy-internationals-legal-action-on-government-surveillance/

Al Sayyad, N., 'Cairo's roundabout revolution', *New York Times*, 13 April 2011, www.nytimes.com/2011/04/14/opinion/14alsayyad.html?pagewanted=all&_r=0

Al-Shabab al-Watani, 1938, in P. Tuson, A. Burdett and E. Quick (eds), *Records of Bahrain 1820–1960*, 8 vols, Archive Editions, Slough, Vol. 5, p. 130.

Al-Shehabi, O., 'Political movements in Bahrain: past, present and future', *Jadaliyya*, 14 February 2012, www.jadaliyya.com/pages/index/4363/political-movements-in-bahrain_past-present-and-fu

AlShehabi, O., 'Divide and rule in Bahrain and the elusive pursuit for a united front: the experience of the constitutive committee and the 1972 uprising', *Historical Materialism*, 21/1 (2013), pp. 94–127.

AlShehabi, O., 'Bahrain's fate', *Jacobin*, January 2014, www.jacobinmag.com/2014/01/bahrains-fate/

Al-Tajir, M.A., *Bahrain, 1920–1945: Britain, the Shaikh, and the Administration*, Routledge, London, 1987.

*Al-Wasat*, 'Crown Prince orders military off Bahrain streets', 19 February 2011, www.alwasatnews.com/3088/news/read/528052/1.html;

*Al-Wasat*, 'The number of Bahrainis using Twitter has increased by 80% during recent events', 6 June 2011, www.alwasatnews.com/3194/news/read/564689/1.html

*Al-Wasat*, 'The Prime Minister sends a cable of good wishes to the General Secretary of Al Wefaq on the occasion of their success in the parliamentary and municipal election', 4 November 2014, www.alwasatnews.com/2981/news/read/496462/1.html

Amnesty International, 'Bahrain: a human rights crisis', November 1995, http:// refworld.org/docid/3ae6a9984.html

Amnesty International, 'Urgent action: Verdict expected for 13 opposition activists', 7 August 2012.

Amnesty International, 'Bahrain: reform shelved, repression unleashed', November 2012, http://amnesty.org/en/library/asset/MDE11/062/2012/en/fe6b00f5-989e-496b-8560-072b14b09152/mde110622012en.pdf

Anderson, D.M., and Killingray, D. (eds), 'Consent, coercion and colonial control: policing the empire, 1830–1940', in *Policing the Empire: Government, Authority and Control, 1830–1940*, Manchester University Press, Manchester, 1991, pp. 1–17.

Anderson, D.M., and Killingray, D. (eds), 'An orderly retreat? Policing the end of empire', in *Policing and Decolonisation: Politics, Nationalism, and the Police, 1917–65*, Manchester University Press, Manchester, 1992, pp. 1–21.

Andoni, L., 'Bahrain's contribution to the Arab Spring', Al Jazeera English, 30 August 2011, www.aljazeera.com/indepth/opinion/2011/08/20118301473301296.html

Arendt, H., *The Origins of Totalitarianism*, new edition, Harcourt Brace, Orlando, 1958.

Austin Holmes, A., 'The base that replaced the British Empire: de-democratization and the American Navy in Bahrain', *Journal of Arabian Studies: Arabia, the Gulf, and the Red Sea*, 4/1 (2014), pp. 20–37.

Baby, S., 'Tribute as top officer mourned', *Gulf Daily News*, 14 July 2005, www.gulf-daily-news.com/newsdetails.aspx?storyid=117021

Badiou, A., quoted in 'Badiou on the revolutions in Egypt and Tunisia' (translated extracts by Anindya Bhattacharyya), bat020.com [blog], 11 March 2011, http://bat020.com/2011/03/11/badiou-on-the-revolutions-in-egypt-and-tunisia/

Bahrain Center for Human Rights, 'Banning one of the most significant historic books in the history of Bahrain', 25 May 2010, www.bahrainrights.org/en/node/3105

Bahrain Center for Human Rights, 'Bahrain's slide to the abyss and the need to defend its people' [press conference], 10 September 2010, London, www.bahrainrights.org/en/node/3343

Bahrain Center for Human Rights, 'Bahraini youth dies after being run over by police car', 19 November 2011, http://bahrainrights.hopto.org/en/node/4843

Bahrain Center for Human Rights, 'Show trial for the policemen accused of torturing two detainees to death, including an online journalist', 13 January 2012, www.bahrainrights.org/en/node/4966

Bahrain Center for Human Rights, 'Bahrain: Ministry of Interior Ombudsman does not prevent or investigate human rights violations', 14 October 2013, http://bahrainrights.org/en/node/6449

Bahrain Center for Human Rights, 'Individuals killed by government's excessive use of force since 14 February 2011', 22 May 2014, www.bahrainrights.org/en/node/3864

Bahrain Independent Commission of Inquiry *see* Bassiouni, M.C., *et al.*

*Bahrain Mirror*, '*Bahrain Mirror* publishes important document regarding Jordanian police: 499 policemen are costing Bahrain 1.8 million dollar per month', 3 April 2014, http://bmirror14feb2011.no-ip.org/news/14724.html

*Bahrain Mirror*, 'CNN: 2500 former Jordanian military personnel also working in Bahrain', 3 April 2014, http://bmirror14feb2011.no-ip.org/news/14762.html

Bahrain News Agency, 'HM King Hamad declares state of national safety', 15 March 2011, www.bna.bh/portal/en/news/449960

Bahrain News Agency, 'Bahrain will always remain an oasis of peace and security, says HRH Premier', 21 April 2011, www.bna.bh/portal/en/news/453767?date=2011-05-3

Bahrain News Agency, 'SIU investigates various cases, Chief Public Prosecutor says', 9 October 2013, www.bna.bh/portal/en/news/583581

Bahrain News Agency, 'UAE martyr of duty honoured', 23 July 2014, www.bna.bh/portal/en/news/627084

Bahrain News Agency, 'Society's Secretary General remanded in custody', 5 January 2015, www.bna.bh/portal/en/news/648334

Bahrain Online, 'Let's choose a specific day to begin the popular revolution in Bahrain' [web forum discussion], 26 January 2011, http://bahrainonline.org/showthread.php?t=258985&page=2

Bahrain Online, 'Sites and possibilities of peaceful protest on Bahrain's Day of Rage on 14 February' [web forum discussion], 31 January 2011, www.bahrainonline.org/showthread.php?t=259208

Bahrain Online, 'Positives and negatives of the two sites Pearl Roundabout and . . .' [web forum discussion], 5 February 2011, www.bahrainonline.org/showthread.php?t=259492

Bahrain Online, 'Positives and negatives of King Faisal Corniche' [web forum discussion], 6 February 2011, www.bahrainonline.org/showthread.php?t=259544

Bahrain Online, 'Positives and negatives of the site Marina Club' [web forum discussion], 7 February 2011, http://bahrainonline.org/showthread.php?t=259563

Bahrain Online, 'Is central organization at the Pearl Roundabout better than in the villages' [web forum discussion], 11 February 2011, http://bahrainonline.org/showthread.php?t=259768

Bahrain Watch, 'Bahrain government hires 18 Western companies to improve image after unrest', 23 August 2012, https://bahrainwatch.org/press/press-release-8.php

Bahrain Watch, 'The IP spy files: how Bahrain's government silences anonymous online dissent', August 2013, https://bahrainwatch.org/ipspy/ip-spy-files.pdf

Bahrain Watch, 'Fabrigate', September 2014, https://bahrainwatch.org/media/#!sameerarajab

Bahrain: Written Question – 220679, Ann Clywd to the Secretary of State, Foreign and Commonwealth Office, 14 January 2015, www.theyworkforyou.com/wrans/?id=2015-01-14.220679.h&s=Bahrain

Bakir, V., *Sousveillance, Media and Strategic Political Communication: Iraq, USA, UK*, Continuum, London, 2010.

Barker, T., and Carter, D.L. (eds), 'Typology of police deviance', in *Police Deviance*, Anderson Publishing Co., Cincinatti, 1994, pp. 3–12.

Barthes, R., *Camera Lucida: Reflections on Photography*, Hill and Wang, New York, 1982.

Barton, B.F., and Barton, M., 'Modes of power in technical and professional visuals', *Journal of Business and Technical Communication*, 7/1 (1993), pp. 138–62.

Bassiouni, M.C., Rodley, N., Al-Awadhi, B., Kirsch, P., and Arsanjani, M.H., 'Report of the Bahrain Independent Commission of Inquiry' [BICI Report], 23 November 2011, BICI, Manama, www.bici.org.bh/BICIreportEN.pdf

Baudrillard, J., *The Gulf War Did Not Take Place*, translated by P. Patton, Indiana University Press, Bloomington, 1995.

Baudrillard, J., *The Conspiracy of Art*, Semiotext(e)/MIT Press, New York, 2005.

Bayat, A., 'Revolution and despair', *Mada Masr*, 25 January 2015, www.madamasr.com/opinion/revolution-and-despair

Bayat, A., 'Revolution in bad times', *New Left Review*, March–April 2013, http://newleftreview.org/II/80/asef-bayat-revolution-in-bad-times

BBC News, 'Bahrain unrest: eight Shia activists sentenced to life', 22 June 2011, www.bbc.co.uk/news/world-middle-east-13872206

BBC News, 'Bahrain and Belarus named "enemies of the internet"', 13 March 2012, www.bbc.co.uk/news/technology-17350225

BBC News, 'Bahraini Embassy roof protester threatens to jump', 16 April 2012, www.bbc.com/news/uk-england-london-17734116

Beaugrand, C., 'The Return of the Bahraini Exiles (2001–2006)', Mapping Middle Eastern and North African Diasporas, BRISMES Annual Conference, Leeds, UK, July 2008.

Beaugrand, C., 'In and out moves of the Bahraini opposition: how years of political exile led to the opening of an international front during the 2011 crisis in Bahrain', in A. Khalaf, O. AlShehabi and A. Hanieh (eds), *Transit States: Labour, Migration & Citizenship in the Gulf*, Pluto Press, London, 2014, pp. 289–322.

Beinin J., and Vairel, F. (eds), *Social Movements, Mobilization, and Contestation in the Middle East and North Africa*, Stanford University Press, Stanford, 2013.

Belgrave, C., *Personal Column*, Hutchinson, London, 1960.

Belgrave, C., Papers of Charles Dalrymple-Belgrave: Transcripts of Diaries, 1926–1957, Library of the University of Exeter.

Belgrave, C., 'Annual report for year 1357 (1938–1939)', *The Bahrain Government Annual Reports 1924–1956*, Vol. 2, Archive Editions, Gerrards Cross, 1986, p. 14.

Belgrave, C., 'The Bahrain municipality', in P. Tuson, A. Burdett and E. Quick (eds), *Records of Bahrain 1820–1960*, 8 vols, Archive Editions, Slough, Vol. 3, 1993, p. 651.

Belgrave, C., to Colonel Loch, 'Government of Bahrain', 28 January 1935, in P. Tuson, A. Burdett and E. Quick (eds), *Records of Bahrain 1820–1960*, 8 vols, Archive Editions, Slough, Vol. 5, 1993, p. 82.

Bhatia, L.S.G., and Shehabi, A., Unpublished interview with Nabeel Rajab [audio recording], 12 August 2014, London.

BICI Follow-up Team, 'BICI Follow-Up Report', November 2012, http://iaa.bh/downloads/bici_nov2012_en.pdf

Black, I., 'Bahrain bans all opposition rallies', *The Guardian*, 30 October 2012, www.guardian.co.uk/world/2012/oct/30/bahrain-opposition-protests-ban

Blom Hansen, T., and Stepputat, F., *Sovereign Bodies: Citizens, Migrants, and States in the Postcolonial World*, Princeton University Press, Princeton, 2009.

Booth, R., and Sheffer, J., 'Bahrain regime accused of harassing UK-based students', *The Guardian*, 16 April 2011, www.theguardian.com/world/2011/apr/15/bahrain-regime-uk-students

Boudreau, V., 'Precarious regimes and match-up problems in the explanation of repressive policy', in C. Davenport, H. Johnston, and C. Mueller (eds), *Repression and Mobilization*, University of Minnesota Press, Minneapolis, 2005, pp. 33–57.

Braithwaite, J.B., 'Rethinking radical flank theory: South Africa', RegNet Research Paper No. 2014/23, http://ssrn.com/abstract=237744

British Embassy Manama, 'British Embassy in Bahrain launches Great British Week', Gov.uk, 6 November 2013, www.gov.uk/government/world-location-news/british-embassy-in-bahrain-launches-great-british-week-2014

'British Political Agency: Letter from Tony Parsons to Michael Weir, Foreign and Commonwealth Office', in A. Burdett (ed.), *Records of Bahrain*, Cambridge University Press, Cambridge, 2006, p. 90.

Brown, W., '"The most we can hope for . . .": human rights and the politics of fatalism', *South Atlantic Quarterly*, 103/2–3 (2004), pp. 451–63.

Brumberg, D., 'Transforming the Arab world's protection-racket politics', *Journal of Democracy*, 24/3 (2013), pp. 88–103.

Buali, S., 'Gulf ads on black cabs', *Visual Urban Cultural* [blog], 10 June 2010, http://humanette.blogspot.co.uk/2010/06/gulf-ads-on-black-cabs.html

Buali, S., 'Digital, aesthetic, ephemeral: the shifting narrative of uprising', *Ibraaz*, 2 November 2012, www.ibraaz.org/essays/48

Buckner, E., and Khatib, L., 'The martyrs' revolutions: the role of martyrs in the Arab Spring', *British Journal of Middle Eastern Studies*, 41/4 (2014), pp. 368–84: 1, doi:10.1080/13530194.2014.918802

Burdett, A. (ed.), *Records of Bahrain*, Cambridge University Press, Cambridge, 2006.

Burke, M., 'Philip Hammond: UK military base in Bahrain to "tackle the security threats"', *The Telegraph*, 6 December 2014, www.telegraph.co.uk/news/worldnews/middleeast/bahrain/11277304/Philip-Hammond-UK-military-base-in-Bahrain-to-tackle-the-security-threats.html

Butler, J., *Frames of War: When Is Life Grievable?*, Verso, London, 2010.

Cameron, D., 'Prime Minister's speech to the National Assembly Kuwait', Gov.uk, 22 February 2011, www.gov.uk/government/speeches/prime-ministers-speech-to-the-national-assembly-kuwait

Campaign Against the Arms Trade, 'Saudi Arabia uses UK-made armoured vehicles in Bahrain crackdown on democracy protestors', 16 March 2011, www.caat.org.uk/media/press-releases/2011-03-16

Cassel, M., 'Even Bahrain's use of "Miami model" policing will not stop the uprising', *The Guardian*, 3 December 2011, www.theguardian.com/commentisfree/2011/dec/03/bahrain-miami-model-policing

Cassel, M., 'Suppressing the narrative in Bahrain', Al Jazeera English, 16 February 2012, www.aljazeera.com/indepth/features/2012/02/201229153055296176.html

Castells, M., *The Rise of the Network Society*, Blackwell, Oxford, 1996.

Cavatorta, F. (ed.), *Civil Society Activism under Authoritarian Rule: A Comparative Perspective*, Routledge, Oxford, 2013.

CBS News, 'Bahrain clashes: "Riot police showed no mercy"', 17 March 2011, www.cbsnews.com/news/bahrain-clashes-riot-police-showed-no-mercy/

Chouliaraki, L., *The Spectatorship of Suffering*, SAGE, London, 2006.

CNN iReport, 'A statement by Bahraini Youth for Freedom', 11 February 2011, http://ireport.cnn.com/docs/DOC-554209

Cornell, V.J., and Henry-Blakemore, V.G. (eds), *Voices of Islam Volume III: Voices of Life: Family, Home and Society*, Praeger Publishers, Westport, 2007.

Crystal, J., 'Human rights in the Arab world', *Human Rights Quarterly*, 16/3 (1994), pp. 435–54.

Curtis, A., 'If you take my advice – I'd repress them', BBC Blogs, 11 May 2012, www.bbc.co.uk/blogs/adamcurtis/posts/if_you_take_my_advice_-_id_rep

Curzon, G.N., *Lord Curzon in India: Being a Selection from his Speeches as Viceroy & Governor-General of India, 1898–1905*, MacMillan, London, 1906.

Daly, C.K., 'Note on the political situation in Bahrain November 1921', 6 January 1922, in P. Tuson, A. Burdett and E. Quick (eds), *Records of Bahrain 1820–1960*, 8 vols, Archive Editions, Slough, Vol. 3, 1993, p. 669.

Davenport, C., Johnston, H., and Mueller, C., *Repression and Mobilization*, University of Minnesota Press, Minneapolis, 2005.

Debord, G., *Comments on the Society of the Spectacle*, translated by M. Imrie, Verso, London, 1998.

Debord, G., *Society of the Spectacle,* translated by K. Knabb, Rebel Press, London, 2000.

Della Porta, D., Peterson, A., and Reiter, H. (eds), *The Policing of Transnational Protest*, Ashgate, Aldershot and Burlington, 2006.

Desmukh, F., 'The internet in Bahrain: breaking the monopoly of information', *Foreign Policy*, 21 September 2010, http://mideast.foreignpolicy.com/posts/2010/09/21/bahrain_government_vs_the_internet

Desmukh, F., 'Myths and lies in the Bahrain infowars' [blog], 11 April 2011, http://revolutionbahrain2.blogspot.se/2011/04/myths-and-lies-in-bahrain-infowars.html

Desmukh, F., 'An epilogue for Liliane Khalil' [blog], 2011, http://chanad.posterous.com/an-epilogue-for-liliane-khalil

Desmukh, F., 'British intelligence gathering firm assists Bahraini regime amidst crackdown' [blog], 2011, http://chanad.posterous.com/british-intelligencegathering-firm-assists-b

Desmukh, F., 'Bahrain government hacked lawyers and activists with UK spyware', Bahrain Watch blog, 7 August 2014, https://bahrainwatch.org/blog/2014/08/07/uk-spyware-used-to-hack-bahrain-lawyers-activists/

Dijk, J.A.G.M. van, *De Netwerkmaatschappij, Sociale aspecten van nieuwe media*, first, second and third editions, Bohn Stafleu van Loghum, Houten, Netherlands, and Zaventem, Belgium, 1991/1993/1997.

Dixon, S., and agencies, 'Facebook "used to hunt down Bahrain dissidents"', *The Telegraph*, 4 August 2011, www.telegraph.co.uk/expat/expatnews/8681230/Facebook-used-to-hunt-down-Bahrain-dissidents.html

Dooley, B., 'Seven helpful things the new ambassador to Bahrain can do', *World Post*, 16 December 2014, www.huffingtonpost.com/brian-dooley/seven-helpful-things-the_b_6336304.html

Dooley, B. '"Troll" attacks on #Bahrain tweets show depth of government attempts to silence dissent', *Huffington Post*, 18 November 2011, http://www.huffingtonpost.com/brian-dooley/troll-attacks-on-bahrain_b_1099642.html

Doward, J., 'UK training Saudi forces used to crush Arab spring', *The Guardian*, 29 May 2011, www.theguardian.com/world/2011/may/28/uk-training-saudi-troops

Doward, J., and Lewis, B., 'UK exporting surveillance technology to repressive nations', *The Guardian*, 7 April 2012, www.guardian.co.uk/world/2012/apr/07/surveillance-technology-repressive-regimes

Ehteshami, A., and Wright, S., *Reform in the Middle East Oil Monarchies*, Ithaca Press, Reading, 2011.

El-Mahdi, R., 'Orientalising the Egyptian Uprising', *Jadaliyya*, 11 April 2011, www.jadaliyya.com/pages/index/1214/orientalising-the-egyptian-uprising

Esseghaier, M., '"Tweeting out a tyrant": social media and the Tunisian Revolution', *Wi: Journal of Mobile Media*, 7/1 (2012), http://wi.mobilities.ca/tweeting-out-a-tyrant-social-media-and-the-tunisian-revolution/

European Center for Constitutional and Human Rights, 'Gamma/FinFisher: no investigation into German-British software company', 12 December 2014, www.ecchr.de/surveillance-technology/articles/human-rights-organisations-file-oecd-complaints-against-surveillance-firms-gamma-international-and-trovicor.html

February 14 Youth Coalition, 'Pearl Charter', 2011, https://docs.google.com/file/d/0B4hFNWHWtbDGZGQyODM2N2MtMGM2ZC00NmJjLWE3MWQtMDQyZTNkMDk3YWYy/edit

Ferrara, F., 'Why regimes create disorder: Hobbes's dilemma during a Rangoon summer', *Journal of Conflict Resolution*, 47 (2003), pp. 302-25.

Fielding, N., and Cobain, I., 'Revealed: US spy operation that manipulates social media', *The Guardian*, 12 March 2011, www.theguardian.com/technology/2011/mar/17/us-spy-operation-social-networks

Fisk, R., 'I saw these brave doctors trying to save lives – these charges are a pack of lies', *The Independent*, 14 June 2011, www.independent.co.uk/voices/commentators/fisk/robert-fisk-i-saw-these-brave-doctors-trying-to-save-lives-ndash-these-charges-are-a-pack-of-lies-2297100.html

Foran, J., *Taking Power: On the Origins of Third World Revolution*, Cambridge University Press, Cambridge, 2006.

Foreign Affairs Committee, 'Bilateral relations with Bahrain', in *The UK's Relations with Saudi Arabia and Bahrain* (HC 2013-14, 88), Ch. 4, www.publications.parliament.uk/pa/cm201314/cmselect/cmfaff/88/8808.htm

Foreign Affairs Committee, 'Written evidence from Dr Mike Diboll', in *The UK's Relations with Saudi Arabia and Bahrain* (HC 2013-14, 88), www.publications.parliament.uk/pa/cm201314/cmselect/cmfaff/88/88vw25.htm

Foucault, M., *Discipline and Punish: The Birth of the Prison*, translated by A. Sheridan, Pantheon, New York, 1977.

Foucault, M., 'Nietzsche, Genealogy, History', in D. Bouchard (ed.), *Language, Counter Memory, Practice: Selected Essays and Interviews*, translated by D. F. Bouchard and S. Simon, Cornell University Press, New York, 1977, pp. 139-64.

Foucault, M., and Miskowiec, J., 'Of other spaces', *Diacritics*, 16/1 (1986), pp. 22-27.

Freedom House, 'Freedom on the Net 2012: Bahrain', 2012, www.freedomhouse.org/sites/default/files/Bahrain%202012_0.pdf

Freedom House, 'Freedom on the Net 2013: Bahrain', 2013, www.freedomhouse.org/sites/default/files/resources/FOTN%202013_Bahrain.pdf

Freedom House, 'Freedom of the Press 2013: Bahrain', 2013, www.freedomhouse.org/report/freedom-press/2013/bahrain

Fuccaro, N., *Histories of City and State in the Persian Gulf*, Cambridge University Press, Cambridge, 2009.

Gamson, W.A., *The Strategy of Social Protest*, Wadsworth, Belmont, CA, 1990.

Gandy Jr, O.H., *The Panoptic Sort: A Political Economy of Personal Information*, Westview Press, Boulder, 1993.

Gardner, F., 'Bahrain's security clampdown divides kingdom', BBC News, 14 April 2011, www.bbc.co.uk/news/world-middle-east-13088600

Gause, F.G., and Yom, S.L., 'Resilient royals: how Arab monarchies hang on', *Journal of Democracy*, 23, 74-88, 15 October 2012.

Geller, W.A., 'Police misconduct: scope of the problems and remedies', *ACJS Today*, 6-8 February 1984.

Gengler, J., 'The most dangerous men in Bahrain', *Religion and Politics in Bahrain* [blog], 5 June 2011, http://bahrainipolitics.blogspot.se/2011/06/most-dangerous-men-in-bahrain.html

Gengler, J., 'A Gulf NATO?: what the new U.S.-GCC security partnership means for Bahrain', *Religion and Politics in Bahrain* [blog], 31 October 2011, http://bahrainipolitics.blogspot.co.uk/2011_10_01_archive.html

Gengler, J., 'Bahrain's Sunni awakening', *Middle East Report Online*, 17 January 2012, www.merip.org/mero/mero011712

Goodman, J.D., '"Twitter Trolls" haunt discussions of Bahrain online', *The Lede* [*New York Times* blog], 11 October 2011, http://thelede.blogs.nytimes.com/2011/10/11/twitter-trolls-haunt-discussions-of-bahrain-online/

Greenwald, G., 'Why didn't CNN's international arm air its own documentary on Bahrain's Arab Spring repression?', *The Guardian*, 4 September 2012, www.theguardian.com/world/2012/sep/04/cnn-international-documentary-bahrain-arab-spring-repression

Gregg, B., 'State-based human rights', Paper presented at the annual meeting of the Midwest Political Science Association, Palmer House Hotel, Chicago, 12 April 2007.

Grossman, L.K., *The Electronic Republic. Reshaping Democracy in the Information Age*, Viking, New York, 1995.

Guilhot, N., *The Democracy Makers: Human Rights and the Politics of Global Order*, Columbia University Press, Chichester, 2005.

*Gulf Daily News*, 'Chaotic scenes outside hospital', 18 February 2011, www.gulf-daily-news.com/NewsDetails.aspx?storyid=299770

*Gulf Daily News*, 'Crown Prince urges restraint', 19 February 2011, www.gulf-daily-news.com/NewsDetails.aspx?storyid=299817

*Gulf Daily News*, 'Security is top wish of young', 15 June 2011, www.gulf-daily-news.com/NewsDetails.aspx?storyid=307981

*Gulf Daily News*, 'Group formed to help policemen', 2 January 2012, www.thefreelibrary.com/Group+formed+to+help+policemen.-a0276117481

*Gulf News*, 'Reforms made Bahrain beacon of democracy', 8 January 2003, http://gulfnews.com/news/uae/general/reforms-made-bahrain-beacon-of-democracy-1.344082

Halvorssen, T., 'PR mercenaries their dictator masters, and the human rights stain', *World Post*, 19 May 2011, www.huffingtonpost.com/thor-halvorssen/pr-mercenaries-their-dict_b_863716.html?

Hama, M.R., and Human Rights Watch. *"Interfere, Restrict, Control": Restraints on Freedom of Association in Bahrain.*

Hammond, A., 'Bahrain media play role in tension after protests', Reuters, 5 May 2011, http://in.reuters.com/article/2011/05/05/idINIndia-56790720110505

Hammond, A., 'Tense Bahrain under spotlight again over uprisings', Reuters, 2 February 2012, http://uk.reuters.com/article/2012/02/02/uk-bahrain-bassiouni-return-idUKTRE8110S720120202

Hanieh, A., *Lineages of Revolt: Issues of Contemporary Capitalism in the Middle East*, Haymarket Books, Chicago, 2013.

Hashem, A., 'The Bahrain Blackout in Arab Media', *Al-Monitor*, 13 January 2013, www.al-monitor.com/pulse/iw/originals/2013/01/bahrain-arab-spring-protests.html

Hashem, A., 'The Arab spring has shaken Arab TV's credibility', *The Guardian*, 3 April 2012, www.theguardian.com/commentisfree/2012/apr/03/arab-spring-arab-tv-credibility

Hasso, F.S., 'Sectarian/gendered police and rupture in Bahrain's Pearl Revolution', in F.S. Hasso and Z. Salime (eds), *Borders, Bodies, and Intimate Politics in the Arab Revolutions* (forthcoming).

Hasso, F.S., and Salime, Z. (eds), *Borders, Bodies, and Intimate Politics in the Arab Revolutions* (forthcoming).

HC Deb 17 Feb 2011.

HC Deb 22 February 2012, Vol. 540, Col. 800W, www.publications.parliament.uk/pa/cm201212/cmhansrd/cm120222/text/120222w0001.htm

Hertog, S., *Princes, Brokers, and Bureaucrats: Oil and the State in Saudi Arabia*, reprint edition, Cornell University Press, Ithaca, 2011.

Heydemann, S., 'Upgrading authoritarianism in the Arab world', Analysis Paper 13, The Saban Center for Middle East Policy at The Brookings Institution, October 2007.

HL Deb 15 May 1903, cited in Sir A.W. Ward and G.P. Gooch, *The Cambridge History of British Foreign Policy 1783–1919: Vol. 1, 1783–1815*, Cambridge University Press, Cambridge, 1922, pp. 320–21.

Hofheinz, A., 'Arab internet usage: popular trends and public impact', in N. Sakr (ed.), *Arab Media and Political Renewal: Community, Legitimacy and Public Life*, I.B. Tauris, London, 2007, pp. 56–79.

Holman, Z., private interview with Sayed Alwadei, 4 June 2013, London.

Holman, Z., telephone interview with Nabeel Rajab, 31 August 2014, London.

Horne, J., 'Who provides the Ministry of Interior with CCTV?', Bahrain Watch, 26 August 2013, https://bahrainwatch.org/blog/2013/08/26/who-provides-the-ministry-of-interior-with-cctv/

Human Rights Watch, 'Routine abuse, routine denial: civil rights and the political crisis in Bahrain', June 1997, http://pantheon.hrw.org/reports/1997/bahrain/

Human Rights Watch, 'Torture redux: the revival of physical coercion during interrogations in Bahrain', 2010, www.hrw.org/sites/default/files/reports/bahrain0210webwcover_0.pdf

Human Rights Watch, 'World report 2011: Bahrain', 2011, www.hrw.org/world-report-2011/world-report-2011-bahrain

Human Rights Watch, 'Bahrain: Nada Dhaif, accidental activist', 2012, www.hrw.org/audio/2012/04/13/bahrain-nada-dhaif-accidental-activist

Human Rights Watch, '"Interfere, restrict, control": restraints on freedom of association in Bahrain', June 2013, www.hrw.org/sites/default/files/reports/bahrain0613webwcover.pdf

Human Rights Watch, 'Criminalizing dissent, entrenching impunity: persistent failures of the Bahraini justice system since the BICI Report', May 2014, www.hrw.org/sites/default/files/reports/bahrain0514_forUpload.pdf

Human Rights Watch, 'Proposed Arab court of Human Rights: an empty vessel without substantial changes to the draft statute', 6 June 2014, www.hrw.org/news/2014/06/06/proposed-arab-court-human-rights-empty-vessel-without-substantial-changes-draft-stat

Humphreys, L., 'Who's watching whom? A study of interactive technology and surveillance', *Journal of Communication*, 61 (2011), p. 575–95.

Ibish, H., 'The Bahrain Uprising: towards confrontation or accommodation', A Henry Jackson Society Strategic Briefing, 2011, www.henryjacksonsociety.org/cms/harriercollectionitems/Bahrain1c.pdf

'Implementation of the Bahrain Independent Commission of Inquiry Report', Hearing before the Tom Lantos Human Rights Commission, House of Representatives, 112th Congress, Second Session, 1 August 2012, http://tlhrc.house.gov/docs/transcripts/2012_08_01_Bahrain/08_01_12_Bahrain.pdf

Information Affairs Authority, 'Press rules and regulations', 2002, www.iaa.bh/policiesPressrules.aspx

Information Affairs Authority, 'Summary of BICI report', November 2012, http://iaa.bh/downloads/BICI_Executive_Summary.pdf

ITN Source, 'UK: Bahraini activist disrupts UK horse show attended by Queen Elizabeth II', 14 May 2013, www.itnsource.com/shotlist/RTV/2013/05/14/RTV010198882/RTV010198882-120?v=2

Ivkovic, S.K., 'Police (mis)behavior: a cross-cultural study of corruption seriousness', *Policing*, 28/3 (2005), pp. 546–66, paraphrased by N.W. Pino and L.M. Johnson, 'Police deviance and community relations in Trinidad and Tobago', *Policing: An International Journal of Police Strategies & Management*, 34/3 (2011), pp. 454–78.

Jacoby, J., 'The Arab Spring', *Boston Globe*, 10 March 2005, www.boston.com/news/globe/editorial_opinion/oped/articles/2005/03/10/the_arab_spring/

Jahshan, P., 'The 2011 Arab uprisings and the persistence of orientalism', *The Arab World Geographer*, 14/2 (2011), pp. 122–27.

Jasper, J.M., *The Art of Moral Protest: Culture, Biography, and Creativity in Social Movements*, University of Chicago Press, Chicago, 1997.

Johnson, D.H., 'From military to tribal police: policing the Upper Nile province of the Sudan', in D.M. Anderson and D. Killingray (eds), *Policing the Empire: Government, Authority and Control, 1830–1940*, Manchester University Press, Manchester, 1991, pp. 151–67.

Jones, M.O., 'Here's looking at YouTube', Masters dissertation, Durham University, 2010, https://marcowenjones.files.wordpress.com/2012/02/dissertations1.pdf

Jones, M.O., 'Sexing up a city: neoliberalism, public space and protest in Bahrain', *Marc Owen Jones* [blog], 4 March 2011, www.marcowenjones.hostbyet2.com/?p=107

Jones, M.O., 'The hunt for #LilianeKhalil', Al Jazeera English, 4 August 2011, www.youtube.com/watch?v=TgCp15kVggI

Jones, M.O., 'Police brutality from five different angles', *Marc Owen Jones* [blog], 16 December 2011, www.marcowenjones.hostbyet2.com/?p=446

Jones, M.O., 'Bahrain special: the steel rods of the police', *EA Worldview*, 16 January 2012, www.enduringamerica.com/home/2012/1/16/bahrain-special-the-steel-rods-of-the-police.html

Jones, M.O., 'Creative resistance in Bahrain', *Marc Owen Jones* [blog], 19 January 2012, www.marcowenjones.hostbyet2.com/?p=512#comment-2356

Jones, M.O., 'Bahrain video feature: celebrating creative resistance', *EA Worldview*, 21 January 2012, www.enduringamerica.com/home/2012/1/21/bahrain-video-feature-celebrating-creative-resistance-owen-j.html

Jones, M.O., 'Some of Bahrain's police are being trained by the US military – but how?', *Marc Owen Jones* [blog], 7 February 2012, http://marcowenjones.word press.com/2012/02/07/are-bahrains-police-being-trained-by-the-us-military/

Jones, M.O., 'Bahrain's PR machine threatens free speech', Index on Censorship, 14 February 2012, http://www.indexoncensorship.org/2012/02/bahrains-pr-machine-threatens-free-speech/

Jones, M.O., 'For the record: police in Bahrain throw Molotov cocktails', *Marc Owen Jones* [blog], 18 March 2012, http://marcowenjones.wordpress.com/2012/03/18/for-the-record-police-in-bahrain-throw-molotov-cocktails/

Jones, M.O., 'Bahrain activists' trouble with trolls', Index on Censorship Uncut, 15 May 2012, http://uncut.indexoncensorship.org/2012/05/bahrain-marc-owen-jones-twitter-trolls/

Jones, M.O., 'A right royal robbery: how the Al Khalifa took a quarter of Bahrain's wealth', *Marc Owen Jones* [blog], 16 August 2012, https://marcowenjones.wordpress.com/2012/08/16/a-right-royal-robbery-how-the-al-khalifas-have-taken-a-third-of-bahrains-wealth/

Jones, M.O., 'Bahrain government flaunt their inadequacy in BICI follow up report', *Marc Owen Jones* [blog], 21 November 2012, http://marcowenjones.wordpress.com/2012/11/21/government-flaunt-their-inadequacy-in-bici-follow-up-report/

Jones, M.O., 'Oppression of Bahrain subjects by the ruling family in Bahrain in the early 1900s: the full list', *Marc Owen Jones* [blog], 31 December 2012, http://marcowenjones.wordpress.com/2012/12/31/oppression-of-bahrain-subjects-by-the-ruling-family-in-bahrain-in-the-early-1900s-the-full-list/

Jones, M.O., 'Member of Bahrain ruling family walks into ministry and threatens to shoot an employee', *Marc Owen Jones* [blog], 5 January 2013, https://marcowenjones.wordpress.com/2013/01/05/member-of-bahrain-ruling-family-walks-into-ministry-and-threatens-to-shoot-an-employee/

Jones, M.O., 'Media distortion and lack of police accountability: the death of Mahmood al-Jaziri', Bahrain Watch, 22 March 2013, https://bahrainwatch.org/blog/2013/03/22/media-distortion-lack-of-police-accountability-the-death-of-mahmood-al-jaziri/

Jones, M.O., 'Social media, surveillance, and social control in the Bahrain Uprising', *Westminster Papers in Communication and Culture: The Role of Social Media in the Arab Uprisings, Past and Present*, 9/2 (April 2013).

Jones, M.O., 'Bahrain's prime minister and his role in the anti-Shia crackdown of the 1980s', *Marc Owen Jones* [blog], 8 April 2013, http://marcowenjones. wordpress.com/2013/04/08/bahrains-prime-minister-and-his-role-in-the-anti-shia-crackdown-of-the-1980s/

Jones, M.O., 'Attitudes of British officials to the Al Khalifa family between 1920 and 1954', *Marc Owen Jones* [blog], 23 May 2013, https://marcowenjones. wordpress.com/2013/05/23/attitudes-of-british-officials-to-the-al-khalifa-family-between-1920-and-1954/

Jones, M.O., 'Methods of a mild Spanish Inquisition: British torture in Bahrain before Ian Henderson', *Marc Owen Jones* [blog], 29 May 2013, https:// marcowenjones.wordpress.com/2013/05/29/methods-of-a-mild-spanish-inquisition-british-torture-in-bahrain-before-ian-henderson/

Jones, M.O., 'The history of British involvement in Bahrain's internal security', openDemocracy, 8 August 2013, www.opendemocracy.net/ opensecurity/marc-owen-jones/history-of-british-involvement-in-bahrains-internal-security

Jones, M.O., 'Bahrain's state unaccountability', *Muftah*, 17 April 2014, http:// muftah.org/bahrains-state-unaccountability/#.VMEojoesXbA

Jones, M.O., 'Satire, social media and revolutionary cultural production in the Bahrain Uprising' [online video], 2014, http://youtu.be/D8EC6EgiaAE

Jones, M.O., email interview with Abdulhadi Khalaf, 13 December 2014.

Jones, T.C., 'Bahrain's revolutionaries speak: an exclusive interview with Bahrain's Coalition of February 14th Youth', *Jadaliyya*, 22 March 2012, www. jadaliyya.com/pages/index/4777/bahrains-revolutionaries-speak_an-exclusive-interv

Jones, T.C., 'Theorizing the Arabian Peninsula roundtable: thinking globally about Arabia', *Jadaliyya*, 22 April 2013, www.jadaliyya.com/pages/index/11294/ theorizing-the-arabian-peninsula-roundtable_thinki

Joyce, M., 'The Bahraini Three on St Helena', *Middle East Journal*, 54/4 (2000), pp. 613–23.

Juska, A., and Woolfson, C., 'Policing political protest in Lithuania', *Crime, Law and Social Change*, 57 (2012), pp. 403–24.

Kafai, N., and Shehabi, A., 'The struggle for information: revelations on mercenaries, sectarian agitation, and demographic engineering in Bahrain', *Jadaliyya*, 29 May 2014, www.jadaliyya.com/pages/index/17912/the-struggle-for-information_revelations-on-mercen

Kareem, M., 'Bahrain: are police cars running over protesters on purpose?', *Global Voices*, 12 November 2011, http://globalvoicesonline.org/2011/11/12/bahrain-are-police-cars-running-over-protesters-on-purpose/

Keck, M., and Sikkink, K., *Activists Beyond Borders: Advocacy Networks in International Politics*, Cornell University Press, Ithaca, 1998.

Kellner, D., *Media Spectacle and Insurrection, 2011: From the Arab Uprisings to Occupy Everywhere*, Bloomsbury, New York, 2012.

Kelly, S., Cook, S., and Truong, M. (eds), *Freedom on The Net 2012: A Global Assessment of Internet and Digital Media,* Freedom House, New York, 2012.

Kember, S., and Zylinksa, J., *Life after New Media: Mediation as a Vital Process*, MIT Press, Cambridge, MA, 2012.

Kerr, S., 'UAE stops using former British officers as military trainers', *Financial Times*, 22 May 2014, www.ft.com/cms/s/0/53cc2584-e1ab-11e3-9999-00144feabdc0. html?siteedition=uk#axzz3LRhlPTrV

Khalaf, A., 'Labor movements in Bahrain', *Middle East Report*, 132 (1985), pp. 24–9.

Khalaf, A., 'Contentious politics in Bahrain: from ethnic to national and vice versa', Paper to the Fourth Nordic Conference on Middle Eastern Studies: The Middle East in a Globalizing World, 13–16 August 1998, Oslo, http://org.uib. no/smi/pao/khalaf.html

Khalaf, A., 'Unfinished business: contentious politics and state-building in Bahrain', Research Reports in Sociology, Department of Sociology, University of Lund, 2000.

Khalaf, A., Opening remarks, 'Bahrain: 30 years of unconstitutional rule', Parliamentary Human Rights Group, House of Lords, 25 August 2005, http:// jaddwilliam2.blogspot.co.uk/2005/08/royal-dream.html

Khalaf, A., 'Arab reform brief: the outcome of a ten-year process of political reform in Bahrain', Arab Reform Initiative, December 2008, www.arab-reform.net/ sites/default/files/ARB.23_Abdulhadi_Khalaf_ENG.pdf

Khalaf, A., 'The many afterlives of Lulu: the story of Bahrain's Pearl Roundabout', *Ibraaz*, 28 February 2013, www.ibraaz.org/essays/56

Khalaf, A., AlShehabi, O., and Hanieh, A. (eds), *Transit States: Labour, Migration & Citizenship in the Gulf*, Pluto Press, London, 2014.

Khalaf, S., 'Poetics and politics of newly invented traditions in the Gulf: camel racing in the United Arab Emirates', *Ethnology*, 39/3 (2000), pp. 46–56.

Khatib, L., *Filming the Modern Middle East: Politics in the Cinemas of Hollywood and the Arab World*, I.B. Tauris, London, 2006.

Khatib, L., *Image Politics in the Middle East: The Role of the Visual in Political Struggle*, I.B. Tauris, London, 2013.

Khouri, R., 'Arab Spring or revolution', *The Globe and Mail*, 18 August 2011, www.theglobeandmail.com/globe-debate/arab-spring-or-revolution/article 626345/

Khuri, F., *Tribe and State in Bahrain: The Transition of Social and Political Authority in an Arab State*, University of Chicago Press, Chicago, 1981.

Kilbride, E., '"Too gay to represent #Bahrain": homophobia and nationalism in the wake of a revolution', *Muftah*, 15 December 2012, http://muftah.org/homophobia-and-nationalism-in-bahrain/

Killingray, D., 'Guarding the extending frontier: policing the Gold Coast, 1865–1913', in D.M. Anderson and D. Killingray (eds), *Policing the Empire: Government, Authority and Control, 1830–1940*, Manchester University Press, Manchester, 1991, pp. 106–25.

Kinninmont, J., *Bahrain: Beyond the Impasse*, Chatham House, London, 2012.

Kinninmont, J., and Sirri, O., 'Bahrain: civil society and political imagination', Research Paper: Middle East and North Africa Programme, October 2014, Chatham House, London.

Krauthammer, C., 'Three Cheers for the Bush Doctrine', *Time*, 7 March 2005, www.time.com/time/magazine/article/0,9171,1034732,00.html

Laguerre, M.S., *Diaspora, Politics and Globalization*, Palgrave Macmillan, New York, 2006.

Law, B., *Bahrain: Policing Protest*, BBC documentary, 26 August 2013.

Lessware, J., 'State of emergency declared in Bahrain', *The National*, 16 March 2011, www.thenational.ae/news/world/middle-east/state-of-emergency-declared-in-bahrain

Louër, L., 'Sectarianism and coup-proofing strategies in Bahrain', *Journal of Strategic Studies*, 36/2 (2013), pp. 245–60.

Lowe, R., 'Bassiouni: new Arab court for human rights is fake "Potemkin tribunal"', International Bar Association, 1 October 2014, www.ibanet.org/Article/Detail. aspx?ArticleUid=c64f9646-15a5-4624-8c07-bae9d9ac42df

Lulu, T. 'In Bahrain, first they came for the athletes', *The Guardian*, 22 April 2011, www.theguardian.com/commentisfree/2011/apr/22/bahrain-counter-revolution-televised-athletes

Lynch, M., 'Obama's "Arab Spring"?', *Foreign Policy*, 6 January 2011, http://lynch.foreignpolicy.com/posts/2011/01/06/obamas_arab_spring

Lyon, D., *Surveillance Society: Monitoring in Everyday Life*, Open University Press, Buckingham, 2001.

McAdam, D., 'Conceptual origins, current problems and future directions', in D. McAdam, J.D. McCarthy, and M.N. Zald (eds) *Comparative Perspectives on Social Movements: Political Opportunities, Mobilizing Structures, and Cultural Framings*, Cambridge University Press, Cambridge, 1996, pp. 23–40.

McDougall, J., 'The British and French empires in the Arab world: some problems of colonial state-formation and its legacy', in S.N. Cummings and R. Hinnebusch (eds) *Sovereignty After Empire: Comparing the Middle East and Central Asia*, Edinburgh University Press, Edinburgh, 2011, pp. 44–65, www.jstor.org/stable/10.3366/j.ctt1r1xmt

Mackinnon, R., *Consent of the Networked: The Worldwide Struggle for Internet Freedom*, Basic Books, New York, 2002 (Kindle edition).

*Mahmood's Den* [blog], '"Just Bahraini" not welcome at checkpoints', 19 March 2011, http://mahmood.tv/2011/03/19/just-bahraini-not-welcome-at-checkpoints//

Mamdani, M., 'Good Muslim, bad Muslim: a political perspective on culture and terrorism', *American Anthropologist*, 104/3 (2005), pp. 766–75.

Manama Document, 'Bahrain's road to freedom and democracy: a joint document by opposition political societies', 12 October 2011, http://alwefaq.net/cms/2011/10/12/5934/

Mann, S., '"Reflectionism" and "diffusionism": new tactics for deconstructing the video surveillance superhighway', *Leonardo*, 31/2 (1998), pp. 93–102.

Mann, S., Nolan, J., and Wellman, B., 'Sousveillance: inventing and using wearable computing devices for data collection in surveillance environments', *Surveillance & Society*, 1/3 (2003), pp. 331–55.

Mapp, H.V., *Leave Well Alone!*, Prittle Brook Publishers, Southend, 1994.

Marczak, B., 'Is Bahrain's government running extremist accounts?', Bahrain Watch blog, 5 August 2013, https://bahrainwatch.org/blog/2013/08/05/is-bahrains-government-running-extremist-accounts/

Marczak, W., 'Bahrain Watch issues urgent advice for activists to stop using @ Zello due to security flaw', Bahrain Watch blog, 7 September 2014, https://bahrainwatch.org/blog/2014/09/07/bahrain-watch-issues-urgent-advice-for-activists-to-stop-using-zello-due-to-security-flaw/

Marczak, W., and Marquis-Boire, M., 'From Bahrain with love: FinFisher's spy kit exposed?', Citizenlab, 25 July 2012, https://citizenlab.org/2012/07/from-bahrain-with-love-finfishers-spy-kit-exposed/

Marczak, W., Scott-Railton, J., Paxson, V., and Marquis-Boire, M., 'When governments hack opponents: a look at actors and technology', 23rd USENIX Security Symposium, 20–22 August 2014, San Diego, www.icir.org/vern/papers/govhack.usesec14.pdf

Matar, M.E., *'Fighting for democracy while supporting autocracy', LobeLog Foreign Policy, 9 October 2014, www.lobelog.com/bahrain-isis-democracy/*

Matthiesen, T., *Sectarian Gulf: Bahrain, Saudi Arabia and the Arab Spring That Wasn't*, Stanford University Press, Stanford, 2013.

Mertens, D.M., 'Philosophy in mixed methods teaching', *International Journal of Multiple Research Approaches*, 4/1 (2010), pp. 9–18.

Mikirova, K., Mueller, K., and Schuhmann, J., 'The influence of civil society activism on regional governance structures in the Russian Federation: cross regional and policy comparisons', in F. Cavatorta (ed.), *Civil Society Activism under Authoritarian Rule: A Comparative Perspective*, Routledge, Oxford, 2013, pp. 111–34.

Mitchell, T., *Colonising Egypt*, University of California Press, Berkeley, 1991.

Mitchell, T., *My Interesting Life* [blog], 4–9 December 2011, https://tonydmitchell. wordpress.com/2011/12/04/hello-world/

Mohan, N., 'Banned books from Bahrain', *Sampsonia Way*, 6 June 2012, www. sampsoniaway.org/blog/2012/06/06/banned-books-from-bahrain/

Monroe, W., 'Prominent shias paint gloomy picture of shia outlook in Bahrain' [diplomatic cable], 9 April 2007, WikiLeaks, https://search.wikileaks.org/ plusd/cables/07MANAMA328_a.html

Morgan, G., 'HMRC faces High Court challenge over spy software sales', V3.co. uk, 16 April 2013, www.v3.co.uk/v3-uk/news/2261787/hmrc-faces-high-court-challenge-over-spy-software-sales

Morozov, E., *The Dark Side of Internet Freedom: The Net Delusion*, Public Affairs, New York, 2011.

Moyn, S., *The Last Utopia: Human Rights in History*, Belknap, London, 2010.

Muhammad, P., 'Foreign relations: tit-for-tat proposed over visa rejections', *The Express Tribune*, 1 April 2014, http://tribune.com.pk/story/689833/foreign-relations-tit-for-tat-proposed-over-visa-rejections/

Musil, R., *Monuments, Posthumous Papers of a Living Author*, translated by P. Worsman, Eridanos Press, Boston, 1987.

@NABEELRAJAB, 'Many #Bahrain men who joined #terrorism & #ISIS came from security institutions and those institutions were the first ideological incubator' [Twitter post], 28 September 2014, https://twitter.com/nabeelrajab/ status/516179409720852480

Nakhleh, E., *Bahrain: Political Development in a Modernizing Society*, Lexington Books, New York, 2011.

Nash, G., *From Empire to Orient: Travellers to the Middle East 1830-1924*, I.B. Tauris, London, 2005.

Neal, D., 'Court rules HMRC must end FinFisher spy software stonewalling', V3.co.uk, 13 May 2014, www.v3.co.uk/v3-uk/news/2344407/court-rules-hmrc-must-end-finfisher-spy-software-stonewalling

Nepstad, S.E., 'Mutiny and nonviolence in the Arab Spring: exploring military defections and loyalty in Egypt, Bahrain, and Syria', *Journal of Peace Research*, 50/3 (2013).

Newman, M., and Wright, O., 'Kazakhstan: PR firm's plan to target Sting after gig boycott', *The Independent*, 8 December 2011, www.independent.co.uk/ news/uk/politics/kazakhstan-pr-firms-plan-to-target-sting-after-gig-boycott-video-6273824.html

O'Connor, T.R, 'Police deviance and ethics', MegaLinks in Criminal Justice, 2005, http://faculty.ncwc.edu/toconnor/205/205lect11.htm

O'Murchu, C., and Kerr, S., 'Bahrain land deals highlight alchemy of making money from sand', *Financial Times*, 10 December 2014.

'Oil and gas regulation in Bahrain: overview', Practical Law: A Thomson Reuters Legal Solution, 2014, http://uk.practicallaw.com/0-525-3563#null

Olton website, www.olton.co.uk/services/reputation-management

Onley, J., *The Arabian Frontier of the British Raj. Merchants, Rulers and British in the Nineteenth-Century Gulf*, Oxford University Press, Oxford, 2007.

Oron, Y. (ed.), *Middle East Record*, Vol. 2, Israel Centre for Scientific Translations, Tel Aviv, 1961.

Physicians for Human Rights, 'Tear-gas related deaths in Bahrain', 2012, http://physiciansforhumanrights.org/issues/persecution-of-health-workers/bahrain/bahrain-tear-gas-deaths.html

Physicians for Human Rights, 'Weaponizing tear gas: Bahrain's unprecedented use of toxic chemical agents against civilians', August 2012, https://s3.amazonaws.com/PHR_Reports/Bahrain-TearGas-Aug2012-small.pdf

Pino, N.W., and Johnson, L.M., 'Police deviance and community relations in Trinidad and Tobago', *Policing: An International Journal of Police Strategies & Management*, 34/3 (2011), pp. 454–78.

Pollack, A., 'Underlying the uprisings', *International Socialist Review*, Issue 93, http://isreview.org/issue/93/underlying-uprisings

Posner, E., 'The case against human rights', *The Guardian*, 4 December 2014, www.theguardian.com/news/2014/dec/04/-sp-case-against-human-rights

Poster, M., *The Mode of Information: Poststructuralism and Social Construct*, University of Chicago Press, Chicago, 1990.

Potter, L.G. (ed.), *Sectarian Politics in the Persian Gulf*, Oxford University Press, Oxford, 2014.

'Privacy International & Gamma International UK Ltd: Final statement after examination of complaint', December 2014, www.gov.uk/government/uploads/system/uploads/attachment_data/file/402462/BIS-15-93-Final_statement_after_examination_of_complaint_Privacy_International_and_Gamma_International_UK_Ltd.pdf

Project on Middle East Democracy, 'One year later: assessing Bahrain's implementation of the BICI report', November 2012, http://pomed.org/wp-content/uploads/2013/12/One-Year-Later-Assessing-Bahrains-Implementation-of-the-BICI-Report.pdf

Punch, M., 'Rotten orchards: "pestilence", police misconduct and system failure', *Policing and Society*, 13/2 (2003), pp. 171–96.

Quinn, B., 'Bahrain to sue newspaper over articles', *The Guardian*, 15 June 2011, www.theguardian.com/world/2011/jun/15/bahrain-sue-independent-newspaper-articles

Ragazzi, F., 'Governing diasporas', *International Political Sociology*, 3 (2009), pp. 378–97.

Rawlinson, K., 'Revealed: lobbyists' plans to hijack "people's petitions"', *The Independent*, 10 April 2012, www.independent.co.uk/news/uk/home-news/revealed-lobbyists-plans-to-hijack-peoples-petitions-7628058.html

REDRESS, Letter to The Rt Hon. Baroness Warsi, 10 April 2014, www.redress. org/downloads/publications/10%20April%202014%20Letter%20to%20 Baroness%20Warsi.pdf

REDRESS and IRCT, 'Bahrain: Fundamental Reform or Torture Without End?', April 2013, www.redress.org/downloads/country-reports/Fundamentalre form.pdf

Reed, J.-P., 'Emotions in context: Revolutionary accelerators, hope, moral outrage, and other emotions in the making of Nicaragua's revolution', *Theory and Society*, 33/6 (2004).

Reisz, T., 'Bahrain: a roundabout way to signify nothing', *World Post*, 4 May 2011, www.huffingtonpost.com/todd-reisz/bahrain-roundabout_b_844276.html

Reporters Without Borders, 'Bahraini and Syrian authorities try to impose news blackout', 4 April 2011, http://en.rsf.org/bahraini-and-syrianauthorities-04-04-2011,39946.html

Reuters, 'Bahraini protester dies after being shot at demonstration', 31 March 2012, http://in.reuters.com/article/2012/03/31/bahrain-death-idINDEE82U05S20120331

Rheingold, H., *The Virtual Community: Homesteading on the Electronic Frontier*, HarperCollins, New York, 1993.

Rihani, A.F., *Around the Coasts of Arabia,* Constable, London, 1930.

Risse, T., and Sikkink, K., 'The socialization of international human rights norms into domestic practices', in T. Risse, S. Ropp, and K. Sikkink (eds) *The Power of Human Rights: International Norms and Domestic Politics*, Cambridge University Press, Cambridge, 1999, pp. 1–38.

Roan, D., 'Bahrain F1 Grand Prix rights complaint "merits examination"', BBC News, 24 October 2014, www.bbc.com/news/uk-politics-29762156

Robinson, A., 'An A to Z of theory: Alain Badiou: the event', *Ceasefire*, 15 December 2014, https://ceasefiremagazine.co.uk/alain-badiou-event/

RTT News, 'Bahrain court orders deportation of 10 people stripped of nationality', 10 October 2014, www.rttnews.com/2405849/bahrain-court-orders-deportation-of-10-people-stripped-of-nationality.aspx?type=gn&utm_source=google& utm_campaign=sitemap

Russia Today, 'Royal treatment: Bahrain princess and princes accused of torturing activists', 25 January 2013, http://rt.com/news/princess-torture-bahrain-detention-665/

Sabla Oman, 'Youth of Manama attacked by thugs manage to arrest them' [web forum discussion], 15 March 2011, http://avb.s-oman.net/showthread.php?t=11 01114&s=3c7a4c0f488fcf7eb259b55d6f654ab6

Saco, D., *Cybering Democracy: Public Space and the Internet,* University of Minnesota Press, Minneapolis, 2002.

Saideman, S., 'Conclusion: thinking theoretically about identity and foreign policy', in S. Telhami and M. Barnett (eds), *Identity and Foreign Policy in the Middle East*, Cornell University Press, Ithaca, NY, 2002.

Scahill, J., 'The Miami model', Democracy Now! on Information Clearing House, 24 November 2000, www.informationclearinghouse.info/article5286.htm

Scarry, E., *The Body in Pain: The Making and Unmaking of the World*, Oxford University Press, New York, 1985.

Sharif al-Sayyid, I., Court of Appeal, Bahrain, 5 June 2012.

Sellin, T., *Culture, Conflict and Crime*, Social Science Research Council, New Jersey, 1938.

Shehabi, A., 'Bahrain's flashy crony capitalism cannot last', *The Guardian*, 20 May 2012, www.theguardian.com/commentisfree/2012/may/20/bahrain-flashy-crony-capitalism

Shehabi, A., 'Bahrain's sovereign hypocrisy', *Foreign Policy*, 9 August 2014, http://foreignpolicy.com/2013/08/14/bahrains-sovereign-hypocrisy/

Shehabi, A., 'Why is Bahrain outsourcing extremism?', *Foreign Policy*, 29 October 2014, www.foreignpolicy.com/articles/2014/10/29/why_is_bahrain_outsourcing_extremism_isis_democracy

Shehabi, A., 'Inviolable sheikhs and radical subjects: Bahrain's recurring sovereignty crisis', *Arab Studies Journal* (forthcoming).

Shehabi, A., and Jones, T.C., 'Bahrain's revolutionaries', *Foreign Policy*, 2 January 2012, http://foreignpolicy.com/2012/01/02/bahrains-revolutionaries/

@SheikhKhalifaPM, 'Bloody typical..hot young women only get in touch with me when they want something from me..like maybe my IP address' [Twitter post], 18 September 2014, https://twitter.com/SheikhKhalifaPM/status/512492182381400064

Silver, V., 'Gamma says no spyware sold to Bahrain: may be stolen copy', Bloomberg, 27 July 2012, www.bloomberg.com/news/2012-07-27/gamma-says-no-spyware-sold-to-bahrain-may-be-stolen-copy.html

Silver, V., and Elgin, B., 'Torture in Bahrain becomes routine with help from Nokia Siemens', Bloomberg, 22 August 2011, www.bloomberg.com/news/2011-08-22/torture-in-bahrain-becomes-routine-with-help-from-nokia-siemens-networking.html

Singh Grewal, S., 'Ex-servicemen to form society', *Gulf Daily News*, 30 October 2011, http://gulf-daily-news.com/NewsDetails.aspx?storyid=316591

Singh Grewal, S., 'Rally to honour security forces', *Gulf Daily News*, 29 December 2011, www.gulf-daily-news.com/NewsDetails.aspx?storyid=320555

Smith, S.C., *Britain's Revival and Fall in the Gulf: Kuwait, Bahrain, Qatar, and the Trucial States, 1950–71*, RoutledgeCurzon, London, 2004.

Snow, D.A., and Benford, R.D., 'Ideology, frame resonance, and participant mobilisation', in B. Klandermans, H. Kriesi, and S. Tarrow (eds) *From Structure to Action: Social Movements Participation Across Cultures*, JAI Press, Greenwich, CT, 1988, pp. 197–217.

Snow, D., Rochford Jr, E.B., Worden, S.K., and Benford, R.D., 'Frame alignment processes, micromobilization and movement participation', *American Sociological Review*, 51 (1986), pp. 456–81.

Sontag, S., *Regarding the Pain of Others*, Penguin, London, 2003.

Spencer, R., 'Philip Hammond praises improvements in Bahrain's human rights records', *The Telegraph*, 20 January 2015, www.telegraph.co.uk/news/worldnews/middleeast/bahrain/11358765/Philip-Hammond-praises-improvements-in-Bahrains-human-rights-record.html

Steinberg, M.W., 'Tilting the frame: considerations on collective action framing from a discursive turn', *Theory and Society*, 27/6 (1998), pp. 845–72.

Strobl, S., 'From colonial policing to community policing in Bahrain: the historical persistence of sectarianism', *International Journal of Comparative and Applied Criminal Justice*, 35/1 (2011), pp. 19–37.

Summary of report submitted by Daniel Walker, Director of the Chicago Study Team, to the National Commission on the Causes and Prevention of Violence, introduction by Max Frankel, E.P. Dutton, New York, 1968, www.fjc.gov/history/home.nsf/page/tu_chicago7_doc_13.html

Tatham, D.E., 'Internal security in Bahrain', 1977, FCO document, www.whatdotheyknow.com/request/164213/response/531538/attach/3/FOI%20 0544%2013%20releasable%20material%20200614.pdf

Terminal X, 'Bahrain deports 500 Pakistani security soldiers over "indiscipline"', 11 May 2014, www.terminalx.org/2014/05/bahrain-deports-500-pakistani-security-soldiers-over-indiscipline.html

*The Daily Show with Jon Stewart*, 'America's freedom packages' [online video], 21 March 2011, http://thedailyshow.cc.com/videos/6x58a1/america-s-freedom-packages

*The Express Tribune*, 'Broken promises: Bahrain deports 450 Pakistanis after alleged torture', 14 March 2013, http://tribune.com.pk/story/520669/broken-promises-bahrain-deports-450-pakistanis-after-alleged-torture/

*The Guardian*, 'Bahrain oil company fires almost 300 over anti-government protests', 11 May 2011, www.guardian.co.uk/world/2011/may/11/bahrain-oil-company-fires-300-protests

*The National*, 'Emirati officer dies in Bahrain bomb explosion', 3 March 2014, www.thenational.ae/world/emirati-officer-dies-in-bahrain-bomb-explosion

The National Archives, 'Commission of inquiry report', 10 July 1954, FO 371/109813.

The National Archives, B.A.B. Burrows, No. 204 Bahrain to Foreign Office, 12 March 1956, FO 371/120544.

The National Archives, B.A.B. Burrows, No. 207 Bahrain to Foreign Office, 12 March 1956, FO 371/120544.

The National Archives, W.O. Little, 'Report by Major Little', in Pamphlet on Bahrain, Part IV, p. 4, 1957, FO 371/126918.

The National Archives, J.P. Tripp to A.D. Parsons, 14 February 1965, FO 371/179788.

The National Archive, J.P. Tripp to M.S. Weir, 5 April 1965, FO 371/179788.

The National Archives, M.S. Weir, 7 October 1965, FO 371/179788.

The National Archives, A.D. Parsons to T.F. Brenchley, 18 December 1965, FO 371/179788.

The National Archives, 'A review of the structure and organization of the Bahraini State Police Force', 1965, FO 371/179788.

The National Archives, 'Annual review of Bahrain affairs, 1965', in Political Agent Bahrain to Political Resident Bahrain, 2 January 1966, FO 371/185327 PRO.

The National Archives, A. Sterling, 'Bahrain: annual review for 1971', FCO 8/1823.

The National Archives, R.M. Tesh, 'Internal political situation', 9 April 1974, FCP 8/2180.

The National Archives, R.M. Tesh to I.T.M. Lucas, 'Internal political situation in Bahrain', 1 March 1975, FCO 8/2415.

The National Archives, 'Bahrain review', 1980, FCO 08/3894.

The National Archives, K. Passmore, 'Internal political situation', 3 December 1980, FCO 8/3489.

The National Archives, W.R. Tomkys, Telegram No. 223, 14 December 1981, FCO 8/3893.

The National Archives, W.R. Tomkys, 'Deportations', 10 February 1982, FCO 8/4332.

The National Archives, W.R. Tomkys, 'Police brutality in Bahrain', 16 February 1982, FCO 8/4332.

The National Archives, W.R. Tomkys, 'Political development in Bahrain', 18 September 1982, FCO 8/4332.

*The Telegraph*, 'Ian Henderson – Obituary', 22 April 2013, www.telegraph.co.uk/news/obituaries/10011292/Ian-Henderson.html

*The Telegraph*, 'New human rights NGO aligned with government', 18 February 2011, www.telegraph.co.uk/news/wikileaks-files/bahrain-wikileaks-cables/8334631/NEW-HUMAN-RIGHTS-NGO-ALIGNED-WITH-GOVERNMENT.html

Trade Arabia, '*Al-Wasat* journalists to stand trial in Bahrain', 12 April 2011, www.tradearabia.com/news/MEDIA_196756.html

Tran, M., 'Bahrain accuses human rights leader of faking pictures of beating', *The Guardian*, 11 April 2011, www.theguardian.com/world/2011/apr/11/bahrain-human-rights-activist-accused

Turk, A., 'Organizational deviance and political policing', *Criminology*, 19/2 (1981), pp. 231–50.

Turk, A., *Political Criminality: The Defiance and Defense of Authority*, Sage Publications, Beverly Hills, 1982.

Ulrichsen, K.C., 'Bahrain's aborted revolution', London School of Economics, 2012, www.lse.ac.uk/IDEAS/publications/reports/pdf/SR011/FINAL_LSE_IDEAS__BahrainsAbortedRevolution_Ulrichsen.pdf

United Nations, 'Report of the Special Rapporteur, Mr. Nigel S. Rodley, submitted pursuant to Commission on Human Rights resolution 1995/37 B', E/CN.4/1997/7, 1997.

US Department of State, 'Bahrain 2013 Human Rights Report', 2013, www.state. gov/documents/organization/220560.pdf

*USA Today*, 'The freest economy in the Middle East', United World supplement, 2 July 2008, www.unitedworld-usa.com/pdf/bahrain.pdf

Virilio, P., *Open Sky*, Verso, New York, 1997.

Wall, J.W., to B.A.B. Burrows, 5 October 1953, in P. Tuson, A. Burdett and E. Quick (eds), *Records of Bahrain 1820–1960*, 8 vols, Archive Editions, Slough, Vol. 7, 1993, p. 22.

Wall, J.W., to FO, 25 October 1954, No. 781, in P. Tuson, A. Burdett and E. Quick (eds), *Records of Bahrain 1820–1960*, 8 vols, Archive Editions, Slough, Vol. 7, 1993, p. 73.

Wall, J.W., to FO, 5 December 1954, No. 781, in P. Tuson, A. Burdett and E. Quick (eds), *Records of Bahrain 1820–1960*, 8 vols, Archive Editions, Slough, 1993, Vol. 7, p. 86.

Watt, N., 'Anger as Cameron invites Bahrain crown prince to No 10', *The Guardian*, 20 May 2011, www.theguardian.com/uk/2011/may/20/cameron-row-bahrain-prince-visit

Weaver, P., 'Bahrain unable to guarantee safety for Formula One says former Met officer', *The Guardian*, 18 April 2012, www.theguardian.com/world/2012/apr/18/bahrain-formula-one-yates-safety

Web 3.0 Lab, 'Bahrain's troll army', 17 February 2011, http://web3lab.blogspot.co.uk/2011/02/bahrains-troll-army.html

Wehrey, F., *Sectarian Politics in the Gulf: From the Iraq War to the Arab Uprisings*, Columbia University Press, New York, 2014.

Welch, M., *Crimes of Power & States of Impunity: The U.S. Response to Terror*, Rutgers University Press, New Brunswick, 2009.

White House, 'President Bush arrives in Bahrain', 12 January 2008, http://georgewbush-whitehouse.archives.gov/news/releases/2008/01/20080112-5.html

WikiLeaks, 'Bahrain security decree' [diplomatic cable], 22 June 1975, https://search.wikileaks.org/plusd/cables/1975MANAMA00716_b.html

WikiLeaks, 'Bahraini political developments: foreign minister's comments' [diplomatic cable], 11 September 1975, https://search.wikileaks.org/plusd/cables/1975MANAMA01057_b.html

WikiLeaks, 'Bahraini political situation' [diplomatic cable], 21 September 1975, https://search.wikileaks.org/plusd/cables/1975MANAMA01086_b.html

WikiLeaks, 'Migrant workers' rights NGO approved by GOB', 2005, www.wikileaks.ch/cable/2005/01/05MANAMA15.html

WikiLeaks, 'A field guide to Bahraini political parties', 4 September 2008, https://wikileaks.org/plusd/cables/08MANAMA592_a.html

Willis, M., 'Britain in Bahrain in 2011', *RUSI Journal*, 157/5, pp. 62–71 (October 2012).

Wilson, Major, 'Selections from the Records of the Bombay Government' [107] (149/733), British Library: India Office Records and Private Papers,

IOR/R/15/1/732 in Qatar Digital Library, www.qdl.qa/en/archive/81055/vdc_100022870191.0x000096

Wyatt, W., 'Special advisers in Bahrain', *Panorama*, BBC, 1960.

Yasin, S., 'Bahrain: where a Facebook "like" gets you expelled', Index on Censorship, 14 October 2011, www.indexoncensorship.org/2011/10/bahrain-where-a-facebook-like-gets-you-expelled/

York, J. 'Twitter trolling as propaganda tactic: Bahrain and Syria', *Jilliancyork*, 11 November 2011, http://jilliancyork.com/2011/10/12/twitter-trolling-as-propagandatactic-bahrain-and-syria/

YouTube, 'Interview with Shaykh Rashid Al Khalifa' [online video], 20 October 2011, www.youtube.com/watch?v=zTdOVFaWfoA

YouTube, 'Dar al-Kulayb: militas throw Molotovs at the people' [online video], 6 January 2012, www.youtube.com/watch?v=mvOaUaaW_zo

YouTube, 'Thugs throw Molotovs at people of Dar al-Kulayb' [online video], 6 January 2012, www.youtube.com/watch?v=pimFQQfGO4w

YouTube, 'Hamad did not fall, 2012 Tn Tn Ttn' [online video], 13 February 2012, www.youtube.com/watch?v=ZPW1FgcttaU

YouTube, 'Bahrain Tin Tin Tytin Movie 2012' [online video], 25 February 2012, www.youtube.com/watch?v=YC1jIqJuedI

YouTube, 'Bahrain: the regime sends its mercenaries to spread hatred of the Shia, describing revolutionaries as "children of muta'a"' [online video], 12 July 2013, www.youtube.com/watch?v=VmpldioCjqk

YouTube, 'The regime carry out a massacre in the village of al-Shakura in Bahrain' [online video], 14 April 2014, www.youtube.com/watch?v=-ZA91Jm4qVM

Yusuf, H., 'Citizens: we must arm the security forces to protect them against terrorists', *Al-Watan*, 2012, www.alwatannews.net/en/post.aspx?id=V6TTTavrPTp4L7unyAVu5mdPf3KB7fokW+p+iKqni4g= (link no longer valid, no alternative).

Zahra, N., 'Confession leak officer spared jail', *Gulf Daily News*, 27 June 2014, www.gulf-daily-news.com/NewsDetails.aspx?storyid=379886

Zawya, 'Rise of Arab social media', 24 July 2012, www.zawya.com/story/Rise_of_Arab_social_media-ZAWYA20120724051637// [link removed].

# Index